Politics and Society in Western Europe

Politics and Society in Western Europe

Jan-Erik Lane and Svante O. Ersson

S SAGE Publications
London · Newbury Park · New Delhi

First published 1987
Second edition 1991

SAGE Publications Ltd
6 Bonhill Street
London EC2A 4PU

SAGE Publications Inc
2455 Teller Road
Newbury Park, California 91320

SAGE Publications India Pvt Ltd
32, M-Block Market
Greater Kailash – 1
New Delhi 110 048

British Library Cataloguing in Publication data
Lane, Jan-Erik
  Politics and Society in Western Europe.
  1. Comparative Government   2. Europe –
  Politics and Government – 1945–
  I. Title   II. Ersson, Svante O.
  320.3'094   JN94.A91

ISBN 0-8039-8406-5
ISBN 0-8039-8407-3 (pbk)

Library of Congress catalog card number 91-052843

Printed in Great Britain by Biddles Ltd, Guildford, Surrey

Contents

Foreword

This second edition of *Politics and Society in Western Europe* not only brings its coverage of events up-to-date but also includes a number of major changes. Firstly, the presentation has been broadened to include the output side of the West European polity and the trends towards intergovernmental coordination in Western Europe. Secondly, much of the technicalities in the first edition have been deleted in an effort to present easily accessible data. Thus, the political party chapter now presents information about each single party instead of the aggregated information in the first edition. Thirdly, the focus of the volume has been substantially broadened from a political stability approach to an elucidation of how a political sociology approach compares with the new institutionalist approach when employed as a framework of analysis for the understanding of West European politics.

Lund and Umeå, January 1991

Introduction: A Changing Scenario

Basic to political phenomena whatever their appearance is change. Transformation characterizes political systems as they comprise dynamic structures adapting to external and internal forces by responding with various mechanisms. Political events have an element of unpredictability built into them. During intervals of time political systems may give the appearance of continuity and rest. However, hardly has the appearance of solidity and calm been interpreted in ideas about the apolitical nature of society, the coming of a technocratic society or the end of ideology when signs of conflict appear, indicating profound divergences based on cleavages. Politics feeds on the conflicts arising from social heterogeneity as well as on the variety of organized groups in the polity. Characteristic of European politics in the post-war period has been the swing back and forth between change and continuity in institutions and politics.

1950–65: End of ideology, and apathy

It used to be believed that the post-war political systems of Europe had stabilized after an unruly transition period at the end of the Second World War. France during the Fourth Republic was a divergent case, but once de Gaulle had created the Fifth Republic France appeared to fit the dominant mode among European democracies. No doubt the state of Italy was also deviant, but scholars interpreted the lack of strife and the overall stability of systems like the United Kingdom, Sweden and the Federal Republic of Germany as due to a disappearance or reduction of ideological conflict (Tingsten, 1955; Aron, 1957; Shils, 1958). Other scholars identified the development of a technocratic and administrative welfare society that would present its inhabitants with security and reduce the disruptive consequences of cleavages (Dahrendorf, 1959; Crozier, 1964; Birnbaum, 1975). The iron curtain was firmly established in the 1950s after considerable turmoil in some of the new people's republics and the East European countries began to embark on a road towards economic recovery by means of a planned economy. The introduction of the NATO organization in 1949 was paralleled by the creation of the Warsaw pact in 1955 setting the parameters for a period of a divided Europe to last up until the fall of 1989.

It was argued that the politics of the post-industrial society would be different from political life in the industrial society (Bell, 1973). West European nations were all thriving from economic growth, leadership seemed remarkably stable and law and order prevailed to an extent that would make analysts of the late 1950s and the 1960s underline stability and continuity. The legitimacy of political institutions was not questioned as political authorities stayed in power for relatively long periods of time, as the regimes or the constitutions of these democracies were regarded as hallmarks of a long constitutional development, as the political community or the political territory of the various democratic states was not questioned by minorities. At the same time the East European political systems seemed more stable after the challenge to the Communist regime had been rejected in East Germany in 1953, in Poland in 1956 and in Hungary in 1956. There politics became routinized in the form of a Communist party monopoly on all major forms of social power, ultimately backed by Moscow and the world power ambitions of the USSR.

Table I.1 presents some basic empirical information about the European scene as it emerged out of the Second World War and the important Jalta agreement about how the empire of the Third Reich was to be divided as well as how Europe was to be structured into Western Europe and Eastern Europe.

Both Western and Eastern Europe comprises small and large countries with regard to both population and land area. The political constitutions of these countries are of different age as the constitutions of some of the West European countries are much older than the East European constitutions. The latter reflect the introduction of so-called peoples' democracies all over Eastern Europe after the Second World War. It may be predicted that the 1990s will witness constitutional revisions or major changes in the political systems of Eastern Europe.

1965–80: Rejection of political authority

Major interpretations of the relationship between society and politics during the 1950s and the early 1960s talked about apathy (Berelson et al., 1954; Sartori, 1962; Lane, 1965; Milbrath, 1965). However, during the 1960s realities made the opposite of apathy, participation, a focus of research (DiPalma, 1970; Dahl, 1971). Participation became a major goal in the political systems in Western Europe as a way of challenging the centralist bias of the industrial state but also as a vehicle of latent cleavages that became manifest during the 1970s.

The late 1960s and the early 1970s showed convincingly how fragile political structures are and how easily the legitimacy of political institutions may be eroded. Signs of change conducive to political instability

Table I.1   *The political systems of Europe 1945–1989*

Country	Population 1950 (000)	Population 1985 (000)	Area 1970 (000 ha)	Date of Current Constitution
Austria	6 935	7 555	83 849	1920
Belgium	8 639	9 903	30 513	1831
Denmark	4 271	5 114	43 069	1953
Germany FR	47 847	61 015	247 973	1949
Finland	4 009	4 902	337 009	1919
France	41 736	55 170	547 026	1958
Greece	7 554	9 934	131 944	1975
Ireland	2 969	3 552	70 283	1937
Italy	46 769	57 128	301 225	1948
Netherlands	10 114	14 484	40 844	1983
Norway	3 265	4 153	324 419	1814
Portugal	8 405	10 157	92 082	1976
Spain	27 868	38 505	504 782	1978
Sweden	7 014	8 350	449 750	1975
Switzerland	4 694	6 470	41 288	1874
United Kingdom	50 616	56 618	244 013	–
Albania	1 215	2 962	28 748	1976
Bulgaria	7 251	8 960	110 912	1971
Czechoslovakia	12 389	15 500	127 869	1960
Germany DR	17 199	16 644	107 771	1968
Hungary	9 338	10 649	93 030	1949
Poland	24 824	37 203	312 677	1952
Romania	16 311	22 725	237 500	1965
Soviet Union	180 075	277 537	22 402 200	1977
Yugoslavia	16 346	23 236	255 804	1974

Sources: United Nations: *Demographic Yearbook*, 1964; 1988; 1971; Britannica World Data (1989)

cropped up in most European democracies as well as in some of the East European countries. Not only did leaders meet with significant difficulties to stay in power for longer periods of time, but the very principles of how the political system of a nation was to be built up became a central political issue in several democracies. Compared to what used to be the case during the 1960s there turned up strong opinions demanding changes in governmental policy and leadership as well as in the structure or the principles of political decision-making. In several European democracies the legitimacy of traditional decision structures was called in question or reduced. And demands for a change of regime were raised in several authoritarian regimes including both Western and Eastern Europe: Czechoslovakia in 1968 and Spain, Portugal and Greece in the early 1970s.

The criticism of the political decision-making systems resulted in demands for institutional autonomy in countries like the United Kingdom, Belgium and Spain. Systems such as those in Sweden, France and West Germany faced a demand for decentralization of political authority to local government and neighbourhood groups (Sharpe, 1979; 1988). In some systems the demand for participation implied decentralization of political authority to the local and regional levels; demands for increased local and regional autonomy appeared during this decade to an extent that surprised the adherents of an efficient centralized welfare state.

The reaction to the progressive development of an industrial state brought out profound cleavages of various kinds, ethnic, religious as well as class-orientated ones. The modern capitalist state implies a centralization of decision-making structures. Concentration of power and resources may bring about a higher level of affluence, but affluence is not a general remedy against contention. In fact, once economic and class cleavages have been attenuated other kinds of cleavages may become stronger (Inglehart, 1977). Affluence may also bring about more of a class struggle, because economic resources even though they are abundant may be distributed unfairly – relative deprivation.

Participation also involved a demand for increased representation for various organized groups in decision-making structures, in particular at the national level, demands which implied that European democracies began to display increasingly accentuated corporatist features (Schmitter and Lehmbruch, 1979; Beyme, 1980; Lehmbruch and Schmitter, 1982). Besides the demands for representation of various élites, a striking feature of the late 1960s was the demand for new types of representation in the form of direct democratic procedures.

Dissatisfaction with government manifested itself in the founding of new political parties or political movements. Party innovation implies that the established structure of parliamentary parties has difficulty in accommodating the appearance of new cleavages or the reappearance of old ones. In some countries new parties implied new directions in the pattern of voter behaviour changing citizen alignments profoundly (Pedersen, 1983). Sometimes the established parties adapted to the reorientation in voter attitudes by making new kinds of policy. Sometimes protest cropped up in loosely organized movements eager to safeguard new values: environmentalist groups, anti-nuclear power groups and various local groups.

The party systems of the European democracies seemed highly stable in the mid-1960s, some scholars stating that these party systems had undergone little change since they were created in the beginning of the twentieth century (Lipset and Rokkan, 1967a; Rose and Urwin, 1970). However, in the mid-1970s the traditional political parties in Western Europe faced some difficult decisions as to what action to take, because not only were they challenged by new political parties and new political movements but they also had to accommodate to an environment for political life that was growing more complex and more uncertain. Traditional ideologies had to be reinterpreted to give direction for the new issues of the 1970s. Increased volatility has characterized the party systems in Western Europe (Mair and Smith, 1989).

The image of the welfare state is that it can deliver policies in response to vital citizen needs. However, the effectiveness of the welfare state has been questioned. In some countries the legitimacy of the political system was challenged because of lack of efficiency. Italy and Denmark belong to this category. The instability of West Germany and the United Kingdom during the 1970s was of a different kind. A new phenomenon in West European politics was the emergence of social disorder that threatened vital state functions. It was believed that guerrilla warfare had its natural roots in underdeveloped countries; the 1970s in Europe showed not only that bloodshed and civil war were possible in advanced societies but that it may prove difficult even for states with large military resources to put an end to the operations of urban guerrillas like in Northern Ireland, Spain, West Germany, Italy. A legitimacy crisis appeared in various nations, though in different shapes.

Countries such as Greece, Portugal and Spain underwent vast changes of their political systems during the 1970s as these nations replaced an authoritarian system of government with a democratic regime, engaging in institution rebuilding. The profound institutional change in Spain, Portugal and Greece was accomplished in revolutionary processes involving severe tension between various groups. During this decade on the one hand democratic regimes faced demands for changes in policy, leadership and structure of the party system as well as of the political system, demands that called for changes in democratic institutions. On the other hand there were processes of democratic transformation of authoritarian political systems. The introduction of democratic institutions in countries which have been under an authoritarian regime for long or short periods meant a political transformation of the European scene; these new democratic systems faced not only the challenge of authoritarian forces eager to turn back to the traditional way of life but also the momentum for change characteristic of the democratic regimes.

The politics of the late 1960 and early 1970s meant not only that participation replaced apathy; cleavages believed to be fading away emerged to an extent that was not predicted. During the 1950s and the 1960s the prevailing theme of modernization implied that ethnic and religious cleavages would diminish as a source of conflict because societies that were modernizing would be dominated by economic or, as they called it, functional orientations (Deutsch, 1961). What actually happened created a need for an analysis of cleavages, in particular the challenges presented to political parties and political systems by the resurrection of traditional loyalties of an ethnic or religious nature. However obsolete the theories of the end of ideology, the apathy of the electorate and the modernization of society are confronted with the turbulence and change of the late 1960s and 1970s or the belief that the welfare state offered a final solution to the political problems in Western Europe, it is also true that the extent of social transformation as well as political instability must not be exaggerated.

1980–90: Crisis of the welfare state and of communism

During the 1970s and early 1980s the economies of Western Europe have undergone vast changes compared to the period of growth after the Second World War. The rate of expansion has slowed down and economic stability has become difficult to achieve with inflation and unemployment figures running high. The certainty and optimism that used to characterize macro-economic policy-making in the wake of the breakthrough of Keynesian principles were shattered during the 1970s as it became increasingly difficult to explain the new phenomenon of 'stagflation'. New ideas in the field of macro-economic management were introduced – monetarism and supply side economics – and tried in some countries but there is as yet no agreement as to how the economy is to be managed, if at all possible (Whiteley, 1986).

The economic crisis in the advanced capitalist economies was bolstered by the shock increases of the oil prices. Similarly, the strong process of economic expansion in the planned economies in Eastern Europe came to a halt in the 1970s. Some of the East European countries faced severe economic difficulties by 1980 which were aggravated and spread all over the Comecon system in the 1980s (Brus and Laski, 1990). Table I.2 has some data about the declining economic performance in Europe and the maturing of the welfare state.

The steady erosion of the planned economies in Eastern Europe meant a decisive blow to the so-called convergence hypothesis or the idea that the market economies in Western Europe and the planned economies in Eastern Europe would grow increasingly alike (Tinbergen, 1967; Galbraith, 1967). Quite to the contrary, the welfare state in Eastern Europe performed less and less well (Castles, 1986; Åslund, 1989). Questions were raised as to the validity of the reported high rates of economic growth during the 1950s and 1960s at the same time as the so-called peoples' democracies admitted grave ecological problems in addition to poor economic performance. The failure of the planned economy in Eastern Europe in combination with the coming to power of Gorbachev in 1985 with the new ideas of *glasnost* and *perestroika* sealed the fate of Communist party hegemony in Eastern Europe, all countries

Table I.2 *Affluence and economic growth in Europe (International US dollar in 1985 prices)*

Country	Real GDP per capita 1950	Real GDP per capita 1985	Growth real GDP per capita		
			1950–1970	1970–1985	1980–1985
Austria	2 318	8 929	7.2	3.3	1.4
Belgium	3 462	9 717	4.5	2.8	0.9
Denmark	4 241	10 884	4.0	2.5	2.2
Germany FR	2 713	10 708	8.3	2.7	1.6
Finland	2 758	9 232	4.9	3.1	1.7
France	3 125	9 918	6.0	2.5	0.4
Greece	986	4 464	9.5	3.2	0.3
Ireland	2 047	5 205	3.7	2.7	0.9
Italy	1 929	7 425	7.7	3.0	0.6
Netherlands	3 404	9 092	4.9	2.0	0.1
Norway	3 802	12 623	4.1	4.9	2.3
Portugal	937	3 729	8.3	2.8	–0.0
Spain	1 640	6 437	8.0	2.9	0.8
Sweden	3 980	9 904	4.1	2.1	2.0
Switzerland	4 886	10 604	4.2	1.0	1.0
United Kingdom	3 993	8 665	2.8	2.3	1.4
Albania	–	–	–	–	–
Bulgaria	1 306	5 113	9.5	2.0	0.7
Czechoslovakia	3 124	7 424	4.0	1.8	1.0
Germany DR	2 119	8 740	8.4	3.1	1.8
Hungary	2 208	5 765	4.7	2.0	0.8
Poland	2 170	4 913	3.8	1.7	–0.3
Romania	1 069	4 273	6.7	4.2	1.4
Soviet Union	1 966	6 266	6.1	2.5	1.9
Yugoslavia	1 101	5 063	7.7	4.7	1.2

Source: Summers and Heston, 1988.

searching for some kind of a democratic polity for the 1990s.

Economic problems in Western Europe were aggravated even though or perhaps because governments began to accumulate huge national deficits to pay for a sustained expansion of the public sector. Some of these public sector deficits reflect the macro-economic crisis, as higher rates of unemployment and inflation drive up public expenditures. But the coming of a state fiscal crisis had other sources also, mainly large-scale public spending. The expansion of the public sectors in the various West European nations after the Second World War was made possible by the rapid increase in income and the taxation revenues derived from income. However, as the rate of economic growth declined during the 1970s the public sector expansion did not adjust but resorted to deficit spending on a scale not seen during the post-war years. The result was a growing concern about the capacity of the welfare state to deliver – a kind of efficiency crisis that interacts with the legitimacy problem.

Up until the mid-1970s many were impressed by the doings of governments at various levels. Public policy seemed to be able to deliver when markets failed or even to deliver in a socially more acceptable or even more efficient manner than markets could allocate. However, the turn to big government has resulted in government overload and the spread of the impression of policy ineffectiveness and policy failure (Rose and Peters, 1978; Wildavsky, 1979; 1980; Rose, 1981; 1984).

Conspicuous evidence of public sector imbalance was the resort to deficit spending during the late 1970s and early 1980s as a response to the fiscal crisis of West European nations. Whereas most of these nations used to run overall public sector surpluses if not central government surpluses the picture in the early 1980s is much more gloomy. Governments in Western Europe have increasingly faced a serious economic predicament of inflation and unemployment, and the addition of a fiscal crisis of the public sector to the private economy problems meant that there was growing concern about the efficiency of the welfare state to meet policy demands in a mixed economy (Table I.3).

The West European welfare state has matured at a steady state level although considerable country differences in welfare state ambitions remain (O'Connor and Brym, 1988). The tax state mobilizes almost 50 per cent of the total income in Sweden, Denmark, Norway, Belgium and the Netherlands. However, in some countries the share of the tax state is only about one-third of GDP: Spain, Portugal, Switzerland, Italy, Finland and Greece. The size of the redistributive branch of government as indexed by the share of social transfer payments indicates a strong commitment to welfare ideals in the Netherlands, France, Belgium, Austria and Sweden when compared with Portugal, Finland and Switzerland. A few countries in Western Europe have persistently had great problems with balancing income and expenditures: Greece, Belgium, Ireland and Italy. It may be predicted that these differences will grow smaller in the 1990s as the welfare state in Northern Europe is under reconsideration whereas the welfare state in the new democracies in southern Europe will be expanded.

1990: The new politics of Europe

The stability of a polity may be threatened by sources external to that society. Other nations may expand their territories or their control at the expense of surrounding nations. During the post war period, however, the sources of instability in European politics have been predominantly internal ones, because the interstate relationships in Europe have remained stable. Not until the late 1980s were there clear signs of a break-up of

Table I.3   *Size of the welfare state in West Europe: public*
expenditures as a percentage of GDP in 1985 (general government)

Country	Current disbursements	Final Government Consumption	Social Transfer Payments	Deficit Spending
Austria	45.2	18.7	20.1	2.5
Belgium	52.3	17.7	22.0	−5.8
Denmark	56.7	25.4	16.5	0.3
Germany FR	43.4	19.9	16.6	2.0
Finland	37.7	20.3	11.6	2.8
France	49.4	16.3	26.6	−0.9
Greece	45.3	20.3	15.0	−10.5
Ireland	50.4	19.2	18.2	−6.1
Italy	44.1	16.6	16.9	−6.6
Netherlands	55.2	16.3	28.5	−0.8
Norway	44.0	18.6	14.8	12.1
Portugal	39.4	15.5	10.9	−3.4
Spain	34.7	13.7	16.0	−1.5
Sweden	60.8	27.4	19.3	−1.4
Switzerland	30.9	13.2	13.7	3.5
United Kingdom	44.9	21.1	14.6	−1.2

Notes: Current disbursements consist of final consumption expenditure, interest on public debt, subsidies and social security transfers to households. Final government consumption covers expenditures for goods and services. Deficit spending is current receipts minus current disbursements which also include other kinds of state income and expenditures.

Source: OECD (1989) *National Accounts 1975–1987.*

the balance of power between NATO in the West and the Warsaw pact in the East. Yet, a most important political trend in Europe has been the growth in a sense of a common European identity, particularly in Western Europe.

The West European countries began in the early 1950s to move towards interstate cooperation which soon resulted in the formation of one economic community – the EC in 1958 – and another trade association – EFTA in 1960. The Economic Community proved to provide a set of viable organizations for the future of Western Europe where interdependencies of various kinds kept growing at a high pace. Disregarding the outburst of conflicts between governments now and then, the EC has grown in strength. At the outset the Rome agreement comprised six countries: France, the Federal Republic of Germany, the Netherlands, Belgium, Luxembourg and Italy. Over time six more countries have entered into the EC: United Kingdom (1973), Denmark (1973), Ireland (1973), Greece (1981), Spain (1986), Portugal (1986). The prospects for European cooperation within various fields look bright indeed with the plans for an internally free market to be introduced in

1992 and the interest on the part of the EFTA countries as well as the emerging democracies in Eastern Europe in becoming part of this united economic system some way or the other.

Democracy as a political regime has reasserted itself with enormous strength in post Second World War Europe. The legitimacy of democratic political institutions has been strongly institutionalized in Western Europe and attracts widespread attention in Eastern Europe although some constitutional problems remain unresolved there. Economically, the future of the welfare state is up in the air in Western Europe. And it remains to be seen if the East European countries can catch up as they turn to market mechanisms. Politically, the future of West European polities is uncertain as it remains an open question how strong the interstate institutions of the EC will become. At the same time the restructuring of the political systems of Eastern Europe is an unpredictable process of numerous changes while basic conflicts between deep-seated social cleavages remain in Western Europe. How can we analyse the political systems in Western Europe? We will focus on two major aspects of these countries: *democracy* and *the welfare state*. Typical of the major countries in Western Europe is their combination of a set of strongly institutionalized democratic procedures and a mixed economy. What would be a proper framework for the analysis of the country variation in Western Europe with regard to these two political aspects?

Framework: democratic institutions in a welfare state

Our aim is to present a comprehensive analysis of political life in the West European democracies, sixteen countries all in all. What sets these countries apart from the political systems in America, Africa and Asia is the legitimate operation of democratic political institutions within state structures that involve big government. A liberal democratic political order is combined with a welfare state and a mixed economy. The public sector plays a major role in the economy of the West European countries allocating and redistributing resources by means of various institutions at different levels of government. How democracy operates within these public institutions in the West European liberal welfare state is the topic of this volume.

West European democracy is very much based on the open competition between political parties for the allegiance of the voter in free elections recruiting a legislative assembly that shares in the exercise of power with government institutions in a national setting. Focussing on political parties, election outcomes and the national party systems in Western Europe we try to show how parties constitute intermediary links between social cleavages, government decision-making mechanisms and political stability, each a complex phenomenon.

The interpretation of European politics calls forth a number of problems concerning how political events and political structures are related to non-political phenomena. There is the political sociology approach of politics as reflecting the forces operating in the social structure (Lipset and Rokkan, 1967b; Rokkan et al., 1970). Here, there is the danger of *structural determinism* which involves political phenomena being looked upon as a function of the structure of society,

The opposite approach assumes that politics has a logic of its own expressed in political institutions – institutionalism (March and Olsen, 1989). Political institutionalism focusses on the organizational level looking at how public institutions have a life of their own maintaining themselves over time or increasing their power in an interorganizational setting. The concept of the state is crucial in the new institutionalist movement (Evans et al., 1985; Almond, 1988), the basic argument being that the structuring of the state has to be understood not by means of political sociology but rather in terms of a political culture framework (Inglehart, 1988a). The institutionalist approach may run into the problem of *social indeterminism* meaning that the social context of political phenomena is overlooked. Political behaviour in an organized democracy focusses on issues which derive much of their sense from the social cleavages between various groups in the social structure.

What is attempted here when interpreting politics in Western Europe is a blend, as it were, of the political sociology approach underlining how cleavages shape politics and political institutionalism which emphasizes the independent logic of political organizations such as political parties as well as governments and bureaucracies. The comparative study of the variety of democratic politics in Western Europe displays how difficult it is to understand the causal interaction between political phenomena and society. Yet, ongoing politics deal with issues that create political conflict before or after policies are made and implemented. To focus on issues is to accept a hypothesis that organized political behaviour matters in the form of electoral competition and in government decision-making and the implementation of policies. The conditions for political behaviour have to be searched for not only in society or in the structure of social cleavages but also in various institutional settings.

Theoretically, we organize our interpretation of West European politics in terms of the concepts of cleavages, political institutions and public policies. Cleavages may be looked upon as the so-called raw materials of politics which political parties mould by aligning themselves in a party system facing the electorate in competitive elections. Public institutions offer decision-making mechanisms for handling issues that somehow relate to the cleavages in the social structure. And the making and implementation of public policies is the resultant of what goes on in political decision-making mechanisms.

Empirical research on the nations in Western Europe presents us with more specific knowledge of what different kinds of cleavage there are and how alternative political decision-making systems may be structured. It also provides us with the possibility of testing hypotheses about the conditions for political stability. In order to state how cleavages and decision-making mechanisms interact we must try to come to an understanding of the entities involved. We devote major parts of the book to a description of: social cleavages, party systems and decision-making structures in the West European context.

We distinguish three fundamental levels in the political system of a country: the social structure, the party system, and the government level. It seems vital to make distinctions between these three levels, because each level deserves its own analysis. It is an unwarranted assumption to believe that cleavages may occur in the same manner in society, in the party system and in government, or to take for granted that the relationship among cleavages at these levels is simple.

One may ask whether cleavages refer to societal lines of conflict or to party system dimensions of contention or the occurrence of issues in government. Cleavages may show up at all three levels, but it must be underlined that there may be crucial differences in appearance at each level. Party systems do not simply reflect cleavages in the social structure, and political parties often reinforce or play down social cleavages; political élites are not just the victims of cleavages in society as the way political parties orientate towards cleavages matters. Issues in the governmental institutions may strengthen or reduce cleavages.

Although all the West European countries adhere to a democratic regime, there are various modes of political decision-making mechanisms. Democracies may be structured differently. Conceptually, one may distinguish a set of mechanisms which provide for *influence* as well as for *autonomy*. On the one hand, into the set of influence mechanisms enter the system of election and representation rules that govern the recruitment of legislative assemblies and the appointment of governments as well as the possibility in some countries of direct citizen participation in political decision-making via the referendum mechanism. On the other hand, political systems also comprise mechanisms that afford different degrees of *individual* autonomy and *institutional* autonomy.

Democratic political systems provide their citizens with a space for individual decision-making, for freedom. The autonomy of individuals is often formalized in legal documents stating the liberties of a nation. Democracies not only offer the freedom of thought, speech and contract but foster the autonomy of organizations and institutions. Institutional autonomy may be a property of national, regional or local institutions. We describe various influence mechanisms and degrees of personal autonomy and institutional autonomy in our sixteen political systems and we analyse the interaction between influence and autonomy. Institutional autonomy may have a *territorial* orientation, which implies a focus on the amount of autonomy of regions and localities. Or institutional autonomy may have a *functional* orientation, which means that autonomy concerns an activity. Whereas cleavages in a sense initiate the political process and decision-making mechanisms offer instruments with which cleavages may be handled, public policies may be regarded as the result of the operation of various decision-making mechanisms. The structure of public policies in West European nations is very much tied up with the European welfare state and its ambition to deliver a number of goods and services to its citizens by means of public programmes. Just as there is a country variation in cleavages, party systems and decision-making mechanisms, so there is a country variation in public policies that is related to the different ways in which the tax state may be institutionalized. We analyse the country variation in public policies by distinguishing between a few major categories related to welfare spending.

It is difficult not to bring in the concept of political stability when one approaches West European politics, although it presents some difficulties of its own. There are two major problems inherent in a political stability approach. First, it is not at all clear how the concept of political stability is to be defined, or more specifically which properties of political systems are to be included or excluded when 'political stability' is applied onto real life phenomena. Second, there is the question of an implicit value bias meaning that the concept of political stability implies a narrow focus on system continuity and a lack of understanding of the importance of change in political life. Here, we will pin down the concept of political stability to a few manageable dimensions which will allow us to point out certain pertinent differences between political systems in Western Europe without placing any explicit or implicit valuation on system maintenance.

Thus, we arrive at the framework for the analysis of political life in the major West European political systems set out in Figure I.1.

Conclusion

The focus on the variation in political democracy institutions and its sources in society as well as its consequences for policy-making means a certain logical structure of the contents of the volume. First, theoretical approaches that are relevant to the study of West European politics are surveyed in Chapter 1. Chapter 2 presents a picture of the social cleavages in Western Europe. The numerous political parties are portrayed in Chapter 3, while Chapter 4 discusses the problem of a connection between the social structure and the electoral strength of political parties. Chapter 5 deals with party systems. These chapters would constitute the basis for the

Figure I.1   *Framework of analysis*

Social structure	Political culture and political institutions		Political outputs and outcomes
Socio-economic dimensions	Parties	Autonomy – individual – institutional	Political stability
Religion	Party systems	Influence	Democracy
Ethnic		– election – government formation	Welfare state
Class	Issues		
		Constitutional devices: parliament, government, interest groups	

social sources of democratic institutions. Second, we turn in Chapters 6 and 7 to the description of fundamental properties of the decision-making systems of West European democracies. Issues are analysed in Chapter 8, while Chapter 9 is devoted to political stability. Third, after the analysis of governmental institutions we come to public policies or the structure of the public sector in the West European countries to be analysed in Chapter 10. Finally, in Chapter 11 we look at the seminal process of West European integration. In the conclusion we summarize the major findings from the separate chapters.

The data base includes sixteen European democracies: Austria, Belgium, Denmark, the Federal Republic of Germany, Finland, France, Greece, Ireland, Italy, the Netherlands, Norway, Portugal, Spain, Sweden, Switzerland and the United Kingdom. The former authoritarian states have been included only in so far as they practise democratic principles of government. Thus, Spain and Portugal will be studied only after the period of the collapse of authoritarianism whereas Greece is covered before and after the authoritarian regime between 1967 and 1974. The time period covered is mainly the post Second World War period meaning that the 'old' FRG is covered and not the 'new' Germany.

1

From Political Sociology to Political Institutionalism

Introduction

Since the 1950s there has been a proliferation of articles and books in the field of comparative politics dealing with politics and society in Western Europe. The number of case studies has grown rapidly, analysing various West European nations from different angles. There has been a rapid increase in analytical and methodological articles, but there have also been major attempts at cross-country comparison which will be surveyed in this chapter. Comparative politics may be contrasted with the conduct of case studies in the way that the latter focusses on one object and the former deals with several objects of analysis in order to identify similarities and differences. This is vague, because each and every political inquiry contains at least a little of comparison between various units of analysis. More specifically, comparative politics involves the analysis of properties of various kinds of *spatial units* like countries, states, societies and sub-national government entities in terms of an explicit framework. A case study would consist of simply an analysis of one such spatial unit whereas comparative politics would focus on how various kinds of government vary from one spatial entity to another. We will follow up this distinction between the case study technique and the comparative approach as we look at the development of comparative politics with special reference to West European politics.

What used to be called the *traditional approach* in comparative politics was basically a narrow focus on case studies of inter alia West European nations. The critique of the traditional approach within comparative politics had implications for the conduct of inquiries into the politics of Western Europe; it argued that the case study mode of conducting comparative studies was deficient both methodologically and substantively, but what was to come in its place?

There is as of today no profound agreement about what comparative politics is, but there is unanimous agreement about what comparative politics should not be, i.e. that comparative politics ought not to be what it used to be. The traditional mode of conducting comparative politics has been identified with the following properties (Bill and Hardgrave, 1973): (1) *configurative description* or the study of political systems was orientated towards a detailed description of some countries without the use of any explicit conceptual framework; (2) *parochialism* or there was a typical Western bias in the selection of relevant variables to be studied in terms of a fixed list of fact finding categories, most of which were legal or formalistically orientated; (3) *formal-legalism* or the constitutional orientation was prevalent in much of the work as it comprised detailed descriptions of the rules supposedly governing the operations of cabinets, legislatures, courts and bureaucracies; (4) *empiricism* or methods or theory were non-existent in traditional comparative politics, at least at the level of intention and recognition; (5) *non-comparative* or most of the texts in the field of comparative government either studied one single country or engaged in parallel descriptions of a few countries.

In the traditional approach concepts were employed without methodological discussions as to their definition and measurement. And frameworks for comparative analysis were not discussed with regard to pros and cons or available alternatives (Macridis, 1955). Stating that model building as well as the elaboration of indicators for concepts is basic to comparative government was no doubt important, but which models, concepts and indicators are we to employ to enhance the comparative understanding of politics within nations?

The analysis of West European politics has struggled with two methodological problems. First, there is the tension between the use of the *case study* method and a genuine *comparative* framework or model. Second, the study of the politics or the polities in Western Europe started from a *political sociology perspective*, but it has gradually moved towards an *institutionalist approach*. The political sociologists entered the scene early and they emphasized social cleavages as influential factors shaping politics in general and political stability in particular. As a matter of fact, the theoretical debate was much concerned with the sources of political instability. However, with the development of new paradigms and frameworks for the analysis of West European politics more and more institutionalism has been inserted. Thus, when surveying the literature on West European politics we need to be aware of these two tendencies, the trend towards more explicitly comparative work and the trend towards more institutional analysis.

Social structure

One influential political sociology theory emphasized the implications of the structure of society arguing that social fragmentation was conducive to political instability. In 1956 Gabriel A. Almond published a brief paper called 'Comparative Political Systems'. The paper summarizes the theoretical situation within the discipline of comparative politics; it opened up new areas for research to be pursued during the 1960s and 1970s. Although it is maintained that the Almond paper was not a very succinct theoretical statement it must be acknowledged that the paper identifies crucial questions and suggests fruitful concepts to be employed by other scholars. As Jean Blondel emphasizes, comparative politics used to be dominated by an empiricist mode of doing research (Blondel, 1969). Much of what was done dealt with formal structures and legal proceedings. Most studies were confined to Western Europe and North America. Actually, comparative politics was less comparative and very much orientated towards the description of facts. In the 1950s attempts were made to reorientate the comparative study of politics towards more theoretical ways of thinking, which would encompass all kinds of political system (Heckscher, 1957; Sutton, 1963). The Almond paper of 1956 is part of that reorientation:

> What I propose to do in this brief paper is to suggest how the application of certain sociological and anthropological concepts may facilitate systematic comparison among the major types of political systems operative in the world today (Almond, 1956: 391).

Almond set out to classify political systems by means of a conceptual schema that focussed on political stability. To Almond it was obvious that there were vital differences between these four types of political system: the Anglo-American, the Continental European, the pre-industrial or partially industrial political systems and the totalitarian political systems. Implicitly Almond mentions a fifth type of political system comprising Scandinavia and the Low Countries. He was uncertain on how to relate these systems to the fourfold classification (Almond, 1956: 392 3).

Almond wanted to introduce a conceptual system that could justify his fourfold classification and he elaborated a number of concepts which were sociological in character to get away from the legalist bias so common in the field of comparative politics. Like other political sociologists at that time Almond was deeply affected by the Parsonian vogue in theoretical sociology in the 1950s. Talcott Parsons and his associates introduced a number of new concepts which proved applicable in cross-country comparative research. As a matter of fact the Parsonian conceptual schemes presented in *Towards a General Theory of Action* (Parsons and Shils, 1951), *The Social System* (Parsons, 1951) and *Economy and Society* (Parsons and Smelser, 1956) became popular in both sociology and political science during the 1950s provoking a sharp reaction against Parsonianism in the late 1960s. Almond's conceptual tools borrowed partly from Parsons and associates have been criticized, but it cannot be doubted that the paper stimulated comparative research (Figure 1.1).

According to Almond the Anglo-American political systems are stable

Figure 1.1   *Almond's typology*

Political role structure \ Political culture	Homogeneous	Fragmented
High degree of differentiation	Anglo-American	Continental European
Low degree of differentiation	Totalitarian	Pre-industrial

systems, because there is a high degree of consensus among the population about political means and ends and because political institutions are clearly defined and separated from each other as well as from other social institutions. The other types of political system are more or less unstable, because either the groups and organizations of these systems are divided into mutually exclusive political cultures or the structure of political roles in these systems is not differentiated into a set of separate, organized and specific institutions.

Classifications and typologies are not the end of comparative political analysis; they are tools for the creation of models by which fundamental processes of interaction may be analysed. Though the Almond typology has been challenged – explicitly excluding a group of the Scandinavian countries and the Low Countries and crudely classifying a number of countries as totalitarian and pre-industrial – the implicit model in Almond's article relating degrees of political stability to political culture and role structure stimulated research into the conditions that promote or operate against stability. The visionary character of Almond's mode of thinking prevented him from stating what was meant by political stability or how the concept was to be operationalized to admit exact measurement procedures. Even if there is some truth to the claim that the Almond analysis was incomplete, asking more questions than it answered, its main contribution was that it opened up new areas for research. It stimulated efforts to understand the conditions that are conducive to stability in various kinds of political systems as well as theoretical modes of thinking in the field of comparative politics. We now turn to these efforts.

Democratic stability

Political Man (1959) by Seymour Martin Lipset was translated into a number of languages, and it greatly influenced research in the field during the 1960s. *Political Man* deals with a topic that is less wide than that of the Almond approach:

> The main problem with which this book deals is democracy as a characteristic of social systems. The principal topics discussed are the conditions necessary for democracy in societies and organizations... (Lipset, 1959: 9).

In his article Almond focusses on conditions conducive to the stability of political systems, whereas Lipset deals with a subset of political systems, the democratic ones. It would seem that there is no conceptual difference between conditions for democracy and conditions for the stability of democratic regimes. However, the fact is not only that Lipset deals with a subset of political systems, but his focus is also slightly different. Lipset looks for conditions that sustain democracy arguing that democracy:

> ... implies a number of specific conditions: (1) a 'political formula' or body of beliefs specifying which institutions – political parties, a free press, and so forth – are legitimate (accepted as proper by all); (2) one set of political leaders in office; and (3) one or more sets of recognized leaders attempting to gain office (Lipset, 1959: 45).

These criteria apply to democracy but not to stability. A political system may possess these properties, but it may not be a stable political system. When Lipset proceeds to speak of 'stable democracies' he means that some political systems have these properties (1) – (3) for some time, but he is not concerned with governmental stability or social order.

There is a relationship between these two concepts – democratic stability and democratic political systems – in so far as if a democracy comes under pressure from groups that want a different kind of regime it shows signs of instability; but the reverse may not be true, since democracies that are not under such pressure may still display signs of instability. This distinction may be further illuminated by a reference to the possibility that political systems which have a democratic regime display instability in other system properties than those pertaining to the regime, for example rapid governmental turnover or social disorder. Actually, the concept of political stability may not be as neatly identifiable as theories about democratic stability sometimes assume.

Lipset's opening passage in *Political Man* states his basic sociological approach to the analysis of the forces that promote democratic rule: 'The study of the conditions encouraging democracy must therefore focus on the sources of both cleavage and consensus' (Lipset, 1959: 21).

Cleavages result in conflict whereas consensus mitigates the disruptive consequences of conflict by defining rules of democratic government to which the contending parties adhere. Democracy implies government as well as opposition; thus democracy cannot exist without cleavages. Yet, too much conflict resulting from fundamental cleavages may strain democratic regimes. Adherence to norms, consensus, is a remedy for societies characterized by heavy cleavages. This is Lipset's starting point and the task he sets himself is to isolate cleavages which may threaten democratic rule and to find factors that may mitigate cleavages because they increase consensus.

Lipset proposes a number of factors that are conducive to democratic stability: economic development, the class structure, the party system, cross-cutting affiliations, the political system and the historical development of conflict resolution. He states:

> Perhaps the most common generalization linking political systems to other aspects of society has been that democracy is related to the state of economic development. The more well-to-do a nation, the greater the chances that it will sustain democracy (Lipset, 1959: 48–50).

The correlation between economic development and democratic regime is well known and perhaps most clearly formulated by Philippe Cutright (Cutright, 1963: 259). Whatever indicator is used, average wealth, degree of industrialization or urbanization and level of education, the hypothesis of a relationship receives a fairly substantial degree of empirical confirmation. What kind of theoretical interpretation could account for the empirically established relation? Lipset takes two different stands on this point. On the one hand he regards economic development as an independent variable explaining the dependent variable, democracy, on its own force. On the other hand he accounts for the relationship by means of an intervening variable, the class structure:

> Economic development, producing increased income, greater economic security, and widespread higher education, largely determines the form of the 'class struggle', by permitting those in the lower strata to develop longer time perspectives and more complex and gradualist views of politics (Lipset, 1959: 61).

Economic development tempers class-based cleavages and contributes to consensus. Poverty in itself is not the main cause of radicalism, but the visibility of poverty when exposed in comparison with the affluence of some strata of the population or with the affluence of other nations affects class-based cleavages. One of the two basic assumptions in *Political Man* relates democratic stability to the stratification system: the less hierarchical the stratification of a country's population is, the higher the probability for democratic rule will be. The class structure or the stratification system affects positively a number of factors conducive to democracy, and economic growth inserts equality into the stratification system. In particular Lipset mentions the contribution of a large middle class to democratic viability tempering conflict by rewarding moderate and democratic parties and penalizing extremist groups.

Lipset states that the nature of political institutions matters, as some institutions enhance a more vital democracy than others, such as two-party systems rather than multi-party systems, the election of officials on a territorial basis rather than proportional representation, and federalism more than a unitary state (Lipset, 1959: 90).

That there is a negative relationship between the number of political parties and democratic stability was argued by several scholars (Duverger, 1954; Neumann, 1956; Almond, 1956). Not only empirical support is adduced, but it is argued that a two-party system fosters a special kind of party the operations of which are conducive to democracy. Lipset distinguishes between representative parties and integrating parties; roughly the same distinction is covered by the well-known differentiation between aggregative parties and articulative parties. By their very nature parties in a two-party system try to pick up support from various groups, thus tending towards the middle. The idea that proportional representation may weaken democracy is but a version of the same theme, since proportional representation operates against a two-party system.

Actually, the hypothesis about a positive relationship between cross-cutting cleavages and democracy is the second basic hypothesis in *Political Man*. The cross-cutting cleavage hypothesis states that a necessary condition for democracy is the presence of cleavages which do not reinforce each other but engage different groups at different times and contribute to cross-pressure on the citizen. The contribution of the party system and the political system to democratic rule is explained theoretically: that these factors are conducive to the existence of cross-cutting cleavages. It is their effect on the cleavage structure, moderating it and creating positive conditions for consensus, that accounts for the relationship between these factors and democracy. An interpretation of the argument about the resolution of historical conflicts gives the same result as the interpretation of the idea that the party system and the political system affect democracy. Resolution of historical conflicts is an intervening variable between cross-cutting cleavages and democracy, because conflicts that remain unresolved in one way or the other are added to each other and foster reinforcing cleavages instead of cross-cutting ones.

The model of political stability in *Political Man* is in effect a hypothesis about two factors, the stratification system and the cleavage structure, conducive to democratic rule (Figure 1.2). These basic factors, low degree of stratification in the class structure and the existence of cross-cutting cleavages, operate on Lipset's basic concepts of cleavages and consensus in a way that satisfies his starting-point to find the sources of variety as well as of cohesion that are necessary for democratic rule. Democracy works nicely when there are enough cleavages to create space for contention and opposition, and also when these cleavages display a

Figure 1.2   *The Lipset approach*

	Mutually reinforcing cleavages	Cross-cutting cleavages
High degree of stratification	Democratic instability	
Low degree of stratification		Democratic stability

structure that does not exclude consensus on the legitimacy of the rules defining democratic procedure.

The concept of democratic stability is different from the concept of political stability. It is one thing to investigate the conditions for a democratic regime and another matter to look for factors that are conducive to stability, because democracies may be unstable and yet remain democratic. Lipset recognizes extremist groups or extremist ideologies as threats against democratic stability, but the stability of democratic regimes may depend on a host of other factors and democracies may become unstable without the existence of large fascist or communist parties. Perhaps it is appropriate to point to a certain circularity in the Lipset argument; the emphasis on the negative impact of extremist parties on democratic viability appears somewhat tautological. Democratic stability is defined as the continued existence of democratic rules; as necessary conditions for democratic stability are adduced two factors that operate against fascist or communist forces which by their very nature oppose democratic stability. Not unexpectedly, democracies thrive if both class and cleavage structures prevent the operation of extremist groups.

Lipset's analysis is in line with the Almond idea that homogeneity contributes to stability. Much research of the 1960s focussed on the analysis of cleavage structures diachronically and synchronically (Lipset and Rokkan, 1967b; Rokkan et al., 1970). If cleavages are so important in explaining the politics of democracies, then it is worthwhile to analyse cleavages and their structure at great length to pin down the impact of the structure of society on political instability.

Cleavages

Among Stein Rokkan's numerous publications there are a few major works that are relevant to our focus – cleavages: 'Cleavage Structures,

Party Systems, and Voter Alignments' (Lipset and Rokkan, 1967a), 'Nation-Building, Cleavage Formation and the Structuring of Mass Politics' (Rokkan et al., 1970) and *Economy, Territory, Identity* (Rokkan and Urwin, 1983).

Rokkan was much in line with a seminal trend in political sociology: political systems are to be interpreted in terms of how they relate to structures of social cleavages; the growth of an industrial society out of a rural one constitutes a process of nation-building, which is heavily influenced by factors that create or may create dissension between people in the form of cleavages; how people at large orientate to cleavages constitutes voter alignments. Rokkan was typical of the political sociology tradition at that time and its approach to understand political phenomena in terms of their social correlates.

Social and political phenomena may be interpreted synchronically or diachronically. Rokkan's interest focussed on the time dimension, on how crucial aspects of political systems and party systems arise from their historical roots. Rokkan dealt in particular with the interpretation of the emergence of West European democracies. These political systems are characterized by mass politics which implies the operation of political parties openly competing for the votes of the citizens in secret ballots, based on universal suffrage; the electorates in these countries are fully mobilized along cleavage lines and the development of cleavages and voter alignments constitute vital aspects of the building process of these nations. If the concept of social cleavages is made central to the interpretation of West European politics, then it becomes vital to understand which the main cleavages are in Western Europe.

Starting from the hypothesis about a freezing of the party systems of Western Europe at the end of the First World War, Rokkan set himself the task to identify the relationship between cleavages in society and the voter alignments as expressed in the party systems of each nation in these countries at the time of the break-through of democratic criteria of government. Rokkan developed a model of the variety of nation-building processes by making distinctions between how different cleavages occurred in alternative combinations in various countries:

> This is a task I shall try to tackle, first for the eleven smaller polities, later for all the fifteen competitive systems in Western Europe: I shall suggest, in crude outline, a model for the explanation of variations in the sequences of democratization and in the structuring of the party systems in these countries... (Rokkan et al., 1970: 78).

The Rokkan model of nation-building relates the process of democratization to election rules and representation criteria and cleavage structures and voter alignments. Rokkan constructed an elaborate classification system to cover the variety of election and representation rules and the different cleavage and alignment structures typical of democratic regimes diachronically.

Figure 1.3   *Types of cleavage: culture and economy versus centre and periphery (Rokkan, 1970: 97)*

Cleavage	National – Centre	Local and regional periphery
Interest–Economy	1A	1B
Ideology–Culture	2A	2B

Rokkan's models are about how democratic institutions and party systems developed in West European political systems. Processes of democratization may occur in various ways and party systems may differ from one country to another. To classify these variations is a valid task, but it is not a substitute for a systematic analysis of party systems and political phenomena today. It is vital to distinguish between questions as to the *origin* of political phenomena and questions as to the *persistence* of political phenomena. Both types of problem are valid objects for scientific inquiry, but they concern different matters of fact.

Rokkan described the variety of party systems that arose along with the process of democratization in West European societies. Using concepts developed by Talcott Parsons Rokkan constructs a figure which covers the basic lines of cleavages political parties orientated themselves towards during the process of democratization (Figure 1.3).

The distinctions refer to two fundamental processes of historical transformation of Western civilization according to Rokkan. Two revolutions have shaped West European societies; the national revolution created unified nation states breaking local and regional affinities and autonomy on the one hand; on the other there is the industrial revolution replacing the diffuse loyalties of the agrarian society, particularly religiously orientated ones, by economically specific lines of interest between various classes.

The basic cleavages are thus: (1A) workers versus employers/owners, (1B) primary versus secondary economy, (2A) church(es) versus government and (2B) subject versus dominant culture. Cleavage (2B) refers to the conflict between the central nation-building culture and the resistance from provincial cultures – be they ethnic or religious ones. Cleavage (2A) covers the contention among the expanding nation state, setting standards and mobilizing resources, and the traditional privileges of the church(es). The first two cleavages are related to the industrial revolution, as (1B) covers the conflict between landed interests and the industrial entrepreneurs whereas (1A) refers to the conflict between the owners of capital, business and employers on the one hand and the tenants, labourers and workers on the other. Rokkan's analysis of social cleavages is relevant for the understanding of the social sources of political phenomena, for example the structuring of the party system as well as political stability.

Conditions for polyarchy

'Polyarchy' is a technical term employed by Robert A. Dahl in his *Polyarchy* (1971) to present a theory of democracy. Dahl makes a distinction between democracy and polyarchy based on theoretical considerations:

> Polyarchies, then, may be thought of as relatively (but incompletely) democratized regimes, or, to put it in another way, polyarchies are regimes that have been substantially popularized and liberalized, that is, highly inclusive and extensively open to public contestation (Dahl, 1971: 8).

Because that work is not the place to discuss the concept of democracy, Dahl refers the reader to his *A Preface to Democratic Theory* (1956) for such matters. He identifies two dimensions of political systems and elaborates a typology by means of these two variables (Figure 1.4): (1) closed hegemonies or a low degree of public contestation and a low degree of participation; (2) inclusive hegemonies or a low degree of public contestation and a high degree of participation; (3) competitive oligarchies or a high degree of public contestation and a low degree of participation; (4) democracies or a high degree of public contestation and a high degree of participation.

Dahl has a simple question and a complex answer, searching for the conditions that are necessary or sufficient for the institutionalization of a democratic regime. Dahl identifies a number of conditions conducive to democratic viability. What are the conditions for democracy?

The way a democracy is created does affect the possibility of its persistence and survival. Dahl mentions the peaceful evolution of democratic institutions that transfer legitimacy from the old regime to the new one, which becomes accepted by large segments of the citizens.

Figure 1.4 *Dahl's dimensions of political systems*

		Participation	
		Low	High
Public Contestation	High	Competitive Oligarchies Switzerland, Ireland	Democracies: Scandinavian Italy
	Low	Closed Hegemonies Portugal*, Spain*	Inclusive Hegemonies GDR*, Hungary*

* Before the introduction of democracy (Hermet, 1978).

Dahl also emphasizes the importance for democracy of a decentralized economy. Ownership of economic assets is not the crucial issue, but a centrally directed economy is not likely to coexist with democratic institutions. Democracy may exist in agrarian societies; again, the degree of hierarchy is the crucial issue, because a society with a system of free farmers is conducive to democracy. Generally, the relationship between socio-economic conditions and democracy depends on how resources are controlled. Most favourable conditions for democracy exist when the control over resources for repression (police and military) and socio-economic sanctions (economic resources, means of communications, education opportunities) are dispersed between groups that have some degree of autonomy versus each other and which may oppose attempts at a monolithic concentration of various kinds of power, political, economic and social. The level of socio-economic development affects democracy; the richer a country is, the more likely is the existence and survival of democratic institutions. However, the connection is a complex one, as there are deviant cases.

Dahl finds a significant connection between equality and democratic institutions:

> Extreme inequalities in the distribution of key values are unfavorable to competitive politics and to polyarchy because this state of affairs ... is equivalent to extreme inequality in the distribution of key political resources and is likely to generate resentments and frustrations which weaken allegiance to the regime (Dahl, 1971: 103).

What is crucial, however, is the question of visibility. Democracies may survive inequalities as long as they do not become a focus for contention among large segments of the population. Dahl's analysis of the relationship between heterogeneity and democracy implies that democracy functions better in homogeneous societies than in fragmented ones, although there are deviant cases. Heterogeneity may be accommodated to democracy by means of a few mechanisms: collaboration between the subcultures, devices which guarantee the various subcultures some influence (veto, proportional representation, federalism).

Dahl also states that belief systems are important for the possibility of creating a democratic regime; moreover, he emphasizes the crucial significance of what various élite groups believe. Democracy needs legitimacy: a belief among political activists that democratic institutions are valid in their own right. Dahl is in agreement with Max Weber that the legitimacy of authority patterns is conducive to stability; and legitimacy is an aspect of belief systems (Weber, 1968). He adheres to an idea proposed by Harry Eckstein that beliefs about one kind of authority (political authority in democratic institutions) must be consonant with beliefs about authority structures in other kinds of institutions like the family, the church and voluntary associations (Eckstein, 1966). In addition Dahl mentions belief in the effectiveness of democratic government to solve problems as well as trust in the sincere objectives of contending political activists.

Political systems, including democratic systems, not only are dependent on the structure of society or political leaders but are vulnerable to the operations of other nations in their environment. Democracy may be threatened by overt foreign intervention. What is the relationship between democracy and foreign control? Dahl states:

> The destiny of a country is never wholly in the hands of its own people. In some cases, domination imposed by people from outside the country can be so decisive as to override the effects of all the other conditions... (Dahl, 1971: 189).

In general overt foreign intervention is not a good thing for a polyarchy. But drawing on the experiences of the West European countries during the Second World War he proposes that foreign intervention may not be fatal to an existing democracy but may strengthen it (Dahl, 1971: 197).

Polyarchy sums up much of the debate concerning the conditions for democratic institutions from a political sociology perspective. Dahl does not employ many measurement procedures or engage in statistical model building, which means that we are left with a few questions: What are the differential effects on democracy of various relevant social conditions? Are some of them more important than others? Dahl like Lipset is preoccupied with democratic rule as if it could be measured along a nominal scale: existent and non-existent. Perhaps one might use general indicators of political stability which admit scales with more properties and which lend themselves to more detailed observations? Perhaps it is just as interesting to look at various kinds of democracy as the institutions of democratic political systems may vary from one country to another reflecting different political cultures? What, actually, is the implication of social heterogeneity or homogeneity for politics?

Political culture

In *Modern Comparative Politics* (1970) Peter H. Merkl argues that functions and structure are not the only elements that comparative analysis involves. Acknowledging the contribution of structural-functionalism and systems theory to the study of various societies and polities Merkl pointed out that there is a rationalist bias in the kind of functionalism associated with Parsons, Almond and Easton, in particular in the notions of 'pattern maintenance', 'stable equilibrium' or 'system persistence'. Merkl states:

> Instead of stability and equilibrium, instability and disequilibrium are far more typical of contemporary societies, whether they be developing or already

highly developed. Basic functions that might be fulfilled in a more stable
setting are sometimes completely in abeyance. (Merkl, 1970: 19)

Moreover, political culture is a basic dimension of politics that cannot
be bypassed when the perspective is a macro one. Merkl underlined that
political attitudes must be included when conditions for the stability of
political systems or states are searched for:

> Where forms of government come and go, sometimes overnight, or turbulence
> is more prevalent than any recognizable structure, as in many developing
> countries, the people and their attitudes are far more constant than anything
> else. (Merkl, 1970: 21)

How is political culture to be analysed in a comparative way? Merkl contrasted the concept of political culture with more traditional approaches
to the analysis of political ideas and orientations: ideology, legitimacy
and national character. These concepts are deficient because they do
not allow the analysis of change in belief systems, whereas the political
culture approach was more flexible, according to Merkl.

Yet, the political culture approach had certain ties with the functionalist
movement, although it lacked its focus on system maintenance. A classic
study was the Almond and Verba volume *The Civic Culture* from 1965
(Almond and Verba, 1989). They started from some Parsonian concepts;
an individual relates to politics on three grounds: interests, participation
and values. And individual action on these bases depends on the cognitive
map of the political system, the affective orientation towards political
objects and symbols as well as the evaluation of political events.

According to Almond and Verba individuals display attitudes towards:
(1) the political system, (2) input activities of citizens like electoral
participation, (3) output activities like public programmes as well as (4)
the self as a political participant. Attitudes whether cognitive, affective or
evaluative tend to be patterned along these political system dimensions.
Thus, *The Civic Culture* derives three archetypes of political culture:
parochial, subject or participant orientations.

A parochial attitude is typical of a political culture where knowledge
and involvement with all aspects of the political system are low whereas
a subject attitude occurs in political cultures where knowledge of the
system is high but involvement low. A participant political culture is
characteristic where knowledge and involvement is high. Almond and
Verba examined data from five countries – Great Britain, West Germany,
Italy, Mexico and the United States – in order to find a participant culture
combined with a democratic polity. There is a limit to the possibilities of
investigating political attitudes in various political systems all over the
world. What has been done is mostly in the form of case studies.

A focus on attitudes and culture may be combined with a political
sociology emphasis on cleavages, or political culture may be approached

as a dimension *sui generis*. At first cultural analysis was tied into much of the cleavage perspective, but it soon disassociated itself from the political sociology approach. Thus, Almond and Verba in *The Civic Culture* (1965) considered social cleavages as fundamental to political life:

> Without some meaningfully structured cleavage in society, it is hard to see how democratic politics can operate. If democracy involves at some point a choice among alternatives, the choice must be about something. If there were no cleavage, if people did not combine into meaningfully opposed political groupings, this would suggest '… a community in which politics was of no real importance to the community' and one in which the alternation of political élites meant little (Almond and Verba 1965: 357-8).

But as cultural analysis developed the question of an association between political attitudes and social cleavages was framed in a more open ended fashion. Political cultures were recognized as belief and value systems with a coherence of their own, which could not be approached in terms of a reductionist perspective, claiming that social conflict somehow was automatically transformed into political issues (Wildavsky, 1987; Inglehart, 1988b). According to *Cultural Theory* (Thompson, Ellis and Wildavsky, 1990) hypotheses about national political cultures may offer illuminating comparative insights into how individuals orientate towards their political context underlining either individualism, egalitarian values, hierarchy or fatalist attitudes. As there is a strong tension in some countries between alternative *political subcultures* the problem of cultural cohesion becomes politically highly relevant.

Social or political cohesion

Fragmentation and polarization in the party system indicate a low degree of value consensus in society, but is the opposite that a high degree of social cohesion will be conducive to political stability also true? In his comparative work reported in *Politics in Western Europe* (1980; 1989) Gordon Smith makes a critique of the political sociology approach by clearly separating between two distinct aspects of cohesion, social cohesion and government cohesion (Figure 1.5).

A fundamental feature of Smith's typology is that there is no necessary or fixed relationship between the levels of government and social cohesion. A low governmental cohesion may be combined with a high social cohesion and vice versa. Smith's two categories of dominant and majoritarian (balanced) party systems may be discussed as it is not necessary that strong governments have to be quasi-authoritarian in societies where cohesion is weak and we cannot make the assumption that majority type governments are always to be found in societies with a large amount of value consensus. The observation of the growing saliency of diffusion among West European nations is essential. Smith states:

The argument presented here is simply that there is an overall movement discernible to the diffused type of party system at the expense of all the other types (Smith, 1979a: 136).

Almond began from the combination of weak social cohesion and weak governmental cohesion whereas Lipset focussed upon the combination strong social cohesion and strong governmental cohesion. Smith identified another possibility: strong value consensus in society but low degree of cohesion in government (Smith, 1986). Evidence may be found in the 1970s when traditional voter alignments have been abandoned without resulting in more political stability. While some traditional cleavages grow less relevant the problems of governmental stability and governmental effectiveness increase as the problems of big government and government overload indicate (Rose, 1981; 1984). To understand politics in representative governments in Western Europe it is evidently not enough to pay attention to the structure of social cleavages. Smith's insistence upon separating politics and society came at a time when a number of cross-country comparative studies showed the complexity of political phenomena at the party level.

Arend Lijphart had early in *The Politics of Accommodation* (1968; 1975) stated a case for a deviance in the political sociology modelling of the relationship between society and politics: the occurrence of fragmentation and strong government cohesion. A basic assumption in prevailing approaches at that time was a hypothesis implicit in much of the work done within political sociology: political phenomena are substantially affected by other kinds of social phenomena like economic development, social stratification and cultural systems. Actually, one trend within political sociology attempted to explain the variation in political phenomena by means of ecological factors. Phenomena such as

Figure 1.5   *Typology of cohesion (Smith, 1986)*

Social cohesion

		Low	High
Governing cohesion	High	Dominance	Balance
	Low	Fragmentation	Diffusion

    Note: The shaded area represents the stable, segmented society.

political parties or political belief systems were to be understood against background information about social structure.

Structural properties were conceived of as determining politics in a somewhat reductionist manner: objective social conditions affect political behaviour in a direct way – what Giovanni Sartori labels 'sociology of politics' (Sartori, 1969). A reductionist approach greatly overemphasized the explanatory power of social factors with regard to political phenomena. Even worse, it missed a crucial property of politics, the behaviour of political élites: their capacity for adaption and innovation, their significance for the explanation of properties of political systems like stability and conflict regulation. The reorientation of comparative politics towards institutionalist frameworks of analysis was a slow process but it showed up in the study of political parties, government and political culture. Let us start with a borderline case between political sociology and institutionalism: the theme of consociational democracy.

Consensus democracy

One basic idea in the theories discussed so far is that social heterogeneity is conducive to instability. The continental European political systems are plagued by the fragmentation of these societies into more or less separate subcultures. Almond states:

> ... these systems have a totalitarian potentiality in them. The fragmented political culture may be transformed into a synthetically homogeneous one and the stalemated role structure mobilized by the introduction of the coercive pattern already described (Almond, 1956: 408).

To Lijphart this was both right and wrong. What was true was the thesis that social heterogeneity affects stability negatively. The more divided a society is along cleavages like religion, language and class the more difficult becomes the task to achieve stable government. However, Lijphart rejected the idea of a direct relationship between heterogeneity and stability. Political systems are not mechanically determined by the prevailing social cleavages, because political institutions can adapt to their environment to overcome negative social conditions.

Lijphart was one among several scholars who from an institutionalist perspective during the 1960s began to investigate the *mechanisms* by which political systems may adapt to and overcome threats to the stability of their institutions. A group of scholars emerged who were much concerned with the capacity of political institutions and political leaders to respond to stimuli from society, the 'incipient school of consociational analysis' according to Hans Daalder. These scholars argued that the negative effects of heterogeneity could be overcome by élite behaviour, by means of so-called consociational devices, which would lessen conflict and contribute to cooperation among the élites of the various subcultures.

These institutionalists argued that there are a number of countries which are plural societies, i.e. which are deeply divided into subcultures, but which have remained stable democracies for a long time due to collaboration between élites and the existence of special mechanisms for élite behaviour. Almond was partly wrong with regard to matters of fact and the crude sociology of politics was wrong with regard to matters of interpretation and explanation, Lijphart argued (Lijphart, 1968). To show that homogeneity is not a necessary condition for political stability and that the effective operation of consociational devices is a sufficient condition for stability these scholars analysed some pertinent cases of heterogeneity and stability among Western European democracies.

Lijphart used the title 'politics of accommodation' in his description of the Dutch political system, and Jürg Steiner called his book on Switzerland *Amicable Agreement versus Majority Rule: Conflict Resolution in Switzerland* (1974). The titles employed by these consociational scholars reveal their approach, their focus on the mechanisms of conflict resolution in plural societies. Val Lorwin analysed Belgium in 'Segmented Pluralism: Ideological Cleavages and Political Cohesion in the Small European Democracies' (1971) whereas Gerhard Lehmbruch wrote about *Proporzdemokratie: Politisches System und Politische Kultur in der Schweiz und in Österreich* (1967). Bingham Powell wrote an Austrian case study entitled *Social Fragmentation and Political Hostility* (1970) and Eric Nordlinger spoke generally of *Conflict Regulation in Divided Societies* (1972).

The Netherlands, Belgium, Switzerland and Austria were selected by these scholars as deviant cases in the Almond typology and their positive contributions to comparative politics consisted of the analysis of the mechanisms in these countries which – according to the theory – safeguard stability in a plural environment conducive to instability. Kenneth McRae added Canada to the set of consociational societies in a book with a typical title: *Consociational Democracy: Political Accommodation in Segmented Societies* (1974). And Lijphart applied the theory to Lebanon and Northern Ireland to state the limits of the theory.

The consociational school wanted to make a contribution to democratic theory; it was concerned not primarily with political stability but with political stability of democratic regimes in plural societies. It is possible to apply the Almond approach to any kind of system, but the consociational analysts looked primarily at democratic political systems. They wanted to refute the thesis implicit in the Almond analysis as well as in other approaches that only the Anglo-American kind of democracy is viable: there are European democracies that are just as stable for different reasons. The stability of the European cases of the Netherlands, Belgium,

Figure 1.6 *Lijphart's typology of regimes (1977a: 106)*

Structure of society

		Homogeneous	Plural
Elite behaviour	Coalescent	Depoliticized democracy	Consociational democracy
	Adversarial	Centripetal democracy	Centrifugal democracy

Switzerland and Austria is due to the presence of consociational devices. Lijphart develops a general theory of democracy in his *Democracy in Plural Societies* (1977a) including a basic typology which indicates the development away from a sociological approach towards some kind of institutionalist perspective (Figure 1.6). Lijphart states:

> The four types in the typology (in Figure 1.6) represent not only different combinations of social pluralism and élite behavior but also different degrees of political stability. The centrifugal type of democracy is unstable, whereas the centripetal and consociational types are stable democracies (Lijphart, 1977a: 107).

Lijphart attributes the fact that consociational democracies are stable to the effective operation within these systems of so-called consociational devices. These devices include: grand coalition, mutual veto, proportionality, autonomy and federalism (Lijphart, 1977a: 25–52). It is argued against the Lijphart hypothesis about consociational devices as conducive to political stability that it remains to be proved that the relationship between consociational devices and stability is a causal relationship (Barry, 1975). Lijphart states:

> Consociational democracy means government by élite cartel designed to turn a democracy with a fragmented political culture into a stable democracy (Lijphart, 1974a: 79).

The model of consociational democracy implies that (a) if a society is fragmented, then its democracy is stable only if it is consociational, and (b) if a society is homogeneous, it is stable. The use of consociational devices is one effective tool to bring about stability – when they are effective. The model raises the question: When are consociational devices effective? If stability means effective government and consociational devices are one way to run a government effectively, then surely Lijphart's proposition (a) is true. Consociational democracies are stable, but are they stable because they are consociational? The stability of consociational democracies

Figure 1.7   *Characteristics of democracy*

The Westminister model	The consensus model
One party and bare-majority cabinets	Executive power-sharing
Fusion of power and cabinet dominance	Separation of powers, formal and informal
Asymmetric bi-cameralism	Balanced bi-cameralism and minority representation
Two-party system	Multi-party system
One-dimensional party system	Multi-dimensional party system
Plurality system of elections	Proportional representation
Unitary and centralized territorial government	Territorial and non-territorial federalism and decentralization
Unwritten constitution and parliamentary sovereignty	Written constitution and minority veto

Source: Lijphart, 1984a.

depends on the extent to which the consociational devices are effective in reducing conflict between groups and organizations. The stability of non-consociational democracies depends on the same condition.

A society may be run on the majority–minority pattern, the minority pattern or the grand coalition pattern. Whether it is stable depends on the political situation, the distribution of control and power among its groups and organizations. In this respect there is no difference between different governmental élite patterns and there is no difference between homogeneous and heterogeneous societies. In short, Lijphart shows convincingly that what Almond called 'Continental European' political systems may be stable, for example the set of consociational democracies, although one may question that the presence of consociational devices is a necessary condition for stability in heterogeneous societies or that the presence of such mechanisms is a sufficient condition for stability.

In his *Democracies* (1984a) Lijphart generalized his model of consociational democracy by means of a distinction between majoritarian and consensus democracy. The so-called consociational devices are only one type of decision-making mechanisms that distinguish what Lijphart refers to as consensus democracy from majoritarian democracy. Lijphart introduces two ideal types of the political system which real polities more or less resemble (Figure 1.7). The emphasis is again on the importance of the structuring of decision processes intermediating between political stability and social cleavages. Lijphart carefully points out that these two models constitute ideal types to which the existing decision-making systems correspond more or less.

A number of pure models of democracy have been proposed as

a distinction between Madisonian, populist and polyarchical models of democracy has been suggested. The growth of corporatization has resulted in suggestions to the effect that we must also recognize a new model of democracy, corporatist democracy (Schmitter, 1984; Streeck and Schmitter, 1985) or organized democracy (Olsen, 1983).

The consociationalist terminology appears to be open to discussion as some basic concepts may need further elaboration. It is not quite clear what a plural society is, what constitutes a consociational democracy or how political stability is defined. Lijphart refers to a definition of heterogeneity employed by Harry Eckstein in his famous study on Norwegian democracy, *Division and Cohesion in Democracy: A Study of Norway* (1966):

> ... a plural society is a society divided by what Harry Eckstein calls 'segmental cleavages'. He writes: 'This exists where political divisions follow very closely, and especially concern lines of objective social differentiation, especially those particularly salient in a society.' Segmental cleavages may be of a religious, ideological, linguistic, regional, cultural, racial, or ethnic nature (Lijphart, 1977a: 3–4).

If one accepts this definition of heterogeneity – what is an objective line of social differentiation? – it is not clear why the Netherlands, Belgium, Switzerland and Austria are designated as the plural societies. There are various kinds of cleavages in the West European political systems and their impact on politics varies. Any sharp line between the homogeneous and the heterogeneous systems is arbitrary, because each and every system has such cleavages, though to a varying extent. There is a more specific meaning of the concept of plural societies. Val Lorwin states that there is a special set of societies that are characterized by religious or ethnic cleavages and which only slightly express economic or functional cleavages (Lorwin, 1974). This seems to be more in line with what most consociational scholars implicitly assume:

> In other words, consociational democracy means segmented pluralism, if it is broadened to include all possible segmental cleavages in a plural society, and combined with concordant democracy (Lijphart, 1977a: 5).

The concept of concordant democracy was developed by Gerhard Lehmbruch to denote a strategy of conflict management by cooperation and agreement among the different élites rather than by competition and majority decision. The restriction of consociational democracy to plural societies is perhaps doubtful, as strategies of cooperation and agreement may occur in all kinds of systems to a varying extent. The idea of concordant democracy – strategies of cooperation and agreement – hardly identifies a few distinct countries.

The idea of a consociational democracy had the same impact as the Almond approach: it stimulated the search for new kinds of typology of political systems thus making comparative politics more theoretically orientated. It counterbalanced the prevailing political sociology way of thinking about political stability and democracy by focussing on deviant cases which combined heterogeneity with stability. More importantly, it expressed the general development of comparative politics towards more institutionalism which may be seen in the way political party as well as comparative government research developed. The idea that corporatist patterns of decision-making were an integral part of democracy in some West European states belongs to the same trend towards institutionalism.

Corporatism

The finding that social cohesion does not necessarily lead to political stability implies that the problem of how cleavages in society are translated into politics must be generalized. Party government may fail to deliver durable governments even where there is low social fragmentation. Although political parties are crucial instruments for the expression of lines of conflict within society they are not the sole vehicles for interest articulation and interest mediation. Even though political parties may be the dominant actors in the issue-making at the governmental level mobilizing groups into camps of conflict as well as resolving matters of contention by participation in the decision-making structures, we must also pay attention to the growing relevance of trade unions – the theme of corporatism. Gerhard Lehmbruch and Philippe Schmitter convincingly argue that West European polities in the 1970s had considerable elements of corporatism in their cleavage structure and their decision-making system. The various nations may be ordered from strong to weak corporatism in relation to how much interest mediation and policy concertation they include in their society and government (Figure 1.8).

The archetype of corporatism is type IV – Austria and partly Sweden – where big interest organizations conduct far-reaching negotiations to reconcile peacefully their interests and where the same hierarchically

Figure 1.8 *Types of interest mediation and modes of policy formation (Lehmbruch and Schmitter, 1982: 263)*

Policy formation by

		Pressure	Concertation
Interest intermediation through	Pluralism	I	II
	Corporatism	III	IV

structured organizations partake in various forms in government policy-making, in the framing and implementation of policies in formally designed channels. The opposite to the pure type of corporatism is the classical image of pure type American pressure politics in a pluralist polity, i.e. type I. Neo-corporatist theory claims that we should not only look for the pure type but devise quantitative techniques that would make possible the description of more or less corporatism. The impure types II and III are crucial for the analysis of cleavages and decision-making in Western Europe today. Interestingly, the corporatism theme states that corporatist decision-making mechanisms are conducive to political stability (Schmidt, 1982), by reducing the levels of unemployment and inflation. At the same time, corporatism has been regarded as a major challenge to the basic institutionalist mode of government in Western Europe: party government.

Place of political parties

Looking at the relationship between politics and social structure one has to recognize political parties as an intervening variable. Political parties and party systems may be looked upon as one of the main links between government institutions and society. Considering the general structure of the West European nations it may not be an exaggeration to maintain that political parties are the main link between society and government. The importance of political parties as expressions of cleavages in the social structure and as vehicles for social movements cannot be doubted; moreover, representative government would be inconceivable without the existence of party systems. However, the question of how political parties operate as mechanisms for the mobilization of social cleavages as well as participants in the formation of governments and the process of political decision-making is an open ended one.

If political parties and the party system are looked upon as a factor intervening between society and government then we must search for how society conditions political parties as well as how political parties operate in a governmental setting. On the one hand it may be asked what are the social correlates of the electoral strength of political parties, nationally as well as regionally. On the other hand it may be inquired into how the parties and the party system relate to political stability.

Giovanni Sartori states in a comprehensive treatment of political parties *Parties and Party Systems* (1976):

> But when the society at large becomes politicized, the traffic rules that plug the society into the state, and vice versa, are established by the way in which a party system becomes structured. At this point, parties become channeling agencies and the party system becomes the system of *political canalization* of the society (Sartori, 1976: 41).

Figure 1.9   *Parties: number and ideological distance (Sartori, 1976)*

Ideological distance

		Small	High
Party fragmentation	Low	Two-partism	Centripetal competition
	High	Segmented multipartism	Polarized multipartism

Sartori's basic argument is institutionalist in intent: political parties are objects worthy of study on their own terms. In particular he warns against any reductionist bias treating parties as simple expressions of social forces that translate to the political system via parties in an automatic fashion. He states:

> However, if we do not identify first the political structures – and particularly the party structuring – we are likely to miss this crucial question: *How is it that similar socioeconomic structures are not translated into similar party systems?* (Sartori, 1976: 180–1)

If political parties are an important link between society and the political system, how are systems of political parties to be analysed? Famous classification schemata and typologies are suggested by Maurice Duverger in his pioneer work *Political Parties* (1954) and by Siegmund Neumann in his important 'Toward a Comparative Study of Political Parties' (1956). Sartori moves beyond the standard criteria of number of parties – one-party system, two-party system and multi-party system – to propose an articulate typology combining number of parties with the extent of ideological distance between the parties in the party system, polarization. The basic concepts may be represented in a 2 × 2 table (Figure 1.9).

The Sartori typology of party systems focusses upon two properties that are particularly relevant for the analysis of the relationship between society and political stability where political parties play an intervening role. Sartori suggests that it is the combination of polarization and fragmentation that distinguishes various party systems. Although Sartori looks more at the party systems themselves than at their causes or effects, we find interesting ideas about the impact of political parties upon government. Sartori states:

> It is important to ask, nonetheless, what are the chances of survival of the polarized polities. Surely, this variety of multipartism is an unhealthy state of affairs for a body politic. A political system characterized by centrifugal drives, irresponsible opposition, and unfair competition is hardly a viable system (Sartori, 1976:140).

Why is it the case that polarized multipartism is particularly conducive to political stability? Is polarized multipartism the only party system type that negatively affects the viability of political systems? Sartori points out the important position of so-called anti-system parties in shaping the party system; the definition reads: 'Accordingly, a party can be defined as being anti-system whenever it undermines the legitimacy of the regime it opposes' (Sartori, 1976:133). Like Lipset Sartori recognizes communist and fascist parties as anti-system and consequently maintains that systems having strong communist and/or fascist parties result in political instability. Although this may be true of the classical examples of political instability, the Weimar Republic, France during the Fourth Republic and modern Italy we must recognize that political instability may have various sources. Moreover, new party research has emphasized that party system volatility and party malfunctioning has become more prevalent in Western Europe in the 1970s and 1980s at the same time as anti-system parties have shrunk in attractiveness in the electorate (Mair and Smith, 1989).

Comparative party research

Government in a representative democracy involves a voter choice in the electorate among party alternatives, but it has remained an issue of contention whether the parties set the agenda for the voter or the electorate decides between the parties (Key, 1966). The rational choice model of democracy was challenged by élite theory that argued that political parties determined the frame of reference of the voter. The standard rational image of government in a representative liberal democracy was replaced by the model of democracy as competition between organized élites influencing the electoral choice between party ideologies expressed in the form of electoral manifestos and election day promises to be kept when the party(ies) got a majority of the vote and to be implemented by means of government action (Schumpeter, 1942). This Schumpeterian model of democracy has in turn been criticized from two different angles, big government resulting in overload politics and implementation deficits as well as the new model of democracy as participation rejecting the claims of party government (Pateman, 1970; Rose, 1980). What is the present condition of the model of democracy as party government?

Recent comparative work has evaluated the competitive model of party government. An ECPR research group gathered in a comparative project 'Recent Changes in European Party Systems' where the focus was on the extent to which political parties perform their traditional functions according to democratic theory in the Schumpeter version: interest articulation and aggregation, policy-making and system legitimation. Under test is the hypothesis that parties and party systems are in a state of crisis due to increased volatility, the bureaucratization of party organization and the expansion of corporatist patterns of policy-making and implementation. *Party Systems in Denmark, Austria, Switzerland, the Netherlands and Belgium* (Daalder, 1987a) comes out of this project.

The concepts of party crisis and party system challenge and response have become central in the institutionalist analysis of political parties and party systems. However, they are ambiguous and need to be assessed in a comparative perspective as the conduct of party functions depends on other properties of the political system as well as the history of the party system. How come there was so little party crisis in Austria and Switzerland, but so much of it in Denmark, the Netherlands and Belgium?

The analysis of political parties from the standpoint of a party systems perspective is without exception about *change* and *durability*. This is the classical focus of the party system problem, particularly with regard to the West European countries. *Parties and Party Systems in Liberal Democracies* (Wolinetz, 1988) exemplifies how these key problems in party research are approached in a semi-comparative fashion. The first step in the typical party system research programme is to classify party systems longitudinally, preferably by means of a number of case studies of the major European democracies. The second step is to model the relation between independent variables and the dependent variable measuring the extent of party system durability either in terms of an explicit comparative model or on the basis of country specific observations pertaining to some implicit comparative model. Several institutionalist studies cover the first step and some even reach the second step, but few if any handle the various party systems in terms of an explicitly comparative model.

The study of differences and similarities in party systems must identify a causal perspective on the set of variables that account for the variation in the set of standard properties of party systems. At first when political sociology had its heydays, the party system was viewed as determined by the structure of social cleavages in the environment, party systems being locked into a long term rigid cleavage structure – Continental Europe – or being freely floating above a cross-cutting system of cleavages – the UK. The advent of the institutionalist paradigm meant that party system continuity was seen as conditioned by both forces of persistency or change in the social environment and the adaptive capacities of parties.

A number of strategies are available for political parties: the mobilization of an electoral niche à la Stein Rokkan, the turn to an Otto Kirchheimer catch-all strategy or the use of the state power structure to create a symbiosis between party and public authority. The probability of success for an adaptive strategy depends not only on the environment of the social structure but also on the choice of strategy by the other remaining parties in the system. Party system instability may also be due to internal party processes which are unrelated to changes in the social cleavage structure. The likelihood of party system durability is high when there is adaptive party change in an uncertain environment. When the strategies of parties are fixed in relation to social change, then there will be considerable party system instability. How stable are political parties, if we focus on electoral outcomes over time or internal party cohesion?

The emergence of a large number of case studies of various elections in different countries has changed the main focus in comparative party research. Traditional party research asked why is there so little change? The Lipset and Rokkan theory about the frozen party systems in Western Europe (Lipset and Rokkan, 1967b) directed research to inquiry into the conditions that sustain political parties. The study edited by Lawson and Merkl, *When Parties Fail: Emerging Alternative Organizations*, is an authoritative statement to the effect that the stability focus has come to an end. Modern party research inquires into the conditions that destabilize political parties and their environment.

Asking not how parties are so stable but why there are parties in the first place means searching for *linkages* between citizens and rulers in relation to which parties derive their functions. The failure of established political parties has meant that alternative organizations have responded to the kinds of linkages between citizen and state that Lawson outlines. The emergent parties are classified in terms of cultural theoretical notions: environmentalist (the Green parties in FRG and Sweden, the Italian Radicals, Swiss civic action groups), supplementary (SDP in the UK, Glistrup in Denmark), communitarian (ethnic groups in the UK) and anti-authoritarian. Merkl interprets the signs of party failure by placing political parties between the two linkage poles. *Citizens* relate differently to parties now because post-materialist cultures emphasize independence, discretion and disloyalty when citizens orientate towards parties. The *state* in a period of overload government creates a new institutional setting for the parties where many groups scramble for power and influence making party life ambiguous, complex and hazardous.

Government, parliamentarians and coalition theory

Taking an institutionalist approach, it becomes vital not to try to reduce the pattern of government formation into a simple description of the social structure of the society. A number of distinctions may be made when describing the properties of government formation in West European nations. Comparative politics needs to strike a balance between the deductive and inductive approaches to the analysis of government formation.

Most West European societies are characterized by a multitude of

social cleavages and West European politics is also to be described by
the formation of a large number of political parties, both of which traits
somehow have an impact on government formation in these countries.
In much of the literature on comparative politics there is a myth of
multipartism as Lawrence C. Dodd points out in his *Coalitions in
Parliamentary Government* (1976):

> (1) governments in multiparty parliaments must be minority cabinets, coa-
> lition cabinets, or both; (2) by their very nature, minority cabinets and
> coalition cabinets are quite transient; (3) multiparty systems are consequently
> undesirable since they produce transient governments (Dodd, 1976: 10).

It is often stated that multi-party systems are conducive to political
instability. A multi-party system makes the formation of one-party majority government difficult. A multi-party setting makes coalition building
a difficult process. This is exactly where Dodd makes his theoretical
argument: it is true that durable governments are primarily minimum
winning coalitions and that minimum winning coalitions may be found
in two-party systems where the majority party is a minimum winning
coalition with one member, i.e. the party itself. But minimum winning
coalitions are possible also within multi-party systems; actually, they
occur quite often.

Dodd's theory about government formation patterns adds a crucial link
to the understanding of the relationships between social structure, political
parties and government. Whether a minimum winning coalition will form
or not is a function of two factors, the willingness of parties to enter
coalitions and the information certainty concerning the bargaining of
potential coalition members. The larger the number of parties is the more
difficult are the calculations of coalition possibilities and advantages; the
more polarized the party system the less the coalition willingness.

Dodd is able to show that although a multi-party system tends to occur
in socially fragmented societies it does not always mean government
instability:

> Yet it is really no truer to maintain that multiparty systems generate transient
> cabinets than it is to argue that party systems as a whole lead to transient
> government. The variation in cabinet durability among multiparty parliaments
> is virtually as great as is the variation among all parliaments including
> majority party systems (Dodd, 1976: 234).

Durable minimum winning coalitions may form in multi-party systems
as long as the fragmentation and polarization are not excessive. Thus,
cabinet stability in multi-party systems is possible contrary to what
multipartism claims. The Dodd analysis showed convincingly that there
is a sort of myth of multipartism, that there may be durable government
among the polities in Western Europe that do not operate on the basis of
a two-party interaction model. However, one may wish to look at more

factors that affect stability than only the pattern of government formation, and there may be more to the equation that only minimum winning coalitions produce stable governments as also minority governments may be stable (Strom, 1985; 1989).

If we take a closer look at government formation at various levels of the public sector, then the institutionalist description will become more and more complex. *Political Parties and Coalitions in European Local Government* (1989) edited by Colin Mellors and Bert Pijnenburg and comprising nine country studies of local government coalition behaviour describes the amorphous nature of local government coalitions. In a few countries local government lacks a local executive body – Britain, West Germany and Ireland – whereas in other countries the range of coalition behaviour includes both a council and an executive of some sort: Belgium, Denmark, Italy, the Netherlands, Spain and France. The making of coalitions ranges from one party dominance to grand coalitions over a variety of constellations where ideology appears to be more salient than size. The strength of the institutional setting for the shaping of local politics is apparent. *Coalitional Behaviour in Theory and Practice: An Inductive Model for Western Europe* (1986) edited by Geoffrey Pridham shows that the patterns of government formation in West European countries depend on a number of factors: history, institutions, motivations, horizontal and vertical relationships, internal party configurations, socio-political as well as environmental/external dimensions. It is simply not possible to catch all the nuances of coalition building at various levels of government in Western Europe by the simple model that social heterogeneity causes a multitude of parties which leads to minority government whereas social homogeneity leads to a two-party system which translates in minimum winning coalitions.

The analysis of patterns of government formation is related to the study of parliamentary behaviour. *Opposition in Western Europe* (Kolinsky, 1987) shows that what is *similar* in patterns of government–opposition interaction in Western Europe is the desertion of the dualistic model of opposition. Political opposition is no longer the strict Westminster model of political competition between two monolithic groups in Parliament, nor the political system struggle between the right and the left classes in Continental Europe. Action complexity and party tactics prevail with consensus on the legitimacy of the rules of political opposition. What is *different* in West European styles of opposition is the location of the centre in the country patterns. In some countries like the UK, the Netherlands and Italy opposition comes from the left of centre whereas the opposite holds in France and Spain. In other countries like the FRG there are considerable extra parliamentary movements of political opposition.

Representatives of the People? Parliamentarians and Constituents in Western Democracies (Bogdanor, 1985) argues that there is some kind of relationship between parliamentary roles and constituency characteristics. There is a cross country variation in the two basic entities: three types of constituencies including single-member, multi-member and one single national constituency as well as four kinds of roles of parliamentarians covering constituency, partisan, interest and policy roles. Single member constituencies without choice of candidates like the British system are conducive to a partisan role of the parliamentarian. When single member constituencies are combined with a selection mechanism between candidates like the primary or the second ballot system the constituency role takes precedence. This is even more emphasized in multimember constituencies which employ the single transferable vote. On the other hand, multimember constituencies with the usual proportional methods tend towards the partisan role where party discipline is strong as well as towards the interest role where the party system is highly segmented in terms of a few salient social cleavages.

Issues

The hypothesis that social forces play a major role if not *the* role in shaping political events appears objectionable as it assumes that political institutions and political behaviour passively mirror the structure of society. This is hardly in line with theories that emphasize the active role of political parties in determining their agenda as well as the notion that political institutions possess a certain amount of autonomy. Social problems cannot crop into political decision-making unless being politicized by the major political actors, i.e. mainly the political parties. The politicization of cleavages in society is a necessary condition for the reflection of social divergences in political life – and the process of politicization needs to be understood on its own terms. Issues provide the missing link between the structure of society with its cleavage bases and government institutions and their properties.

In their *Explaining and Predicting Elections* (1983) Ian Budge and Dennis J. Farlie argue convincingly that issues are important elements in the electoral processes in democracies, determining the fate of political parties and paving the way for the selection of political leaders in government. In elections the social problems of nations are politicized in issues to which the electorate orientates itself on the basis of ideological and interest considerations. Without the politicization process politics could not relate to cleavages in society. But the politicization process has its own logic meaning that parties may emphasize issues that are not related to social cleavages or may find it to their advantage to suppress or underline some social cleavages more than others. And – as Budge and Farlie show – issue orientation has a profound impact on electoral outcomes which must be recognized in addition to such factors as party loyalty and party identification ('basic vote' or 'normal vote'). Issue orientation is a way to reduce the complicated calculations of the pros and cons of various party proposals for both electors and leaders meaning that issue identification replaces the intricate interest calculation as conceived in rational choice theory.

The fundamental importance of issues in political life makes it necessary to deal at some length with the process of politicization of problems. Issues not only are relevant to the understanding of party choice in an electoral setting but have a profound impact on political stability. Political instability results from contention between political actors which is focussed on issues. Which are the main types of issues in European democracies? We attempt to broaden the analysis of issues by relating it to the social structure searching for the social sources of the politicization process without any implicit reductionist conception.

Political outputs and outcomes

The reorientation of comparative politics from a political sociology approach towards institutionalist lines of inquiry did not only mean an interest in understanding the peculiar logic of political parties or decision-making mechanisms. It also involved the identification of new substantive areas of interest. One of the most striking innovations is the emerging field of comparative public policy. Traditionally nothing was said about what governments in fact did, as the focus of interest was on the structure of the state. To look at policy outputs or governmental programmes and policy outcomes or social results in a comparative perspective added a new dimension to comparative politics, particularly in relation to the problem of interpreting the West European welfare state.

Comparative Public Policy: The Politics of Social Choice in Europe and America (1983) underlines the neglect of output studies in the field of comparative government. The authors state:

> Comparative public policy is the study of how, why, and to what effect different governments pursue particular courses of action or inaction (Heidenheimer et al., 1983: 2–3).

Public policy rests on choice in an environment of opportunity and constraint. The variety of policy-making may be approached as involving the choice of scope, policy instrument, distribution and innovation in relation to different policy areas as for example education, health, housing, economic policy, taxation policy, income maintenance and urban planning. The importance of a policy perspective in comparative politics derives from two considerations: on the one hand it complements the traditional focus on input and structure and on the other hand it offers a new way to look at what different types of government mean concretely for the citizens of a country. In order to explain various national policy patterns we resort to information about inputs and structure. The study of comparative policy-making is to a considerable extent an attempt to link the variation in policies to the country differences in state structure and the opportunities and constraints that follow from structural considerations.

For example, look at education policies in terms of this perspective. The differences between mass education programmes and élite programmes reflect the decentralization and centralization variation between the political systems. Change and innovation come about differently in accordance with this separation. There are policy differences between highly centralized France and Sweden on the one hand and more decentralized United Kingdom and the Federal Republic of Germany. The Netherlands is different due to its strong state support of private church organized education. Policy-making reflects deeper forces in the social structure, but of crucial importance is the existence of opportunity and restraint inherent in the structure of existing institutions.

Health care policy is also an example which reflects political structure. British health care displays the pros and cons of a totally nationalized system whereas the West German health care policy reflects both the traditional reliance on third payers and the decentralized political structure in the 1949 constitution whereas Swedish health care policy is orientated towards a reliance on a socialized but decentralized solution of the supply problem. The policy variables – scope, instrument, distribution, restraints and innovation – are different in these different health care policies reflecting the basic structures.

The hypothesis about a close link between politics and policy is not born out equally clearly in the variety of housing policy. Housing policy is too complicated a matter to be reducible to a few simple categories. However, the United Kingdom and Sweden have favoured public alternatives more than private whereas the opposite is true of France and West Germany. And Sweden and West Germany have relied very much on the third sector. The reorientation of housing policy towards the demand side instead of the supply side has been a universal one with various consumer subsidies replacing producer incentives.

What is the range for variation in economic policy? The growing interdependency between the countries in the world means that the different nations are hit by similar economic changes like the oil crises phenomena in the early and late 1970s as well as the combination of inflation and depression – stagflation – since the mid-1970s. However, the policy responses do vary as some countries emphasize traditional Keynesian techniques whereas others have tried monetarist or supply side policies. A distinction may be made between those countries that underline employment and those that emphasize the fight against inflation as a solution to the trade-off between either high unemployment or high inflation. What matters here is the nature of the political system, as the policy choice is affected by the position of the left in state and society (Schmidt, 1982). Corporatist patterns of policy-making have been tried in order to increase economic stability and consensus (Schmitter and Lehmbruch, 1979). It is, however, very much an open question how much political variables matter for economic outcomes (Whiteley, 1986).

Taxation policy is closely tied to general economic policy and has followed its general development. As long as there was economic growth governments increased their tax ratios. When hit by the combination of slow economic growth and high inflation taxation policy had to be reorientated as marginal tax rates were cut back and deficit spending resorted to. Countries tend to differ in the redistributional emphasis of their taxation systems depending on the strength of the left. And with the type of taxation policy goes a certain kind of income maintenance policy. Certain policy instruments in social insurance and means-tested assistance are employed in many countries, but in alternative combinations. The transition from individual equity to social adequacy in insurance concepts has been a long-term trend in Western Europe. But countries with the strongest base of working-class politics seem to make the greatest efforts at conscious redistribution (Heidenheimer et al., 1983: 236). Policy differences between countries may show up in all the dimensions of policy: scope, instrument, distribution and innovation.

Granted that there exist policy patterns – how extensive are these? And are they consistent between nations, times and policy sectors? According to the political structure hypothesis the policy patterns vary more between nations than along policy sectors, because policy-making and implementation reflect the decision-making structures more than the problem nature of a policy sector. The policy sector hypothesis argues the other way around underlining the similarities between policies in various countries in one and the same policy sector and the differences between policy sectors in one and the same country. Finally, there is the policy style hypothesis which argues that nations approach their various policy sectors in terms of a unique and general mode of policy-making and implementation which may reflect both structural characteristics but also change with time and tradition. How are these hypotheses to be evaluated? The study of comparative public policy would have to include several countries and test more precise policy models before one could move towards a general hypothesis about the sources of patterns of policy-making.

Following the general systems model of the political system, the comparative study of government may focus on either the input side, the output side or the political system itself. No doubt the traditional approach heavily emphasized the structure of the political system whereas the reaction to the traditional approach – functionalism, behaviouralism and the developmental approach – underlined the input side and the implications of broad social change for the nature of the political system. The policy orientation thus added the output perspective asking whether inputs or structure matter for outputs or outcomes, the actions of the polity and their consequences for society respectively.

The hypothesis that politics matters for policies may be framed in two ways; a weak version would claim only that different patterns of policies covary with various regimes whereas a strong version states that this covariation is independent of any link between the structure of society and the political system. It could be the case that social transformation implies political system change which also leads to policy change. However, it is often claimed that the polity means a difference for policies independently of the social correlates of regime characteristics. We face two problems raised in the public policy analysis of the West European state: (1) What is the public policy variation between various political systems? (2) Which factors – social or political – are associated with patterns of policy variations?

Taxation and budgeting differ between regimes in Western Europe. Public finance data may be employed as evidence for these policy differences. In fact, when looking at taxation and budgetary differences it is necessary to look at the time and space variation within the set of West European regimes. May we expect widely different expenditure patterns in various democracies depending on whether the right-wing or left-wing forces dominate – the famous 'Does politics matter?' theme?

Output measures as well as outcome measures like the total size of the tax state, general government outlays, transfer payments, central government disbursements and military versus various types of civilian expenditures may differ between countries. Are there any clear differences between right-wing and left-wing regimes? Or perhaps general social conditions like the level of affluence are more important than the political institutions that prevail? Could one substantiate the controversy in the 'Does politics matter?' debate by a more minute analysis of public finance data? The same applies to the findings about education, culture and social welfare. Here it is essential to look at the differences both between countries but also over time (Wildavsky, 1986).

The difficult problem of accounting for the variation in the size of the state in general and the welfare state in particular remains a puzzling research task (Swank, 1988; O'Connor, 1988; Pampel and Williamson, 1988; O'Connor and Brym, 1988; Alber, 1988). It parallels our concern with the contrast between a political sociology approach and an institutionalist approach to the understanding of politics in Western Europe. Two hypotheses remain crucial in the debate over the sources of policy differences: on the one hand the affluence hypothesis predicting policies by means of the variation in the level of affluence and on the other hand the political hypothesis explaining the size of the state in terms of the strength of the left in government or society.

Democratic performance

Once one accepts the notion that politics is not a simple reflection of societal cleavages but that political élites may take action that successfully overcomes the divisive implications of heterogeneity it becomes essential to move towards an analysis of how various kinds of political phenomena intervene between the structure of society and political stability. A far-reaching analysis of the relation among society, political organization and political stability is *Contemporary Democracies: Participation, Stability, and Violence* (1982) by Bingham Powell. Looking for factors that have an impact upon voting participation, government durability and social order Powell has a number of findings derived from statistical modelling of cross-sectional data concerning a wide set of democracies.

Firstly, and foremost, Powell shows convincingly that the occurrence of various kinds of cleavages is not enough to account for the country variation in democratic performance. Various political factors such as constitutional rules, election procedures, party system and élite behaviour may not only increase or reduce the environmental implications but have an impact *sui generis*, in particular upon government durability and the occurrence of riots and violent phenomena. Secondly, Powell is able to pinpoint a number of specific relationships between the dependent and the independent variables which are not quite in accordance with traditional theoretical notions. It appears that consociationalism is present in political systems characterized by a high degree of political stability but it is not quite correct to draw the conclusion that the existence of consociational practices accounts for the occurrence of political stability. It is a matter of the well-known distinction between the coexistence of phenomena and a causal relation between these.

Moreover, Powell offers some interesting support for the Lipset notion that the position and strength of extremist political parties are crucial for democratic performance. Majoritarian political systems tend to bring about a two-party competition that leaves no space for an extremist party whereas representative party systems, multi-party systems, characterized by fractionalization offer a real opportunity for the operation of such parties. When the rules of the political game more or less exclude extremist parties there is more social disorder, whereas when these parties are strong within a fractionalized system the instability problem concerns government longevity.

The main conclusions include: that political stability is not a uni-dimensional entity; that majoritarian party systems are conducive to executive stability but are accompanied by more social disorder than the representative party systems where a high degree of fractionalization results in government instability; that democratic polities display a considerable extent of political responsiveness as measured by the capacity of parties to influence policy outputs at the government level. Powell's approach is orientated towards a careful empirical analysis of empirical data which contrasts with the more theoretically orientated contributions dealt with so far. No doubt Powell has proved the fertility of econometric modelling to the analysis of comparative politics. It remains to be seen if his results are corroborated when a smaller set of nations – West European democracies – is investigated with methods that have an affinity with the Powell approach although the data set is more extensive.

Conclusion

We borrow from the political sociology approach the notion that there is some relationship between society and politics, although this certainly cannot be modelled in terms of causal determinism. We take from the sociological approaches the idea that cleavages have some impact on democratic political systems, but we also wish to take into account the insight of the emergent institutionalist perspective that political parties and public institutions have a logic of their own. We have learned from the consociational scholars that élite behaviour and political institutions constitute a dimension of its own. We focus upon political parties as expressing cleavages in a society following a recognition of the fundamental importance of parties, party systems and party government in Western Europe.

More specifically, we approach the study of politics in terms of a number of middle-range theories. Instead of the general sociological notion about the implications for politics of cleavages in society we search for specific relationships between various types of social cleavage and diverse political phenomena like parties, issues and political stability, substantiated in an empirical argument that covers the variation in our set of countries. In a similar manner we open up the institutionalist idea that political parties and governmental structure are particularly important for political phenomena by their own way of functioning by looking at the empirical evidence that there is a variation in political institutions and public policies that cannot be explained by sociological factors. Public policies result from decision-making and implementation in political institutions where there is a certain amount of discretion on the part of policy-makers in relation to environmental forces.

Thus, what follows in the coming chapters is not a new theory about cleavages and political institutions, but a number of middle-range hypotheses substantiated by a large amount of empirical data, which all imply that the relationship between society and politics is anything but simple. We steer away from the use of the case study technique, as the employment of comparative frameworks and models is the best way to enhance comparative politics as a discipline. In the present state of knowledge middle-range theories offer the best route to new insights into comparative politics, as Blondel argued early in his *An Introduction to Comparative Government* (1969).

Much of what follows in the various chapters may be interpreted generally as a critique of the idea of the existence of *one* single abstract model of the interplay between society and political phenomena or of the variety of political institutions. In particular, we wish to warn against simple general answers concerning how social structure and politics interact as well as how various kinds of political phenomena are related. By-passing the reductionist fallacy in some political sociology approaches we search for identifiable relationships between structural properties in society and political variables. At the same time we are hesitant towards the new institutionalism that seems to imply that politics – issue-making and political stability – is completely independent of the social setting (March and Olsen, 1989). Looking for middle-range hypotheses between clearly specified variables appears to offer a middle course between sociological reductionism and institutionalist indeterminism.

Let us begin with a description of the structure of society and social cleavages in European democracies since influential approaches to politics in general and political stability in particular place such an emphasis on homogeneity versus heterogeneity.

2
Social Cleavages

Introduction

The needs, wishes and demands of the individuals and organizations that make up societies are unlimited, but resources – material ones as well as nonmaterial ones – are scarce. Basic to social life is contention between individuals or collectivities for scarce opportunities. Political systems are necessary for the regulation of conflict in society as well as for the translation of demands for public activities into government policies. A variety of demands or needs in society is relevant for politics, as the cleavage structure in Western Europe shows.

As some countries, among others the West European democracies, experienced staggering economic growth after the Second World War some scholars began to speak of the affluent society (Galbraith, 1958) and the welfare state (Wilensky, 1976); yet it is striking that prosperity is fragile even in some advanced countries and how vulnerable the economies of Western Europe have become in terms of for example unemployment. Even though the amount of resources to be allocated to citizens in West European societies has grown in a way that has made poverty less visible human and organizational motivations remain the same. Allocation of resources of every nature involves the resolution of conflicts about priorities.

Resource allocation implies relating goods to goals in situations of uncertainty. Whatever the size of the amount of resources to be allocated the distribution of utilities in societies raises vital moral questions about equity, equality and justice. Such matters activate interests, which define groups and motivate individuals or collectivities to move against each other (Wildavsky, 1986). Political systems deal with conflicts as political institutions present opportunities for regulating the level of conflict. The incompatibility of goals and demands of individuals and organizations require institutions for the regulation of conflicts to avoid anarchy. Political systems provide mechanisms of conflict resolution by means of decision-making structures. And patterns of conflict depend on cleavages.

Concept of a cleavage

A cleavage is a division on the basis of some criteria of individuals, groups or organizations among whom conflict may arise. The concept of cleavage is thus not identical with the concept of conflict; cleavages may lead to conflict, but a cleavage need not always be attended by conflict. A division of individuals, groups or organizations constitutes a cleavage if there is some probability of a conflict. Cleavages occur in society, in party systems and in government. Cleavages operate in the social structure dividing it into various collectivities; sometimes such structural cleavages become the target of conscious orientation and a variety of interests are defined.

Political parties organize themselves on the basis of identification of cleavages, through which the alignment of the electorate takes place. Cleavages crop up in the political system as issues to be dealt with by the decision-making structures of government. Interest organizations are structured along cleavage lines.

We use the concept of cleavages to describe and analyse *latent* and *manifest* patterns of conflict within our sixteen nations; we deal with cleavages at three levels: in society, party system and government. We investigate what cleavages exist at the various levels, how they interact at each level and what the interrelationships between the levels are. The crucial problem is: What cleavages are to be identified? How many? Let us turn to the literature on cleavages, which is substantial.

A concise treatment of cleavages is presented in *The Analysis of Political Cleavages* (1970) by Douglas W. Rae and Michael Taylor. They identify cleavages in the following manner:

> Cleavages are the criteria which divide the members of a community or subcommunity into groups, and the relevant cleavages are those which divide members into groups with important political differences at specific times and places (Rae and Taylor, 1970: 1).

Which cleavages are politically important? The problem is similar to that of the forest and the trees, because to understand politics some cleavages setting groups and organization apart from each other must be identified, but when these cleavages are to be identified it is not enough to talk about criteria that divide people into groups, because there are many such criteria and groups may be amalgamated in a myriad of ways.

Rae and Taylor must find the criteria among several alternative sets of criteria since cleavages are to be employed to identify 'important political differences'. Rae and Taylor suggest that there are three types of cleavage worthy of study: (1) ascriptive or 'trait' cleavages: race or caste; (2) attitudinal or 'opinion' cleavages: ideology or preference; and (3) behavioural or 'act' cleavages: those elicited through voting and organizational membership. If the typology proposed is illuminating it does not solve a principal problem in research on cleavages: Which cleavages are to be singled out for description and analysis? Rae and Taylor state:

> A cleavage is merely a division of a community – into religious groups, opinion groups, or voting groups, for example. Formally, we define a 'cleavage' as a family of sets of individuals (Rae and Taylor, 1970: 23).

A large community such as the United Kingdom or France may be divided into an unlimited number of groups. The problem remains: Which cleavages are to be picked out as the significant ones (Pesonen, 1973; Zuckerman, 1975, 1982; Knutsen, 1989)?

Scott C. Flanagan proposes another typology of cleavages. To Flanagan cleavages are 'potential lines of division within any given society', which can be classified in the following way: segmental cleavages: racial, linguistic or religious differences; cultural cleavages: young–old, urban–rural, traditional, modern, authoritarian–libertarian; economic–functional cleavages: class, status or role differences (Flanagan, 1973: 64). It is often considered that classifications are to be mutually exclusive, i.e. the entities to be classified should fall into one and only one of the classification boxes. It may be argued against the Flanagan classification that linguistic and religious cleavages may be classified as cultural ones and the urban–rural cleavage and the traditional–modern cleavage could be placed under economic–functional cleavages. Segmental cleavages 'tend to divide a country into exclusive communities' (Flanagan, 1973: 64). This may be true: if so, class cleavages may certainly be segmental cleavages.

Social science concept formation is often considered ambiguous and the amount of intersubjective agreement as to the employment of words is low; compare the use of terms between Flanagan and Harry Eckstein's *Division and Cohesion in Democracy* (1966). Eckstein makes a distinction among three types of cleavage, one of which is the segmental one:

> A third kind of division is segmental cleavage. This exists where political divisions follow very closely, and especially concern, lines of objective social differentiation ... (Eckstein, 1966: 34).

As examples of 'objective social differentiation' Eckstein mentions tribe, race, region, rural–urban, sex, young–old, language, religion and occupation. While Flanagan reserves the word segmental for a very special set of cleavages Eckstein seems to include almost all kinds of cleavage, because there may exist many lines of objective social differentiation. Perhaps it is appropriate to mention the other two political divisions that Eckstein refers to: one kind is composed of disagreements as to policy issues and the other kind refers to cultural divergences in general belief and value systems (Eckstein, 1966: 33–4). Could it not be the case that segmental cleavages like religion and language often concern cultural lines of division, and that segmented cleavages are often identified through their appearance at the policy level?

If it is difficult to construct valid typologies of cleavages, then perhaps it is better simply to enumerate them. Hans Daalder turns to historical inquiries to arrive at a list of cleavages, where the most important dividing lines in Europe have tended to be (a) class or sectional interest: parties representing sections of industry or commerce, labour or agriculture; (b) religion: modernists, fundamentalists, Catholics, Protestants, clericals, anti-clericals, Anglicans, and non-conformists; (c) geographical conflict: town versus country and centre versus periphery; (d) nationality or nationalism: ethnic parties and nationalist movements; and (e) regime: status quo parties, reform parties, revolutionary and counter-revolutionary parties (Daalder, 1966a: 67–8). What are the criteria for deciding what is an important dividing line? How is importance measured? Are there perhaps other kinds of cleavage that should be mentioned? What about ideologies? Or the cleavage young–old or modern–traditional? The problem concerning cleavages remains even if a procedure of enumerating kinds of cleavages is resorted to: How many are to be listed? And what procedure guarantees that some cleavages are not neglected?

In his *Party Strategies in a Multiparty System* (1968) Gunnar Sjöblom relates the concept of cleavage to concepts such as politicization, fighting line, dividing line and conflict dimension (Sjöblom, 1968: 122). To Sjöblom a cleavage is a permanent conflict dimension though it may be a latent one. And he states that cleavages are based on value and belief systems (Sjöblom, 1968: 169). David Easton points out that it is often assumed that cleavages imply diversity in points of view (Easton, 1965: 223–4). Easton argues affirmatively that such a narrow conception is not quite adequate, since the concept of cleavage may refer to how groups act, not to what they believe or value. How do we distinguish among act, belief and value, as people reveal their opinions through the actions they perform? What is the justification for the argument that a line of division has to include values or beliefs or become the target of action to qualify as a cleavage?

Cleavages may be distinguished on the basis of a typology identifying different kinds of cleavage; but a seminal theme in the study of comparative politics is that it is equally important how cleavages occur. On the one hand there is the hypothesis about the differential impact of mutually reinforcing cleavage structures as against the effects of cross-cutting patterns of cleavages; Blondel speaks of sectionalism in relation to the former type (Blondel, 1969: 52–8). On the other hand we have hypotheses about the implications of intensity of cleavages for the structuring of political life, what Val Lorwin and Kenneth McRae refer to as segmented pluralism (Lorwin, 1974). According to McRae segmented pluralism involves that:

> the cleavage in question should be sufficiently intense and durable to give members of the respective groups a distinctive and persistent outlook or cultural orientation that is different from that of other sectors, a raison d'être for maintaining organized segmentation (McRae, 1974: 6).

But, how do we measure intensity and duration of a social cleavage?

Choice of cleavages

In the literature on cleavages there is no agreement on either what the necessary and sufficient conditions are for a cleavage or what a fruitful typology over cleavages would look like. A cleavage necessarily involves a line of division; but not all lines of division are cleavages. Some scholars demand that the line of division becomes the focus of value and belief systems. Others add criteria that are difficult to operationalize like 'important political difference' or 'meaningfully structured' or 'sufficiently intense'. The difficulties inherent in the concept of a cleavage reflect a deeper problem which is our concern here: how to justify that one set or type of cleavage is selected for inquiry to the exclusion of any other set of cleavage. We do not believe that there is valid justification for one criterion that would identify the set of lines of division which would comprise all cleavages.

The identification of the cleavages to be studied depends upon theory or theoretical assumptions. The concept is used as a construct to summarize forces that are conducive to conflict. What forces tend to cause contention and dissension among people and organizations cannot be specified for all times, places and levels. The choice of cleavages to be included in the analysis may be justified not on the basis of a typology or on the basis of an enumeration of types of cleavage found, but on the basis of theoretical arguments about interrelationships between cleavages and the other properties to be studied. Whether a proper choice of cleavages has been made depends on the amount of explained variation in the other variables which are assumed to be interrelated to cleavages.

It is vital to distinguish between latent and manifest cleavages, because belief, value or action are not by necessity properties of cleavages. In consequence we distinguish between cleavages in the structure of societies and cleavages in the consciousness of societies. In our framework to be applied on sixteen countries in Western Europe today we assume that we can shed some light on crucial political phenomena if we identify and describe the following types of cleavage:

– Religious
– Ethnic

– Class-based
– Regional

Whether our choice is correct cannot be decided a priori: the test of a selection of theoretical constructs is the amount of understanding of the phenomena singled out. If we choose these cleavages, can we learn something about society, parties and issues? Let us first begin by describing the overall socio-economic structure of West European democracies.

Socio-economic dimensions may become the target of social cleavages although they themselves do not constitute cleavages. This is a matter of definition to be decided on the basis of theoretical deliberations. If it is required of the concept of cleavage that it has an inherently subjective frame of reference in terms of belief systems and ideologics, then the argument is correct. Since we distinguish between manifest and latent cleavages, it may be argued that socio-economic dimensions such as industry and wealth may constitute latent cleavages.

Socio-economic structure

In modern political sociology it has become commonplace that the development of the socio-economic structure of a nation affects its political life. Typical concepts employed in the analysis of processes involved in socio-economic development are modernization or social mobilization. Perhaps these concepts do not cover identical facts, because concepts like modernization and social mobilization belong to a category of grand social science concepts operationalized by means of a host of indicators. Samuel Huntington and Jorge I. Dominguez state:

> Modernization presumably involved industrialization, urbanization, increasing literacy and mass media consumption, economic growth, greater social and occupational mobility, and related processes (Huntington and Dominguez, 1975: 4).

Although they mention several variables entering into the concept of modernization the list is by no means exhaustive, which is indicated by the addition of the residual: related processes. Some scholars use the concept not only for the analysis of socio-economic development but for the description of all kinds of social change.

Wolfgang Zapf and Peter Flora talk about subdimensions of the modernization process including cultural transformation, political development, economic development, social mobilization and integration, psychic mobilization and transformation of international relations (Zapf and Flora, 1973: 172). When the concept is used in such a wide fashion as almost synonymous with the general notion of development of social systems it loses discriminatory power. It may not be advantageous to devise a concept that covers changes in the social structure, the economy and the polity. It is vital to remain alert to the variety of social development and to investigate by means of empirical methods the extent to which change in various kinds of social system, the society, the party system and the political system may be related.

The concept of modernization implies some theory about the uniformity of various kinds of social development – a 'process of social change whereby less developed societies acquire characteristics common to more developed societies' (Lerner, 1968: 386). The general change that Daniel Lerner refers to may cover almost all kinds of phenomena – social structure, economics or politics. The interrelationships between these aspects are far too complex to be summarized in a simple concept, as Karl Deutsch argues:

> Social mobilization is a name given to an overall process of change, which happens to substantial parts of the population in countries which are moving from traditional to modern ways of life. It denotes a concept which brackets together a number of more specific processes of change, such as changes of residence, of occupation, of social setting, of face-to-face associates, of institutions, roles and ways of acting, of experiences and expectations, and finally of personal memoirs, habits and needs, including the need for new patterns of group affiliation and new images of personal identity (Deutsch, 1961: 493).

It is not quite clear how much is achieved in understanding these complex phenomena when they are labelled mobilization. Lerner also uses the concept of modernization in a narrow fashion:

> Modernization, therefore, is the process of social change in which development is the economic component. Modernization produces the societal environment in which rising output per head is effectively incorporated (Lerner, 1968: 387).

The narrow concept of modernization is employed by scholars dealing with the political implications of socio-economic change. They use 'modernization' and 'mobilization' as a summary variable covering socio-economic change to state the consequences for political life of these changes. Problematic in the narrow use of the concept is the specification of variables and indicators to be employed. Some scholars use a great number of indicators whereas other scholars mention only a few (Lipset, 1959: 50; McGranahan, 1971: 70; Mughan, 1979: 29; Jackman, 1975: 35; Banks, 1970: 406).

Leaving problems of operationalization at the moment, it is evident that socio-economic structure and socio-economic development are believed to be explanatory factors in the analysis of political life in general and the occurrence of cleavages in particular. Although we refrain from the use of words like modernization and mobilization, we employ the narrow concept of modernization in relation to contemporary West European societies to find the inter-societal differences in the socio-economic structure.

West European social structure

The employment of the concept of socio-economic structure for systematic description must start from the fact that there is no generally accepted definition of the concept. When the socio-economic environment of politics is spoken of the meaning of the concept often remains implicit and a variety of operational indicators are considered relevant. To the socio-economic structure of a country belongs variables that enter into one or the other headings: income, employment, education and population statistics. By looking at the standard literature we arrive at a list of variables typically included in the concept, from which we select a small set of socio-economic dimensions that may be employed for the analysis of West European nations (Hofferbert, 1968; Morgan and Lyons, 1975; Banks, 1981).

The comparison of socio-economic differences between European democracies refers to the post-Second World War period. Two socio-economic dimensions are selected based on socio-economic variables for the sixteen nations at five points of time: 1950, 1960, 1970, 1980 and 1985. These two dimensions account for much of the variation in the indicators on socio-economic structure in Western Europe: an affluence dimension and an industrialization dimension. To the static aspect which is thus well-covered must be added a dynamic aspect. Typical of the modern society is the rapid change of the socio-economic structure.

Affluence
In order to measure the affluence dimension we employ data about GDP per capita for the years 1950–1985. A standardized national income series has been compiled by Summers and Heston (1988) which comprises comparable data, because the various country data have been recalculated in real money terms and at specified exchange rates. Table 2.1 presents the comparable country data.

Looking at the variation in affluence as measured by the indicator GDP (Gross Domestic Product) per capita (constant prices) at various times since the Second World War we find that the country variation as measured by the coefficient of variation has gone down as prosperity has increased considerably in each country. At the same time wealth of the West European nations still varies; the country variation has a conspicuous North–South appearance. Among the most affluent nations in 1985 were Norway, Switzerland and Denmark which also ranked high in 1950. On the other hand Portugal, Greece, Spain, Ireland and Italy

Table 2.1   *Real GDP per capita in international prices (constant prices; US$ 1980 at 1980 exchange rate in thousands)*

	1950	1960	1970	1980	1985
Austria	2.318	3.908	5.843	8.230	8.929
Belgium	3.462	4.379	6.750	9.228	9.717
Denmark	4.241	5.490	7.776	9.598	10.884
F R Germany	2.713	5.217	7.443	9.795	10.708
Finland	2.758	4.073	6.186	8.393	9.232
France	3.125	4.473	7.078	9.688	9.918
Greece	986	1.474	2.952	4.383	4.464
Ireland	2.047	2.545	3.628	4.929	5.205
Italy	1.929	3.233	5.028	7.164	7.425
Netherlands	3.404	4.690	6.915	9.036	9.092
Norway	3.802	5.001	7.104	11.094	12.623
Portugal	937	1.429	2.575	3.733	3.729
Spain	1.640	2.425	4.379	6.131	6.437
Sweden	3.980	5.149	7.401	8.863	9.904
Switzerland	4.886	6.834	9.164	10.013	10.640
United Kingdom	3.993	4.970	6.319	7.975	8.665
CV	40.7	36.9	30.7	27.1	29.1

Eta-squared by time = .59
Eta-squared by country = .36
Source: Summers and Heston (1988)
Note: Real GDP per capita is adjusted for differences in the purchasing power of currencies, i.e. efforts have been made to make intercountry comparisons.

are to be found among the less affluent countries, speaking in terms of a comparison within this set of rich countries in the world.

One may always ask in relation to GDP per capita data whether they really measure national welfare or individual well-being. After all, aggregate income figures do not tell everything about welfare or its distribution. We test if there is a correlation between our index and affluence indices in the literature on West European societies. McGranahan (1971: 80) gives an account of a developmental index for 1960, Banks (1974: 334) renders a socio-economic index for the same year and Castles (1978: 69) presents a social welfare index for circa 1975. The correlations between these indices and our measure for corresponding points of time are: $r = .91$, $r = .91$ and $r = .82$ respectively, which would justify the statement that they measure rather similar phenomena.

Industrialization
The industrialization dimension may be measured by industrial employment where high values express high industrial employment and low values express the opposite (Table 2.2). The variation in the industrialization dimension is not as extensive as the variation noted

Table 2.2   *Employment in industry as a percentage of economically active in civilian employment*

	1950 (1)	1960 (2)	1970 (3)	1980 (4)	1985 (5)
Austria	36.6	41.7	42.3	39.7	36.5
Belgium	48.8	45.0	42.0	34.1	29.7
Denmark	33.3	36.9	37.8	30.4	28.1
F R Germany	44.9	47.0	48.5	44.1	41.0
Finland	27.7	32.6	34.6	34.6	31.9
France	32.9	38.4	39.2	35.9	32.0
Greece	19.4	17.4	25.0	30.2	27.3
Ireland	24.3	23.7	29.9	32.5	28.9
Italy	32.1	33.9	39.5	37.9	33.6
Netherlands	36.9	40.5	38.9	31.4	26.5
Norway	36.4	35.6	37.3	29.7	27.8
Portugal	24.9	31.3	32.9	36.6	35.3
Spain	25.5	30.3	35.5	36.1	31.8
Sweden	38.2	40.3	38.4	32.2	29.9
Switzerland	46.7	46.5	45.9	39.7	37.7
United Kingdom	49.1	47.7	44.7	37.7	32.3
CV	26.3	23.1	15.6	11.5	12.8

Eta-squared by time = .10
Eta-squared by country = .63
Sources: (1): Mitchell (1981); (2)–(5): OECD (1983; 1987)
Note: Industry includes employment in mining and quarrying, manufacturing, electricity, gas and water, construction.

in the affluence dimension, and industrialization does not vary along the North–South axis. Heavy industrialization characterizes in particular central and western Europe: Austria, Belgium, Germany, Switzerland and the United Kingdom. In northern and southern Europe the socio-economic structure is not distinguished by comparatively high levels of industrial employment, but for different reasons. In Portugal and Greece there is still a substantial amount of employment within the agricultural sector whereas in the Scandinavian countries and Finland the modern sector has expanded at the expense of industrial employment.

When analysing the CV and the Eta-squared scores in Table 2.2 it appears once again that the differences between the West European countries have become less pronounced as their economies have developed along similar lines during the post-war period. Yet, there is a persistent country variation at the same time as the data indicate substantial changes in industrial employment since 1945.

Perhaps the most conspicuous finding concerning the socio-economic structure of West European nations is that affluence and industrialization are almost completely independent of each other at present (1985).

Figure 2.1   *Affluence and industrialization in 1985*

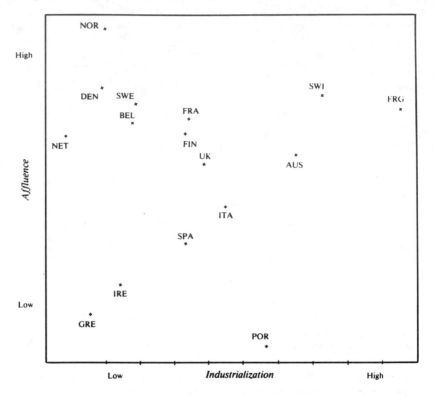

Whereas affluence varies along the North–South axis, the degree of industrialization has a different geographical connotation (see Figure 2.1).

From Figure 2.1 it appears that these two socio-economic dimensions – affluence and industrialization – divide European democracies into four clusters: a high level of affluence and a low level of industrialization distinguishes Sweden, Denmark and Norway; a medium level of affluence and industrialization sets Finland, Belgium, the Netherlands, France, Austria and the United Kingdom apart; Switzerland and the Federal Republic of Germany are characterized by a high level of industrialization and a high level of affluence whereas a low level of affluence as well as industrialization is to be found in Italy, Spain, Portugal, Greece and Ireland.

Formerly, industrialization used to produce affluence but Figure 2.1 does not corroborate this hypothesis. Perhaps the old truth about wealth as a function of industrialization is not false but simply old. Actually, the correlation coefficient between affluence and industrialization displays a variation that indicates some fundamental facts about West European social structure. During the expansion period of the welfare state the relationship between wealth and industrialization is strong; in 1950 the association is $r = .75$ (Pearson's coefficient), in 1960 it amounted to .80 and in 1970 we find $r = .70$. However, in 1980 the link between affluence and industrialization was broken as indicated by the absence of any real association between the two dimensions, viz., $r = .08$ or for 1985, $r = .07$.

It seems plausible to interpret the findings to mean that affluence used to be dependent upon industrialization, but that this is no longer the case. The expansion of the service sector and the public sector in the maturing welfare state implies both a reduction in industrial employment and an increase in affluence. The findings in Figure 2.1 confirm the observations of the coming of a post-industrial society (Myrdal, 1961; Galbraith, 1967; Bell, 1973; 1976). More and more the wealth of a nation has become a function of factors other than the degree of industrialization of its socio-economic structure.

Economic growth rates

The post-war period in Western Europe is the period of the coming of an abundant society; the rate of transformation of the level of affluence has been most spectacular which Table 2.3 indicates. All West European nations have experienced this growth in wealth although not to the same extent. The weakening of the association between affluence and industrialization has implications for the average growth rates in the economy. Some nations that have a quite substantial positive change in affluence display a negative trend in the relative size of the population working in industrial employment. Belgium and Norway should be mentioned as examples of the combination of a substantial increase in wealth between 1950 and 1985 while the level of industrialization has been reduced. When the West European nations change in their relative level of industrialization there will not necessarily be a corresponding change in the affluence level between the countries. Among the nations where there has been a substantial increase in industrialization we also find a high rate of growth in wealth, viz., Greece and Spain, whereas the growth rate in wealth is lower for Ireland.

The average rate of economic growth varies not only between countries but also with regard to the time period studied. Looking at the developments since 1960 countries with a low starting point in terms of affluence tend to grow at a faster rate than countries at a high level of affluence: compare Portugal and Greece with Switzerland and the United Kingdom. But if we concentrate on data for 1980–85 the picture is not that simple. Norway and Finland display high rates of economic growth whereas the Netherlands, Sweden and Greece score low.

Table 2.3   *Economic growth per capita in Western Europe (yearly per cent averages)*

	1950 –85 (1)	1950 –60 (2)	1960 –70 (3)	1970 –80 (4)	1980 –85 (5)	1960 –80 (6)	1960 –85 (7)	1979 –87 (8)
Austria	8.1	6.9	5.0	4.1	1.7	4.1	3.4	1.6
Belgium	5.2	2.6	5.4	3.7	1.1	3.8	3.1	1.4
Denmark	4.5	2.9	4.2	2.3	2.7	3.3	2.7	1.9
F R Germany	8.4	9.2	4.3	3.2	1.9	3.3	2.7	1.5
Finland	6.7	4.8	5.2	3.6	2.0	4.0	3.5	2.9
France	6.2	4.3	5.8	3.7	0.5	3.9	3.1	1.2
Greece	10.1	4.9	10.0	4.8	0.4	5.8	4.3	0.6
Ireland	4.4	2.4	4.3	3.6	1.1	3.1	2.9	1.6
Italy	8.1	6.8	5.6	4.2	0.7	3.6	3.2	2.0
Netherlands	4.8	3.8	4.7	3.1	0.1	3.2	2.4	0.6
Norway	6.6	3.2	4.2	5.6	2.8	3.5	3.6	2.9
Portugal	8.5	5.3	8.0	4.5	–0.0	5.0	4.2	1.5
Spain	8.4	4.8	8.1	4.0	1.0	4.5	3.7	1.5
Sweden	4.3	2.9	4.4	2.0	2.3	2.3	2.5	1.6
Switzerland	3.4	4.0	3.4	0.9	1.3	1.9	1.8	1.5
United Kingdom	3.3	2.4	2.7	2.6	1.7	2.2	1.9	1.6

Note: (1)–(5) are calculated from Table 2.1; (6) is based on *World Development Report* (1982); (7) is based on *OECD Historical Statistics* (1987); (8) is based on *OECD Historical Statistics* (1989).

The relationship between affluence and industrialization is far more complex than stated here; the findings do not allow the interpretation that a negative development in industrialization could not have a negative impact upon the wealth of a nation. What matters is how the shrinking of the population in industrial employment comes about and in which sector the part of the population that is not active within industrial employment works. The point to be underlined is that a high level of industrialization does not mean a high level of affluence, and a process of industrialization does not necessarily mean large increases in the wealth of a nation – as things used to be in the coming of the welfare state before and after the Second World War.

Religious cleavages

During the twentieth century West European societies have passed through a process of secularization meaning that church attendance has declined considerably (Mol, 1972; Martin, 1978). Although the attendance at church has decreased and the memberships of the churches have diminished as reflected in a decline in the frequency of church baptisms, weddings and burials, it does not follow that religion has lost its importance as a cleavage among people in society, the party system or in the government. The religious cleavages established in Europe through the Reformation and the French Revolution persist in today's society even though processes of modernization and secularization have made them less conspicuous. Religion still plays a significant role in the politics of several countries (Rose and Urwin, 1969).

The occurrence of religious cleavages, it has been argued, works against political stability:

> The linkage between democratic instability and Catholicism may also be accounted for by elements inherent in Catholicism as a religious system. Democracy requires a universalistic political belief system in the sense that it accepts various different ideologies as legitimate (Lipset, 1959: 84).

Besides the influence on the party system and the government it has been assumed that religion has special effects on the development of society. It is unnecessary to enter into the unending battle concerning Max Weber's argument that Protestantism has a positive influence on the development of capitalist institutions (Weber, 1965; Tawney, 1938; Samuelsson, 1961). It seems possible to demonstrate that different religions are coupled with differences in attitudes to the development of society. In the words of Gerhard Lenski:

> socio-religious group membership is a variable comparable in importance to class, both with respect to its potency and with respect to the range, or extent, of its influence (Lenski, 1963: 326).

Interesting problems for research concern the existence of religious political parties. What is the significance of religious cleavages in society for the electoral success of religious parties? Is the formation of religious parties facilitated by the existence of a large Catholic population (Rose and Urwin, 1969: 20–21)? Under what conditions could religious parties lose in importance and become marginal parties (Yinger, 1970: 430)? Now let us describe in more detail just how important religious cleavages are in society.

Religious Structure

A religious structure is composed of groups, whose sizes are measured by means of the number of members. There is a large variety of religious groups of differing size and official status. Our description of the religious structure of West European democracies takes account of a few major groups and their relationships: Protestants, Catholics, Other Christians, and persons explicitly adhering to no creed. We neither cover the varieties of Protestantism nor measure the extent of secularization because the size of the group of persons explicitly adhering to no creed at all cannot be used as an indicator on secularization. Many people remain members

Table 2.4　*Religious structure and fragmentation*

Country	Protes-tants (1)	Catho-lics (2)	Other Chris-tians (3)	No Creed (4)	Index 1 1960s (5)	Index 2 1900s (6)	Index 3 1970s (7)
Austria	7	89	1	3	.20	.15	.20
Belgium	1	93	1	5	.14	.02	.15
Denmark	97	1	0	2	.06	.02	.08
F R Germany	51	45	1	3	.54	.52	.55
Finland	96	0	2	2	.08	.03	.10
France	2	82	0	14	.30	.06	.34
Greece	0	1	94	5	.12	.04	.01
Ireland	5	94	1	0	.12	.19	.09
Italy	0	91	0	9	.17	.01	.17
Netherlands	38	40	0	22	.65	.50	.59
Norway	99	0	1	0	.02	.02	.03
Portugal	0	94	1	5	.12	.00	.06
Spain	0	100	0	0	.00	.00	.05
Sweden	100	0	0	0	.00	.02	.41
Switzerland	44	43	0	13	.62	.49	.52
United Kingdom	62	9	0	29	.53	.17	.41

Note: Columns (1)–(4) denote estimates of percentages of the population adhering to different creeds as of the 1960s (Taylor and Hudson, 1972); column (5) represents the fragmentation index based on the preceding estimates; column (6) presents estimates of the fragmentation index for the early 1900s, whereas column (7) presents similar estimates for the early 1970s; index 2 and index 3 are calculated from data reported in Barrett (1982).

of some church though they refrain from religious practices except on some major occasions during their lives. Data concerning religious heterogeneity appear in Table 2.4. These data apply to the late 1960s or early 1970s, but essentially they are still valid for today. An index on religious fragmentation has been computed from these data which shows the likelihood that two random persons belong to different religious creeds or do not adhere to any creed.

The religious map of Western Europe has not changed its basic structure since the end of the religious wars in the middle of the seventeenth century. Northern Europe as well as Southern Europe has a religious structure that is homogeneous, the North adhering to Protestantism and the South to Catholicism. Between these two blocks there is a set of countries which display a heterogeneous religious structure, having substantial portions of both Protestant and Catholic population. This set includes the Netherlands, Switzerland, West Germany, Great Britain and Northern Ireland. The religious fragmentation of Western Europe has remained almost unchanged over the last century. What has really changed is the coming of a broad process of secularization.

The Nordic countries score very low on the fragmentation index. All have a Lutheran state church. The majority of the population in these countries are members of the state church and the proportion of those not adhering to any creed is small. There are, however, many varieties of Protestantism in these countries that are not covered by the index. Revival movements during the nineteenth century resulted in regional variety in the religious structure. In Norway the revival movements were particularly strong in Vestlandet around Bergen, in Denmark in West Jutland around Limfjorden and in Sweden on the west coast and in the province of Småland.

The countries in the South do not score as low as the Nordic countries, because there are groups that do not belong to the majority of Roman Catholics. The population of Greece is Orthodox Catholic whereas Spain, Portugal, France, Austria, Italy and Belgium have a predominantly Roman Catholic population. France and Austria score about .20 or .30 on the index, because they have substantial minorities of Protestants.

In Austria the Protestants are dispersed all over the country and in France they live mainly in the Alsace area and around Paris. In these countries there is no formal state church, but the connection between the state and the church has been close during certain periods in Spain (Franco), Portugal (Salazar), Ireland, Italy, Austria and Belgium. The opposite is true of France, where these relations were broken off in the beginning of the twentieth century. Between 1934 and 1938 the church of Austria was a state church, but after the war this relation has been broken. The position of the church in Greece is peculiar, as there is neither a state church nor a complete separation between state and church.

Between the North and the South, both presenting a homogeneous religious structure, there is a group of countries which show a heterogeneous structure. There are Roman Catholics, Lutherans and above all Calvinists and Presbyterians in the Netherlands, Switzerland and West Germany, but to a certain extent also in the United Kingdom. In some of these countries the difference between the North and the South is reflected as the Protestants are found in northern provinces and the Catholics in the southern ones.

The most heterogeneous country is the Netherlands, the probability that two persons belong to different religions being .65. The two major groups, the Catholics and the Protestants, are about equal size. The Catholics dominate in southern Holland, close to the borders of Belgium. Up to the end of the nineteenth century they constituted a rejected minority, because they were regarded with suspicion by the non-Catholic part of the population and a number of restrictions had been placed on Catholic practices. At the end of the century these restrictions were abolished. The Protestants are Reformists, but there are two different groups. The Reformed Church of the Netherlands (Hervormde) was founded during

Table 2.5   *Religious structure in the Netherlands, 1971 (percentages of the population)*

Province	Roman Catholics	Hervormde	Gereformeerde	Other religion	No religion
Groningen	7	28	15	11	39
Friesland	8	30	22	9	31
Drenthe	9	42	13	9	27
Overijssel	32	30	8	10	20
Gelderland	38	35	6	7	14
Utrecht	31	29	7	10	23
Noord Holland	30	15	5	9	41
Zuid Holland	24	30	8	9	29
Zeeland	27	37	11	12	13
Noord Brabant	84	6	2	3	5
Limburg	91	3	1	2	3
Total	40	23	7	8	23

Source: Lepzy, 1979: 38f.

the Reformation and its position was that of a semi-state church up to the end of the nineteenth century. In 1892 the Reformed Church (Gereformeerde) was founded in fundamentalist opposition to the Church of the Netherlands as a reaction against the liberal development of the latter. The religious distribution of the Netherlands appears in Table 2.5.

Almost as heterogeneous as the Netherlands is Switzerland, scoring .62 on the index. It is not clear whether the Protestants or the Catholics are in the majority in Switzerland. Among those living in the country the Catholics outnumber the Protestants, whereas the Protestants constitute a majority among Swiss citizens. The Protestants are concentrated in the cantons in the North and the West; it should be remembered that Calvin was active in Geneva and Zwingli in Zürich. The Catholics predominate in the southern and eastern cantons on the borders of Italy and Austria (Table 2.6).

From Table 2.6 it appears that the extent of religious domination varies from canton to canton. In some of them the ratio between the two groups is almost even, whereas in others one of the groups dominates substantially. The federal structure of Switzerland dates back to the federation that was agreed upon in 1848 by the cantons, which resulted from a short civil war between the Protestant and the Catholic cantons. Today there is no connection between the churches of Switzerland and the federal state. However, there is a close relationship between state and church in the catholic cantons (Campiche, 1972: 511 ff). Two more countries score significantly on the index, West Germany and the United Kingdom. The religious structure of the Federal Republic of Germany appears in Table 2.7.

Table 2.6   *Religious distribution map of Switzerland, 1980*
(percentages of the population)

Canton	Protestants		Roman Catholics	
	Population	Citizens	Population	Citizens
Zürich	54.7	63.1	35.4	29.2
Bern	76.8	82.3	17.5	12.9
Luzern	12.9	13.3	82.4	83.7
Uri	5.9	5.8	91.0	92.6
Schwyz	10.0	10.3	86.6	88.1
Obwalden	5.3	4.9	92.1	94.1
Nidwalden	11.0	10.9	86.1	87.3
Glarus	51.7	61.5	43.0	36.8
Zug	18.4	18.9	75.3	78.0
Fribourg	13.6	14.2	83.2	83.7
Solothurn	36.5	40.7	54.9	53.0
Basel Stadt	44.4	51.2	35.5	31.3
Basel Landschaft	54.3	61.1	36.3	31.5
Schaffhausen	60.5	70.1	27.7	22.6
Appenzell A.Rh.	64.1	71.4	28.7	24.0
Appenzell I.Rh.	6.8	7.1	90.5	91.8
St Gallen	33.5	37.2	61.0	60.0
Graubünden	45.2	50.0	51.0	47.8
Aargau	45.1	51.3	46.5	42.8
Thurgau	53.1	60.8	41.0	36.0
Ticino	7.6	8.6	87.1	86.8
Vaud	55.7	67.1	35.7	25.9
Valais	4.7	4.8	92.8	93.5
Neuchatel	53.0	63.1	36.2	26.5
Genéve	30.6	40.2	51.1	43.7
Jura	13.3	14.4	83.6	83.0
Total	44.3	50.4	47.6	43.6

Source: Statistisches Jahrbuch der Schweiz, 1983: 42–3.

The Protestants outnumber the Catholics in West Germany. The Protestants are concentrated to the North and the East, while the Catholics dominate in the South and in the West. There is a Protestant church in each of the Länder of the republic and they are all united in the EKD (Evangelische Kirchen in Deutschland). The churches have the status of 'corporations of the public law'; they are entitled to state subsidies as recompense for the confiscation of their possessions in 1806, they also have the power to raise church taxes, and some of them have concluded 'state treaties' with the Länder.

What makes the United Kingdom score high on the index is the existence of Catholics in some parts of the country. The Protestants dominate the Kingdom, but there are varieties of Protestantism. England and Wales

Table 2.7   *Religious structure of the Federal Republic of Germany, 1970 (percentages of the population)*

State	Protestants	Roman Catholics
Schleswig-Holstein	86.5	6.0
Hamburg	73.6	8.1
Niedersachsen	74.6	19.6
Bremen	82.4	10.2
Nordrhein-Westfalen	41.9	52.5
Hessen	60.5	32.8
Rheinland-Pfalz	40.7	55.7
Baden-Würtemberg	45.8	47.4
Bayern	25.7	69.9
Saarland	24.1	73.8
Berlin West	70.2	12.5
Total	51.1	44.1

Source: Statistisches Jahrbuch für die Bundesrepublik Deutschland.

belong to the Church of England, the episcopal church, whereas the Scots belong to the Presbyterian Church of Scotland. The Church of England is a state church, whereas the Church of Scotland is independent of the state. Catholics live mainly in English and Scottish cities where the number of immigrants from Ireland is large, for example, in Liverpool. Northern Ireland is the part of the Kingdom that is religiously most divided (Table 2.8).

The Catholics have their strongholds in the southern and western counties. One may note the moderate rise in the number of catholics over the years. The Protestants are not all of a kind, as they are divided

Table 2.8   *Religious structure of Northern Ireland: proportion of Roman Catholics, 1951, 1961 and 1971 (percentages)*

County	Proportion Roman Catholics			
	1951	1961		1971
		(a)	(b)	
Belfast	26.1	28.2	27.4	31.4
Antrim	22.1	24.9	24.5	28.1
Armagh	46.5	47.9	47.5	50.3
Down	30.3	28.9	28.5	27.9
West	52.8	53.3	–	54.1
Londonderry	–	–	42.9	–
Fermanagh	–	–	52.9	–
Tyrone	–	–	54.5	–
Northern Ireland	34.5	35.2	34.9	36.8

Sources: 1951, 1961(a), 1971: Compton, 1976: 437; 1961(b): Rose, 1971: 90.

between the Presbyterians and the Anglicans, who are orientated towards the episcopal church. There are also some fundamentalist groups (Highet, 1972: 250 ff; Martin, 1972: 229 ff; Ward, 1972: 295 ff; Rose, 1976: 126 ff).

Religious Awareness
Religious cleavages may be latent or manifest. Manifest cleavages are those cleavages which become the focus of orientation of the citizens. Religious structure is by definition a latent, or unconscious, structure which can be transformed into a manifest structure through a process in which religious cleavages become tied to some kind of religious awareness. Religious awareness operates on religious structure in such a way that the higher the religious awareness is the more likely it is that the cleavages become conspicuous.

How to measure religious awareness is problematic. What indicator is to be used? We use data showing the frequency of attendance at church during a certain period and we assume that the greater the frequency, the greater the religious awareness. The data we set out from are of two kinds: on the one hand we use data collected at election surveys from the late 1960s or early 1970s into which questions about frequency of attendance at church entered; on the other, we use data from a Gallup poll on attendance at church in a number of western countries in 1968 (Social Compass, 1972), data from interviews conducted in 1970–71 in the countries belonging to the EEC (Inglehart, 1977) and estimates made in more recent investigations (Eight nation study, 1979; European value survey, 1982).

Data on church attendance must be interpreted with caution. Church attendance is a sign of religious devoutness, but devoutness may imply different patterns of attendance in different churches. To be a Catholic may mean that one attendance a week is devoutness, whereas to a Protestant one attendance a month may be enough to qualify as a devout Protestant. Not only is the validity of data concerning church attendance questionable, but so is their reliability. There is a clear tendency among people when being questioned to state too high a frequency of attendance at church. In reality the frequency is lower. Data are not available to the same extent for all the countries. Table 2.9 presents data on church attendance. We have constructed two scales, one for attendance once a week and the other for attendance once a month, and computed values from various sources.

A comparison of the data available shows marked differences between the countries. The Nordic countries and the United Kingdom have the lowest degree of religious awareness. Two types of country present a high degree of religious awareness, viz., those with a heterogeneous religious structure and the one with a homogeneous Catholic population.

Table 2.9   *Religious awareness: church attendance (percentages)*

	Various surveys (1)		Inglehart (2)	European value survey (3)		Eight nation study (4)		Social compass (5)	
	W	M	W	W	M	W	M	W	M
Austria	26	43	–	–	–	32	50	38	68
Belgium	41	–	54	30	38	–	–	–	–
Denmark	–	–	–	3	12	–	–	–	–
F R Germany	23	51	29	21	37	23	36	27	54
Finland	–	–	–	–	–	3	10	5	33
France	21	60	22	12	18	–	–	25	47
Greece	–	–	–	–	–	–	–	28	88
Ireland	90	–	–	82	88	–	–	–	–
Italy	48	–	51	36	52	36	53	–	–
Netherlands	29	42	38	27	40	43	55	42	55
Norway	–	10	–	–	–	–	–	14	37
Portugal	54	83	–	–	–	–	–	–	–
Spain	38	60	–	41	53	–	–	–	–
Sweden	–	10	–	–	–	–	–	9	28
Switzerland	44	–	36	–	–	24	43	30	60
United Kingdom	–	26	14	15	24	16	22	–	23

Note: Sometimes when weekly or monthly attendance is not stated we let practising, regular attendance or churchgoing equate with weekly attendance while less strong attachment equals monthly attendance; obviously the distinctions are not always clearcut.
Sources: (1) A: Nick, 1988: 411; B: Delruelle-Vosswinkel and Frognier, 1980: 28; D: Berger et al., 1986: 283; F: Michelat and Simon, 1977a: 74; IRL: Whyte, 1974: 640; I: Barnes, 1974: 217; NL: Miller and Stouthard, 1975: 221; N: Valen, 1981: 150; P: Bruneau and Macleod, 1986: 114; E: Linz, 1980: 261; S: Holmberg and Gilljam, 1987: 206; CH: Nicola, 1975: 196; GB: Rose, 1974a: 518. (2) Inglehart, 1977: 224. (3) European Values Survey 1982. (4) *Political Action: An Eight Nation Study*, 1979: 291. (5) *Social Compass*, 1972: 282.

To the former group belong Switzerland and the Netherlands. To the latter group belong Italy, Austria and Belgium. The United Kingdom is an exception to the relationship between heterogeneity and church attendance; France, Portugal and Spain do not quite exemplify the close relation between Catholic homogeneity and church attendance. In the last three countries there are some regional variations so far as church attendance is concerned. By tradition religion has a stronghold in Brittany, Vendée, Alsace-Lorraine, in French Flanders and in Southwest France; church attendance is low in the Paris area. In Spain and Portugal church attendance is high in the northern provinces. In the southern provinces, Andalusia and Alentejo, there is a strong anti-religious tradition (Querido, 1972: 428; Duocastella, 1975; Martin, 1978: 272; Isambert and Terrenoire, 1980; de Franca, 1980).

Summary

Religious fragmentation and religious consciousness do not correlate. The extent of fragmentation in the religious structure of a country neither affects nor is affected by the degree of religious consciousness typical of the various denominations constituting the religious structure. Our data corroborate the null hypothesis: religious awareness is not heightened due to the existence of competing or conflicting denominations. Actually, this finding is somewhat surprising as it could have been expected that the existence of a diversified religious structure would stimulate religious consciousness. Perhaps the lack of a significant relationship between these two variables constituting the religious cleavage is a phenomenon typical of the twentieth century secularization process of Europe.

There is a strong connection between type of denomination and religious awareness: Catholics tend to have a high degree of religious consciousness whereas the opposite is true of Protestants. Thus, what conditions religious awareness is not if a country is split between various denominations. Religious awareness is a function of the size of the Catholic denomination whether religious consciousness is measured by weekly church attendance ($r = .74$) or monthly church attendance ($r = .85$). Since the relationship is stronger for monthly church attendance than for weekly church attendance it may be assumed that the high correlation indicates a higher level of religious awareness in nations where the Catholic Church dominates rather than simply that the Catholic Church tends to demand more formal religious practice.

Ethnic cleavages

The 1970s made it clear that ethnic cleavages constitute a powerful source of change and contention in societies. Perhaps the implications of ethnic cleavages for a society and its political system have been neglected, as one scholar states:

> Social science theorists have until recently paid little attention to enduring ethnic or cultural identity as a primary social force comparable to nationalism or class affiliation (De Vos, 1975: 7).

Today it is generally believed that ethno-linguistic cleavages are just as important as religious or class-based cleavages for the development of society (Ragin, 1979). Perhaps ethnicity was neglected because its role was underestimated or misunderstood? Some scholars believed that the modernization of society implied that functional cleavages such as class or economic structure would replace traditional cleavages such as ethnicity and religion (Geertz, 1963). The variety that stems from language and culture would disappear as a result of growing communications.

Theories of modernization were popular during the 1960s and they implied that ethnic cleavages and ethnic mobilization would decrease and not increase in importance. Lipset and Rokkan argued that ethnic cleavages belong to a category whose importance will decrease as societies become fully mobilized or modernized. What happened in Western Europe during the 1970s proved that these theories were out of touch with reality in Northern Ireland, the Basque provinces, and the Flemish provinces (Anderson, 1978). As ethnic cleavages have proved their relevance to politics the interest in ethnicity is growing. Some scholars talk about 'ethnonationalism' (Connor, 1977), and 'minority nationalistic movements' (Birch, 1978); others speak of 'ethnic political mobilization' (Ragin, 1979), 'peripheral nationalisms' (Gourevitch, 1979) and 'territorial identities' (Rokkan and Urwin, 1982). The basic problem is to understand and account for this resurrection of ethnicity (Allardt, 1979; Blaschke, 1980; Krejci and Velimsky, 1981; Smith, 1983, Rudolph and Thompson, 1989; Meadwell, 1989; Zariski, 1989).

One explanation is a version of the modernization theme: if modernization is not successful it will result in a revitalization of ethnic cleavages and ethnic conflict. Already one of the prophets of modernization, Deutsch, pointed out that modernization 'may tend to strain or destroy the unity of states whose population is already divided into several groups with different languages or cultures or basic ways of life' (Deutsch, 1961: 501).

No doubt, there is a core of truth in this since attempts at modernization tend to bring about a disruption of ethnic structure and ethnic loyalties – a development which may offset successful counter-tendencies to strengthen ethnicity (Ragin, 1979). However, the nucleus of the problem remains: Under what conditions do efforts at modernization fail and result in a resurrection of ethnicity? More complex explanations of ethnicity point out that the revival of ethnic loyalties depends on economic diversification (Ragin, 1979), on regional differences (Mughan, 1979), and the balance between the centre and the periphery (Hechter, 1975). These explanations employ some kind of theory of relative deprivation. The cause of the revival of ethnicity is not that ethnic structures are threatened in modern society, but the combination of a break-up of ethnic structures and an uneven economic development to the disadvantage of ethnic groups.

Some scholars speak about the need for a balance between transaction and integration (Lijphart, 1977b: 55; Birch, 1978: 334). As societies modernize there must come about a balance between the transaction among various groups in society and the institutions that integrate these groups. If the development is too rapid and the transactional pattern gets too far away from the integration pattern the solidarity and consensus of society will be hurt (Hechter, 1971: 42).

These explanations emphasize the interregional development in a society; the important issue is not the level or the stage of the modernization process but, decisively, how the various regions develop in relation to each other. What matters is the problem of congruence, i.e. whether regions develop more or less evenly in relation to each other. If the modernization process is congruent with the regions, then the prospects for peripheral nationalism are not as bright as when the process results in non-congruent situations where an ethnic potential may become exploited (Gourevitch, 1979: 306).

To Walker Connor economic factors have been overemphasized. Ethno-nationalism in Europe has a long tradition and may be interpreted as a continuation of nationalistic tendencies so strong in Europe. Today it is a commonplace that ethnic cleavages affect politics and political stability. Ragin states that they constitute 'a potentially disintegrative force in the modern polity' (Ragin, 1979: 619). According to Richard Rose and Derek Urwin cleavages and the size of ethnic parties affect the party system of a country (Rose and Urwin, 1969: 41; 1970: 308). Our selection of ethnic cleavages needs no more argument. Data on ethnic minorities are presented in Appendix 2.1.

Ethnic Structure
An ethnic group or an ethno-linguistic group is a collection of people who share the same language or have a common culture based on language. We start our analysis of the occurrence of ethnic cleavages in the social structure by distinguishing between ethnic structure and ethnic consciousness. A society is ethnically homogeneous or heterogeneous if its citizens belong to one and the same cultural tradition in language or if there is a division of the population into two or more different cultural groups in point of language. Societies may be classified on the basis of their degree of ethnic heterogeneity by means of indices that measure the distribution of the population on ethno-linguistic fragmentation measured through an estimate of the likelihood that two random persons in a society belong to different ethno-linguistic groups. Another way of presenting the data is to look at the percentage of the population that uses the dominant language or belongs to a dominant ethno-linguistic group. A picture of ethno-linguistic fragmentation in the social structure appears in Table 2.10.

Two countries display a high ethnic fragmentation, viz., Belgium and Switzerland; Spain, the United Kingdom and France also score high on the index. This in particular is true of Spain which is almost as ethnically diversified as Switzerland and Belgium. Some countries, the Netherlands, Finland, Greece and Austria, score high on the index, because they have relatively large ethnic minorities within their borders. Other countries, Denmark, Ireland, Italy, Norway, Portugal, Sweden and West Germany, are more or less homogeneous.

Table 2.10   *Ethnic structure and fragmentation*

	Ethnic fragmentation				Percentage of population using the dominant language/belonging to dominant ethno-linguistic group	
	Index 1 1920s (1)	Index 2 1960s (2)	Index 3 1970s (3)	Index 4 1970s (4)	1950s (5)	1970s (6)
Austria	.04	.13	.02	.13	99	93.3
Belgium	.55	.55	.50	.54	50	58.5
Denmark	.02	.05	.00	.05	97	97.5
F R Germany	.00	.02	.00	.12	100	93.6
Finland	.16	.16	.13	.15	92	92.0
France	.50	.26	.40	.33	86	82.0
Greece	.03	.10	.09	.10	98	94.9
Ireland	.22	.04	.37	.07	97	96.3
Italy	.06	.04	.10	.08	99	95.9
Netherlands	.08	.10	.06	.11	95	94.1
Norway	.01	.04	.00	.05	100	97.7
Portugal	.00	.01	.00	.01	100	99.5
Spain	.50	.44	.39	.44	73	72.8
Sweden	.01	.08	.00	.19	98	89.9
Switzerland	.45	.50	.52	.56	69	63.2
United Kingdom	.05	.32	.03	.37	98	78.5

Note: Columns (1)–(4) denote different estimates of ethnic fragmentation based upon different sources; index 1 is calculated from Tesnière (1928); index 2 is based upon Taylor and Hudson (1972); index 3 is calculated from data in Stephens (1976); and index 4 is calculated from Barrett (1982). Columns (5) and (6) present estimates of percentages of the population using the dominating language/belonging to the dominant ethno-linguistic group; data in column (5) stem from Rustow (1967) and data in column (6) stem from Barrett (1982).

Belgium   There are two major ethnic groups in Belgium, the Flemings who speak Dutch and the Walloons who speak French. In addition, there is a small group of German-speaking people. The distribution of the population of these groups appears in Table 2.11. The Flemings have remained somewhat more numerous than the Walloons, and they have increased their numbers since the Second World War, although the relationship between the two remains intact. The Flemings are concentrated in the northern parts of the country, more specifically in the provinces of Oost Vlaanderen, West Vlaanderen, Antwerpen and Limburg. The French-speaking Walloons are found in the provinces of Hainaut, Namur, Liège and Luxembourg, i.e. the South of Belgium. The German-speaking groups live in the East, in the provinces of Liège and Luxembourg. The

Table 2.11   *Language groups in Belgium (percentages of the population)*

Year	French	Dutch	German
1846	42	57	1
1910	45	54	1
1920	46	53	1
1930	45	54	1
1947	44	55	1
1961*	40–1	58–9	1
1970*	39–40	59–60	1

Note: *Estimations computed from Rayside. There are no official data later than 1947 because of the political delicacy of the ethnic cleavage in Belgium.
Sources: Zolberg, 1977: 107; Rayside, 1977: 103.

capital city of Brussels has a special position being situated within Flemish territory but having a majority of French-speaking inhabitants. The French-speaking make up roughly two-thirds of the population of Brussels and they live in the central parts whereas the remaining third, Flemings, live in the surrounding parts. Ethnic fragmentation is high in Belgium, the probability being more than one half that two randomly selected persons do not belong to the same ethnic group.

Switzerland   The basic data on the ethnic structure of Switzerland are given in Table 2.12. There are two ways of describing ethnicity in Switzerland, either by using data on the Swiss population or on the Swiss citizens. These data are not entirely congruent, because the proportion of Gastarbeiter ('guest labourers') makes a difference. The ethnic structure has remained stable for the last hundred years, though there are some small but important changes during the last twenty years.

Three major languages are spoken in Switzerland. The predominant language is German, spoken by roughly 65 per cent of the population. It is

Table 2.12   *Language groups in Switzerland (percentages of the population)*

Year	German	French	Italian	Romansh	Others
1850	70.2	22.6	5.4	1.8	–
1900	69.7	22.0	6.7	1.2	0.4
1930	71.9	20.4	6.0	1.1	0.6
1950	72.1	20.3	5.9	1.0	0.7
1970	64.9	18.1	11.9	0.8	4.3
1980	65.0	18.4	9.8	0.8	6.0

Sources: Almanach der Schweiz, 1978: 29; Statistisches Jahrbuch der Schweiz, 1983: 88.

Table 2.13   *Language groups in Spain (percentages of the population)*

Language	Per cent
Spanish	72.5
Catalan	17.2
Basque	2.2
Galician	7.8

Source: Haarman, 1975: 65.

spoken by the majority of the population in nineteen out of the twenty-six cantons of Switzerland. French is spoken by somewhat more than 18 per cent. It is the majority language in five cantons, those situated in Western Switzerland, closest to France. The third major language in Switzerland is Italian, spoken by barely 12 per cent of the population. Only in the canton of Ticino in the south is Italian the majority language, but the size of the Italian group has increased since 1945. Besides these languages Romansh is spoken by a small minority, barely 1 per cent.

Several cantons have a mixed population as regards language. In the canton of Bern this state has been conducive to conflicts among the various language groups. Within Bern there was a minority of French-speaking people constituting 15 per cent of the population of the canton, concentrated into the seven districts forming the Jura region. However, the Jura region is not homogeneous in point of language, as there is a German-speaking minority there making up somewhat more than 20 per cent of the population, to be found in larger numbers in the southern districts. There exists a religious cleavage between the northern and the southern districts in Jura in addition to the ethnic one. In the North the majority are Catholics, whereas in the South the majority are Protestants. In 1978 the northern districts broke out of the canton of Bern and formed the canton of Jura (Steiner, 1974; Bassand, 1976; McRae, 1983). Switzerland is only slightly less fragmented than Belgium, the probability being one half that two persons do not belong to the same ethnic group.

Spain   The boundaries of present day Spain have remained very much the same since the beginning of the sixteenth century, yet Spain is a multi-ethnic society. Spanish, i.e. the Castilian dialect, is the predominant language. The other big language groups are Catalan, Galician and Basque. Table 2.13 contains the data on ethnic structure in Spain.

People in the eastern coastal areas speak Catalan which is the dominating language in the provinces of Gerona, Lérida, Barcelona, Tarragona, Castellón, Valencia and Alicante as well as in the Balearic Islands. The Basque language is spoken in the North of Spain on the

Table 2.14   *Celtic language groups (percentages of the population)*

Language	1891	1911	1931	1951	1971
Wales: Welsh	54.0	43.0	37.0	28.9	20.8
Scotland: Scottish Gaelic	5.2	3.1	2.7	1.6	1.8

Source: Stephens, 1976: 51f, 145f.

borders of France, in the provinces of Alava, Vizcaya, Guipuzcoa but also in Navarra. Finally, Galician is spoken in the Northwest corner of the country: the provinces of La Coruna, Lugo, Orense, and Pontevedra (Stephens, 1976: 605). Spain is ethnically diverse to a considerable extent (.44) but it is not a bilingual society in the way Belgium and Switzerland are. It is composed of several language groups and the differences between the languages are pronounced.

The United Kingdom   Great Britain and Ulster, the six northernmost counties in Ireland, form the United Kingdom, which comprises three different language groups. The Anglo-Saxon dialects, which form the basis of Modern English, predominate. There are Celtic language groups; on the one hand we have the Q-Celts: Irish, Manx (spoken in the Isle of Man) and Scottish Gaelic; on the other hand there is the P-Celts: Welsh and Cornish; and Breton is spoken in Brittany in France (Rose, 1976: 121). The Celtic language groups are small today. The use of the Celtic languages in present-day Great Britain is shown in Table 2.14.

In Wales Welsh is spoken by a fairly large proportion of the population, which may constitute the basis for national identification. Language does not play the same role in Scotland and in Ulster, because national identification is based more on the patterns of communication that have developed in these areas and which separate them from other parts of Great Britain (Kellas, 1975: 10). In Ulster differences survive between the Irish and the descendants of the Scottish and the English colonists who immigrated in the beginning of the seventeenth century. On the whole these differences coincide with religious differences, the colonists being Protestants and the Irish Catholics (Rose, 1971: 18). Ethnic fragmentation is substantial in the United Kingdom (.32) and its relevance for political action and identification has became apparent during the 1970s.

France   The ethno-linguistic minorities in France are found in the periphery of the country, where other languages also besides French are spoken (Table 2.15).

In Brittany groups speak Breton, a Celtic dialect. On the borders of Spain there are in the South Basque-speaking clusters and in the Southeast, Catalan-speaking clusters. In Corsica Corse is spoken, which is in reality an Italian dialect. German is spoken in Alsace (das Elsass) on the

Table 2.15   *Language groups in France (percentages of the population)*

Language group	According to Haarman	According to Stephens
Bretons	2.1	1.4
Basques	0.2	0.2
Catalans	0.4	0.6
Corsicans	1.6	0.4
Alsatians	2.4	2.5
Flemings	0.4	0.2
Occitans	21.8	19.8

Sources: Haarman, 1975: 58; Stephens, 1976: 298 ff.

borders of West Germany, an area that has been French since the end of the First World War, the years of German occupation excepted. (Alsatia was French from 1648 to 1871.) Flemish is spoken by small groups living near the borders of Belgium, in the Northwest. These ethno-linguistic minorities constitute in all slightly more than three million out of a total population of fifty million people.

A special case is the province of Occitania, in the south-eastern part of France. It covers the provinces of Languedoc, Provence, Limousin, Auvergne, Gascogne, Guyenne and Dauphiné. There are those who claim that the people in this area form an ethno-linguistic unit. However, it is doubtful whether the language in this area is to be regarded as a dialect or as a language of its own. Le Roy Laduire comments: 'The Occitanian language has reconquered an active and seductive minority. It has not quite been able to persuade the silent and still francophone majority of the land of Oc' (Le Roy Laduaire, 1977: 30; cf. Hobsbawm, 1977: 19–20).

Finland   There is still a Swedish-speaking minority in Finland, though it decreased in one hundred years as shown in Table 2.16. The Swedish

Table 2.16   *Swedish minority in Finland*

Year	Percentage of total population
1880	14.3
1900	12.9
1920	11.0
1940	9.6
1960	7.4
1970	6.6
1980	6.2

Source: Statistical Yearbook of Finland.

Table 2.17 *Language groups in Austria (percentages of the population)*

Year	Slovenians in Kärnten	Croatians in Burgenland
1951	8	13
1961	5	10
1971	4	9

Source: Stephens, 1976: 3ff.

minority is concentrated in the province of Österbotten, to the coastal area between Åbo and Helsingfors and to the island of Åland. During the last eighty years the Swedish minority has decreased to half its size and it has maintained a majority position only in the island of Åland.

Austria Austria is less ethnically diversified than Finland. The Dual Monarchy of Austria and Hungary was a nation deeply troubled by its ethnic diversity. Compared with this Great Power of the past today's Austria has a homogeneous population. Most people speak German, but there are ethnic minorities. A Slovenian minority lives in Kärnten and there is a Croatian minority in Burgenland, areas that are situated on the borders of Yugoslavia (Table 2.17).

Italy In some countries which score low on the measure of ethnic diversity there are small but important minorities. Italy is one instance. There is a number of minorities in Italy that use languages other than Italian. They constituted roughly 4 per cent of the population in 1970 and their size is shown in Table 2.18. The Sards live in the island of Sardinia, where Sardish is the dominating language. It is an old version of Italian. In the region of Friulia-Venezia on the borders of Austria some people speak Friulish, which comes close to the Romansh language. The Slovenian language is spoken in the area of Trieste on the borders of Yugoslavia. The Trieste area has long been a source of contention between Italy and Yugoslavia. Trieste went to Italy after the First World War. During the years 1945–54 the area was under the mandate of the UN, but has subsequently been Italian territory.

In the extreme North, in South Tyrol, on the borders of Austria there is a minority of German-speaking people. As was the case with Trieste there have been divergent opinions about where South Tyrol should belong. It became Italian territory after the First World War, but in 1939 an agreement was made between Hitler and Mussolini according to which the German-speaking population of South Tyrol was to be transferred to the German Reich. The status of the area was again debated after the Second World War, but South Tyrol remained Italian. Austria and Italy have negotiated treaties which provide for certain guarantees concerning

Table 2.18   *Language groups in Italy*

Groups	Millions
Sards	1.0
Friulian	0.4
German	0.2
Slovenian	0.1
French	0.1

Source: Haarman, 1975: 51.

the status of South Tyrol within Italy. The first agreement was concluded in 1946 and the one now in force dates from 1972. In the same year the Italian government granted South Tyrol autonomy within the state of Italy. The percentage of German-speaking people in the area of South Tyrol or the province of Bolzano has declined during the twentieth century, but it has stabilized since 1960 (Table 2.19).

In the West on the borders of France and Switzerland there is a minority of French-speaking people in Valle d'Aosta. The area has been Italian ever since the country was united in 1860. The proportion of those speaking French in Valle d'Aosta is diminishing. In 1901 roughly 92 per cent spoke French, whereas in 1971 the proportion amounted to 65 per cent; these people live mainly in the countryside, while most Italian-speaking people in this area live in the urban areas (Stephens, 1976: 508, 514; Janin, 1975: 79).

Denmark   Another example of a country that cannot be classified as ethnically diversified but still contains a minority is Denmark. The area of Slesvig has been a cause of conflict between Denmark and Germany. From 1866 up to 1920 the whole of Slesvig was part of Prussia, and later Germany. The referendums that were held in 1920 as a result of the Versailles peace treaty led to a new solution. The area was divided into two parts, and North Slesvig was integrated into Denmark. This solution is still in force, though there were other boundaries during the Second

Table 2.19   *Percentages of German-speaking people in South Tyrol*

Year	Percentage
1910	97
1921	87
1939	72
1945	66
1961	62
1971	63

Sources: Stephens, 1976: 526; Katzenstein, 1977: 209.

Table 2.20 *National identification in Belgium (percentages of the population)*

| Group | Identification | |
	Belgian	Other
All Belgians	41.5	58.5
Flemings	32.5	67.5
Brussels	56.5	43.5
Walloons	50.3	49.7

Note: Data based on samples.
Source: Computed from Delruelle-Vosswinkel and Frognier, 1980: 9.

World War. A consequence of the division of Slesvig was the creation of a German-speaking minority in North Slesvig and a Danish-speaking minority in South Slesvig. The German minority has remained about 20 000 and their proportion of the population of the South of Jutland is about 10 per cent. It is not easy to estimate the size of the Danish minority living in the province of Slesvig-Holstein, but it could amount to 50 000, which means roughly 2 per cent of the population (Stephens, 1976: 233, 421; Elklit et al., 1972: 386).

Ethnic consciousness
Ethnic diversity may cause conflict and even civil war. The relation between ethnic structure and action orientated towards ethnic conflict is, however, by no means a simple one. In order that action may be taken on behalf of the interests of ethnic groups an ethnic consciousness must exist. The mere occurrence of various languages within a political system is not in itself a threat to political stability. When the ethnic structure becomes the object of serious and sustained identification, then ethnic contention is close. It is by no means evident that an ethnic diversity will carry over into ethnic ideologies or ethnic consciousness. Ethnic fragmentation works like a potential for conflict. In some cases during certain intervals of time such a potential may be turned into actuality, dividing a nation into groups with separate national identification.

An ethnic consciousness cannot be described as existent or non-existent. There are degrees of ethnic identification. In some countries and for some groups the ethnic identification may even outbalance the national identification. When this occurs the step to action is not far away. Let us look at the data. The three countries that are most diversified ethnically are Belgium, Switzerland and Spain. To what extent is there some kind of ethnic consciousness in these countries? It should be stressed that it is difficult to measure the attitude dimension of ethnic and national identification. Data from various countries may not be

Table 2.21   *National identification in Switzerland (percentages of the population)*

| Groups | Identification | | |
	Nation	Language group	Canton
German-speaking	53	16	31
Romance-speaking	40	40	31

Note: Data based on samples.
Source: Kerr, 1974: 21.

comparable, because different indicators have been used and the data may be given different interpretations. Besides, these kinds of data are not in abundance.

Table 2.20 shows that national identification in Belgium is, indeed, a questionable matter, as only 41 per cent of the population display such an identification. The country faces a severe ethnic cleavage in both extension and intensity. The Flemings seem to identify considerably with Flemish culture, whereas the Walloons appear to be more split between an ethnic orientation towards Walloon culture and an orientation towards the geographical area of Brussels. The orientation towards Brussels covers both an ethnic cleavage and an urban–rural cleavage. Besides the ethnic dimension there is the identification with the metropolis of Brussels, which for people living in that area is stronger than the national identification. Belgium is a country where ethnic diversity seems to be combined with a crisis of cultural and national identity.

Switzerland is somewhat different from Belgium, because ethnic fragmentation is not paralleled in the consciousness of the Swiss population. Data concerning the German-speaking population show that national identification is stronger than ethnic loyalties (Table 2.21). Although the Romance-speaking population is less identified with the nation, they do as a group identify more with the nation than with any other competing object.

The data concerning ethnic identification in Spain present a picture that is different from both Switzerland and Belgium. There is nothing comparable to the general lack of national loyalty among all groups in Belgium, because some regions display a highly positive orientation towards the nation (Castile), whereas other regions show at least somewhat of a national identification (Catalonia). Conversely, there are regions in which the ethnic identification is greater than that typical of Switzerland (Table 2.22).

National loyalties are a fragile matter within the provinces of Galicia, Vasco and Navarra (Basque provinces). Ethnic diversity in Spain has no parallel as far as ethnic consciousness is concerned, but there are

Table 2.22 *Identification in Spain (percentages of the population)*

	Identification	
Regions	Spanish	Regional*
Asturias	93	5
León	92	3
Castilla la Nueva	83	6
Madrid	81	6
Castilla la Vieja-León	77	10
Valencia	72	13
Extremadura	70	16
Andalucia	68	21
Barcelona	66	22
Cataluña-Baleares	65	23
Murcia	65	11
Aragón	61	31
Canarias	44	49
Vasco-Navarra	43	47
Galicia	38	53

Note: *These data concern primarily regional identification. We use them, because of the overlap between regional identification and ethnic loyalties in Spain. Data are based on samples.
Source: Blanco, J.J. et al., 1977: 47.

minorities in the ethnic structure which are very much orientated towards their own groups.

The United Kingdom scores significantly on the extension index though the score is not comparable to the scores of the other nations dealt with. The data on the United Kingdom show convincingly that ethnic extension and ethnic intensity may differ. The United Kingdom does not score among the three highest on the index of ethnic fragmentation, but there are regions in which ethnic intensity seems to be higher than it is in Switzerland and Spain (Table 2.23).

Table 2.23 *National identification in the United Kingdom (percentages of the population)*

	Identification					
Region	British	Scottish	Welsh	English	Ulster	Irish
Scotland	29	67	1	–	–	–
Wales	15	1	69	13	–	1
N. Ireland	29	–	–	–	21	43

Note: Data based on samples.
Source: Rose, 1976: 127.

The British identification is about the same in Scotland, Wales and Northern Ireland and it is low. Whereas those in Scotland and Wales who do not share deep loyalties to the nation are united, the ethnic identification in Northern Ireland is – as is well-known – severely split into two contending orientations.

France and Finland have ethnic minorities, but data concerning identification are almost totally lacking. It is difficult to state anything about ethnic consciousness in these countries. Efforts have been made to survey the orientations of the people in Occitania, but they show that only a tiny portion of the population has some kind of ethnic identification. Perhaps it is not too daring a hypothesis that the same weak ethnic identification recurs within the other areas of the French ethnic structure. However, matters are probably not quite the same in Finland, because the ethnic identification among the Swedish minority can be expected to be substantial. Their language is different from that of the Finnish majority and they have a culture of long-standing characteristic of this minority. There is an ethnic identification among the Swedish Finns, but there is no data available to tell us how strong the identification is (Allardt and Miemois, 1979).

Data are available for some minorities within countries that are not particularly diversified ethnically. Among the German-speaking minority in North Slesvig there is a high ethnic identification (Elklit et al., 1972). It seems as if the ethnic identification within minorities is strong to the extent that they speak a language different from the national one and to the extent that they may identify themselves with the majority of the population of a bordering nation. This means that ethnic consciousness should be rather strong among the German-speaking in South Tyrol, among the French-speaking in Valle d'Aosta, and among the Slovenians and the Croatians in Austria. Available data on Austria only measure the extent to which the population is orientated towards Austria or Germany (Bluhm, 1973: 220).

Migration in Western Europe
To give a more complete picture of the ethno-linguistic cleavages of Western Europe it is necessary to supplement the preceding account with data on migration in Western Europe. An uneven economic development in Europe has paved the way for a large migration process after the Second World War, the countries in the South providing the countries in the North and the West with labour. At the same time the countries that used to be colonial powers have had to receive immigrants from their former colonies; this applies primarily to the United Kingdom, France and the Netherlands.

Let us first look at migration in Western Europe beginning with the early 1970s. Although migration tends to vary over time, we note

Table 2.24   *Migration (per thousand in relation to the population)*

	Net migration rates		
	1970	1980	1985
Austria	2.3	1.2	1.1
Belgium	0.4	–0.4	0.1
Denmark	2.4	0.2	1.8
F R Germany	9.3	5.1	1.5
Finland	–7.8	–0.6	0.6
France	3.5	0.8	–0.1
Greece	–4.4	5.0	1.1
Ireland	–1.0	–0.3	–7.3
Italy	–0.9	0.1	1.5
Netherlands	2.6	3.7	1.4
Norway	–0.3	1.0	1.4
Portugal	–16.5	–12.9	2.3
Spain	–0.6	0.0	0.4
Sweden	6.1	1.2	1.3
Switzerland	–1.0	2.7	2.2
United Kingdom	–0.5	–0.9	1.3

Note: Net migration means immigration minus emigration.
Source: OECD (1988) *Labour force statistics.*

clear differences between the various countries. In Finland, Greece and Portugal emigration was larger than immigration whereas the opposite is true of the Federal Republic of Germany, Sweden and the Netherlands. In the 1980s no country except Ireland displays a negative migration balance and the positive migration balance is rather small in the other countries (Table 2.24).

In addition, migration in West Europe may be described by looking at data about the size of the minority population (Table 2.25) as well as data about the proportion of the population of a country that lives abroad (Table 2.26). Admitting that these estimations are somewhat shaky we find a country pattern that agrees with earlier observations. The following countries have a large proportion of immigrants: Switzerland, Belgium, United Kingdom, the Federal Republic of Germany, France, Sweden and the Netherlands. On the other hand, the countries with a large proportion of its population living abroad include: Ireland, Portugal, Italy, Greece, Finland and Spain.

Most countries have emigration, which is the reason why we count those countries as emigrant countries where the proportion of emigrants exceeds the proportion of immigrants. Even if these data are to be interpreted cautiously it is evident that Ireland is the major emigration country. The migration waves have had political consequences resulting in or reinforcing cleavages.

Table 2.25   *Migration in Western Europe: minority population as a percentage of total population*

	1950*	1960*	1970*	1975*	1980*	1982**	1984***
Austria	–	–	–	–	–	–	3.6
Belgium	4.3	4.9	7.2	8.5	9.2	8.9	9.1
Denmark	–	–	–	–	–	–	–
F R Germany	1.1	1.2	4.9	6.6	7.2	7.6	7.2
Finland	–	–	–	–	–	–	–
France	4.5	5.4	6.5	7.9	7.7	6.8	8.2
Greece	–	–	–	–	–	–	–
Ireland	–	–	–	–	–	–	–
Italy	–	–	–	–	–	–	–
Netherlands	1.1	1.0	1.8	2.6	3.4	3.8	3.9
Norway	–	–	–	–	–	–	–
Portugal	–	–	–	–	–	–	–
Spain	–	–	–	–	–	–	–
Sweden	1.8	2.5	5.1	5.0	5.1	4.7	4.7
Switzerland	6.1	10.8	15.8	16.0	14.2	14.5	13.0
United Kingdom	3.2	4.3	7.4	(7.8)	8.5	–	3.2

Sources: *Castles (1984: 88), **OECD Employment Outlook* (1985), ***Layton-Henry (1988: 590)

The post-war migration has resulted in large foreign populations in several West European countries like Switzerland, Belgium, France, West Germany, Sweden, the Netherlands, Austria and the United Kingdom. The size of these groups is not easily established as it depends upon the various definitions of citizenship in different countries (Layton-Henry, 1990). Yet, post-war immigration is large enough to present severe problems to the political élites in several West European countries.

Conclusion

The ethnic cleavage may be separated into three dimensions: ethnic structure, ethnic consciousness and migration. Whereas ethnic structure may adequately be described by the fragmentation index or a measure of the percentage of the population that speaks the dominant language, it is far more difficult to arrive at a measure of the extent of ethnic consciousness typical of a nation. Ethnic identities belong to ethnic groups, not to nations. For the national level the relationship between ethnic fragmentation and ethnic consciousness may be summarized thus: a high degree of fragmentation is conducive to the existence of highly conscious groups, but it is not a sufficient condition.

A high level of fragmentation does not automatically produce intense ethnic awareness as Switzerland shows, and it is not that the higher the fragmentation the more intense the awareness. Ethnic consciousness in parts of the United Kingdom is probably as high as it is in Spain and in

Table 2.26   *Migration in Western Europe: estimated population and labour force living abroad (as a percentage of the total population)*

	Estimated population living abroad			Estimated labour force living abroad	
	In Europe c.1970*	In Europe c.1982**	In World c.1982**	In Europe c.1977***	In Europe c.1982**
Austria	–	–	–	–	–
Belgium	–	–	–	–	–
Denmark	–	–	–	–	–
F R Germany	–	–	–	–	–
Finland	–	3.7	4.8	4.5	4.7
France	–	–	–	–	–
Greece	4.1	–	–	5.7	4.1
Ireland	25.1	–	–	–	–
Italy	3.4	4.1	9.4	4.0	4.6
Netherlands	–	–	–	–	–
Norway	–	–	–	–	–
Portugal	6.0	11.8	40.3	10.6	13.9
Spain	2.9	2.3	5.6	3.2	3.1
Sweden	–	–	–	–	–
Switzerland	–	–	–	–	–
United Kingdom	–	–	–	–	–

Sources: *Castles and Kosack (1973), **OECD Employment Outlook (1985), *** OECD Observer (1979).

Belgium, although the fragmentation is lower in the United Kingdom. Intense ethnic identification may occur in a country that is not highly fragmented ethnically. Ethnic awareness may be found in France, Finland and Denmark even though these countries are not highly fragmented. To make more detailed comparisons between ethnic structure and ethnic awareness regional data should be consulted.

Class-based cleavages

There is unanimity among scholars that class is an important cleavage between people in industrialized societies in Western Europe (Bottomore, 1966; Goldthorpe et al., 1969). Class seems to be an important explanatory variable (Korpi, 1983). The class a person belongs to affects his/her pattern of action as Robert Lane argues (Lane, 1965: 220). The concept of class has not only an individual dimension but above all a social dimension. Walter Korpi maintains that it helps in understanding of how privileges and chances in life are distributed in society as well as how conflict between groups arises and how society changes (Korpi,

1978). Divergent opinions in the theoretical debate concerning class deal not with whether class is an important cleavage but with the relative importance that is to be attached to class compared with other types of cleavages. These differences recur in the approaches to the concept of class (Carlsson, 1969).

Outlooks differ in the debate concerning the extent conflicts based on class cleavages decrease or increase in importance as industrial societies are transformed into welfare societies or 'the post-industrial society'. Above all among American scholars the view may be found that class conflicts would lose in importance in these societies. Another line of reasoning akin to such statements was that ideologies based on class cleavages were fading away; the slogan was 'the end of ideology' (Tingsten, 1955; Aron, 1957; Shils, 1958; Bell, 1960; 1973; Lipset, 1964; DiPalma, 1973).

In *Class and Class Conflict in Industrial Society* (1959) Ralf Dahrendorf maintained that class conflicts were declining at the same time as they proved to be easier to solve in welfare societies. Developments during the late 1960s and early 1970s have made the opposite interpretation more common: the salience of class conflict increased in industrialized societies. David Matheson writes:

> The May 1968 events in France and the turbulent reaction of labor to the world economic crises of the 1970s, particularly in Italy but also in other European countries, like Finland, seemed to mark the working class as anything but passive and accommodating to the established order (Matheson, 1979: 12–13).

Class-based cleavages – whether latent in the class structure or manifest in class consciousness – are assumed to be influenced by the economic-social development of a society, although opinions are divided about the magnitude and direction of the influence. The question is an old one as already Friedrich Engels in his description of the situation of the English working class considered that it had deteriorated as a consequence of the process of industrialization (Engels, 1958; Hobsbawm, 1964). In later discussions the positive effect of industrialization on the decrease of class distinctions is stressed. Lenski holds that both the process of industrialization and the rate of economic growth lead to reduced class distinctions (Lenski, 1966; Cutright, 1967). However, opinions are divided about whether the connection is a linear or a curvilinear one (Jackman, 1975: 43). Too rapid economic growth may have the opposite effect and lead to increased class distinctions (Olson, 1963: 536). When attempts have been made to clarify these connections, weak connections have been found in some cases (Jackman, 1975: 128), and stronger ones in others (Hewitt, 1977: 459; Dryzek, 1978: 407).

Another related set of problems focusses on how class consciousness changes. Does class consciousness diminish as societies become increasingly modern and achieve higher levels of economic growth? – that is the theme of the 'end of ideology' debate. So far we have looked upon class structure and class consciousness as a dependent variable. But class based cleavages should also be regarded as a causal variable, as an independent variable, which influences party and politics in different respects. A general model of politics in Western Europe has to take into account the implications of class-based cleavages for society, the party system, as well as for government. It is not necessary to adhere to orthodox Marxism to justify the inclusion of class-based cleavages (Crouch and Pizzorno, 1978).

Class Structure
The main problem when describing class structure is the operationalization of the concept of class. To be able to describe class-based cleavages in societies comparatively we must choose some measure or indicator. We take the distribution of income in society as our starting-point assuming that societies which have an uneven distribution of income present a class-based stratification system, whereas societies with a more even class structure display a more even income distribution. We measure class structure by income distribution because of the availability of various kinds of data. Although the data on income structure are plentiful, the quality varies, which often renders comparisons between countries difficult. This has led some scholars to repudiate this type of data altogether (Therborn et al., 1978: 27 f). We believe, however, that income data used judiciously can give a picture of the class structure of today's societies. Data that admit historical comparisons are not available.

Another circumstance is that the measures used to describe income distribution are not indisputable (Allison, 1978). In order to catch something of a country variation in the degree of inequality in the distribution of income we employ some measures that may be derived from the so-called Lorenz-curve. On the one hand we have the Gini-index which is an overall measure of the extent of income inequality. On the other hand we also use a measure of the proportion of the total disposable household income that goes to the top quintile.

Several data series of the income distribution among households and individuals have been presented during the 1970s and the 1980s (Paukert, 1973; Roberti, 1974; Uusitalo, 1975; Sawyer, 1976; Cromwell, 1977; Bornischer, 1978; Deutsch, 1980; Lecaillon et al., 1984; OECD, 1986). The quality varies and it is not always clear what has been included; some of the series are inadequate as a basis for comparisons between countries. The best of these series and the best overview up to now that we know of is the one made by Malcolm Sawyer. Sawyer does not present

Table 2.27   *Income distribution: Gini-indices*

	Index Yr (1)	Index Yr (2)	Index Yr (3)	Index Yr (4)	Index Yr (5)
Austria	–	0.369(67)	–	–	–
Belgium	–	–	–	–	–
Denmark	0.37(63)	0.365(66)	–	0.38*(71)	–
FRG	0.45(64)	0.392(70)	0.396(73)	0.383(73)	0.31**(78)
Finland	0.46(62)	0.463(67)	–	0.37*(71)	0.30**(78)
France	0.50(62)	0.421(70)	0.416(70)	0.414(70)	0.43(75)
Greece	0.38(57)	0.394(57)	–	–	–
Ireland	–	–	–	–	–
Italy	0.40(48)	0.397(69)	–	0.398(69)	0.37(80)
Netherlands	0.42(62)	0.393(67)	0.385(67)	0.354(67)	0.31**(77)
Norway	0.35(63)	0.361(70)	0.354(70)	0.307(70)	0.32**(79)
Portugal	–	–	–	–	–
Spain	–	0.391(64)	–	0.355(73)	0.39(80)
Sweden	0.39(63)	0.350(72)	0.346(72)	0.302(72)	0.33**(79)
Switzerland	–	0.401(68)	–	–	0.29(80)
UK	0.38(64)	0.346(62)	0.344(73)	0.318(73)	0.33(80)

Sources: (1) Paukert (1973): pre-tax; (2) Bornischer (1978): pre-tax; (3) Sawyer (1976): pre-tax; (4) Sawyer (1976): post-tax; * = Uusitalo (1975); (5) OECD (1986); **authors' computations.

Note: The Gini-index ranges from 0 to 1 with 0 being maximum equality and 1 maximum inequality. See Sawyer (1976) and OECD (1986) for a discussion of methodological problems. The number within brackets stands for the year of measurement.

comparable data for all the countries in Western Europe, but they may be complemented by other sources rendering reasonable estimates possible. Household incomes are compared and there are comparable data based on similar definitions of both income and household. The data collected are not based on income-tax statements but on survey investigations concerning after-tax income.

Table 2.27 gives these data on the income distribution in Western Europe varying from the 1960s to the 1980s. The Gini-index goes from 0 to 1, where 0 implies equality and 1 the opposite, i.e. a few have a very large amount of the resources, whereas the many have a very small share. The higher the value of the index is the more unequal is the distribution. When the different series are compared, there is an acceptable agreement with regard to the ranking order of the countries. Sawyer constantly shows lower values, which is probably because he consistently uses data on after-tax income.

In the ranking order of the countries clear differences appear between countries with high values (those which are above .400) and countries that have low values (those which are below .350). The countries in between are more difficult to distinguish from each other as the difference between

Table 2.28 *Income distribution: share of top 20 per cent*

	Share (Yr) (1)	Share (Yr) (2)	Share (Yr) (3)	Share (Yr) (4)	Share (Yr) (5)	Share (Yr) (6)
Austria	–	–	–	–	–	–
Belgium	–	–	–	–	36.0(78)	–
Denmark	43.2(63)	47.6(68)	–	–	38.6(81)	–
FRG	45.6(70)	52.9(64)	45.6(70)	46.2(73)	39.5(78)	38(78)
Finland	49.3(62)	49.3(62)	–	–	37.6(81)	37(78)
France	53.7(62)	53.7(62)	46.9(70)	46.9(70)	45.8(75)	47(75)
Greece	–	49.5(57)	–	–	–	–
Ireland	–	–	–	–	39.4(73)	–
Italy	–	48.4(48)	46.5(70)	46.5(69)	43.9(77)	44(80)
Netherlands	–	48.5(67)	42.9(70)	42.9(67)	36.2(81)	37(77)
Norway	40.5(63)	40.5(68)	37.3(70)	37.3(70)	38.2(82)	37(79)
Portugal	–	–	–	–	49.1(73)	–
Spain	45.2(64)	45.7(65)	42.2(70)	42.2(74)	40.0(80)	42(80)
Sweden	42.5(70)	44.0(63)	37.0(70)	37.0(72)	41.7(81)	39(79)
Switzerland	–	–	45.9(70)	–	38.0(78)	37(78)
UK	39.2(68)	39.0(68)	39.4(70)	38.8(73)	39.7(79)	39(80)

Sources: (1) Ahluwalia (1976); (2) Musgrave and Jarrett (1979); (3) Muller (1985); (4) World Bank (1979) *World Development Report*; (5) World Bank (1986, 1988) *World Development Report*; (6) OECD (1986).

Austria and Belgium is small (and uncertain) and so is the difference between Belgium and the Netherlands. It appears that the class cleavage is most conspicuous in southern Europe including France whereas northern Europe, in particular the Scandinavian countries, is characterized by a more even income distribution. The case of Switzerland illustrates the lack of consistency between various estimates. Actually, the different estimates for Switzerland result in a weak association between index (5) and index (2) ($r = .06$). Let us turn to an alternative measure of income distribution.

Another measure of the amount of income inequality in a country is the top quintile, which states the share of total income that goes to the 20 per cent most well off. The association between the various estimates of the share of the top quintile is higher ($r = .92$ for index (6) and index (5)) meaning that the top quintile measure is a more robust indicator. Table 2.28 has the data which complement Table 2.27. The extent of income inequality is higher in the southern parts of Europe than in the northern parts.

Class consciousness
After considering the class structure in Western Europe let us look at the consciousness dimension of class-based cleavages. We choose to do so by describing the degree of class consciousness within the working class,

Table 2.29   *Estimates of class voting (Alford Index) in the 1950s/1960s and the 1970s/1980s*

	1950s/1960s		1970s/1980s	
	Index	(year)	Index	(year)
Austria	31	(1967)	25	(1986)
Belgium	25	(1956)	25	(1974)
Denmark	44	(1963)	29	(1987)
FRG	27	(1959)	14	(1987)
Finland	59	(1958)	39	(1987)
France	15	(1956)	18	(1978)
Greece	–		18	(1981)
Ireland	19	(1969)	06	(1987)
Italy	19	(1959)	31	(1976)
Netherlands	26	(1956)	26	(1986)
Norway	46	(1957)	29	(1985)
Portugal	–		26	(1983)
Spain	–		20	(1979)
Sweden	53	(1955)	34	(1985)
Switzerland	26	(1963)	15	(1975)
UK	37	(1959)	30	(1983)

Sources: 1950s/1960s: Lijphart, 1971, except IRL: Whyte, 1974. 1970s/1980s: A: Plasser and Ulram, 1988: 85; B: Frognier, 1975: 480; DK: Worre, 1989: 51; SF: Berglund, 1988: 70; F: Colliard, 1982: 228–29; D: Dalton, 1989: 287; GR: Tsokou et al., 1986: 277; IRL: Laver et al., 1987: 111; I: Allum, 1979: 148; NL: Daalder, 1987b: 226–27; N: Aardal and Valen, 1989: 321; Bacalhau, 1988: 247; E: Gunther et al., 1986: 195; S: Holmberg and Gilljam, 1987: 179; CH: Kerr, 1987: 156; UK: Heath et al., 1985: 21.

which can be done in various ways. We select two indicators to describe class consciousness. On the one hand we have the Alford index on class voting as an expression of class identification. On the other hand we have the degree of trade union organization in a country as an expression of a union orientation and how class consciousness manifests itself in action through membership in trade unions.

Table 2.29 contains the Alford index measures for two time periods, the late 1950s and early 1960s on the one hand and the late 1970s and early 1980s on the other hand. It should be pointed out that the overall degree of class voting is lower in the late 1970s than in the late 1950s, but the country variation persists over time to a considerable extent (r = .69). Class voting tends to be low in southern Europe, for example France, central Europe, for example Switzerland and western Europe, for example Ireland whereas it tends to be high in northern Europe, i.e. Finland, Norway and Sweden.

The second indicator on class awareness shows how large a proportion of the economically active population is organized in trade unions. The

Table 2.30   *Estimates of work force unionized (percentages)*

	1946–60 (1)	1961–76 (1)	1978–80 (2)	c. 1980 (3)	1985 (4)
Austria	54	56	60	58	61
Belgium	42	52	72	75	83
Denmark	48	50	71	79	89
F R Germany	36	34	40	33	42
Finland	30	47	70	75	87
France	28	19	20	22	18
Greece	–	–	27	–	–
Ireland	33	40	–	52	61
Italy	27	18	50	37	42
Netherlands	31	33	39	38	34
Norway	47	44	58	55	68
Portugal	–	–	40	–	–
Spain	–	–	37	–	–
Sweden	65	76	89	85	94
Switzerland	25	22	38	35	34
United Kingdom	43	44	56	54	50

Sources: (1) Korpi (1983); (2) Hartmann (1984); Smith (1984); Mielke (1983); Hellman et al. (1980); (3) Therborn (1984); (4) Armingeon (1989).

data in Table 2.30 represent various estimates of the trade union density from the 1950s to the early 1980s. There appears to be a certain measure of agreement between different estimates of unionization as the association between estimate (4) and (3) and (2) is $r = .98$ and $r = .93$.

The trade unions organize a high percentage of the work force in the Scandinavian countries in particular. Austria, Belgium and the United Kingdom also have strong unionization. Most interestingly, the data indicate that the rate of unionization has not declined in the 1980s in the advanced capitalist countries in Western Europe.

Summing up

The class cleavage is the most homogeneous dimension of the types of cleavage that we consider. Class structure and class consciousness interact to a considerable extent. The correlations between the income distribution of a nation (the Gini-measure (4) and (5) and the Quintile measure (5)) and our measures of class consciousness (the estimates of trade union density (measure (2) and of class voting)) tend to be negative ($r = -.53, -.39$; $r = .45, -.20$; $r = -.36, -.01$, respectively). The finding is that the more even the income distribution between various strata in the class structure the higher the class consciousness and the degree of unionization. The correlation between class voting and trade-union organizing ($r = .74$) is to be expected, but what is a good explanation of the relationship between class structure and the two measures of class consciousness?

Firstly, we may conclude that it is hardly true that a more equal income distribution between economic strata softens class awareness. Class consciousness as measured by two different kinds of indicators, identification and unionization, is not necessarily higher in nations characterized by a hierarchical distribution of income. Secondly, we explain the findings by reversing the relationship: a high level of class consciousness results in an equalization of incomes; and a high level of class consciousness may persist for a long time even though the income distribution is no longer as unequal as it used to be. The explanation fails to account for the origin of a high level of class consciousness: If a high level of class consciousness explains the evenness of income distribution, what explains the low level of class consciousness in unequal countries? Perhaps a diachronic interpretation of each of the countries could account for the origin of the levels of class consciousness. Since our interest lies in the synchronic interpretation of data we note the coexistence of a high level of class consciousness in countries with a more even income distribution; and we suggest that class consciousness operates against economic inequalities.

Regional cleavages

Cleavages may occur between collectivities, between Protestants and Catholics, between ethnic groups and between economic strata, and cleavages may take on a territorial dimension within a nation. Nations are typically organized on the basis of some territorial division, and it may become the target of political action. The territorial dimension of cleavage structures may be expressed in centre–periphery tension, metropolis–hinterland imbalances, the growth of regional identities and the adherence to local government autonomy (Rokkan, 1980; Rokkan and Urwin, 1982; Rokkan and Urwin, 1983). By territorial cleavages we refer to cleavages between groups of people that happen to coincide with territorial distinctions; ethnic and religious cleavages may comprise a territorial dimension as in Belgium and Switzerland. In the occurrence of regional cleavages territorial distinctions not only are accidental epiphenomena but constitute the main focus of the cleavage.

Latent regional cleavages constitute a source of political conflict as differences in social-structure dimensions may become the target of systematic orientation resulting in the rise of specific regional identities or so-called manifest regional cleavages. When religious, ethnic or class-based cleavages take on a territorial dimension a process of interaction is often initiated in which the non-territorial and territorial cleavages reinforce each other. Although it is important to separate between region as a surface dimension in the cleavage structure that is the outcome of the operation of other dimensions in the social structure and region as an independent dimension on its own term (Janda and Gillies, 1983), a regional cleavage dimension is often a concomitant to the spatial distribution of cleavages such as religion, ethnicity or industry. The regional cleavage could reinforce the other cleavages and it may acquire a life of its own as a result of which the polity is divided between distinctly different regional identities which have their own political tradition.

A major theme in political sociology has been the analysis of centre periphery relations at various levels of political organization (Frank, 1967; Langholm, 1971; Galtung, 1971; McKenzie, 1977; Seers et al., 1979). Centre–periphery models have attempted to explain developmental differences between economically backward and advanced regions at whatever level regions are specified. Underdevelopment is assumed to be a consequence of transactions between the centre and the periphery, the centre exploiting the backward regions by accumulating profits at the centre. The transaction pattern between the centre and the peripheral regions is biased to the advantage of the metropolitan areas, whatever the transaction may concern. These developmental models stem from Hobson and Lenin and their analyses of the development of the capitalist economy. They have been reinterpreted against new data by several scholars (Baran, 1957; Myrdal, 1957; Frank, 1967; Galtung, 1971; Wallerstein, 1974). Centre–periphery models focus on the distribution of various values within a nation; Stein Rokkan, Edvard Shils and Charles Tilly have argued forcefully that the centre–periphery concept provides a meaningful tool for the analysis of intra-societal value distribution (Rokkan, 1980; Rokkan and Urwin, 1983; Shils, 1975, Tilly, 1975).

In the centre–periphery models it is perhaps not always clear what is meant by the concept of a centre or how the centre–periphery relations are measured empirically. Often there seems to be tautology: a centre is that which has central control. However, the crucial point is that the existence of a centre cannot be taken for granted and it remains a matter of empirical investigation to present evidence of the extent to which some entity controls some specified values. It seems conceivable that different centres may exercise different degrees of control over basic values in the political system. Moreover, the centre may exercise different degrees of control over different values. If centre–periphery theory predicts only the existence of a centre which has more access to goods and services than the peripheries, then centre–periphery theory would be rather trivial. Sometimes a centre–periphery model appears to be little more than a conceptual scheme. Sometimes centre–periphery models assert far more interesting and challenging hypotheses than simply that political power is unevenly distributed in a country. It is claimed that the transactions between the centre and the periphery result in the underdevelopment of the periphery or that variations in the possession of values between the periphery and the centre may cause opposition and political instability.

However, the centre–periphery framework is not easily employed to study regional cleavages; its concepts about regional underdevelopment, centre domination, regionally distinct identities and region-specific patterns of voter alignments are difficult to apply in the analysis of interactions between politics and society in Western Europe. Firstly, it may be difficult to pinpoint a centre due to the competition between several metropolises. Although one may speak of monocephalic and polycephalic systems it is not quite clear how many centres are to be identified and how national centres are to be distinguished from regional centres. Secondly, even if one recognizes a multiplicity of centres regional cleavage is still a broader concept than centre–periphery tension. Although there may be a metropolis or centre in a region dominating its hinterland the region as a whole may still be characterized by a striking dissimilarity in comparison with other regions in material and cultural resources.

When the centre–periphery model is applied to regional cleavages within a country the starting point is the distribution among its regions of both human and material resources. Rokkan uses an index of economic backwardness and an index of population density to operationalize the concept (Rokkan and Valen, 1962: 116–17). In another study also dealing with Norway the indicators used to describe regional cleavages were: gross regional product; percentage employed in non-primary sectors; average income/capita; index for private consumption; index for economic asymmetry; net out-migration; index for industrial concentration; index for industrial monoculture (Naustdalslid, 1977: 206). It must be emphasized that there is no given way to describe the occurrence of regional cleavages. Various indices may be employed and it is difficult to single out one or two as the important ones. The availability of data is also a limiting factor. In addition, when comparing the countries in Western Europe various types of regional divisions are conceivable: regions that are of equal size in area or regions that are of equal size in population or the existing administrative regions. Finally, it is difficult to find a meaningful measure for comparing regional distributions between countries. Here, we refrain from presenting data about the occurrence of regional cleavages, but we note this additional cleavage dimension.

Conclusion

According to a major theory in political sociology social heterogeneity and cleavages have a profound impact on politics, including political stability. The concept of social fragmentation may be applied to the structure of West European societies by the employment of indicators on cleavages. In this chapter we described a few major cleavage bases,

Table 2.31   *Indices on social heterogeneity (T-Scores)*

	Structure			Summary index	
	Religious	Ethnic	Class	Narrow	Broad
Austria	48.7	44.2	48.3	46.4	47.1
Belgium	46.1	71.1	37.6	58.6	51.6
Denmark	42.5	43.1	44.7	42.8	43.4
F R Germany	63.7	43.1	47.2	53.4	51.3
Finland	43.4	50.3	42.0	46.9	45.2
France	53.1	48.7	64.6	50.9	55.5
Greece	45.2	48.1	61.3	46.6	51.5
Ireland	45.2	45.3	46.9	45.2	45.8
Italy	47.4	48.7	59.3	48.0	51.8
Netherlands	68.6	46.4	38.1	57.5	51.0
Norway	40.8	43.1	43.6	41.9	42.5
Portugal	45.1	43.1	73.7	44.1	54.0
Spain	39.9	64.9	48.6	52.4	51.1
Sweden	39.9	43.1	53.3	41.5	45.4
Switzerland	67.2	72.2	43.1	69.7	60.8
United Kingdom	63.3	44.8	47.8	54.0	52.0

Note: The indices are standardized measures derived from Tables 2.4, 2.12, 2.28. The narrow index only consists of the indices for religious and ethnic structures whereas the broad index includes all three indices. Values on class for Austria and Greece are estimates.

religion, ethnicity and class. In addition we portrayed the socio-economic structure of the societies in Western Europe. The findings may be partly summarized in two indices on social fragmentation, which refer to the latent dimension of cleavages. Table 2.31 gives one broad index on social heterogeneity consisting of an average for the ratings of the various nations on religious structure, ethnic structure and class-based cleavages as well as one narrow index on social fragmentation consisting of an average for the scores on religious and ethnic cleavages. The table also contains the scores on the various dimensions.

The two indices on social fragmentation – the broad one and the narrow one – give a somewhat different picture of West European societies. Although the various country scores are related, the correlation is not perfect, $r = .76$. When it is spoken of divided societies the reference is usually to the religious or ethnic structures. Divided societies in this sense are first and foremost Switzerland, Belgium and the Netherlands. Perhaps one should also mention the Federal Republic of Germany and Spain in this context. Socially heterogeneous in a broader sense, including other types of cleavage as well, are: Switzerland, Portugal, Greece and France. When we also consider cleavage bases such as class and region, then the most socially fragmented nations are not quite the same as the typically divided societies. The Scandinavian countries may be characterized as socially homogeneous in this country comparison. It is thus important when one refers to the structure of West European societies to specify how social fragmentation is measured. Various cleavage bases may be identified, and they do not always give the same picture. In any case, there is a real variation in the extent of social heterogeneity in West European societies whether measured by means of the narrow or the broad index.

What are the implications for political phenomena? According to one hypothesis social fragmentation has a profound impact on politics by means of its impact on the political parties and the party system. Let us next look closely at this theory of social structure determinism, explaining various political phenomena with direct reference to cleavages. We begin with the hypothesis that political parties are very much a reflection of the cleavage structure in society. Later on we will deal more with the theory that political stability depends on social heterogeneity. Firstly, we present an overview of the political parties in Western Europe.

Appendix 2.1 Ethno-linguistic structure in Western Europe during the twentieth century (thousands)

		Stephens (1976)	Haarman (1975)	Straka (1970)	Blaschke (1980)	Heraud (1974)	Muller (1964)	Tesnière (1928)
Austria	Slovenes	28	38	25		15	20	91
	Magyars	19	5	4		6		12
	Croats	32	28	37	24	24		43
	Tot.pop.	7 456				.		6 669
Belgium	Flemings	5 700	5 375		5 700	5 600	5 000	4 015
	Walloons	3 800	3 750	3 300	4 000	3 900	4 000	3 471
	Germans	62	58	110	100	60	180	94
	Tot.pop.	9 656						7 903
Denmark	Germans	23	23	23	20	15	10	41
	Tot.pop.	4 937						3 435
FR Germany	Danes	50	35	50	20	35	10	11
	Frisians	60	12	60		80	17	29
	Tot.pop.	61 210						63 332
Finland	Sw. Finns	303	303	330	330	330	400	392
	Aalands	21		31	21			
	Lapps	3	2	3	4	2	5	2
	Tot.pop.	4 606						4 573
France	Occitans	10 000	11 000		10 000			10 490
	Catalans	260	200	250		273	200	186
	Basques	90	130	90		90	100	100
	Corsicans	200	770	190	130		1 000	291
	Alsatians	1 300	1 200	1 500			1 800	1 289
	Flemings	90	200	400	90		20	200
	Bretons	685	1 100	1 400	400	1 000	1 000	1 000
	Tot.pop.	49 750						38 280

Appendix 2.1 (continued)

		Stephens (1976)	Haarman (1975)	Straka (1970)	Blaschke (1980)	Heraud (1974)	Muller (1964)	Tesnière (1928)
Greece	Turks		350		90	105	200	2
	Albanians		50	92		90	100	100
	Tot.pop.	8 770						6 600
Ireland	Gaels	55	716			400	900	390
	Tot.pop.	2 971						3 166
Italy	Occitans	200		100		250		
	Friulians	600	430	800	500		520	383
	Ladins	30	12	24	30	23		16
	Valdotains	70	85	60		70	300	97
	Germans (Tyrol)	260	230	232		260	450	295
	Slovenes	75	125	65	50	75	20	371
	Sards	1 200	1 000	1 200	1 000		1 000	
	Greeks	10	30	36	20	6		34
	Albanians	260	80	261	100	115	100	98
	Tot.pop.	54 105						40 971
Nether-lands	Frisians	400	300	500		420	250	317
	Tot.pop.	13 120						7 403
Norway	Lapps	20	10	35	40	20	25	17
	Tot.pop.	3 890						2 777
Portugal	Tot.pop.	8 663						5 854
Spain	Catalans	5 000	5 500	6 750		8 000	5 000	4 753
	Basques	500	700	525	525	525	700	600
	Galicians	2 500	2 500	2 600	2 600	2 600	2 000	2 248
	Tot.pop.	33 800						23 237
Sweden	Lapps	10	5	10	17	10	10	7
	Finns	30	35	40		40	30	31
	Tot.pop.	8 095						6 060
Switzer-land	Rhaetians	50	50	38	49	50	40	44
	Germans		4 070				4 000	2 868
	French		1 135				1 300	859
	Italians	744	746				400	248
	Tot.pop.	6 187						4 046
United Kingdom	Gaels (Sco)	89	81		80	80	100	148
	Gaels (Wa)	542	656	2 600		660	700	1 058
	Manx	56		50	55	50		1
	Ch. Islanders	121	60		130		100	46
	Tot.pop.	55 707						45 390

3

Political Parties

Introduction

Political parties may be approached as intermediators between social cleavages and political decision-making in government structures. In political systems characterized by representative government political parties are the principal vehicles for political action. Interacting with citizens and interest organizations parties express and organize political demand and support in relation to social cleavages; parties recruit government decision-makers whose behaviour has a profound impact upon society by means of the implementation by bureaucracies of government decisions and actions.

Party government is characteristic of democracy in large scale polities. Not even small Switzerland with its tradition of direct democracy in numerous referendums can do without political parties and governments recruited by them. If the electorate were to decide on each and every issue by means of a referendum, the transaction costs would be overwhelming. It is no wonder that the study of political parties has attracted the attention of political sociologists. In the words of Blondel:

> Political parties are thus one of the most fascinating as well as most modern institutions of political life. They are multiform and they are at the cross-roads between the institutional and behavioural aspects of politics (Blondel, 1969: 221).

The fact that modern democracy in the form of representative government has proved to be the only viable institutional framework for the exercise of popular will does not prove the existence of party systems all over Western Europe. Political parties may be regarded as organized collectivities capable of intentional action in order to promote their own interests. Democracy opens up the opportunities for political parties, but how the challenges of party government are confronted depends on the goals and capacities of the political parties themselves.

A major theme in the study of West European politics is the viability of the political parties. K. Lawson and Peter H. Merkl argue that political parties operate under increasing stress – see their *When Parties Fail: Emerging Alternative Organizations* (1988). On the one hand, the traditional parties have more and more difficulties in maintaining their electoral support, particularly the large parties in Western Europe. On the other hand, new and emerging parties that challenge the traditional large parties face an uncertain future as their electoral base is easily undermined. Lawson and Merkl state:

> It is complex, as becomes even more clear when we turn away from the failing major parties to their would-be surrogates. Dissatisfaction with the world's major parties is widespread, but the exact nature of that discontent, and the action it prompts the disaffected to take, vary widely (Lawson and Merkl, 1988: 5).

The West European countries are described as typically *multi-party systems*, because a basic trait of the major democracies in Europe is the operation of more than two parties in each country under rules of competition and cooperation. The political parties in Western Europe may be classified in various ways (Raschke, 1978; Smith, 1989; McHale, 1983; Steed and Hearl, 1985; Humphreys and Steed, 1988). We make a distinction between structural parties and non-structural parties allowing for borderline cases. The structural parties may be divided into ethnic, agrarian, religious and class-based parties like socialist and communist parties though some conservative parties could be regarded as class-based parties. Among the non-structural parties we distinguish between centre, liberal, conservative, environmental, discontent (populist) and ultra-rightest parties. How many parties are there according to these party type categories in the West European political systems? What are their characteristic properties? These are the kind of questions this chapter attempts to shed light on.

Number and types of political parties

The multi-party system format is the characteristic mode in Western Europe, because in most countries we find examples of the different types of party identified above. Let us briefly survey the existing political parties in Western Europe and suggest a tentative classification of them according to a few well-known criteria. It should be pointed out that some of the political parties in Western Europe are difficult to classify unambiguously like the Irish parties (Gallagher, 1985; Mair, 1987) or the French and Greek political parties.

Political parties may be classified as religious parties on the basis of four criteria: name, programme, appeal and international relations. It is an open question whether or not some of the very large religious parties like CDU and DC should really be classified in this category. It may be argued that CDU and DC belong to the conservative party type. However, classifications are not true in an absolute sense but only more or less

Table 3.1   *Religious parties*

Austria	ÖVP	Österreichische Volkspartei
Belgium		Parti Social Chretien/Christelijke Volkspartij
	PSC	Parti Social Chretien
	CVP	Christelijke Volkspartij
Denmark	KRF	Kristeligt Folkeparti
Finland	SKL	Suomen Kristillinen Liitto
France	MRP	Mouvement Républicain Populaire
F R Germany	CDU/CSU	Christlich Demokratische Union/
		Christlich Soziale Union
Ireland	FG	Fine Gael
Italy	DC	Democrazia Cristiana
Netherlands	CDA	Christen Democratisch Appel
	ARP	Anti-Revolutionaire Partij
	KVP	Katholieke Volkspartij
	CHU	Christelijk-Historische Unie
	SGP	Staatkundig Gereformeerde Partij
	PRR	Poelitike Partij Radicalen
Norway	KrF	Kristeligt Folkeparti
Portugal	CDS	Partido do Centro Democratico Social
Sweden	KDS	Kristdemokratiska Samhällspartiet
Switzerland	CVP	Christlichdemokratische Volkspartei
	EVP	Evangelische Volkspartei

plausible. The parties we count as religious parties are shown in Table 3.1 (Fogarty, 1957; Irving, 1979; Brezzi, 1979).

Typically, an ethnic party is formed for the purpose of protecting the interests of the group it represents. Often the orientation appears in the choice of party denomination. Perhaps the orientation is marked still more strongly in their programmes (Rudolph and Thompson, 1989)? We count the organizations shown in Table 3.2 as ethnic parties in present-day Europe.

Table 3.2   *Ethnic parties*

Belgium	VU	Volksunie
	FDF	Front Démocratique des Bruxellois Francophones
	RW	Rassemblement Wallon
Finland	SFP	Svenska Folkpartiet
Italy	SVP	Südtiroler Volkspartei
Spain	PNV	Partido Nacionalista Vasco
	CiU	Convergencia Democratica de Catalunya
	HB	Herri Batasuna
United Kingdom	SNP	Scottish National Party
	PC	Plaid Cymru
	SDLP	Social Democratic and Labour Party
	Unionists	Ulster Unionists and Loyalists

Table 3.3 *Rural parties*

Denmark	V	Venstre
Finland	KESK	Keskustapuolue
Norway	SP	Senterpartiet
Sweden	CP	Centerpartiet
Switzerland	SVP	Schweizerische Volkspartei

Perhaps there are no rural or agrarian parties today in the sense that such parties pursue mainly agrarian interests or are supported predominantly by rural voters. Yet, there exist parties that may be considered as the heirs of agrarian or rural political traditions (Gollwitzer, 1977). As rural parties today we characterize those in Table 3.3.

Socialist parties may be identified on the basis of historical tradition, party programme and international cooperation (Paterson and Thomas, 1977; 1986; Pelinka, 1980). Socialist parties are easily identified on the basis of membership in the Socialist International. Member parties are to be found in all the West European countries, Greece excepted as the PASOK is formally not a member of the Socialist International. The most recent social democratic party was the British SDP. Formed in 1981 it was dissolved in 1990 after major parts of the party had been amalgamated with the Liberal Party into the Social and Liberal Democrats (SLD). The SDP acted on the electoral arena in an alliance with the Liberal Party

Table 3.4 *Socialist parties*

Austria	SPÖ	Sozialistiche Partei Österreichs
Belgium		Belgische Socialistische Partij/Parti Socialist Belge
	BSP	Belgische Socialistische Partij
	PSB	Parti Socialiste Belge
Denmark	SD	Socialdemokratiet
Finland	SSP	Suomen Sosialdemokraattinen Puolue
France	PS	Parti Socialiste
F R Germany	SPD	Sozialdemokratische Partei Deutschlands
Greece	PASOK	Pan-Hellenic Socialist Movement
Ireland	LAB	Irish Labour Party
Italy	PSI	Partito Socialista Italiano
	PSDI	Partito Socialista Democratico Italiano
Netherlands	PvdA	Partij van der Arbeid
Norway	DNA	Det Norske Arbeiderpari
Portugal	PSP	Partido Socialista Portuguesa
Spain	PSOE	Partido Socialista Obrero Espanol
Sweden	SAP	Socialdemokratiska Arbetarpartiet
Switzerland	SPS	Sozialdemokratische Partei der Schweiz
United Kingdom	LAB	Labour Party
	SDP*	Social Democratic Party

Note: *abolished in 1990

Table 3.5   *Communist parties*

Austria	KPÖ	Kommunistische Partei Österreichs
Belgium	KPB/PCB	Kommunistische Partij van Belgie/
		Parti Communiste de Belge
Denmark	DKP	Danmarks Kommunistiske Parti
Finland	SKDL	Suomen Kansan Demokraattinen Liitto
	DV	Demokraattinen Vaihtoehto
France	PCF	Parti Communiste Francais
F R Germany	KPD/DKP	Kommunistische Partei Deutschlands
Greece	KKE	Communist Party of Greece
	EDA	United Democratic Left
	KKEes	Communist Party of the Interior
Ireland		Communist Party of Ireland
Italy	PCI	Partito Comunista Italiano
Netherlands	CPN	Communistische Partij Nederland
Norway	NKP	Norges Kommunistiske Parti
Portugal	PCP	Partido Communista Portugues
Spain	PCE	Partido Comunista de Espana
Sweden	VP	Vänsterpartiet (Kommunisterna)
Switzerland	PDA	Partei der Arbeit der Schweiz
United Kingdom	CPGB	Communist Party of Great Britain

(Pelinka, 1980). The parties to be counted as socialist parties are shown in Table 3.4.

Communist parties can be identified on the basis of their names, programmes and historical traditions. All the parties have some form of the word 'communist' in the party label (Rubbi, 1979; Timmermann, 1987; Waller and Fennema, 1988; Courtois, 1986). The only exception in Western Europe is the Swiss party so far, but it may be predicted that several of the West European communist parties will drop the label 'communist' as the Swedish communist party did in 1990. By tradition all West European communist parties take their origin from the time of the formation of the Comintern in 1919 and – sooner or later – became members of the Comintern, but the re-orientation of the party ideology in the early 1990s will involve a movement towards the image of a broadly based popular left-wing party.

After the Second World War the parties regarded themselves as members of the communist world movement; attendance at the European communist meeting held in East Berlin in June 1976 may be considered a criterion if the party is to be counted as communist. Communist parties exist in all the West European countries. The party that was legalized last was the Spanish party in 1976. The communist parties of today are shown in Table 3.5.

The set of left-wing socialist parties is not easily identified, but the employment of both organizational and ideological criteria helps

Table 3.6   Left-socialist parties

Denmark	SF	Socialistik Folkepartei
	VS	Venstresocialisterne
France	PSU	Parti Socialiste Unifié
Ireland	WP	Sinn Fein – The Workers Party
Italy	PDUP	Partito di Unita Proletaria per il Comunismo
Netherlands	PSP	Pasifistisch-Socialistische Partij
Norway	SV	Sosialistisk Venstreparti
Switzerland	POCH	Progressive Organisationen der Schweiz

considerably (Baumgarten, 1982). Typically, these parties originate from social democratic or communist parties from which they have split. The difficulty in identifying such a party is that they are not easily separated from social democratic or communist parties, and they tend to be short-lived. Besides the ideological criterion is not clear-cut as the emergence of an environmentalist ideology has attracted the attention of left-wing groupings as, for example in West Germany where 'Die Grüne' comprises groups that adhere to some kind of left-wing orientation. The set of left-socialist parties we include in Table 3.6.

We find Liberal – or Centre Liberal – parties in practically all West European party systems as they are often easy to identify because of their name. Ideology may also be used for the identification of liberal parties. It is true that the classical liberal ideology developed subsequently in different directions, but enough of this tradition may be found in parties characterized as liberal or centre liberal parties in contemporary politics (Kirchner, 1988).

International cooperation constitutes another criterion for the identification of liberal parties. During the inter-war years cooperation which took place between the liberal parties developed further especially within the European Community. Within the frame of the International, extended regional cooperation in Europe has developed resulting in the formation of 'The Federation of Liberal and Democratic Parties of the European Community' in 1976. The federation was formed in view of the first elections to the European Parliament that took place in 1979; it also constitutes a group in this parliament. Thus we arrive at the list of parties in Table 3.7.

The prototypes of the modern conservative party are to be found in Great Britain and in the Nordic countries. As they adhere to a tradition of conservative ideas they are placed to the right in the party systems of their countries, which typically appears from the names of the parties (Layton-Henry, 1982; Morgan and Silvestri, 1982). In France these parties use a designation like 'Indépendants' or similar appellations and the adherence to a tradition of conservative ideas is not equally self-evident in continental countries. How to classify a party like 'Les

Table 3.7   *Liberal parties*

Austria	FPÖ	Freiheitliche Partei Österreichs
Belgium		Partij voor Vrijheid en Vooruitgang/Parti
		de la Liberté et du Progrés
	PVV	Partij voor Vrijheid en Vooruitgang
	PLP	Parti de la Liberté et du Progrés
Denmark	RV	Radikale Venstre
	RF	Retsforbundet
	CD	Centrum-Demokraterne
Finland	LKP	Liberaalinen Kansanpuolue
France	RAD	Parti Républicain Radical et Radical Socialiste
F R Germany	FDP	Freie Demokratische Partei
Greece	KF	Liberal Party
	EDHIK	Union of the Centre
Ireland	FF	Fianna Fail
	PD	Progressive Democrats
Italy	PRI	Partito Repubblicano Italiano
	PLI	Partito Liberale Italiano
	PR	Partito Radicale
Netherlands	VVD	Volkspartij voor Vrijheid en Democratie
	D66	Democraten'66
Norway	V	Venstre
Portugal	PSD	Partido Social Democrata
	PRD	Partido Renovador Democratico
Spain	UCD	Union del Centro Democratico
	CDS	Centro Democratico y Social
Sweden	FP	Folkpartiet
Switzerland	FDP	Freisinnig-demokratische Partei
	LPS	Liberale Partei
	LdU	Landesring der Unabhängigen
United Kingdom	LIB	Liberal Party

Giscardiens' or 'Parti Republicain' is anything but self-evident (Colliard, 1982; Frears, 1988). The international cooperation of the parties gives some guidance. In many cases it is difficult to distinguish conservative parties from Christian democratic parties like the CSU and the ÖVP. To the set of conservative parties we count those in Table 3.8.

The concept of a discontent party is not a generally accepted notion. Yet, the phenomena that we intend to cover with the concept are well-known. Often these parties have been formed around some concrete issue as the starting point channelling peoples' discontent. The element of populism in the programmes of these parties is also obvious. Another characteristic is that the discontent parties are headed by charismatic leaders. We include the parties shown in Table 3.9 in the set of discontent parties.

After the Second World War it is difficult to point out parties that belong to the set of ultra-right parties. The set of ultra-right parties

Table 3.8 *Conservative parties*

Denmark	KF	Konservative Folkeparti
Finland	KOK	Kansallinen Kokomos
France		Gaullistes:
	RPR	Rassemblement du peuple francais
	UNR	l'Union pour la nouvelle republique
	UDR	l'Union démocratique du travail
	RPR	Rassemblement pour la république
		Républicains indépendents:
	CNIP	Centre national des indépendants et paysans
	RI	Républicains independants
	PR	Parti républicain
Greece		Conservative parties:
	LK	Peoples Party
	ES	Greek Rally
	ERE	National Radical Union
	ND	New Democracy
Norway	H	Höyre
Spain	AP/CD	Alianza Popular
Sweden	M	Moderata Samlingspartiet
United Kingdom	CONS	Conservative Party

comprises above all parties that in one respect or another can be said to belong to the tradition laid down by the fascist parties of the inter-war period. Juan Linz points to certain features common to the majority of fascist parties: the ideology, the style and the organization (Linz, 1979). The ideological dimension ties the ultra-right parties of today to the fascist parties of the inter-war years, because the anti-democratism as well as nationalism survive, whereas attempts have been made to efface the elements of racism and anti-semitism – at least on the surface. As the set of ultra-right parties in the West European party systems of today we list those shown in Table 3.10.

In the 1970s rejuvenated ideologies were introduced into the political sphere in the form, for example, of a post-materialist ideology

Table 3.9 *Discontent parties*

Belgium	UDRT	Union Démocratique pour le Respect du Travail/ Respect voor Arbeid en Demokratie
Denmark	FRP	Fremskridtspartiet
Finland	SMP	Suomen Maaseudun Puolue
France	UDCA	Union pour la Defence des Commercants et Artisans
Norway	FRP	Fremskrittspartiet
Switzerland	NA	National Aktion für Volk und Heimat
	REP	Schweizerische Republikanische Bewegung

Table 3.10   *Ultra-right parties*

France	FN	Front national
F R Germany	NPD	Nationaldemokratische Partei Deutschlands
Italy	MSI	Movimento Sociale Italiano – Destra Nazionale
Spain	FN	Fuerza Nueva

(Inglehart, 1977). There was a growing reaction against the costs of a highly industrialized society and an emergent awareness of other values than economic growth and material prosperity. The emphasis upon the environment of social systems and the ecological context of human behaviour was displayed conspicuously at conferences: The UN Conference on the Human Environment in Stockholm in 1972 as well as the Club of Rome's presentation of *The Limits to Growth* (1972). Moreover, the 1970s witnessed a strong reaction against certain uses of nuclear power, uniting a large number of citizens in various countries against what was regarded as the excesses of a materialist ideology. The virtues of an urbane and affluent society were no longer taken for granted as considerable groups of citizens searched for rural or anti-system values. Although the post-materialist ideology was hardly a coherent one, its ideas and sentiments constituted the basis for attempts at political organization.

New parties – environmentalist or ecology parties as well as green movements – were formed in some West European nations and they participated in elections at various levels of government (Pilat, 1980;

Table 3.11   *Green parties*

Austria	VGÖ	Vereinte Grüne Österreichs
	ALÖ	Alternative List Österreichs
Belgium		AGALEV
		Ecologistes
Denmark		Groene
Finland		Green
France		Ecologistes
F R Germany		Die Grüne
Greece		Green
Ireland		Green Alliance
Italy		Lista Verde
Netherlands		Federatieve Groenen
Norway		Miljoe
Portugal		Partido 'Os Verdes'
Spain		Verdes
Sweden	MP	Miljöpartiet
Switzerland		Grüne
United Kingdom		Ecology Party

Müller-Rommel, 1982; 1985; 1989). The groups that emerged out of a concern about ecology and a reaction against materialist growth policies are different in various nations as far as organization and political access are concerned, but we identify (Table 3.11) a set of Green parties using party labels as the identification criterion.

We have arrived at a total number of some 120 parties, which constitute the party systems of present-day West European politics. Can we describe some of their main characteristics in a comparative framework?

Party properties

Several definitions of a political party have been suggested (Downs, 1957; Sjöblom, 1968; Sartori, 1976; Epstein, 1980). The problem of stating necessary or sufficient conditions for the identification of an organization as a party is more relevant in the analysis of party systems outside of the West European context in the post-war period. Although it may sometimes be difficult to make a sharp separation between organizations that are parties and those that are not, political parties in Western Europe are those organizations that have been registered in election statistics. They may be compared with regard to some common properties often stated in the literature on political parties. The derivation of some relevant aspects of party organization and party behaviour is based on the findings from the nowadays extensive literature on political parties (Sartori, 1976; Janda, 1980; von Beyme, 1982).

When were the major parties in Western Europe formed? The history and development of parties are relevant in a comparative perspective, as it is a widely accepted hypothesis that the major political parties in Western Europe have been highly stable over time – *the stability hypothesis*. In a well-known article Lipset and Rokkan state:

> The most important of the party alternatives got set for each national citizenry during the phases of mobilization just before or just after the final extension of the suffrage and have remained roughly the same through decades of subsequent changes in the structural conditions of partisan choice (Lipset and Rokkan, 1967a: 52).

Much of the party research has aimed at a criticism or rejection of the Lipset and Rokkan hypothesis. Party change or party instability has been underlined more and more as we move into the 1990s. How much stability and continuity remains is, however, a matter of dispute. We will sketch the origins of the modern parties in Western Europe and look at the crucial question about developmental trends in electoral support.

Political parties live in an uncertain world which they strive to cope with to secure stability for themselves (Rose and Mackie, 1984). In multi-party systems parties attempt to maintain themselves to reach a satisfactory level of voting support as well as keep their organization and membership intact (Epstein, 1980). Parties seek to avoid extinction as well as various internal threats like splits to their maintenance. As with any organization political parties search for security. Parties try to survive, if not expand, in an uncertain environment. Often they define some minimum level of electoral support and membership as a necessity for continued operations. If parties find that there is a risk that they will sink below this threshold, then they will take measures to break the negative development.

Parties try to maintain some basic level of support in society. They may score electoral successes, but they also know that today's victory may be followed by tomorrow's defeat. Extinction is something parties fear most. How stable are parties over time? Not only the volatility of the electorate is a threat to party survival, but so is internal party cohesion. Parties may suffer substantially because it is decided to create a new party. Or parties may split into several parties. How common are party splits?

Parties use a number of strategies to reduce the risk of a negative electoral development, ending in organizational extinction. Parties search for electoral niches at a certain level of electoral support. In multi-party systems it is unrealistic to dream of vote maximization, because the fierce competition between several parties over the support of marginal voters forces the parties to focus on less than majority support. Political parties try to identify key groups on whose continuous support they hope to rely (Campbell et al., 1960; Converse, 1966). These core groups often have special social characteristics defining the social niche of the party. However, the support of these key groups has to be nurtured to be counted on in the future. If parties propose measures that could attract marginal voters from other camps, then they may face serious problems in maintaining the support of their key groups. To what extent do parties tend to count on special key groups in the social structure?

An analysis of the way parties mobilize the political implications of social cleavages must recognize that the electoral bases of parties change. The transformation of the social structure presents parties with a necessity to adapt to maintain their electoral strength – a process of adaptation that some parties handle successfully whereas others have to face substantial changes in their electoral strength. The adaptive capacity of parties depends upon several things, among which we pay attention to the organizational features of parties as well as their capacity to enter governments. Parties may react differently to social structure change. Some stick to their traditional clientele whereas others try to identify new key groups.

Political parties are organized collectivities orientated towards the pursuit of some combination of the goal of electoral success and the end of political effectiveness or the capacity of parties to have an impact upon government policy-making (LaPalombara and Weiner, 1966a). And the various modes in which political parties are organized may affect the capacity of political parties to maintain themselves. It may make a difference whether a party is centralized, whether it has close connections with interest organizations of various kinds, and how large its membership is. Political parties vary more or less in these organizational features. Organizational differences between parties may help explain the variation in the capacity of parties to reach the goal of coping with a changing if not turbulent environment.

Political parties take different views to the question of stability and system maintenance in democracies. Some identify themselves as governing parties as they seek to form governments themselves or in some coalition. Some stay in power for long periods of time and take on the image of a ruling party or an étatist party. Others identify as protest or dissent parties. Their objective is not to form governments to engage in piecemeal social engineering but to offer an image of an alternative to the existing order. If they come to power, their objective is grand social change. Still other parties confine themselves to expressing an ideology or a system of beliefs to which some groups adhere. The articulation of these ideas is their main rationale, not vote maximization or government participation.

We present some data pertaining to the party properties discussed above for a number of political parties classified according to the type of party. Thus, we focus on the following: age and continuity, relevance, party strength at elections, organization and membership, government participation, left–right orientation and working-class support. It must be admitted that the information is not comprehensive meaning that each and every party is covered, nor do we offer a full account for each party. Much of the data has been taken from Wende (1981), McHale (1983) and Day and Degenhardt (1984) when not stated otherwise.

Age and continuity
One indicator on party stability is party longevity, or the time span since it was born. One may make a distinction between birth of a present party and birth of a predecessor party. Another indicator is party continuity measured by the mutation score, or the frequency of splits. This measure involves a somewhat crude ranking of the parties in relation to the number of splits that they have experienced, a low score indicating continuity whereas a high score stands for discontinuation. The political parties that dominate in present-day party systems have a long history. Several political parties in Western Europe became a political factor to be reckoned with shortly after their formation. Let us look briefly at data about the age of the present or its predecessor party (Table 3.12 at the end of this chapter).

It is no coincidence that the birth of the predecessor to the present-day political party usually dates back to the period around 1900 when the traditional order was challenged by organizations calling for democratic principles of rule. This holds in particular with regard to the large parties along the right–left dimension: socialist parties, communist parties, liberal parties and conservative parties. There are three innovations in the party landscape since 1945: the left-socialist parties, the discontent parties and the environmental parties of the late 1970s and early 1980s. The overall image is one of continuity when the 1980s are compared with the late 1940s.

However, if we take a longer time-perspective there is less stability. Firstly, there is a clear difference between the birth of a present party and that of a predecessor party, meaning that there has been substantial organizational change. Secondly, the mutation scores indicate that no party type has not experienced internal dissent resulting in party splits and organizational transformation. Let us take a brief but closer look at each party type.

The oldest religious parties, Catholic as well as Protestant, were founded during the later part of the nineteenth century; eight out of the now active parties emerged during the period before the First World War. The party identity of the old religious parties has been transformed, as several of the now active parties can be characterized as new parties in relation to their predecessors. Most of the ethnic parties originated at the time before the Second World War. The oldest parties, the Basque PNV and the Finland-Swedish SFP, were formed at the end of the nineteenth century, whereas the Walloon and the Italian parties were not founded until after the Second World War. About half the parties have been transformed after their first formation; yet, on the whole the ethnic parties prove to have changed little during the twentieth century.

The rural parties were formed during the decades immediately after the turn of the century, although the Danish Venstre was already formed in 1870. In particular the Danish Venstre has suffered a number of splits from the parent party. The rural parties have gone though a process of reorientation after the Second World War adapting to the social transformation involving a declining rural population.

Most of the socialist parties were formed during the decades before the turn of the century. Some were transformed after the Second World War (SPÖ, PSB/BWP, PvdA), but as late as the end of the 1960s a transformation of the parties in Italy and France took place. Several socialist parties have thus undergone changes.

The communist parties date their origin to the years immediately after the Russian revolution. Some parties broke with the reformist parent party somewhat earlier (the Netherlands and Sweden), whereas in most countries this split took place either directly after the Russian revolution (Finland, Germany) or in the early 1920s after years of internal conflicts (Italy, France, and Norway). As a consequence of state intervention party transformations became necessary in Finland, Germany and Switzerland; mutations have also come about as a result of internal party conflicts – ideological as well as personal ones.

Left-socialist parties can be said to be a phenomenon of the late 1950s and the early 1960s. It is true they had their counterparts during the inter-war years, but not in the countries in which they later developed. These parties are to be found in the Nordic countries, central Europe (the Netherlands) and southern Europe (France, Italy). They resemble each other in that they constitute splits from existing parties, but they differ in that some of them come from socialist parties like the PSIUP, PSP, and SV, whereas one party definitely can be said to have its origin in a communist party, the Danish SF; the French PSU is of mixed origin; the VS is a breakaway from the SF.

Most liberal parties date from the later part of the nineteenth century or the beginning of the twentieth century; the PVV takes its origin as far back as 1846. The parties that were formed later on can either be characterized as splits like the D66 and the CD or as parties that were given the legal possibility to operate at a rather late date. However, about half the liberal parties have undergone profound changes since their first formation.

The origin of the conservative parties dates back to the turn of the century and the immediately preceding decades. The parties in France constitute an exception, Gaullism clearly belonging to the post-war period. It is obvious that conservative parties have undergone small changes during the twentieth century; however, the French parties again constitute an exception.

In relation to discontent parties we have deliberately restricted ourselves to parties active during the post-war years, because little continuity before the Second World War is to be found for any of these. Immediately after the war this party type appeared in Italy and West Germany to be followed in France by the Poujade movement. It is not possible to speak of any particular period when these very parties were formed, since those in Denmark and Norway were founded in the 1970s.

The basic change in political climate between the inter-war period and the years after the Second World War appears in the drastic decline in support for fascist parties. Actually, only three or four parties can be described as ultra-right in the 1980s. For these parties there were parties during the inter-war years that can be regarded as their predecessors. Their successors after the war were formed only a short time after the activities of their predecessors had been prohibited. The ultra-right parties have had a high frequency of mutations.

Present-day political parties tend to have a long tradition as most have existed for a long time with the major exception of the so-called Green parties. They were founded in the 1970s or 1980s. The average age of the party systems in the West European democracies is substantial as measured by the average longevity of their constituent parties. The organizations that once challenged the traditional undemocratic political order demanding party government as part of a democratic regime have grown into established institutions themselves. There is a country difference in the average age of the parties dominating the national political scene. Generally speaking, the older and established parties are to be found in the Scandinavian countries, in the United Kingdom and in Switzerland whereas young and recently established parties operate in Greece, Portugal and Spain.

Party relevance
Several political parties in Western Europe became a political factor to be reckoned with shortly after their formation. For some types there is a close connection between parliamentary introduction and government participation whereas for others government positions could only be reached after several years of parliamentary work for various reasons. Let us look briefly at the different political parties (Table 3.12).

Concerning the old religious parties there is a close connection in time between the formation of the parties, their representation in parliament and cooperation in government indicating the political relevance of the religious party. However, this is not the case in Italy, France and Germany (FRG) where the parties existing after the Second World War have a definitely stronger position than their predecessors had. The small religious parties have had some success, but have remained tiny in the electorate, not becoming a political factor, for example the EVP, GPV and KDS.

With the exception of the parties in the United Kingdom the ethnic parties became represented in parliament fairly early. Rural parties became represented in parliament at an early date, whereas their first participation in government came somewhat later. It was not until 1901 that Venstre held office and as the last of the rural parties the Swedish Farmers' Union joined the government in 1936. Operating between the left and the right the rural parties were able to play a role in government not long after they had been founded.

The socialist parties became represented in parliament at an early date in most cases in the 1920s. Up to the First World War the question of participation in government was a matter of dispute, but during the war at least eight of the parties were represented in governments. The resistance to participation in government persisted longest among the Norwegian DNA and the Dutch SDAP (later PvdA).

Most of the communist parties succeeded in getting returned to parliament a few years after their formation. Communist parties held office on some occasions for the first time in connection with the end of the war; the exception is the PCE which entered into the Spanish

Popular Front government during the years 1936–9. The sharp rise in the attraction of communist parties immediately after the war dwindled just as rapidly, however. Most communist parties had to give up government participation and most of them were not able to repeat their astonishing level of political influence at the end of the war. All the left-socialist parties became represented in parliament shortly after their formation.

The political break-through of the liberal parties came very close in time on their formation. During the decades before and after the turn of the century they had a strong position in parliament as well as in government. For some parties like the VE, the LKP and the LIB this period constituted the time of prosperity, when they reached a position in parliament as well as in government that they were not able to repeat later. The liberal parties that were founded early were most active in the process of introducing democratic rule in the early years of the century which rendered them their powerful position.

For conservative parties we hold that the political break-through took place at the same time as the formation of the party; the practice was often that parliamentary groups united and formed a political party which resulted in a close connection between the dates of parliamentary representation and participation in government. One exception is the Gaullists in France, because the RPF never became a factor of power during the Fourth Republic.

Although discontent parties entered the political scene after the war it was not until the late 1960s and early 1970s that they scored considerable electoral success, with the exception of Poujadism which had its high season in the 1950s. Most of the discontent parties became represented in parliament during the 1960s, but their electoral break-through occurred in the early 1970s. Since this party type has been looked upon with considerable suspicion by other parties, few have managed to participate in government. Of the small ultra-right parties in the post-war years the MSI and the predecessors of the NPD appeared shortly after the war. None of the successors to the fascist movement of the inter-war period has been able to participate in government. The recently founded environment parties or the Green parties have not been regarded as potential coalition partners when governments have been formed. Their main preoccupation is to receive or maintain enough support to be represented in Parliament.

Speaking generally, one may identify three different time periods when the West European political parties became represented in Parliament. Firstly, rural, liberal, conservative and socialist parties managed to reach parliamentary representation before the First World War when the traditional order was challenged by the movement towards democracy. Secondly, a number of religious, ethnic, fascist and communist parties entered the legislative assembly during the inter-war years. Thirdly, discontent parties and ecology parties emerged after the Second World

War without becoming accepted as legitimate government participants. Whereas the conservative and liberal parties participated early in government it took some time before it was considered appropriate, particularly among the socialists themselves, to bring socialist parties into government. The same applies to religious parties. Government participation by the ethnic, communist, left-socialist and discontent parties has taken place since the Second World War.

Electoral strength

Electoral support is the crucial determinant of party continuity. The electoral arena is the test of the viability of parties. If a party fails to maintain its attraction for voters, then the party faces the need for change. Either it takes action to reverse a negative electoral trend or it may be crushed by the shifting allegiance of voters. Parties may handle small changes in electoral outcomes, but a long-term downward trend creates enormous pressure on the party. Let us look at the various types of parties in Table 3.13 (at the end of this chapter) where the average level of electoral support for a party during a decade is presented.

Several religious parties have lost some of their attraction since the 1940s. After the Second World War the electoral support for the religious parties hovered somewhat going up immediately after the war to decline later on. The KrF, SKL, SGP and EVP had an upward trend in the 1940s and 1950s, whereas the big DC and CDU/CSU were smaller before the war than they were after it. The medium-sized MRP had a short period of prosperity during the 1940s. In the 1980s the overall impression concerning the developmental trend for this party type is one of decline. Although some religious parties such as the Dutch CDA, the Irish Fine Gael and the German CDU/CSU have been able to maintain their electoral support, it is a fact that other religious parties have not done equally well in a decade characterized by intensive secularization. The religious parties in Austria, Belgium and Italy have suffered from a decline.

The ethnic parties have prospered during the post-war period, although there are definite signs of declining attraction in the 1980s. Trends over long periods can be inferred for some of the parties. If we look at the development after the Second World War we find that the majority display an upward tendency; again the Finland-Swedish SFP is the exception with an even downward trend. The years of advance vary somewhat but can be dated approximately to the late 1960s and the early 1970s; notable is that most parties display a decline for the late 1970s and early 1980s. There was a kind of ethnic revival in the 1960s which was manifested in political support for ethnic parties in the early 1970s; ethnic parties managed to mobilize the ethnic potential in the electorate at that time. In the 1980s the electoral trend for the parties orientated towards regionalism has come to a stand still. In the following countries regional or ethnic parties have been able to maintain but not increase their support: Belgium, Finland, Spain and United Kingdom.

The rural parties are not to be found in all the countries. It seems as if there is a growing problem for these parties to maintain themselves. Before the First World War Venstre was the largest party in Denmark, but it has not been able to maintain this position. The Finnish KESK was a small party before the First World War but has later been one of the four large parties in Finland. The other three parties have been small parties throughout most of the twentieth century, but during the 1970s the Centre party in Sweden developed into a strong party in point of voters. There is no trend common to all the rural parties. An almost continuous downward trend is shown by Venstre, whereas the Norwegian and Swedish Centre parties rose at times. Looking more closely at developments during the 1980s we find that the KESK and the SVP display a slight upward trend, whereas the opposite is true of the Danish Venstre, the SP and CP. Thus, a simple environment hypothesis fails as one cannot connect the decline of agricultural occupations throughout the twentieth century with the electoral development of the rural parties.

The socialist parties have maintained themselves rather well over the years since 1945. Only four out of seventeen parties are below 20 per cent if we look at average values; nine parties have a mean exceeding 30 per cent, which justifies the assertion that socialist parties have a strong electoral position in most of the West European countries. The 1940s involved a certain decline whereas their position was reinforced during the 1950s and the 1960s. In the 1970s and 1980s, however, a decline to a lower level set in in some countries. But in France as well as in Greece and in Spain the socialist parties are stronger in the 1980s than during the 1970s.

The social democratic parties have by tradition received much electoral support in all the West European societies. In some countries where the labour movement was split into two major groups the social democrats have not managed to achieve something similar to the somewhat hegemonic position held in some countries where the left united more or less unanimously behind one labour party. However, in the 1980s the large and established social democratic parties have not been able to keep up their support, at least not in the following countries: Austria, Denmark, Federal Republic of Germany, Norway, Portugal, Sweden and United Kingdom. The spectacular successes in Spain and Greece constitute exceptions to the major development trend which is downward for the big socialist parties. In the 1989 elections also the large PASOK suffered a decline. Actually, the medium-sized socialist parties have done better than the large ones, relatively speaking, as in the following countries: Belgium, Finland, Italy and the Netherlands.

At most five or six of the communist parties have been able to rally any considerable support over a long period of time. The large parties are the PCI, PCF, SKDL/SKP and from the 1970s the PCP, whereas the other parties have had electoral successes merely for short periods of time. The parties that were large in the 1940s are the parties that can be characterized as large also in the 1970s and 1980s. From the time of the formation of the parties and onward we find some continuity though the KPD as the largest party during the inter-war years has become the smallest during the post-war period, whereas the PCI – one of the minor parties during the inter-war years – has developed into the largest of the communist parties during the post-war era.

In some West European countries large communist parties have a long tradition. During the 1980s they have all had to face declining support. In other countries communist movements have always received tiny support which has not increased during the 1980s. Among countries with large but retarding communist movements we find: Italy, Finland, Greece, Portugal, France and Spain. With the exception of the Swedish communist party which has moved in the other direction towards an electoral support of about 6 per cent the communist parties in the other countries where they are active do not reach support of more than about 1 per cent: Austria, Denmark, the Netherlands and Switzerland.

The left-socialist party type is represented by a few, small parties that have been able to attract increasing voter support during the post-war period. Only occasionally has any left-socialist party had support from more than 10 per cent of the electorate, such as the SF in 1966 and in the 1980s or the SV in 1973 and 1989. Only the SF in Denmark and the SV in Norway have been able to maintain considerable support during the post-war period although their electoral outcomes have fluctuated.

There has been a major debate about a negative development trend for the liberal parties. Although some liberal parties had a powerful position in the early decades of the century, liberal parties did not develop into large parties after the introduction of universal suffrage, speaking generally. Liberal parties have had their strongest position in Ireland (FF), in Greece (EDHIK) and in Switzerland (FDP). If the FDP is excepted, these parties cannot be counted among the group of classical liberal parties. Liberal parties have had weak support in Italy, at least after the Second World War, and also in Finland, Austria and France.

If different periods are compared it appears that the liberal parties were strongest before the First World War, weakened during the inter-war period to become still smaller during the post-war period. There are exceptions to the general picture as the liberal parties in Belgium and the Netherlands were larger during the 1970s and 1980s than during the 1940s. If the 1940s involved a continuation of the decline, a change took place during the 1950s which resulted in an upward trend for a majority of the parties during the 1960s. This trend is again broken in the 1970s, but only about half of the parties display a downward trend, which means that it cannot be asserted that the 1970s and 1980s meant a general decline for liberal parties.

The overall trend for most of the conservative parties appears to be the opposite compared with the liberal party type. The conservative parties have stayed at the same level from the inter-war period onward, on the whole. The conservatives in the United Kingdom were larger in the 1950s than during the inter-war years, just as the Danish KF was stronger in the 1960s than during the inter-war period. It is more difficult to find a common trend for the post-war period. Most of the parties declined during the 1940s, but showed a slight upward trend during the 1960s. The data confirm the hypothesis of a conservative revival in the 1970s and 1980s, which also applies to a few of the Christian Democratic parties. However, in the 1980s the conservatively orientated parties in the following countries have not been able to maintain their earlier successful momentum: Denmark, France, Norway, Spain and Sweden. Again, the picture is not altogether unambiguous as some conservative parties as in Greece and the United Kingdom have maintained their support, if not increased it.

Discontent parties may be considered a phenomenon of the post-war period. Typical of the discontent parties is that they have managed to gain support from a considerable portion of the electorate on isolated election occasions. The only party that to some extent succeeded in breaking this pattern was the Danish FRP (Glistrup) in the 1970s. The period when the parties show an advance is the late 1960s and early 1970s; for the 1970s as a whole the parties display a clear downward trend. Yet, in some countries a major development in the 1980s has been a strengthening in the support for anti-system parties. These protest parties cannot be regarded as successors to the fascist parties in Western Europe as their source of support is more a welfare state backlash or anti-system vote towards the welfare state élites than explicit authoritarianism. What is similar is the sometimes hostile attitude towards immigrants. In Denmark and Norway, protest parties have played a significant role in the politics of the 1980s.

Viewed over the whole post-war period the ultra-right parties have been small in terms of voters. In West Germany ultra-right parties scored successes at the election in 1949, and at the election in 1969 the NPD was almost returned to parliament. The Italian MSI on the other hand had its greatest successes at the election in 1972. In the 1970s both parties display a decline; during the same period the Spanish FN on the other hand shows an advance, even though the party is the smallest as regards size of the electorate. Surprisingly Le Pen's Front National scored an electoral success in the European Election in the summer 1984 reaching a high 11 per cent of the vote, almost repeated in the 1986 and 1988 elections, meaning that the ultra-right movement has not lost its appeal, at least not in France (Plenel and Rollat, 1984; Charlot, 1986; Mayer and Perrineau, 1989).

Most countries have witnessed the appearance on the political scene of green parties in the form of politically organized environmental groups. And the ecologists have not been without success as they have scored more than 5 per cent in some elections. Let us rank the various countries after the strength of their environmental parties in the 1980s: Switzerland, FRG, Sweden, Austria, Finland, Belgium, Italy and France. In several countries the green parties have been strong enough to reach parliamentary representation which has caused problems for the traditional separation of political parties into left- and right-wing parties, in some countries diminishing the support for the left block and in other countries causing problems for the right block.

In electoral development the green parties are still in their infancy period, and there is a risk that they may never develop into mature political parties. However, the number of green parties is growing; the largest one is the German ecology party – Die Grünen – with a 5 per cent average vote share in the 1980s, but it failed to enter the new Bundestag in the all German elections in 1990. The British ecology party used to be the weakest one, but the Green Party received 15 per cent of the vote in the 1989 Euro-election. It is very difficult to predict what the future of the green parties will look like (Urwin, 1990). It is important to separate the electoral fate of green parties, which is uncertain, and the growing relevance of ecological considerations in policy-making.

Typical of the ecology movement is that the adherents do not easily reach unanimity with regard to broader social problems, some favouring socialist alternatives whereas others argue against a 'politicization' of the ecology movement. The fate of the green parties hinges upon what will happen to their image in the eyes of the voters as well as how the saliency of the environmental issues develops.

Looking at the data on average electoral support the Lipset and Rokkan stability hypothesis must be qualified. The fortunes of the parties in the electoral arena have differed considerably over time. It is true that the electoral outcomes of some parties have stayed within a rather narrow range of fluctuations over time, but there is also the finding that others have experienced heavy fluctuations. Some parties were like 'flash' parties (Pedersen, 1982) as they grow rapidly and then declined just as fast. There is, in addition, a set of parties that have faced a long-term trend of advance or decline reinforced at each election.

Organizational structure

Political parties are vulnerable to the threat of a decline in voter support; they also seek to maintain or if possible increase other kinds of support. The organization of political parties depends on how membership is defined, how they maintain their organization by emphasizing integration as well as how they structure their contacts with other groups.

The membership aspect of party organization is related to how the party itself defines the strategy of including members in the party. The orientation of the party towards the membership concept may differ. Some parties organize a higher proportion of their voters as party members than other parties do (membership ratio). And some parties are at the same time large parties (absolute membership number). In a similar way, we have to pay attention to how integration and segregation as important aspects of the organization of parties differ from one party to another. The concept of integration refers to structure, centralization and unity. When speaking of the degree of integration of parties we mean that integrated parties present a firmer structure, are more centralized and have stronger unity.

According to Duverger it is possible to distinguish two parts in the structure of party organization: form and element (Duverger, 1954). The form of organization refers to the way members are affiliated to the party. The most common form of affiliation is direct membership, whereas other forms are indirect membership or various mixed forms. Organization element refers above all to the character of the basic organization of the parties. Duverger distinguishes among caucus, branch, cell and militia. There are differences between these types in level of activity, geographical extension and degree of autonomy in superordinate bodies. The militia is typically to be found in the armed groups of the fascist parties and an equivalent in present-day Western Europe could be 'Brigate Rossi' in Italy and 'Rote Armee Fraktion' in West Germany, but they have no ties whatever with any political party.

For comparative purposes a simple typology of party structure may be proposed which identifies different kinds of element of political parties: primitive organization (approximately caucus) with little unity, little activity and a high degree of autonomy; weak branch, i.e. rather little unity, a certain amount of activity, but a medium degree of autonomy; strong branch, i.e. greater unity, rather high activity and a small degree of autonomy; cell-like organization where the characteristic feature is the occurrence of organizations in working places (Pride, 1970; Ozbudun, 1970).

Another crucial property of party structure is the amount of centralization. To reduce ambiguity and uncertainty parties devise a hierarchical decision-making mechanism which may be more or less centralized. The degree of centralization typical of a party may be measured by various indicators. The position of the party leader has a bearing on centralization:

Are there often changes in party leadership? The relationship between the national party and the corresponding party group within parliament is another aspect of centralization: How often do the leadership of the party and the parliamentary group coincide? How often a party has congresses matters under the working hypothesis that the less frequent the congresses, the more centralized are the decision functions.

It is also relevant to look at which level within the party decisions on nominations of candidates to parliamentary elections are made. It should be pointed out that the relationship between these organizational aspects – type of party element, the position of the party leader, the power of party congresses and the nomination procedure – and party integration is not straightforward; various interpretations are possible, but taken together these may help us distinguish between parties.

Political parties try to stabilize their environments by maintaining support from other organizations. Parties not only structure their internal life, they handle their external environment by the organizational identification of their friends – segmentation. Parties engage to a considerable extent in the segmentation of their milieu, increasing predictability in support. The concept of segmentation includes three aspects: extent, i.e. the number of organizations with which the party has relations; orientation, i.e. the type of organizations with which it has relations (industry, agriculture, employers, employees, religious or ethnic organizations); connection, i.e. how close the relationships are between the party and these organizations. The extent, orientation and connection of segmentation may vary and a party may be said to be highly segmented if it has organized relations that are close to the way political parties penetrate their environments to erect a foundation for their activities.

Table 3.14 at the end of this chapter contains data about the organization structure of several of the West European political parties. The information has been gathered from various sources and must be interpreted with care and caution. It has not been possible to cover all parties with the kind of intractable data that is involved in relation to these organizational properties of political parties.

Looking at membership data one may use either a relative measure, i.e. the membership ratio between the number of party members and voters for a party, or an absolute membership figure. Since a high relative membership proportion may stand for both low and high absolute membership figures we concentrate on data about the latter measure. It is true though that the structural parties organize a higher proportion of their voters as party members than the non-structural parties do (membership ratio). Some of these structural parties are at the same time large parties (absolute membership number). The socialist parties must be characterized as mass parties. Depending on how the size of the membership of the Irish Labour Party is calculated practically all the parties have membership exceeding 100 000; the largest parties, the SAP and Labour, have more than a million members. During the post-war period certain parties increased their memberships strongly like the SPÖ, SAP, Labour, PSB/BWF, whereas others display a decline like the SD and the DNA. The development of membership in communist parties reflects the electoral development of the parties fairly well. In most of the parties the membership is largest during the 1940s, and then declines strongly, particularly so among the smaller ones.

The well-developed organization of the rural parties is reflected in their memberships which are high both in absolute and relative figures. This is partly because the KESK as well as the CP also include their supporting organizations in the number of their members, yet rural parties can be said to have a high membership and a high membership ratio. With the exception of the Danish Venstre, the development of the membership shows an upward tendency; with the Centre Party this resulted in a diminishing membership ratio, since the number of votes for the party increased more than its membership in the 1970s.

Small parties may have a high membership ratio. Although it is particularly difficult to get membership data for periods other than the 1980s, the membership in ethnic parties shows an upward tendency up to the mid-1970s. The ethnic parties in Western Europe cannot be described as mass parties since none counts more than 100 000 members. However, this type of party is apparently skilful in turning the electoral support into an active party membership as the high membership ratios of these parties indicate a high level of mobilization and political consciousness.

As a rule large religious parties provide information about the number of members whereas membership information is often lacking for the small ones. Allowing for the mixed quality of the data it seems to be that at least five of the religious parties have had more than 100 000 members; the DC over a million members. These five parties are also the parties that must be characterized as electorally strong. The development trend of the parties' membership is not uniform, but the ÖVP as well as the CDU/CSU and the DC have an upward tendency, whereas the KVP represents the most obvious example of a downward trend; from having had more than 400 000 members around 1945 the number was only some 50 000 in the mid-1970s. If we look at the whole post-war era we find that only a handful of the liberal parties, the PLI, FP, FDP and the British Liberal party, have had more than 100 000 members during some period, which justifies the characterization of these parties as fairly small in point of members.

The absolute membership figures of the conservative parties make it possible to classify some of the parties as mass parties; the RPF counted nearly one million members for some years in the early 1950s and the conservatives in Britain have had over a million members throughout the post-war era. Only two of the parties, the Spanish AP and the Finnish KOK, have not had a membership exceeding 100 000 members at some time or other.

What distinguishes discontent parties from other parties is that they go to elections on specific issues appealing to particular groups. As regards membership and membership ratios these parties must be described as small. Among the ultra-right parties the NPD has never become a party with a large membership, whereas the MSI must be characterized as a large party in point of members in absolute as well as relative figures.

Turning next to the other two aspects of the organization structure, we may assume that political parties search for internal stability by devising an organizational structure which is to be a bulwark against party splits and party dissension. Some types of party, mainly the communist and socialist, emphasize the value of a high degree of party integration. The uniformity of the communist party structure reflects that communist parties were founded during the Comintern period when all the parties were sections of the Comintern. A firm hierarchic organization – democratic centralism – is applied by most of the parties. In consequence of the schism within the communist world movement all parties have been unable to maintain organizational unity. More or less clearly built-up factions have existed in the KKE, PCE, VPK, CPGB or contributed to the split of the the the SKP/SKDL, which was inconceivable during the Comintern period. Characteristic of the left-socialist parties is instead a weakly built-up organization. The leadership has a weak position and deliberate attempts to decentralize decisions within the parties have led to the emergence of party factions as has happened in the Danish VS.

The socialist parties served as a model for the type of parties Duverger called 'branch parties', as the socialist parties are more strongly integrated than other types, manifested in the strongly built-up organization and the position of the leadership within the party. During the post-war era the unity that characterized the parties earlier has declined due to the more or less open formation of factions, in particular in the parties in France and Belgium. The rural parties must also be characterized as fairly well integrated with a stable leadership and great unity within the parties.

Some types of parties are characterized by a low degree of organizational integration. Most religious parties are weakly integrated as organization and the position of the party leadership are weak and there is not always homogeneous behaviour within the party. There are some exceptions, above all the ÖVP and the ARP which display the most integrated party structure among the religious parties. Typical of most liberal parties is that the organization of the parties is held weakly together and that the position of the leadership is not as strong as in, for example socialist parties. However, that the parties can be seen as open coalitions between different currents explains why factions within the parties seldom lead to party divisions.

For a long time conservative parties were primarily parliamentary parties, meaning that the unity within the party organization was weak. The strong position of party leadership compensated for this which rendered it possible for the parties to be held together. The ethnic parties also cannot be characterized as strongly integrated parties. This is apparent among other things through the existence within some of the parties of more or less open factions, which is a consequence of the fact that a common attitude of the group interest need not coincide with common interests in other matters.

Common features to be found in the organization of modern ultra-right parties is the strong position of the party leadership, even if it can hardly be compared to the leader worship occurring within the parties of the inter-war years. Also, the parties of today are dissimilar to their predecessors of the inter-war period in organization stability. The MSI has initiated the build-up of a central trade-union organization of its own, the CISNAL, and has also well-developed branch organizations which are not present in the West German NPD.

The degree of segmentation is high within most of the socialist parties as the party organization is well developed internally, and nearly all the parties have close cooperation with the trade-union branch of the labour movement; the only exception would be the Greek PASOK. Many parties are also closely tied to consumers' cooperation (PSB/PWB), tenants' movements (SAP) or sports movements (SSP).

The ties of the communist parties with other organizations reflect above all their support within the working class, manifested in their contacts with the trade union movement. Every large party is or has been closely allied with one of the major central trade-union organizations of the country (SKP/SKDL – FFC, PCF – CGT, PCI – CGIL, PCP – CGTP, PCE – CCOO) whereas the small parties have influence only on lower levels or within certain unions. As a rule the major parties also have ties to smallholders' and agricultural organizations, and close ties to numerous peace organizations, friendly societies with the socialist states and other similar organizations. As a contrast to the communist parties one may look upon the left-socialist parties which display a weakly segmented organization as there is no organization pattern emanating from the parties and their contacts with other organizations are few.

It appears that segmentation occurs in large and old religious parties as segmentation is typical of the broad Catholic people's parties, the ÖVP, PSC/CVP, CDU/CSU, DC and the CVP. The degree of segmentation is clearly lower among the small parties, most of which are Protestant parties; the exception to the general picture is the Protestant ARP which had formal ties with both religious organizations and trade unions.

Religious parties tend to have one type of formal contact, i.e. with non-political religious organizations. In addition some of these parties have ties with either agricultural organizations or trade unions which reflects two different lines of development of the religious party type.

The outer organization of conservative parties has been well developed as there have been frequent contacts with many organizations, by tradition those orientated towards industrial and employers' interests. Most of the ethnic parties have at least some organizations tied to them and as a rule they have well developed connections with organizations which defend the interests of their groups. One party, the SVP, occupies a special position in relation to other parties because of its strong ties with other kinds of organizations within Tyrol.

With regard to structure there are obvious similarities between the rural parties. They are fairly well integrated with a stable leadership and great unity within the parties. This applies above all to the Nordic parties, whereas the Swiss SVP deviates to some extent. Characteristic of the rural parties is their close connections with farmers' and agricultural organizations within their respective countries as well as their fairly well-developed organization nets: youth organizations and women's organizations.

Not all types of party score high on segmentation. It is true that liberal parties themselves have few organizations attached to them and that these parties have few close ties to other organizations. Irrespective of which indicator is chosen it is obvious that the discontent parties have a weak organization. These parties are typically built around a leader which implies that the fate of the party is crucially tied to the leadership role in a way that echoes Weber's famous analysis of the basic problem of institutionalizing charismatic leadership. This party type also has a feeble network of contacts with other types of organization outside the party.

To sum up: parties differ substantially in terms of organizational structure. The green parties are not only special in terms of their ideology or belief-system, but they also have a characteristic organization with a small membership in absolute though not in relative terms as well as little integration and segmentation. An opposite organizational structure is displayed by the socialist parties which have considerable membership, strong integration and a large degree of segmentation. The other types of political parties tend to fall somewhere in between these two with polar types of organizational structure.

Government participation and ideology
Political parties like other organizations attempt to survive in an uncertain world. As vehicles for citizen opinion they orientate themselves towards government and the exercise of political power. Political parties may

differ substantially in their attitudes to government and their willingness to assume government responsibility. Some parties emphasize the objective of exercising power by means of government positions. Other parties take a sceptical or negative attitude to coalition formation and pay more attention to proclaiming their distinctiveness.

We must distinguish between attitude towards government and actual experience of governmental work. Some parties view government participation as their main goal. They may play down their ideology to become so-called 'catch-all parties', looking for a maximization of their votes to form a majority government by themselves. Other parties that could not hope to reach such a dominating position by themselves search for coalition partners to come to government power.

In 'The Transformation of the Western European Party Systems', Otto Kirchheimer (1966) argued that the integrative tasks of political parties have become stronger than their articulative functions, meaning that they tend to emphasize broader ideological themes and party appeals:

> Under present conditions of spreading secular and mass consumer-goods orientation, with shifting and less obtrusive class lines, the former class-mass parties and denominational mass parties are both under pressure to become catch-all peoples' parties (Kirchheimer, 1966: 190).

The revitalization of traditional loyalties in the late 1960s and early 1970s means that we have to qualify the hypothesis about the coming of catch all parties. However, Kirchheimer is no doubt correct in emphasizing the general orientation of the major West European parties towards a broad voter appeal to reach government power.

It is true that the most programmatically orientated parties are to be found on the extremes of the traditional left–right continuum. We must note too that discontent parties as well as ethnic parties tend to be highly orientated towards specific political agendas. However, the large West European parties are with few exceptions not very programmatically orientated as may be predicted from their goal of electoral success to reach government power.

There are parties that take a negative view of government participation. They emphasize their own party organization and their ideology. Some of these parties take a sceptical view of government, in principle rejecting the traditional society. If they come to power their promise is to change the basic principles of government, in one direction or the other. Another group of parties plays down government participation all together viewing the party as an expression of a vital citizen opinion.

Data on the programmatic orientation as well as government participation of some political parties are presented in Table 3.15 (see the end of this chapter). The scores on programmatic orientation, where a low score means a pragmatic attitude and a high score stands for a programmatic attitude, are intended as a way to characterize the parties in a general fashion. The extent of government participation is measured in terms of the length of time in months that a party has participated in government or held the post as premier.

Not all parties manage to get to participate in government. And there are wide differences between the parties in their government experience. During the post-Second World War period socialist, agrarian and religious parties participated frequently in government. Liberal and conservative parties have also at times been accepted in government, but ethnic, communist, discontent, left-socialist and ultra-right parties seldom managed to reach government power.

All the rural parties were in office during the post-war era, the Finnish KESK for the longest period, which shows the strong position of the party in Finnish politics. On the whole the rural parties have a strong position in the Nordic countries. The Swiss SVP is a special case, but its participation in government indicates its position in the Swiss model of government. Again, we find that the position of the rural parties in the middle of the political spectrum has been conducive to making them attractive as a coalition partner.

Considering the capacity of the socialist party type to attract large number of voters in several West European nations it may be expected that the party participates frequently in the formation of governments. Looking at the data it appears that the socialist party has almost become the party of the state in some nations such as Austria, Norway and Sweden. With the exception of a few nations socialist parties have been effective in being considered relevant in deliberations about government coalitions since 1945. The party that before the war was thought of as a dubious participant in governments – not least by itself as a result of the principle that socialists could not enter a government in a bourgeois society – appears very much responsible for the conduct of national affairs after the war.

Religious parties have no doubt been attractive in deliberations about government formation; only four of the parties did not hold office during the post-Second World War period. There is a clear connection between the size of the religious party and its capacity to participate in government, as only one of the small parties, the Dutch PPR, entered into some government. Moreover, size also has implications for the length of the participation of religious parties in governments. The Italian DC and the Swiss CVP constitute the extremes as they have been represented in every government since the end of the Second World War.

Although the post-war era involved a decline for liberal parties this does not mean that they lost all political influence; only six liberal parties held no office during this period and of these it is only one, the British Liberal party, that can be described as a medium-sized party.

During the post-war era all the conservative parties, the Spanish AP excepted, held office for two years at least. The Nordic parties were in power for a much shorter time than the continental conservative parties which indirectly reflects the position of the social democrats in these countries.

Ethnic parties are much orientated towards the protection of minority interests; the potential to enter the formation of national governments derives solely from their attractiveness as coalition partner. It may be established that few ethnic parties are considered when government coalitions are built up. The picture would be different if regional governments were considered. Only four ethnic parties participated in government during the post-war period, and only the SFP (Finland) has been able to participate for any considerable period of time.

Most communist parties were regarded only as politically viable for a few years as a coalition partner in the formation of governments. The only communist party that remained politically relevant after the beginning of the cold-war period was the Finnish SKP/SKDL, although their participation in Finnish governments since 1966 has something to do with the special relation between the USSR and Finland. The PCI was able to participate in governments between 1944 and 1948, but the hopes for a real government responsibility for the PCI in some combination with other parties thus far have been frustrated. The French election in 1981 meant a radical shift for the communist party; again it participated for some years in government up to 1984 which it had had to leave in 1947.

The anti-governing parties used to be the two extremist parties, the communist parties and the ultra-right parties. To this category must be included the innovation among party types after the Second World War – the discontent parties. Among this party type only the Finnish Rural party (SMP) has been able to enter government (in May 1983). So far the ecology parties also belong to this set of highly programmatic parties with little or no experience in government participation. There is a clear connection between actual participation in governing a country and the degree to which a party is pragmatically orientated. Probably there is a mutual interaction between the two, a pragmatic orientation leading to being accepted in government and vice versa.

Self-location and working-class support
The standard approach to the programmatic orientation of political parties is to employ the left–right continuum. Although it is true that the politics of Western Europe have become less and less unidimensional, and that the simple left–right model is too crude to capture crucial distinctions between party ideologies and party practices, we resort to a classification of the political parties on the basis of the subjective adherence of the

voters, the self-location. The extent to which the electorate still tends to orientate towards a classical left–right scale is substantial in the data presented in Table 3.16 (at the end of this chapter).

Political parties do not look for support everywhere; party action is focussed upon what is referred to as their 'key group of voters'. Some parties are highly orientated towards certain categories of citizen which is indicated in their programmatic orientation, if not in the party labels. Thus, political parties tend to receive support from certain social groups but not from others. The simple image of parties is that left-wing parties attract the vote of the working class and the farmers support agrarian parties whilst the non-socialist parties either turn to entrepreneurs or businessmen or mobilize their support from a religious or ethnic base.

In reality the connection between a party and some key group is a complicated matter (Budge and Farlie, 1977). These social connections may change considerably over time, as a result of voter volatility (Pedersen, 1979; Borre, 1980; Holmberg, 1984; Crewe and Denver, 1985; Dalton et al., 1985). We use two indices which show the relative size of the support of the working class for a party, because these afford the possibility of comparing data cross-nationally. The indicators on the amount of working-class support only tap a part of the variety of relations between party support and the structure of social groups. Table 3.16 presents data on the extent of working-class support for various parties.

A distinctive feature of the electoral basis of the rural parties is their weak support within the working class. Summing up the profile of the electoral basis of the socialist parties it is evident that they have strong support within the working class, although a few parties deviate from this general pattern like the French PS and PSDI as well as the German SPD. The communist parties are strongly orientated towards the working class and in general the communist parties receive their votes from the working class. An increasingly large share of the small communist parties' votes is derived from intermediate strata instead of from the working class. In their party programmes the left-socialist parties appeal to voters within the working class, but all the parties cannot be said to have strong support within this class.

Generally speaking, religious parties do not have their social bases in the working class. The share of workers among the electorate of the religious parties is far lower than the relative size of the working class in the population; there are a few exceptions to this general rule (the KVP, CVP, DC, PSC/CVP). Conservative parties, also, have a weak backing in the working class. Ethnic parties have a few strongholds among broader social groupings in society, generally speaking. In some nations the ethnic party is supported by farmers in particular, but in others this may not be the case. It appears from the data for the ethnic parties in Belgium, Finland and the United Kingdom that the working class is under-represented in the electorate of these parties. Instead they are most strongly supported by independents.

It is not possible to point out any particular group where only liberal parties have support. These parties have their strongest support in the group of independents, but this is not characteristic only of liberal parties. Correspondingly, the support within the working class is weak; this is not true of Fianna Fail which again illustrates that the Irish party system is somewhat special. The electoral support of the discontent parties among voters from the working class seems on the whole to correspond to its share of the population; actually, for the Swiss NA a slightly positive score is discernible.

If it is at all possible to make any generalization it may be said that ultra-right parties get fairly even support from all social groupings. They are somewhat over-represented among independents, but only slightly under-represented among the working class (MSI) or there is even a very slight over-representation (NPD) illustrating the ambition of the party to fulfil their own image of a party for all the classes.

Although it is often emphasized that the class structure and class orientation means less and less for the electoral choice of the voters, it is still the case that class voting is a relevant concept when understanding the differences in the electoral support of various social groups for socialist parties and conservative parties.

Conclusion

It is difficult not to be impressed by the capacity of the political parties in Western Europe to maintain themselves in such an uncertain world as that of politics. We find that the major political parties of today date back to the beginnings of the century, that their political relevance was established rather soon after their formation and that their electoral record during the post-Second World War period has meant that they remain politically salient. It must, however, be recognized that there have been changes since the Second World War. Some types of party have declined generally speaking (religious, liberal and communist parties) whereas other types have advanced (socialist and conservative parties). A spectacular phenomenon was the sudden instability caused by the rise in attraction of discontent parties. Another new phenomenon was the revitalization of ethnic parties. And the emergence of environmental or green parties has been a highly important innovation in the party landscape in some countries.

It seems as if the stability of the political parties in Western Europe depends more on their capacity to adapt than on lingering social ties. The political parties appear to be able to handle the uncertainty that derives from less traditional voter loyalty and voter identification. This does not mean that parties have abandoned their basic party appeal or party ideology. Parties still tend to orientate towards their voters in a set of issues that to a considerable extent has a left–right dimension (Budge and Farlie, 1983). It appears that the electorate places the parties in very much the same way.

The Lipset and Rokkan hypothesis about West European party systems implies that in most countries the structure of political parties was *frozen*, meaning that a few major political parties introduced in the process of democratization and mass mobilization have been able to maintain themselves at very much the same level of voter support over the decades. However, the data above suggest that not everything has remained the same and that profound changes have taken place with regard to both the parties in the party systems and the transformation of the established parties. New types of parties have been introduced in the post-Second World War period and new parties have replaced old ones. Yet, there is some truth to the claim that present-day political parties tend to have a long tradition as most have existed for a long time.

It is neither possible to confirm nor disconfirm the party stability hypothesis – that the major political parties of Western Europe tend to remain intact over time. It is true that there is much continuity but we also find change, electorally, organizationally and in voter alignments. As Richard Rose and Thomas Mackie state, political parties have a large adaptive capacity but some fail, others are transformed and a few innovate (Rose and Mackie, 1988). The political parties in Western Europe are not as stable as the famous stability hypothesis claims but the major parties in these nations take a positive view on system persistence in the sense of democratic rule. The strength of anti-system parties has declined although it must be admitted that discontent parties have attracted an interest from time to time, particularly in the 1970s. Some of the large parties have developed into government parties, as guarantees of system maintenance. These parties tend to participate frequently in government formations and they have a moderate programmatic orientation indicating their development towards catch-all parties.

The Lipset and Rokkan stability hypothesis not only maintains that the political parties of Western Europe tend towards continuity but also asserts that this stability is a function of the close ties between political party electoral support and social cleavages. Is it true that political parties mirror the structure of society?

Table 3.12 *Age and continuity, first-time representation*

Country	Party	Age and continuity			First-time representation	
		Date of Present	Date of Predecessor	Continuity	in Parliament	in Government
Religious parties						
Austria	ÖVP	1945	1889	2	1890	1907
Belgium	PSC/CVP	1945	1884	5	1884	1884
	PSC	1968	1945			
	CVP	1968	1945			
Denmark	KRF	1970		1	1973	1982
Finland	SKL	1958		1	1970	
France	MRP	1944	1912	4	1924	1944
	REF	1971	1944	5		
F R Germany	CDU/CSU	1950	1870	5	1870	1919
Ireland	FG	1933	1922	2	1922	1922
Italy	DC	1943	1919	2	1919	1920
Netherlands	CDA	1980	1975	1	1977	1978
	ARP	1879		5	1888	1901
	KVP	1945	1904	5	1888	1901
	CHU	1908	1897	2	1897	1908
	SGP	1918		1	1922	
	PRR	1968		1	1971	1973
Norway	KrF	1933		1	1933	1945
Portugal	CDS	1974		2	1975	1978
Sweden	KDS	1964		1	1985	
Switzerland	CVP	1912		2	1896	1919
	EVP	1919		1	1919	
Ethnic parties						
Belgium	VU	1954	1919	3	1919	1977
	FDF	1964		2	1965	1977
	RW	1968	1961	3	1965	1974
Finland	SFP	1906	1894	1	1894	1894
Italy	SVP	1945		2	1946	
Spain	PNV	1890		1	1910	
	CiU	1977	1906	3	1910	
	HB	1979		1	1979	
United Kingdom	SNP	1934	1928	2	1967	
	PC	1925		1	1966	
	SDLP	1970	1949	1	1974	
	Unionists	1974	1886	3	1974	

Table 3.12 *continued*

Country	Party	Age and continuity			First-time representation	
		Date of Present	Date of Predecessor	Continuity	in Parliament	in Government
Agrarian parties						
Denmark	V	1870		4	1870	1901
Finland	KESK	1906		3	1907	1907
Norway	SP	1920	1896	2	1921	1931
Sweden	CP	1921	1913	3	1917	1936
Switzerland	SVP	1971	1917	3	1919	1929
Socialist parties						
Austria	SPÖ	1945	1889	4	1897	1918
Belgium	BSP/PSB	1945	1885	4	1894	1916
	BSP	1978	1945			
	PSB	1978	1945			
Denmark	SD	1871		4	1884	1915
Finland	SSP	1899		3	1907	1907
France	PS	1969	1905	5	1893	1914
F R Germany	SPD	1875	1863	5	1871	1918
Greece	PASOK	1974		1	1974	1981
Ireland	LAB	1912		2	1922	1948
Italy	PSI	1892		5	1895	1944
	PSDI	1947	1892	4	1947	1947
Netherlands	PvdA	1946	1894	5	1897	1939
Norway	DNA	1887		5	1903	1927
Portugal	PSP	1973	1875	2	1911	1919
Spain	PSOE	1879		5	1910	1931
Sweden	SAP	1889		2	1902	1917
Switzerland	SPS	1870		2	1893	1943
United Kingdom	LAB	1900		3	1900	1915
	SDP	1983		1	1983	
Communist parties						
Austria	KPÖ	1918		2	1945	1945
Belgium	KPB/PCB	1921		2	1925	1944
Denmark	DKP	1919		4	1932	1945
Finland	SKDL	1944	1918	3	1922	1944
	DV	1986	1944		1987	
France	PCF	1920		2	1924	1944
F R Germany	KPD/DKP	1968	1918	5	1920	
Greece	KKE	1918		3	1926	1989
	EDA	1951			1951	
Italy	PCI	1921		2	1921	1944
Netherlands	CPN	1918	1909	3	1918	1945

Table 3.12 *continued*

Country	Party	Date of Present	Date of Predecessor	Continuity	First-time representation in Parliament	in Government
Norway	NKP	1923		2	1923	1945
Portugal	PCP	1921		1	1975	1974
Spain	PCE	1920		4	1933	1936
Sweden	VPK	1917		5	1917	
Switzerland	PDA	1944	1921	3	1922	
United Kingdom	CPGB	1920		4	1922	

Left-socialist parties

Country	Party	Date of Present	Date of Predecessor	Continuity	in Parliament	in Government
Denmark	SF	1958		2	1960	
	VS	1967		2	1968	
France	PSU	1960		3	1962	1988
Ireland	WP	1977	1907	2	1977	
Italy	PDUP	1974	1964	3	1968	
Netherlands	PSP	1957		2	1959	
Norway	SV	1975	1961	3	1961	
Switzerland	POCH	1971		2	1975	

Liberal parties

Country	Party	Date of Present	Date of Predecessor	Continuity	in Parliament	in Government
Austria	FPÖ	1955	1885	5	1890	1930
Belgium	PVV/PLB	1961	1846	4	1846	1847
	PVV	1979	1961			
	PLP	1979	1961			
Denmark	RV	1905	1870	1	1906	1909
	RF	1919		1	1926	1957
	CD	1973		1	1973	1982
Finland	LKP	1965	1894	4	1894	1894
France	RAD	1901		3	1901	1899
F R Germany	FDP	1948	1861	5	1870	1880
Greece	KF	1910			1910	1910
	EDHIK	1974	1961	3		
Ireland	FF	1933	1905	2	1922	1932
	PD	1987		1	1987	1989
Italy	PRI	1894		2	1897	1947
	PLI	1848		2	1922	1922
	PR	1955		1	1976	
Netherlands	VVD	1948	1885	5	1888	1891
	D66	1966		1	1967	1973
Norway	V	1884		3	1884	1884
Portugal	PSD	1974		2	1975	1974
	PRD	1985		1	1985	
Spain	UCD	1977		1	1977	1977

Table 3.12   *continued*

Country	Party	Age and continuity			First-time representation	
		Date of Present	Date of Predecessor	Continuity	in Parliament	in Government
	CDS	1982	1977	1	1982	
Sweden	FP	1934	1900	4	1893	1905
Switzerland	FDP	1894		1	1894	1894
	LPS	1911		2	1893	
	LdU	1936		1	1936	
United Kingdom	LIB	1876	1839	4	1876	1880

Conservative parties

Denmark	KF	1916	1850	2	1876	1876
Finland	KOK	1918	1894	2	1894	1894
France	Gaullistes	1976	1947	5	1951	1959
	PR/CNIP	1977	1949	4	1876	1896
Greece	LK	1902			1902	1902
	ES	1950	1902		1950	1950
	ERE	1955	1950		1955	1955
	ND	1974	1955	3	1974	1974
Norway	H	1884		2	1884	1889
Spain	AP/CD	1976	1910	2	1910	1910
Sweden	M	1968	1902	3	1904	1905
United Kingdom	CONS	1867	1830	2	1867	1867

Discontent parties

Belgium	UDRT/RAT	1978		1	1978	
Denmark	FRP	1972		1	1973	
Finland	SMP	1959		2	1966	1983
France	UDCA	1953		1	1956	
Norway	FRP	1973		2	1973	
Switzerland	NA	1961		2	1967	
	REP	1971	1961	1	1971	

Ultra-right parties

France	FN	1972		2	1986	
F R Germany	NPD	1964	1920	4	1949	
Italy	MSI	1946		4	1948	
Spain	FN	1976	1934	5	1979	

Green parties

Austria	VGÖ	1982			1986	
	ALÖ	1982			1986	
Belgium	AGALEV	1981			1985	

Table 3.12   *continued*

Country	Party	Age and continuity			First-time representation	
		Date of Present	Date of Predecessor	Continuity	in Parliament	in Government
	Ecologistes	1978			1981	
Denmark	Groene	1985				
Finland	Green	1982			1983	
France	Ecologistes	1978				
F R Germany	Die Grüne	1980			1983	
Greece	Green	1988			1989	
Ireland	Green Alliance	1987			1989	
Italy	Lista Verde	1987				
Netherlands	Federatieve Groenen	1986			1989	
Norway	Miljoe	1989				
Portugal	Partido'Os Verdes'	1986			1987	
Spain	Green	1989			1989	
Sweden	MP	1981			1988	
Switzerland	Grüne	1982			1983	
United Kingdom	Ecology Party	1979				

Note: The measure of party continuity ranges from 0 to 5 where a low number stands for more continuity and a high number for more discontinuity including the occurrence of divisions, splits, amalgamations and changes of name.

Table 3.13   *Party strength at national elections, per cent*

Country	Party	1940s	1950s	1960s	1970s	1980s
Religious parties						
Austria	ÖVP	46.9	43.8	46.9	43.2	42.2
Belgium	PSC/CVP	43.0	45.1	35.9	30.1	–
	PSC	–	–	–	9.7	7.6
	CVP	–	–	–	25.2	20.2
Denmark	KRF	–	–	–	3.5	2.4
Finland	SKL	–	0.2	0.6	2.9	2.8
France	MRP	26.4	11.6	–	–	–
	REF	–	–	10.6	16.2	–
F R Germany	CDU/CSU	31.0	47.7	46.3	46.8	45.9
Ireland	FG	19.8	28.1	33.4	32.8	33.9
Italy	DC	41.9	41.3	38.6	38.6	33.6
Netherlands	CDA	–	–	–	31.9	32.5
	ARP	13.1	10.2	9.3	8.7	–
	KVP	30.9	30.7	29.2	19.8	–
	CHU	8.5	8.5	8.4	5.6	–
	SGP	2.3	2.3	2.2	2.2	1.9
	PRR	–	–	–	2.8	1.7
Norway	KrF	8.2	10.4	9.0	12.4	8.7
Portugal	CDS	–	–	–	13.7	14.5
Sweden	KDS	–	–	1.7	1.6	2.4
Switzerland	CVP	21.2	23.0	22.8	21.1	20.2
	EVP	0.9	1.2	1.6	2.1	2.1
Ethnic parties						
Belgium	VU	2.1	2.1	6.6	9.6	8.6
	FDF	–	–	3.6	4.2	2.2
	RW	–	–	–	5.5	–
Finland	SFP	8.1	7.1	6.2	5.2	5.3
Italy	SVP	0.5	0.5	0.5	0.5	0.5
Spain	PNV	–	–	–	1.7	1.5
	CiU	–	–	–	3.2	4.6
	HB	–	–	–	1.0	1.1
United Kingdom	SNP	0.1	0.0	0.4	1.9	0.4
	PC	0.1	0.2	0.3	0.6	0.4
	SDLP	–	–	–	0.5	0.5
	Unionists	–	–	–	1.4	1.3
Agrarian parties						
Denmark	V	25.5	22.9	20.0	15.1	11.4
Finland	KESK	22.8	23.5	22.1	17.1	17.6
Norway	SP	8.0	9.2	9.9	9.8	6.6
Sweden	CP	12.4	11.0	15.0	21.8	12.2
Switzerland	SVP	12.1	12.1	11.2	10.8	11.0

Table 3.13 *continued*

Country	Party	1940s	1950s	1960s	1970s	1980s
Socialist parties						
Austria	SPÖ	41.7	43.3	43.3	50.0	45.4
Belgium	BSP/PSB	31.2	37.4	31.0	27.0	–
	BSP	–	–		12.4	14.0
	PSB	–	–	–	13.0	14.0
Denmark	SD	36.4	40.2	39.1	33.6	30.9
Finland	SSP	25.7	25.3	23.4	24.5	25.4
France	PS	20.9	15.0	16.0	22.1	35.6
F R Germany	SPD	29.2	30.3	39.4	44.2	39.4
Greece	PASOK	–	–	–	19.5	43.5
Ireland	LAB	8.7	10.9	14.8	12.7	8.6
Italy	PSI	14.8	13.5	11.8	9.7	12.9
	PSDI	7.1	4.6	5.4	4.1	3.6
Netherlands	PvdA	27.0	30.7	25.8	28.6	31.0
Norway	DNA	43.4	47.5	45.5	38.8	37.4
Portugal	PSP	–	–	–	35.2	27.5
Spain	PSOE	–	–	–	30.4	43.4
Sweden	SAP	46.1	45.6	48.4	43.7	44.5
Switzerland	SPS	26.8	26.5	25.1	24.1	20.7
United Kingdom	LAB	48.0	46.3	46.1	39.1	29.2
	SDP	–	–	–	–	10.7
Communist parties						
Austria	KPÖ	5.3	4.3	1.7	1.2	0.5
Belgium	KPB/PCB	10.1	3.4	3.7	2.9	1.4
Denmark	DKP	9.7	4.2	1.0	3.0	0.9
Finland	SKDL	21.8	22.1	21.6	17.6	11.8
	DV	–	–	–	–	4.2
France	PCF	27.0	23.9	21.4	22.0	12.4
F R Germany	KPD/DKP	5.7	2.2	–	0.3	0.2
Greece	KKE	–	–	–	10.8	12.0
	EDA	–	12.9	13.6	–	–
Italy	PCI	20.6	22.7	26.1	30.7	28.3
Netherlands	CPN	9.2	4.4	3.2	3.4	1.3
Norway	NKP	8.9	4.3	1.8	0.4	0.2
Portugal	PCP	–	–	–	16.1	16.1
Spain	PCE	–	–	–	10.1	5.9
Sweden	VPK	6.3	4.2	4.2	5.1	5.6
Switzerland	PDA	5.1	2.7	2.6	2.4	0.8
United Kingdom	CPGB	0.4	0.2	0.2	0.1	0.0
Left-socialist parties						
Denmark	SF	–	–	7.2	6.0	12.6
	VS	–	–	2.0	2.3	1.9
France	PSU	–	–	2.8	3.3	1.1
Ireland	WP	–	–	–	1.4	3.3

Table 3.13　*continued*

Country	Party	1940s	1950s	1960s	1970s	1980s
Italy	PDUP	–	–	–	1.2	1.6
Netherlands	PSP	–	1.8	3.0	1.3	1.8
Norway	SV	–	–	3.9	7.7	6.8
Switzerland	POCH	–	–	–	1.4	1.8
Liberal parties						
Austria	FPÖ	11.7	8.4	6.2	5.6	7.4
Belgium	PVV/PLB	12.2	12.0	18.3	16.4	–
	PVV	–	–	–	9.5	11.8
	PLP	–	–	–	8.1	9.3
Denmark	RV	7.6	8.1	8.4	8.3	5.6
	RF	3.2	5.7	1.2	2.5	1.2
	CD	–	–	–	4.9	5.6
Finland	LKP	4.6	6.5	6.2	4.8	0.9
France	RAD	11.7	10.9	7.6	–	–
F R Germany	FDP	11.9	8.6	9.4	8.2	8.9
Greece	KF	33.7	–	–	–	–
	EDHIK	–	37.0	42.8	16.2	–
Ireland	FF	41.9	46.0	45.7	48.4	45.1
	PD	–	–	–	–	8.5
Italy	PRI	3.7	1.5	1.7	3.0	4.4
	PLI	5.3	3.3	6.4	2.4	2.5
	PR	–	–	–	2.3	2.4
Netherlands	VVD	7.2	9.9	10.5	14.2	18.1
	D66	–	–	4.5	5.5	7.4
Norway	V	13.5	9.8	9.5	3.5	3.4
Portugal	PSD	–	–	–	27.7	31.8
	PRD	–	–	–	–	11.7
Spain	UCD	–	–	–	34.9	6.7
	CDS	–	–	–	–	6.7
Sweden	FP	22.7	22.1	17.0	11.8	10.8
Switzerland	FDP	23.0	23.7	23.6	22.7	23.2
	LPS	3.2	2.4	2.3	2.5	2.7
	LdU	4.4	5.4	7.1	5.9	4.2
United Kingdom	LIB	9.0	5.1	9.9	14.7	13.3
Conservative parties						
Denmark	KF	15.3	17.1	19.3	10.5	19.5
Finland	KOK	16.0	14.2	14.2	18.9	22.6
France	Gaullistes	1.6	15.4	33.0	23.2	20.6
	PR/CNIP	13.0	17.2	12.0	16.1	19.0
Greece	LK	55.1	–	–	–	–
	ES	–	40.0	–	–	–
	ERE	–	–	41.8	–	–
	ND	–	–	–	19.5	43.5

Table 3.13   *continued*

Country	Party	1940s	1950s	1960s	1970s	1980s
Norway	H	17.7	18.8	20.2	19.6	28.1
Spain	AP/CD	–	–	–	7.5	25.9
Sweden	M	12.3	17.0	15.1	15.4	21.1
United Kingdom	CONS	36.8	47.6	42.7	41.0	42.5
Discontent parties						
Belgium	UDRT/RAT	–	–	–	0.9	1.3
Denmark	FRP	–	–	–	13.8	6.6
Finland	SMP	–	–	1.6	7.0	8.0
France	UDCA	–	6.5	–	–	–
Norway	FRP	–	–	–	3.5	7.1
Switzerland	NA	–	–	0.6	2.3	3.4
	REP	–	–	–	2.5	–
Ultra-right parties						
France	FN	–	–	–	–	9.7
F R Germany	NPD	–	–	3.2	0.5	0.3
Italy	MSI	2.0	5.3	4.8	6.7	6.4
Spain	FN	–	–	–	1.3	–
Green parties						
Austria	VGÖ				–	2.2
	ALÖ				–	1.9
Belgium	AGALEV				–	4.1
	Ecologistes				0.6	3.2
Denmark	Groene				–	1.4
Finland	Green				–	2.7
France	Ecologistes				2.2	0.9
F R Germany	Die Grüne				–	5.1
Greece	Green				–	0.6
Ireland	Green					
	Alliance				–	0.4
Italy	Verde				–	2.4
Netherlands	Federatieve					
	Groenen				–	2.1
Norway	Miljoc				–	0.8
Portugal	Partido'Os					
	Verdes'				–	0.4
Spain	Verdes				–	1.4
Sweden	MP				–	2.9
Switzerland	Grüne				–	5.4
United Kingdom	Ecology					
	Party				–	0.3

Note: Mackie and Rose, 1982; *European Journal of Political Research* yearly updating of *International Almanac of Electoral History*.

Table 3.14 *Party membership and organizational structure*

		1950	1960	1970	1980	1985	Integ-ration	Segmen-tation
Religious parties								
Austria	ÖVP	616	710	716	720		1.7	2.3
Belgium	PSC/CVP	99	212	147	167		1.3	2.5
	PSC							
	CVP							
Denmark	KRF						1.1	1.3
Finland	SKL		9	27			1.0	1.3
France	MRP						1.3	1.7
	REF				43		1.3	1.5
F R Germany	CDU/CSU	265	270	418	880	920	1.3	2.3
Ireland	FG			20	30	31	1.4	1.5
Italy	DC	885	1500	1760	1395		1.3	2.5
Netherlands	CDA				143	129	1.3	1.8
	ARP	103	98	81	55		1.7	2.0
	KVP	319	386	97	49		1.3	1.8
	CHU	48		29	26		1.3	1.5
	SGP							
	PRR							
Norway	KrF		30	39	70		1.3	1.5
Portugal	CDS				30		1.3	1.8
Sweden	KDS			15	22	27	1.6	1.3
Switzerland	CVP		111		60		1.4	2.0
	EVP		10		4		1.0	1.2
Ethnic parties								
Belgium	VU		3	36	47		1.4	1.5
	FDF				12		1.6	1.5
	RW						1.0	1.5
Finland	SFP	48	50	49	42	45	1.4	1.5
Italy	SVP						1.3	2.2
Spain	PNV							
	CiU							
	HB							
United Kingdom	SNP				40		1.0	
	PC				30		1.4	1.3
	SDLP							
	Unionists							

Table 3.14 *continued*

		1950	1960	1970	1980	1985	Integ-ration	Segmen-tation
Agrarian parties								
Denmark	V	198	189	129	95		1.7	1.7
Finland	KESK	143	253	288	306	290	1.8	1.7
Norway	SP			60	54	50	1.5	1.5
Sweden	CP	122	119	117	137	125	1.7	1.8
Switzerland	SVP		54		80		1.3	1.5
Socialist parties								
Austria	SPÖ	616	710	716	720		2.0	1.7
Belgium	BSP/PSB	150	197	225	295		1.3	2.0
	BSP							
	PSB							
Denmark	SD	306	253	185	106		1.7	1.7
Finland	SSP	73	46	61	100	93	1.7	2.0
France	PS	140	100	71	225		1.4	1.5
F R Germany	SPD	680	650	800	1000	930	1.9	1.7
Greece	PASOK				40		1.7	1.3
Ireland	LAB			4	5	6	1.7	1.5
Italy	PSI		465	537	502	554	2.0	1.7
	PSDI				200		1.7	1.5
Netherlands	PvdA	106	143	99	119	101	1.4	1.7
Norway	DNA	201	165	155	154	171	2.0	2.0
Portugal	PSP					139	1.7	1.3
Spain	PSOE				150		1.6	1.5
Sweden	SAP	669	796	908	1189	1204	2.0	2.0
Switzerland	SPS	54	57	54	57		1.7	1.8
United Kingdom	LAB	5920	6328	6223	7206		1.7	1.8
	SDP					50		
Communist parties								
Austria	KPÖ	150	60	26	17		2.1	1.7
Belgium	KPB/PCB	35	14	13	10		2.0	1.7
Denmark	DKP	45			10		2.1	1.8
Finland	SKDL	65	60	51	55	34	2.0	2.2
	DV							
France	PCF	483	300	380	520	380	2.1	2.2
F R Germany	KPD/DKP						2.0	1.5
Greece	KKE				15		1.8	1.7
	EDA							
Italy	PCI	2113	1793	1507	1751	1636	2.2	2.2
Netherlands	CPN						2.0	1.8
Norway	NKP						2.0	1.3
Portugal	PCP			10	187	200	2.2	2.0

Table 3.14   *continued*

		1950	1960	1970	1980	1985	Integ-ration	Segmen-tation
Spain	PCE				110		2.0	1.7
Sweden	VPK	34	20	16	17	17	1.9	1.5
Switzerland	PDA		4		4		1.8	1.3
United Kingdom	CPGB				16		1.9	1.3

Left-socialist parties								
Denmark	SF		4	5	5		1.5	1.3
	VS						1.0	1.3
France	PSU				7		1.3	1.3
Ireland	WP							
Italy	PDUP							
Netherlands	PSP							
Norway	SV		3	2	10		1.7	1.5
Switzerland	POCH				1			

Liberal parties								
Austria	FPÖ		22	28	37		1.3	1.5
Belgium	PVV/PLB			78	126		1.1	1.3
	PVV							
	PLP							
Denmark	RV	33	35	25	13		1.3	1.2
	RF							
	CD				2		1.5	1.0
Finland	LKP			18			1.0	1.2
France	RAD				20		1.1	1.0
F R Germany	FDP	80		56	90	70	1.4	1.3
Greece	KF							
	EDHIK						1.4	1.3
Ireland	FF				55		1.3	1.3
	PD							
Italy	PRI		55		107		1.4	1.2
	PLI			150		39	1.2	1.3
	PR							
Netherlands	VVD	21	35	38	86	87	1.3	1.7
	D66			6	15	9		1.0
Norway	V		28	13	12	12	1.2	1.2
Portugal	PSD					80	1.3	1.3
	PRD							
Spain	UCD				150		1.5	1.3
	CDS							
Sweden	FP	93	89	76	51	45	1.4	1.2

Table 3.14 *continued*

		1950	1960	1970	1980	1985	Integ-ration	Segmen-tation
Switzerland	FDP		115		120		1.3	1.8
	LPS		10		10		1.3	1.0
	LdU		6		8		1.0	1.5
United Kingdom	LIB					100	1.6	1.2

Conservative parties

		1950	1960	1970	1980	1985	Integ-ration	Segmen-tation
Denmark	KF	79	114	110	45		1.2	1.5
Finland	KOK	76	82	81	73	75	1.5	1.5
France	Gaullistes				300		1.4	2.0
	PR/CNIP				100		1.6	1.5
Greece	LK							
	ES							
	ERE							
	ND				50		1.3	1.7
Norway	H	49	97	110	152	170	1.3	1.7
Spain	AP/CD				25		1.4	1.3
Sweden	M	143	207	123	128	137	1.4	1.3
United Kingdom	CONS	2800			2000		1.6	1.7

Discontent parties

		1950	1960	1970	1980	1985	Integ-ration	Segmen-tation
Belgium	UDRT/RAT					5		
Denmark	FRP				15		1.5	1.0
Finland	SMP			3			1.6	1.3
France	UDCA							
Norway	FRP			1	10		1.6	1.0
Switzerland	NA				8		1.7	1.2
	REP				1		1.3	1.0

Ultra-right parties

		1950	1960	1970	1980	1985	Integ-ration	Segmen-tation
France	FN							
F R Germany	NPD						1.5	1.3
Italy	MSI						1.7	1.7
Spain	FN							

Green parties

		1950	1960	1970	1980	1985	Integ-ration	Segmen-tation
Austria	VGÖ							
	ALÖ							
Belgium	AGALEV							
	Ecologistes					2		
Denmark	Groene							
Finland	Green							

Table 3.14 *continued*

	1950	1960	1970	1980	1985	Integ-ration	Segmen-tation
France	Ecologistes						
F R Germany	Die Grüne			20	40		
Greece	Green						
Ireland	Green Alliance						
Italy	ListaVerde						
Netherlands	Federatieve Groenen						
Norway	Miljoe						
Portugal	Partido'Os Verdes'						
Spain	Verdes						
Sweden	MP				4		
Switzerland	Grüne						
United Kingdom	Ecology Party						

Note: Party membership is measured in thousands. The reliability of the membership data may sometimes be questionable whereas the validity of the measures on integration and segmentation is open to doubt, as they in a tentative way sum up how the parties score on the various aspects that make up integration and segmentation. The scaling runs from a low degree to a high degree of integration and segmentation. The degree of integration refers to the existence of a firm structure, a more centralized structure and the extent of strong unity. Segmentation refers to the extent of ties with organizations outside the party, the orientation of these contacts as well as their closeness.

Sources: Austria: Gerlich, 1987: 82; Belgium: Dewachter, 1987: 314–15; Denmark: Worre, 1982: 31, Pedersen, 1987: 35; Finland: Sundberg, 1989: 30; France: Criddle, 1987: 60; F R Germany: Dalton, 1989: 271, Smith, 1979b: 128; Greece: Featherstone and Katsoudas, 1987; Ireland: Mair, 1987: 104; Italy: Farneti, 1985: 148, Pridham, 1988: 49, Ghini, 1982: 237, Hine, 1977: 84, Morlino, 1984: 59; Netherlands: Daalder, 1987b: 234; Norway: Svåsand, 1985, Heidar, 1983; Portugal: Fernandez Stock, 1988: 160; Spain: Donaghy and Newton, 1987; Sweden: Wörlund et al., 1989; Switzerland: Gruner, 1969: 210, Tschäni, 1979, Bauer et al., 1980: 497; United Kingdom: Minkin and Seyd, 1977: 149.

Other sources: von Beyme, 1982, Day and Degenhardt, 1984, Buton, 1988.

Table 3.15 *Government participation and programmatic*
orientation

Country	Party	Govt particip. Months	Govt particip. Per cent	Prime Min. Months	Prime Min. Per cent	Programmatic orientation
Religious parties						
Austria	ÖVP	328	62	292	55	4
Belgium	PSC/CVP	238	46	209	40	4
	PSC	215	41	0	0	
	CVP	215	51	200	38	
Denmark	KRF	69	13	0	0	6
Finland	SKL	0	0	0	0	6
France	MRP	183	35	25	5	5
	REF	142	27	0	0	4
F R Germany	CDU/CSU	327	68	327	68	3
Ireland	FG	183	34	183	34	3
Italy	DC	522	100	461	88	4
Netherlands	CDA	145	28	145	28	5
	ARP	254	49	27	5	5
	KVP	318	61	167	32	5
	CHU	175	34	0	0	4
	SGP	0	0	0	0	7
	PRR	55	11	0	0	5
Norway	KrF	117	22	12	2	6
Portugal	CDS	61	32	0	0	3
Sweden	KDS	0	0	0	0	6
Switzerland	CVP	507	100	136	26	4
	EVP	0	0	0	0	5
Ethnic parties						
Belgium	VU	21	4	0	0	7
	FDF	30	6	0	0	7
	RW	36	7	0	0	7
Finland	SFP	430	78	5	1	5
Italy	SVP	0	0	0	0	5
Spain	PNV	0	0	0	0	5
	CiU	0	0	0	0	5
	HB	0	0	0	0	7
United Kingdom	SNP	0	0	0	0	6
	PC	0	0	0	0	6
	SDLP	0	0	0	0	6
	Unionists	0	0	0	0	6
Agrarian parties						
Denmark	V	211	40	73	14	4
Finland	KESK	474	86	179	33	4
Norway	SP	117	22	65	12	4

Table 3.15   *continued*

Country	Party	Govt particip. Months	Per cent	Prime Min. Months	Per cent	Programmatic orientation
Sweden	CP	132	25	60	11	4
Switzerland	SVP	507	100	132	26	4
Socialist parties						
Austria	SPÖ	481	91	237	45	5
Belgium	BSP/PSB	191	37	98	19	4
	BSP	99	19	0	0	
	PSB	99	19	15	3	
Denmark	SD	326	61	326	61	4
Finland	SSP	427	78	263	48	5
France	PS	171	32	113	21	4
F R Germany	SPD	190	39	156	32	3
Greece	PASOK	95	22	92	21	4
Ireland	LAB	183	34	0	0	4
Italy	PSI	231	44	44	8	5
	PSDI	331	63	0	0	3
Netherlands	PvdA	235	45	179	35	4
Norway	DNA	394	74	394	74	4
Portugal	PSP	69	36	54	28	5
Spain	PSOE	83	56	83	56	5
Sweden	SAP	462	87	462	87	5
Switzerland	SPS	435	86	111	22	4
United Kingdom	LAB	206	39	206	39	4
	SDP	0	0	0	0	3
Communist parties						
Austria	KPÖ	23	4	0	0	6
Belgium	KPB/PCB	19	4	0	0	6
Denmark	DKP	6	1	0	0	6
Finland	SKDL	190	35	28	5	6
	DV	0	0	0	0	
France	PCF	60	11	0	0	6
F R Germany	KPD/DKP	0	0	0	0	6
Greece	KKE	7	2	0	0	6
	EDA	0	0	0	0	
Italy	PCI	11	2	0	0	6
Netherlands	CPN	0	0	0	0	6
Norway	NKP	0	0	0	0	6
Portugal	PCP	15	8	0	0	6
Spain	PCE	0	0	0	0	5
Sweden	VPK	0	0	0	0	5
Switzerland	PDA	0	0	0	0	5
United Kingdom	CPGB	0	0	0	0	6

Table 3.15 *continued*

Country	Party	Govt particip. Months	Govt particip. Per cent	Prime Min. Months	Prime Min. Per cent	Programmatic orientation
Left-socialist parties						
Denmark	SF	0	0	0	0	6
	VS	0	0	0	0	7
France	PSU	36	7	0	0	5
Ireland	WP	0	0	0	0	7
Italy	PDUP	0	0	0	0	7
Netherlands	PSP	0	0	0	0	6
Norway	SV	0	0	0	0	6
Switzerland	POCH	0	0	0	0	5
Liberal parties						
Austria	FPÖ	44	8	0	0	3
Belgium	PVV/PLB	133	25	0	0	3
	PVV	136	26	0	0	
	PLP	136	26	0	0	
Denmark	RV	157	30	44	8	3
	RF	48	9	0	0	6
	CD	69	13	0	0	4
Finland	LKP	238	43	6	1	3
France	RAD	249	47	69	13	3
F R Germany	FDP	400	83	0	0	3
Greece	KF	41	9	41	9	
	EDHIK	48	11	45	10	3
Ireland	FF	363	66	363	66	3
	PD	6	1	0	0	
Italy	PRI	315	60	17	3	3
	PLI	191	37	0	0	3
	PR	0	0	0	0	
Netherlands	VVD	371	72	0	0	3
	D66	69	13	0	0	3
Norway	V	78	15	0	0	3
Portugal	PSD	143	75	104	54	3
	PRD	0	0	0	0	
Spain	UCD	65	44	65	44	3
	CDS	0	0	0	0	
Sweden	FP	72	13	12	2	3
Switzerland	FDP	507	100	132	26	3
	LPS	0	0	0	0	4
	LdU	0	0	0	0	3
United Kingdom	LIB	0	0	0	0	3

Table 3.15   *continued*

Country	Party	Govt particip. Months	Govt particip. Per cent	Prime Min. Months	Prime Min. Per cent	Programmatic orientation
Conservative parties						
Denmark	KF	138	26	88	17	3
Finland	KOK	95	17	33	6	3
France	Gaullistes	320	60	244	46	3
	PR/CNIP	395	75	79	15	3
Greece	LK	48	11	25	6	
	ES					
	ERE	128	29	113	26	
	ND	94	22	91	21	3
Norway	H	125	24	60	11	3
Spain	AP/CD	0	0	0	0	4
Sweden	M	43	8	0	0	3
United Kingdom	CONS	317	61	317	61	3
Discontent parties						
Belgium	UDRT/RAT	0	0	0	0	
Denmark	FRP	0	0	0	0	4
Finland	SMP	81	15	0	0	5
France	UDCA	0	0	0	0	
Norway	FRP	0	0	0	0	4
Switzerland	NA	0	0	0	0	5
	REP	0	0	0	0	5
Ultra-right parties						
France	FN	0	0	0	0	5
F R Germany	NPD	0	0	0	0	4
Italy	MSI	0	0	0	0	4
Spain	FN	0	0	0	0	4
Green parties						
Austria	VGÖ	0	0	0	0	5
	ALÖ	0	0	0	0	5
Belgium	AGALEV	0	0	0	0	5
	Ecologistes	0	0	0	0	5
Denmark	Groene	0	0	0	0	5
Finland	Green	0	0	0	0	5
France	Ecologistes	0	0	0	0	5
F R Germany	Die Grüne	0	0	0	0	5
Greece	Green	0	0	0	0	5
Ireland	Green Alliance	0	0	0	0	5
Italy	ListaVerde	0	0	0	0	5

Table 3.15 *continued*

Country	Party	Govt particip. Months	Govt particip. Per cent	Prime Min. Months	Prime Min. Per cent	Programmatic orientation
Netherlands	Federatieve Groenen	0	0	0	0	5
Norway	Miljoe	0	0	0	0	5
Portugal	Partido 'Os Verdes'	0	0	0	0	5
Spain	Verdes	0	0	0	0	5
Sweden	MP	0	0	0	0	5
Switzerland	Grüne	0	0	0	0	5
United Kingdom	Ecology Party	0	0	0	0	5

Note: Government participation refers to the number of months the party has been in government or held the position as premier in a government measured in both actual number of months and in terms of a percentage of the total number of months over the entire time period 1945–89. Programmatic orientation of a party refers to the party programme: degree of pragmatism, extent of target orientation and comprehensiveness of programmes. Party pragmatism is the extent to which programmes guide parties when acting on issues; target orientation is the inclusiveness of the groups to which the programmes are directed; comprehensiveness means the degree to which the programme covers issues on a piecemeal basis or in terms of basic principles.

Table 3.16 *Left–right placement of parties and working-class support*

		(1)	(2)	(3)	(4)	(5)	Alford's Index	Rose–Urwin Index
Religious parties								
Austria	ÖVP	7.6				5.8	−.20	.12
Belgium	PSC/CVP	7.3	7.1				.00	.00
	PSC			6.9		6.3		
	CVP			7.2		5.8		
Denmark	KRF			6.1		6.2	−.01	−.06
Finland	SKL					6.8		
France	MRP							
	REF	5.3	6.0	5.8				
F R Germany	CDU/CSU	7.0	7.4	7.1	7.9	7.3	−.12	−.06
Ireland	FG		6.7	6.5		6.8	−.14	−.13
Italy	DC	5.9	5.6	5.7	5.7	5.4	−.15	−.12
Netherlands	CDA			7.2		5.7	−.03	−.01
	ARP	7.0	7.8	7.5				
	KVP	6.9	7.3	6.9				
	CHU	7.2	7.9	7.5				
	SGP			8.2		9.2		
	PRR					1.8		
Norway	KrF				6.4	6.1	−.02	−.06
Portugal	CDS					8.5	−.07	−.14
Sweden	KDS					6.5	−.02	−.15
Switzerland	CVP	7.1				6.8	.03	.02
	EVP					6.1		
Ethnic parties								
Belgium	VU	6.8	6.4	6.6		6.8	.02	.07
	FDF		5.3	5.9		5.6	−.14	−.27
	RW			5.7		2.6	−.02	−.12
Finland	SFP					6.1	−.08	−.35
Italy	SVP							
Spain	PNV					6.7	.00	−.02
	CiU					6.6		
	HB					0.5	.00	.03
United Kingdom	SNP					4.4		
	PC					3.4		
	SDLP							
	Unionists					8.3		
Agrarian parties								
Denmark	V		6.4	6.4		6.7	−.07	−.15
Finland	KESK	6.3				5.2	−.09	−.15

Table 3.16 *continued*

		(1)	(2)	(3)	(4)	(5)	Alford's Index	Rose–Urwin Index
Norway	SP				6.0	5.8	−.07	−.22
Sweden	CP				6.2	5.9	−.03	−.07
Switzerland	SVP	6.4				6.4	−.04	−.07
Socialist parties								
Austria	SPÖ	4.9				3.0	.25	.14
Belgium	BSP/PSB	4.6	3.9	4.1			.24	.21
	BSP					2.9		
	PSB					2.5		
Denmark	SD		5.0	5.2		3.8	.27	.22
Finland	SSP	3.9				3.0	.27	.21
France	PS	3.8	3.9	3.8		2.6	.03	.03
F R Germany	SPD	4.5	4.4	4.5	2.7	3.3	.20	.13
Greece	PASOK						.08	.04
Ireland	LAB		5.0	5.3		3.6	.03	.15
Italy	PSI	3.7	3.2	3.2	3.5	3.1	.02	.04
	PSDI	4.8	4.2	4.3	5.1	5.4	−.02	−.14
Netherlands	PvdA	4.2	4.2	3.9		2.6	.26	.13
Norway	DNA				4.2	3.0	.30	.18
Portugal	PSP				4.7		.01	.01
Spain	PSOE	3.9				3.6	.13	.10
Sweden	SAP				3.6	2.9	.34	.19
Switzerland	SPS	4.7			4.0		.13	.10
United Kingdom	LAB	4.4	3.6	4.5		2.3	.30	.23
	SDP					4.6	−.07	−.06
Communist parties								
Austria	KPÖ					0.5		
Belgium	KPB/PCB			3.4		1.4	.01	.23
Denmark	DKP			2.7		1.0	.01	.03
Finland	SKDL	2.3				1.8	.12	.33
	DV							
France	PCF	2.2	2.6	2.5		1.4	.16	.20
F R Germany	KPD/DKP					1.4		
Greece	KKE						.10	.15
	EDA							
Italy	PCI	2.5	1.8	2.0	2.3	1.6	.29	.16
Netherlands	CPN			2.6		0.8		
Norway	NKP						.00	.12
Portugal	PCP				1.8		.25	.24
Spain	PCE	2.7				2.7	.07	.14
Sweden	VPK				2.6	1.2	.00	.04

Table 3.16 *continued*

		(1)	(2)	(3)	(4)	(5)	Alford's Index	Rose–Urwin Index
Switzerland	PDA				2.8			
United Kingdom	CPGB							
Left-socialist parties								
Denmark	SF		3.2	3.4		1.9	.01	.01
	VS			2.3		0.8		
France	PSU		2.3	2.2			.01	.06
Ireland	WP						.03	.27
Italy	PDUP					0.6		
Netherlands	PSP			3.5		0.6		
Norway	SV			3.3		1.2	−.01	−.04
Switzerland	POCH							
Liberal parties								
Austria	FPÖ					6.8	−.02	−.05
Belgium	PVV/PLB	6.4	6.3	6.5			−.11	−.17
	PVV					7.8		
	PLP					7.6		
Denmark	RV		5.8	5.4		4.8	−.05	−.16
	RF							
	CD			6.1		5.7	−.02	−.13
Finland	LKP	6.3				5.6		
France	RAD						−.02	−.07
F R Germany	FDP	5.8	5.5	5.4	6.3	5.1	−.05	−.22
Greece	KF							
	EDHIK							
Ireland	FF		6.6	6.2		6.3	.15	.06
	PD						−.07	−.10
Italy	PRI	4.8	4.8	5.0	4.9	4.8	−.03	−.26
	PLI	6.5	6.6	6.8	6.6	5.9		
	PR					2.3		
Netherlands	VVD	6.8	7.4	7.3		7.4	−.21	−.20
	D66		4.3	5.3		4.4	−.03	−.07
Norway	V				4.3	4.0	−.01	−.05
Portugal	PSD					7.1	−.19	−.18
	PRD							
Spain	UCD	5.9				7.1	−.13	−.06
	CDS							
Sweden	FP				6.3	5.5	−.11	−.17
Switzerland	FDP	6.6				6.2	−.12	−.11
	LPS					6.2		
	LdU	5.5				5.2	−.01	−.04
United Kingdom	LIB	5.6	5.6	5.4		5.0	−.07	−.06

Table 3.16   *continued*

		(1)	(2)	(3)	(4)	(5)	Alford's Index	Rose–Urwin Index
Conservative parties								
Denmark	KF		7.4	7.2		7.3	−.15	−.17
Finland	KOK	8.1				7.2	−.24	−.21
France	Gaullistes	7.3	7.2	7.0		8.2	−.04	−.05
	PR/CNIP	6.8		6.6		6.6	−.04	−.10
Greece	LK							
	ES							
	ERE							
	ND						−.16	−.15
Norway	H			7.4		7.7	−.21	−.16
Spain	AP/CD	7.0				8.4	−.05	−.23
Sweden	M			7.7		7.7	−.17	−.20
United Kingdom	CONS	7.2	7.5	7.1		7.8	−.24	−.11
Discontent parties								
Belgium	UDRT/RAT					9.2		
Denmark	FRP		6.1	6.5		8.7	.01	.05
Finland	SMP					5.8	.03	.13
France	UDCA							
Norway	FRP				7.7	9.4	.01	.10
Switzerland	NA				6.0			
	REP				5.5			
Ultra-right Parties								
France	FN					9.8	−.01	−.06
F R Germany	NPD							
Italy	MSI	8.3	8.7	9.0	7.9	9.1	−.06	−.27
Spain	FN					9.8	−.02	−.24
Green parties								
Austria	VGÖ						−.03	−.11
	ALÖ						−.03	−.11
Belgium	AGALEV							
	Ecologistes					4.5		
Denmark	Groene							
Finland	Green						−.01	−.07
France	Ecologistes					3.5	−.02	−.21
F R Germany	Die Grüne				1.6	2.8	−.04	−.22
Greece	Green							
Ireland	Green Alliance							

Table 3.16   *continued*

		(1)	(2)	(3)	(4)	(5)	Alford's Index	Rose–Urwin Index
Italy	ListaVerde							
Netherlands	Federatieve Groenen							
Norway	Miljoe							
Portugal	Partido'Os Verdes'							
Spain	Verdes							
Sweden	MP				5.0		−.01	−.17
Switzerland	Grüne							
United Kingdom	Ecology Party							

Note: The index on self-location of the voter on the left–right continuum is based on a scale from 1 to 10 where the higher the score the further to the right is the party. Both Alford's and the Rose–Urwin index measure the extent of support for the party within the working classes. Positive scores mean that a party has a more than proportionate support within the working classes considering the share of the working classes within the electorate. Negative scores imply that the party is under-represented within the working classes whereas zero scores mean that the party has relative support from the working classes that is close to the relative size of the working classes in the electorate: Alford, 1963: 79–80; Rose and Urwin, 1969: 10–11; Zuckerman and Lichbach, 1977: 526.

Source: *Left–right placement*: (1) Sani and Sartori, 1983: 322–3; (2) Inglehart and Klingemann, 1975: 253–4; (3) Eurobarometers 5 and 6; (4) F R Germany: Dalton, 1989: 281; Italy: Daalder, 1983: 227; Norway: Aardal and Valen, 1989: 31; Portugal: Bruneau and Macleod, 1986: 88; Sweden: Holmberg and Gilljam, 1987: 258; Switzerland: Inglehart and Sidjanski, 1974: 98; (5) Castles and Mair, 1984.

Class voting or working-class support: Austria: Plasser and Ulram, 1988: 85; Belgium: Frognier, 1975: 480; Denmark: Worre, 1989: 51; Finland: Berglund, 1988: 70; France: Colliard, 1982: 228–9; F R Germany: Berger et al., 1986: 277; Greece: Tsokou et al., 1986: 448; Ireland: Laver et al., 1987: 111; Italy: Allum, 1979: 148; Netherlands: Daalder, 1987b: 226–7; Norway: Aardal and Valen, 1989: 321; Portugal: Bacalhau, 1988: 247; Spain: Gunther et al., 1986: 195; Sweden: Holmberg and Gilljam, 1987: 179; Switzerland: Kerr, 1987: 156; United Kingdom: Heath et al., 1985: 21.

4

Political Parties and the Social Structure

Introduction

The structural approach to the relation between society and politics emphasizes the implications of social structure for political phenomena. We wish to test a version of this theory looking at the relationship between the structure of society and political party support. How valid is environmental determinism? The search for the cleavage bases of party systems is a dominant theme in political sociology. A standard theoretical framework maintains that the support for political parties expresses the cleavages that prevail in society. The cleavage approach in political sociology received much of its impetus from the Seymour Martin Lipset and Stein Rokkan article 'Cleavage Structures, Party Systems, and Voter Alignments: An Introduction'. They state:

> ... we shall give attention to alignments by such obvious criteria as region, class, and religious denomination, but also to alignments by strictly political criteria of membership in 'we' versus 'they' groups. We shall consider the possibility that the parties themselves might establish themselves as significant poles of attraction and produce their own alignments independently of the geographical, the social, and the cultural underpinning of the movements (Lipset and Rokkan, 1967a: 3).

The extent to which the electoral strength of political parties varies as a function of structural properties is a task for comparative research (Janda, 1989). Our purpose is to compare the implications for voter alignments of cleavage structures within sixteen European democracies. We focus on the systematic relationship between political party support and social structure at the regional level. A cross-national comparison reveals whether the same structural properties have similar impact in various countries as well as whether the same type of party is dependent upon similar structural properties. Since we focus on structural effects on party strength, we use data on votes cast for parties within geographical areas, i.e. we will use the ecological approach (Dogan and Rokkan, 1969).

Cleavage bases

In the Lipset–Rokkan quotation, four factors are mentioned that affect voter alignments: class, religion, region, and political tradition. We introduce a distinction between structural and non-structural factors to identify the implications of the social structure for party support. Structural factors refer to enduring social classifications that differentiate people into various collectivities, for example class, religion, and ethnicity. Non-structural factors are transitory, such as candidates and issues, which interact with structural properties as the bases for electoral choice. Our objective is to estimate how much variation in electoral strength of a party over time can be accounted for by social structure, treating non-structural factors as residual effects.

Region enters the analysis in two different ways. The dependent variable – the electoral strength of a political party – is measured at the regional level. Although 'region' is also used as a nominal variable to explain differences in party strength, it is not viewed as a structural property. Political parties may vary considerably in their electoral outcomes between regions, but it does not follow that region accounts for the variation. We approach the regional variable using the distinction by Adam Przeworski and Henry Teune between idiographical and nomothetical variables, and we attempt to explain as much as possible of the regional variation by means of structural properties.

> The basic assumption is that names of nations, or of social systems in general, are treated as residua of variables that influence the phenomenon being explained but have not yet been considered. Thus such concepts as 'culture', 'nation', 'society', and 'political system', are treated as residua of variables, which can be incorporated into a general theory (Przeworski and Teune, 1970: 29).

It is, of course, an empirical question to what extent it is possible to substitute structural variables for region in ecological analysis. An exploration in regional analysis using the ecological method may not arrive at a comprehensive answer to the problem concerning the possibility of a political sociology. We refrain from the debate concerning an implicit reductionist bias in structural models (Sartori, 1969). Our goal is to estimate whatever links to the social structure the political parties in Western Europe may have.

It is uncommon for comparative ecological research to focus on the aggregate election results of the political parties at some regional level as the explanandum. The most ambitious attempt is the 1975 study by Richard Rose and Derek Urwin, *Regional Differentiation and Political Unity in Western Nations*, which concludes:

> In most nations of the Western world, there is either little dispersion in electoral support for the parties, and thus a low cumulative inequality rating, or else a cumulative inequality rating above the minimum does not lead to regionally distinctive parties because deviations from pure proportionality are based upon status rather than spatial concerns (Rose and Urwin, 1975: 31).

The Rose and Urwin distinction between status and spatial properties parallels our separation between structural and non-structural variables, though our concept of structural factors is a broader one. Assuming that spatial factors (i.e. idiographical properties summarized in a regional label) do not account for much of the variation in political party support, we must search for general explanatory variables – the explanans.

If political parties are modelled as somehow dependent upon the cleavages in the social structure for their electoral outcomes, then identifying the set of structural dimensions becomes a crucial problem. From a theoretical point of view, it seems appropriate to include both religion and ethnicity. Ethnicity can be interpreted broadly as a cultural structure dimension. The distinction between behaviour and consciousness is valid in relation to these two dimensions as it does matter for party outcomes whether a cleavage is manifest or simply latent. Class is a basis for cleavage in the social structure; the concept of class is, however, difficult to measure with aggregate data. We use industry, size of agricultural holdings, and affluence (wealth). These variables pertain to class cleavages but may differ independently from each other. The specification of the set of structural variables follows the findings in political sociology as reported in several well-known studies (Bendix and Lipset, 1957; Lipset and Rokkan, 1967; Janowitz, 1968; Rose and Urwin, 1969; Rose, 1974b; McRae, 1974; Linz, 1976). Data on the independent variables have been collected by means of the following indicators:

Industry: indicators measuring the proportion of those employed within different branches of industry as reported in censuses
Agriculture: data on the size of farms or types of farmers, for example per cent freeholders or sharecroppers
Affluence: indices measuring the distribution of income between regions
Religious structure: indicators for the share of the population belonging to a certain creed as well as the share of the population that is religiously active
Ethnic structure: an index measuring the share of the population that belongs to a certain linguistic group or that adheres to a distinct regional culture

An effort has been made to choose as similar indicators as possible for each country. There are two problems involved here; the measurement problem concerns the link between the indicators specified and the ecological property to be measured; the model specification problem relates to identifying those ecological variables that result in the best fit. It is difficult to find comparable variables and indicators for a large set of parties in sixteen countries. Other variables and indicators could

Table 4.1   *Regional units and average size*

	Regional unit	Number	Population	Mean
Austria	Politischer Bezirk	117	7 522 000	64 290
Belgium	Arr. electoral	30	9 831 000	327 700
Denmark	Kommune	277	5 096 000	18 397
F R Germany	Wahlkreis	248	61 520 000	248 065
Finland	Kommun	496	4 746 000	9 569
France	Departement	95	53 353 000	561 000
Greece	Nomos	52	9 251 000	177 904
Ireland	County	19	3 199 000	168 368
Italy	Provincia	92	56 722 000	616 543
Netherlands	Regio	40	13 891 000	347 275
Norway	Kommun	454	4 054 000	8 930
Portugal	Concelho	274	9 830 000	35 876
Spain	Provincia	50	36 542 000	730 840
Sweden	Kommun	275	8 254 000	30 015
Switzerland	Kanton	25	6 307 000	252 280
United Kingdom*	Constant unit	161	55 925 000	347 360

Note: Data on population are for 1978, taken from Kurian (1979).
We find no significant relationship between the population in a region and either Eta-square or R-square for these sixteen countries. So differences in region size by country do not appear to bias our ecological analysis.
*In this chapter Great Britain.

be considered in an ecological analysis of one party or a set of political parties in a single country.

There are also problems in defining region in cross-national analysis. We operated on the following considerations: (a) the division into regions should be nation-bound, i.e. regions are contained within national borders; (b) regional levels should coincide with administrative boundaries; (c) the regional unit should be about equally large in every country studied; (d) the division into regions must satisfy the requirement that the application of the regression technique is well-founded, i.e. the number of cases must not be too small. Our conceptual criteria were then compromised by the availability of data for party strength and social structure in the 1970s. Our choices of regional units are rendered in Table 4.1.

As shown in Table 4.1, the combination of data availability, country population, and national differences in region size results in regional units with widely different populations – from 8 930 for Norway to 730 840 for Spain. The effect of region size on ecological analysis is complex. The expected size of the correlation between ecological variables tends to increase with the degree of homogeneity of units and with the size of the units, measured in number of observations. However, the influences of homogeneity and size generally balance each other, as small units tend to be more homogeneous than large ones. It should be emphasized that different sets of units produce different matrices of correlations (Janson, 1969: 331–2).

Mattei Dogan and Daniel Derivry argue that an analysis of the ecology of French political parties requires a focus on a very small unit, i.e. the French *canton* (Dogan and Derivry, 1988). Some previous studies within single countries suggest that higher levels of aggregation (i.e. more populous regions) tend to produce higher correlations between social attributes than do smaller regions (Gurr, 1972: 34). Although the choice of the regional or local entity as the unit of analysis is a crucial one, practical considerations about available data force us to focus on a rather high level of aggregation.

Method of analysis

The first step in the analysis is to arrive at how much regional variation there is to be explained. Among the measures for describing variations in distributions the variability coefficient (*CV*) is considered to be both simple and handy (Blalock 1960: 73–4; Allison 1978: 877). The *CV* adjusts for different means in different distributions and therefore renders comparisons between groups possible. The *CV* is obtained by dividing the standard deviation by the mean value, i.e.

$$CV = s / \bar{x}$$ [1]

The *CV*-measure is sensitive to changes in the number of units, which renders it less attractive to cross-country comparisons than cross-party comparison within a country. The standardized coefficient of variability takes these difficulties into account. We will employ both measures, in particular a weighted version of the standardized coefficient (SCV_w) (see Martin and Gray, 1971; Smithson, 1982). The SCV_w is derived by first taking the population size of the regional units into account and then standardizing the scores by means of the square root of the number of units in the country. Since there exists no single indicator on the extent of regional variation that meets all requirements we employ two indicators that balance each other; the *CV* is biased due to a large number of units whereas the SCV_w is biased due to small number of units.

A special approach may be used to estimate the stability of environmental effects on regional voting from one election to the next. If regional factors determined party voting, the percentage of vote cast for party *i* in a given region would be constant across adjacent elections. However, if candidate and issue factors were determining, the vote for party *i* would vary idiosyncratically from election *t* to *t* + 1. In the aggregate, the amount of variability in the percentage of vote for party *i* between elections but within the same regions can be computed using the analysis of variance

Figure 4.1   *Dependent factors in party choice*

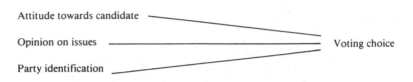

Attitude towards candidate

Opinion on issues   Voting choice

Party identification

and the associated measure of relationship, *Eta-squared*. The general formula for Eta-squared is:

$$E^2 = \frac{TSS - WSS}{TSS}$$ [2]

where: *TSS* equals Total Sum of Squared Deviation and *WSS* equals Within Group Sum of Squares.

It is applied in the following way. Consider the vote in per cent for party i in region j in 1972 and again in 1975. Given 30 regions in a country, the total number of election per cents for party i is 60. Compute the mean per cent vote for party i over all 60 instances. *TSS* is the total sum of squared deviations of the election per cents from the mean party vote. To arrive at *WSS*, compute the mean party vote in each region for 1972 and 1975 and total the squared deviations of the 1972 and 1975 percentages from their mean. *WSS* is the sum of all such squared deviations within regions added together over all regions. If there is no difference between the per cent vote for party i between elections within all regions, *WSS* will be 0 and E^2 will be 1. The greater the difference between 1972 and 1975 is, the larger *WSS* and the smaller E^2 will be.

In effect, this analysis relies on the identity of the region as a nominal variable predicting the similarity of party voting in adjacent elections. It thus captures the configuration of all environmental variables – social, political, economic, and geographic – in estimating the effect of region on party voting (see Harmel and Janda, 1982: Chapter 2).

The object of our ecological analysis is to explain why the same party receives differential support in various regions. In ecology models, party votes at some level of aggregation are regressed on environmental properties of the same aggregate unit. How much environmental dependence could theoretically be expected? The finding in the survey tradition is that party choice depends upon factors other than environmental ones. In traditional survey research, an individual's voting choice in an election at time t is regarded as a function of the voter's attitude towards a particular candidate or party leader, the voter's opinion on the current election issues, and the voter's party identification (Figure 4.1).

The first two variables, attitudes towards candidates and opinions on

Figure 4.2   *Party preference determinants*

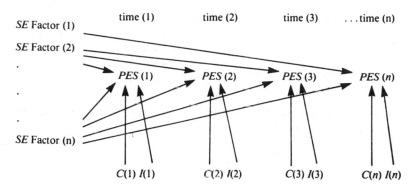

issues, tend to be election-specific and thus are regarded as short-term forces. The third, party identification, is regarded as a long-term voting predisposition resulting from the process of political socialization (Campbell et al., 1954; 1960).

In ecological research, data are unavailable on the short-term forces associated with voters' views of candidates and issues. In ecological research one also lacks data on voters' party identification, but one can probe the causal structure by studying the structural characteristics of the voters' social environments. Thus, the focus of ecological research of electoral behaviour tends to be on underlying ecological causes of party preferences rather than on the determinants of candidate choice more generally. Such ecological research assumes that environmental characteristics change relatively slowly.

Consequently, the long-term forces that determine party preference will tend to be constant within the same space (the same aggregation of voters) from time *t* to time *t* + 1 and will thus tend to exert the same effects in adjacent elections, with equality of effects varying according to the length of time between elections (Figure 4.2).

According to this Figure 4.2 and assuming little change in structural characteristics over time *t* to *t* + 1, factors *SE* (1) to *SE* (*n*) should have the same effects on party strength in each election year. Ecological analyses of the social environment and party strength over time will never explain all the variance in party strength over regional areas due to the missing factors: candidates and issues. Not only will the overall explanatory power be less than perfect but the exact effects of the ecological factors in each election will be inaccurately estimated because of the missing factors. In practice, this means that the *R*-squared values in a regression analysis will be less than unity and the coefficients in the associated equations will vary across elections. The greater the candidate and issue effects are, the lower the *R*-squared value from regressing party strength on structural factors and the greater the variation in coefficients across equations. These observations are not new, but reconsidering them can lead to a different approach to ecological analysis of electoral behaviour to provide a better estimate of environmental effects on party strength (see Appendix 4.1).

Our ecological model introduces into the analysis the differential effects of candidates and issues in adjacent elections to produce alternative estimates of environmental effects on party strength. We employ a pooled model approach that attempts to remove the differential effects of candidates and issues across elections by using the socio-economic factors to predict the per cent vote cast for the same party across elections (Ersson et al., 1982). Thus, we have

$$PES_t + PES_{t+1} + PES_{t+2} = F(EF) \qquad [3]$$

where PES = party electoral strength. Social structures are not constant, meaning that the equation [3] has to be applied with care. When the time spans between the election years become large, there is every reason to expect that the environmental impact will be reduced simply because the social structure has changed. Our regional ecology analysis covers mainly a single decade. We use the set of social structure variables to predict average electoral outcomes for three consecutive elections in the 1970s (see Appendix 4.2).

The estimation of the ecology model equation [3] is based on multiple regression equations, where the model estimation will be done on the basis of tests of the significance of the parameters: parameters that do not meet the restriction of a significance level lower than .05 will not be considered. The significance test is resorted to as a method of sorting out chance results from real relationships, 'significant' here meaning 'very probably not by chance alone' in a statistical decision approach (Winch and Campbell, 1969).

Findings

Political parties may be said to be dependent on the social structure to the extent that the variance in party strength can be explained by structural properties. We employ the pooled party model to estimate the extent of environmental influence on party electoral outcomes. The findings of separate regression analyses for each party in the sixteen countries – ninety-three regression analyses in all – appear in sixteen tables in Appendix 4.2. The results are presented by focussing either on the country in which a party operates or on the type of party to which a party belongs according to the criteria discussed in Chapter 3.

The ecological analyses presented in the sixteen tables in Appendix 4.2 rely on two measures of the variation in the electoral support of the political parties, the CV-scores and the SCV_w-values. These

Table 4.2 *Average regional variation by country and type of party*

	CV	SCV_w	Type of party	CV	SCV_w
Austria	0.475	0.420	Communist	0.809	0.657
Belgium	0.710	1.147	Socialist	0.346	0.332
Denmark	0.436	0.236	Religious	0.621	0.711
F R Germany	0.270	0.169	Liberal	0.461	0.394
Finland	0.951	0.384	Conservative	0.396	0.296
France	0.473	0.443	Agrarian	0.639	0.489
Greece	0.319	0.383	Ethnic	2.198	2.351
Ireland	0.284	0.603	Other	0.608	0.444
Italy	0.405	0.388			
Netherlands	0.616	0.931			
Norway	0.765	0.339			
Portugal	0.642	0.324			
Spain	0.739	0.928			
Sweden	0.464	0.248			
Switzerland	0.943	1.097			
United Kingdom	1.494	1.549			

Source: Appendix 4.2.

measures display a pattern by types of party as well as countries. We classify the political parties into eight party types: communist, socialist, religious, liberal, conservative, agrarian, ethnic, and other. Whereas the CV measure is appropriate for the regional variation within a country, the SCV_w measure reveals the regional variation between political parties in various countries (Table 4.2).

It is typical of Western Europe that countries as well as types of political party differ extensively in the regional variation in party support. Some nations like Great Britain, Belgium, and Switzerland display very high SCV_w scores due to the presence in these party systems of parties that put up candidates in some but not all constituencies. Among the regionally dispersed party systems we also count the Netherlands and Spain which have considerably higher SCV_w scores than regionally homogeneous party systems, as in Germany and Sweden. Not surprisingly ethnic parties have a regional variation that sets them apart from the other types of party. It may be pointed out that communist parties tend on the average to be more regionally dispersed than the other types.

The preceding findings concerning the regional variation in party strength suggest that an ecological analysis is promising. There is enough regional variation in electoral outcomes (the CV and the SCV_w-scores) to warrant the estimation of an ecology model. Moreover, the regional pattern in the variation in support for political parties tends to remain rather stable over time (the Eta-squared scores). The average E^2-scores for countries and party types, respectively, are given in Table 4.3.

Table 4.3   *Average regional effects (E²) by country and type of party*

	Number of parties	Regional effect (E^2)	Party type	Number of parties	Regional effect (E^2)
Austria	4	0.86	Communist	12	0.85
Belgium	6	0.91	Socialist	17	0.76
Denmark	11	0.64	Religious	14	0.92
F R Germany	3	0.79	Liberal	17	0.64
Finland	9	0.84	Conservative	11	0.64
France	5	0.75	Agrarian	6	0.70
Greece	4	0.40	Ethnic	6	0.94
Ireland	3	0.89	Other	10	0.63
Italy	7	0.75			
Netherlands	10	0.78			
Norway	8	0.73			
Portugal	3	0.89			
Spain	5	0.48			
Sweden	6	0.86			
Switzerland	4	0.69			
United Kingdom	5	0.87			

Source: Appendix 4.2.

We see in Table 4.3 the powerful effects of 'region' on party strength in Western Europe as measured by the Eta-squared statistic. The percentages of votes cast for parties in a country tend to vary systematically across regions over multiple elections. Regional factors explained more than half the variance in party strength in every country except Spain and Greece, where region accounted for only .48 and .40 of the variance, respectively. In eleven of the sixteen countries, regional factors explained more than .75 of the parties' electoral strength. Belgium reaches the high point in regional effects, with – on the average – more than 90 per cent of the vote cast for six Belgian parties associated with voting patterns in Belgium's 30 regions.

The European democracies show a stable regional variation in voter alignments for the different types of party. In Austria, for example, the ÖVP has an E^2 of .98, which means that region 'explained' 98 per cent of the ÖVP's percentage of vote won in the three elections studied. That is, the ÖVP won about the same percentage of the vote in 1975 as it did in 1971 and even in 1962 in each of Austria's Bezirke. The SPO ($E^2 = .93$) and the FPO ($E^2 = .90$) also showed stable regional variation, but the KPO ($E^2 = .61$) did not. Not surprisingly, parties without programmatic social ties are less stable in their regional outcomes (liberal and conservative parties) than political parties that explicitly appeal to particular social groups (religious, ethnic, and communist parties). This indicates the relevance of social structure variables as potential determinants of the

Table 4.4   *Average structural explanation (R^2) by country and type of party – within-nation differences*

	Number of parties	Structural explanation (R^2)	Party type	Number of parties	Structural explanation (R^2)
Austria	4	0.46	Communist	12	0.41
Belgium	6	0.71	Socialist	17	0.41
Denmark	11	0.31	Religious	14	0.60
F R Germany	3	0.51	Liberal	17	0.21
Finland	9	0.42	Conservative	11	0.29
France	5	0.23	Agrarian	6	0.47
Greece	4	0.06	Ethnic	6	0.66
Ireland	3	0.62	Other	10	0.30
Italy	7	0.29			
Netherlands	10	0.52			
Norway	8	0.29			
Portugal	3	0.49			
Spain	5	0.21			
Sweden	6	0.42			
Switzerland	4	0.38			
United Kingdom	5	0.52			

Source: Appendix 4.2.

variation in political party strength at the regional level. Let us turn to the regression analyses (Table 4.4).

The structure of the tables in Appendix 4.2 is devised for the purposes of comparative analysis; a general ecology model is estimated for all the political parties in Western Europe which gives us a number of values of various parameters to be employed for a comparative meta-analysis. It should be pointed out that wealth and religious orientation have been measured by an index covering several indicators, based on a test procedure to arrive at the most suitable ones. Moreover, the partial effects of the different social structure dimensions are measured by standardized coefficients following the advice to look for latent variables in ecological research (Hammond, 1979; see also Hargens, 1976). It was considered necessary to insert a measure of multi-collinearity (R^2D) as it may be expected that some social structure dimensions may not be independent of each other in all countries. This mass of coefficients is difficult to interpret in toto, but patterns emerge when the coefficients are averaged by country and party type.

Our ecological approach leads us to probe beyond simple regional effects to determine the underlying structural properties affecting party strength. Our attempts at 'recapturing' these regional effects with only five structural variables – industry, agriculture, affluence, religion, and ethnicity – varied in success from country to country. When included in regression equations and run for all ninety-three parties, these variables produced R-squares that approached the Eta-squares for some parties but fell far short for others. Summarized by country in Table 4.4, the mean R-square was highest again for Belgium – where our structural factors came close to 'reproducing' the regional effects – and lowest in Greece – where structural factors explained almost none of the variance.

Belgium, where the ecological approach appears to have worked best, deserves closer study for insight into the analysis. Examination of the six regression equations for Belgium in Appendix 4.2 reveals that religion (religious orientation) and ethnicity (per cent speaking French or Dutch) tend to have high coefficients over all six parties. This reflects the strong coincidence of religious and ethnic patterns with regions within Belgium.

We wish to emphasize one major source of regional variation in voter alignments not included in our analysis: political tradition. There is no way to estimate the impact of this factor on the basis of data reported on here. Political tradition remains a residual in our analysis, and it is not possible to separate it from a genuine regional factor. However, the major finding is that structural determination is fundamental to most party systems in Western Europe. Taking into account the impact on electoral outcomes of non-structural factors (issues, candidates, political tradition, region) we may rank the various party systems in extent of structural determination, from high to low: Belgium, Ireland, the Netherlands, Great Britain, the Federal Republic of Germany, Portugal, Austria, Finland, Sweden, Switzerland, Denmark, Italy, Norway, France, Spain, and Greece. Some types of political party are structurally determined parties. The following ranking distinguishes between the political parties on the same basis: ethnic, religious, agrarian, communist, socialist, conservative, and liberal parties.

The Beta-weights and the t-statistics contained in Appendix 4.2 indicate some interesting comparative findings about cleavage structures. Most party systems in Western Europe display the impact of social structure dimensions. Only with Greece is it difficult to establish a structural basis for voter alignments. In France, the Netherlands, and Sweden the social structure implications for the variation in party strength derive in particular from religion, whereas in Finland, language constitutes the most salient cleavage dimension. In Italy it is a matter of religion, wealth and agricultural structure whereas the cleavage structure of Irish politics consists of language, religion, and industry. Voter alignments in Norway express the cleavage dimensions of industry, religion, and language.

The overall findings indicate that language or ethnicity and religion usually do not constitute cleavage dimensions simultaneously. The pure case of a cleavage structure constituted of religion and language is Belgium. Religion tends to enter together with either industry or agricultural structure as cleavage dimensions in Switzerland, Spain, Portugal, and Austria.

Ethnicity is combined with class-orientated cleavage dimensions in Great Britain. When ethnicity constitutes a cleavage basis, it is usually of great importance, but ethnicity as a cleavage is typical of only a few countries. However, religion either as confession or religious orientation is present in most West European countries as a cleavage dimension. The same applies to industry.

The cleavage pattern characteristic of the different types of political party is less complex than the country pattern. Mono-causal relationships characterize three types of political party: ethnic, religious, and agrarian. The electoral strength of socialist parties tends to vary as a function of two cleavage bases: industry and religion. Communist parties have only one common structural denominator, (no) confession and/or religious orientation. Most interestingly, the strength of communist parties is not generally affected by such structural properties as industry, size of agricultural units or wealth. These structural properties may have considerable impact on the electoral strength of a communist party in one country, but such relationships are not invariant. Finally, we should mention that liberal and conservative parties also lack invariant structural connections.

The findings of the model estimations show convincingly that a social structure model is relevant to the explanation of party electoral outcomes in Western Europe. Predicting for the outcomes of three elections, a general model of properties of the social structure captures roughly 40 per cent of the variation in support for the political parties in Western Europe. Moreover, we find that the social structure implications account for a considerable portion of the variation in electoral outcomes that remains when time-specific circumstances are discounted (mean of E^2 = .75). Relating the average value of the R^2 to the overall very high average of the E^2-statistic we find that a general structural model explains well on the whole (Table 4.5).

The difference between the values for Eta-square and R-square in each country measures our success in finding structural factors that explain variations in party strength by region. The difference of .20 for Belgium between Eta-square (.91) and R-square (.71) contrasts sharply with the difference of .53 for France, where region accounts for .75 of the variance in party strength but our five structural factors recapture only .23 of the variance. About .75 of the variance in voting for parties in each of the sixteen countries can be attributed to 'region', but about .40 of the variance in party voting can be explained by our five structural factors. On the average, the difference between the regional and structural explanations of party strength is .35.

We also hypothesize that the implications of the social structure

Table 4.5   *Differences between regional effect and structural explanation ($E^2 - R^2$)*

	Number of parties	Difference ($E^2 - R^2$)	Party type	Number of parties	Difference ($E^2 - R^2$)
Austria	4	0.40	Communist	12	0.44
Belgium	6	0.20	Socialist	17	0.35
Denmark	11	0.33	Religious	14	0.32
F R Germany	3	0.38	Liberal	17	0.43
Finland	9	0.42	Conservative	11	0.35
France	5	0.52	Agrarian	6	0.23
Greece	4	0.34	Ethnic	6	0.23
Ireland	3	0.27	Other	10	0.33
Italy	7	0.46			
Netherlands	10	0.36			
Norway	8	0.44			
Portugal	3	0.40			
Spain	5	0.27			
Sweden	6	0.44			
Switzerland	4	0.31			
United Kingdom	5	0.35			

Source: Appendix 4.2.

for electoral outcomes are stronger the less the regional variation in party support is influenced by time-specific circumstances. Thus, we expect that the more stable the regional variation as measured by the E^2-score, the more relevant social structure is for the determination of electoral outcomes. The data support our expectation as the correlation between the E^2- and the R^2-scores is .69. However, the association is not perfect, meaning that factors other than social structure are relevant to the explanation of a regionally stable variation.

Another hypothesis is that large regional variations are more stable over time than small regional variations are, because large regional variations would be clearly the result of structural factors that would be stable over time. Small variations on the other hand could be accounted for by means of other factors like issues or candidates. However, the correlation between extent of regional variation and stability over time is weak (.24). Interestingly, small regional variations may be stable over time reflecting a social niche. Thus, even if the extent of regional variation in Western Europe were small, we would still have to conclude that an ecological analysis may be useful.

We find that the size of a political party is relevant to the regional variation expressed in the SCV_w scores and the E^2 statistics. One may expect that the larger the political party, the less its regional variation. Large parties by their very nature would display a tendency to penetrate every region of nation. It is surprising that the correlation between party size and extent of regional variation is not pronounced (−.40), although the direction of relationship is as hypothesized. This means that many small parties make an effort to receive support in most regions. Only the set of ethnic parties shows a tendency to focus narrowly upon special regions.

Conclusion

The findings of the regional investigations of the relationship between social structure and political party support neither of the two prevailing approaches to politics. European politics are not characterized by extensive social determinism as argued by political sociology, because the within-nation variation in political party outcomes can not be reliably predicted on the basis of knowledge of social structure dimensions. The data do not confirm the contrary hypothesis − political institutionalism − that political parties have a life completely of their own unaffected by their environments. Social cleavages matter but they do not explain everything. Political parties reflect their environment to a certain extent, meaning that there is also ample room for autonomous political action. We must now move to the analysis of the system level of political parties or how political parties constitute elements in national party systems. What is a party system?

5

Party Systems

Introduction

When West European political parties were analysed at length in Chapters 3 and 4 the focus was on the single parties, their continuity and social bases. However, political parties also constitute so-called party systems which require their own analysis. Let us now focus on systems of political parties by looking at the West European party system in order to establish what could be meant by the systemic aspect. If a national party system is something more than simply the set of political parties in a country, then which are the emergent properties at the system level?

A well-known hypothesis in comparative party research claims that the West European party systems are characterized by a high degree of continuity. Thus, the so-called frozen party system hypothesis argued that change is not a typical feature of the party systems of Western Europe. Seymour Martin Lipset and Stein Rokkan stated in their famous analysis of the development of party systems since these political systems were transformed into democracies:

> the party systems of the 1960s reflect, with few but significant exceptions, the cleavage structures of the 1920s. This is a crucial characteristic of Western competitive politics in the age of 'high mass consumption': *the party alternatives, and in remarkably many cases the party organizations, are older than the majorities of the national electorates* (Lipset and Rokkan, 1967a: 50).

Richard Rose and Derek Urwin came to the same conclusion with a refined analysis of the development after the Second World War:

> Whatever index of change is used – a measure of trends or any of several measures of fluctuations – the picture is the same: the electoral strength of most parties in Western nations since the war had changed very little from election to election, from decade to decade, or within the lifespan of a generation. The consistency of this finding increases confidences in the indicators used. In short, the first priority of social scientists concerned with the development of parties and party systems since 1945 is to explain the absence of change in a far from static period in political history (Rose and Urwin, 1970: 295).

This widely accepted interpretation of the party systems in Western Europe may be challenged by relating it to the new theme of party failure (Wolinetz, 1988; Lawson and Merkl, 1988; Mair and Smith, 1989). When one sets out to inquire into how much party system change has taken place in West European party systems since the democratization of the political systems, then the notion of party system change becomes crucial. The concepts of party system change or instability both require theoretical clarification which is also true of the concept of a party system itself. How much is there of party system stability in Western Europe?

What is a party system?

A party system like any system consists of parts and relationships between these parts. According to systems analysis a system is a set of objects together with relationships between the objects and between their attributes (Hall and Fagen, 1956: 18). The parts of a party system are, of course, the political parties, but the specification of relationships is not as simple as the specification of the parts (Daalder and Mair, 1983). It is generally agreed that a party system is an entity that is different from a political party or a simple set of political parties, as a party system involves organization. A party system consists of a set of political parties operating within a nation in an organized pattern, described by a number of party-system properties. This is where the agreement ends, as scholars do not identify the same set of properties. There are a number of relevant party-system properties and little justification for the use of one or two of these to the exclusion of the others. The study of party systems faces a conceptual problem about what the semantically relevant properties of party systems are. A semantically relevant property is a property that typically occurs in a set of phenomena and that characterizes part of the similarities and differences between phenomena in that set, which makes it useful for definition purposes (Achinstein, 1968).

Lipset and Rokkan as well as Rose and Urwin approach the problem of party system change as a matter concerning the development of the parts of party systems. However, it seems that the concept of party system change must be tied to that of party system property, which covers the parts of the system studied as well as the systems relationships between them (Mair, 1989; Smith, 1989; Mair and Smith, 1989). It is a matter of research strategy which parts and which relationships are to be singled out as crucial in the analysis of party system change. It seems appropriate to base any judgement of the occurrence of change on an investigation of how basic properties of the party systems in Western Europe have developed since 1945. The concept of party system stability relates to the development over time of basic properties in party systems.

It has been argued that the identification of the parts of a national party system should start from the concept of a *relevant* political party. Sartori lays down rules for what parties are to be counted as relevant within a party system: on the one hand the parties must show continuity over time, on the other hand they should have a coalitional potential (applies to small parties in the political centre) or a blackmail potential (applies to large extremist parties) (Sartori, 1976: 122–3). Actually, various definitions, stating necessary and/or sufficient conditions for the application of the term 'party system', have been suggested. Duverger states that a party system is defined by a particular relationship amongst characteristics such as numbers, respective sizes, alliances, geographical localization, political distribution, and so on (Duverger, 1954: 203). To Eckstein a party system comparison between the various parties makes it possible to identify new elements that do not exist for each party community considered in isolation (Eckstein, 1968: 438). Rae underlines the network of competitive relationships between political parties. This system of competition constitutes the party system and it provides democratic political parties with their unique importance (Rae, 1971: 47). Similarly, Sartori focusses on the system of interactions resulting from inter-party competition, i.e. how the parties relate and react to each other, competitively or otherwise, to the other parties (Sartori, 1976: 44).

The definitions fall into two sets; the proposals of Eckstein, Rae, and Sartori are general since they state that a party system is more than the sum of its parts; on the other hand, the suggestion by Duverger may result in an infinite enumeration of properties. We need a set of minimal properties by which to characterize a maximum amount of actual party-system variation. Perhaps at the present stage of knowledge concerning political parties the search for a definition stating the necessary and sufficient properties is premature. The best strategy may be to derive a tentative list of semantically relevant properties, even though such a list would need revision before a definition is arrived at.

Party system dimensions

Most typologies of party system identify one or two properties or dimensions along which various party systems are classified. Besides electoral participation the number of parts in a party system is a property that is almost always considered a basic dimension; Duverger is famous for his classification scheme of the single-party, the Anglo-Saxon two-party, and the multi-party system (Duverger, 1954: 203). In the same vein Blondel talks of two-party systems, two-and-a-half-party systems and multi-party systems with or without dominant parties (Blondel, 1968: 187). Sartori's model includes besides party fragmentation (number of parties) ideological distance (Sartori, 1976: 282–93). Mogens Pedersen states that polarization and fragmentation have, by tradition, been identified as the party system dimensions and adds a typology based on volatility to the growing literature on party systems (Pedersen, 1979: 3). The Lipset and Rokkan model focusses upon the cleavage lines that distinguish the various parties in a party system from each other (Lipset and Rokkan, 1967a: 33–50). Thus, typologies of party system identify either relationships between the constituent parts of the system or properties of the parts of the system. However, the basic conceptual problem is still unresolved: How many dimensions are to be included in a party-system model (Gross and Sigelman, 1984)?

A number of indicators are used to characterize party systems. The proper procedure for describing party system dimensions depends on the resolution of the conceptual problem of identifying the dimensions of party systems. We argue that those properties should be selected that cover as much as possible of the variation in a set of West European party systems. Thus, the dimensions we focus upon are, hopefully, the semantically relevant properties of the concept of party systems as it relates to Western Europe. Which are the indicators when the relevant dimensions or relevant party-system properties are operationalized by means of indicators measuring party system variation in Western Europe?

A number of party system indicators may be identified considering existing typologies; thus, we arrive at the following sets of indicators corresponding to the one- or two-dimensional models previously referred to: electoral participation, number of parties, ideological distance between parties, realignments behind the parties, and cleavage lines in the party system. Let us study the West European party systems with the aid of a number of indicators that have been measured in relation to 201 elections from 1945 to 1989 in our set of sixteen countries.

Indicators

A basic indicator when describing party systems in operation is some measure on electoral participation. We use a standard measure such as the total number of votes cast as a percentage of eligible votes. There are a lot of indicators connected with the number of parties and the strength of parties. One indicator we consider in this connection is the number of parties, i.e. the number of parties that have taken part in parliamentary elections and become represented in parliament as well as the number of other parties, irrespective of how small they are. It includes also certain non-represented parties like the minor communist parties. As an operational definition we suggest the political parties represented in parliament and the parties included in Mackie and Rose: *International Almanac of Electoral History* (1982).

Another indicator is the number of effective parties calculated as:

$$N = 1 \Big/ \sum_{i=1}^{n} p_i^2; \qquad [1]$$

where p_i is the fractional share of the i-th party component and Σ (sigma) refers to the summation over all components according to the Laakso and Taagepera formula (1979). A fourth indicator would be the fractionalization index where:

$$F = 1 - \sum_{i=1}^{n} p_i^2; \qquad [2]$$

Rae is the one to whom the credit is due for this index which measures both the number of parties and their size. Much has been written about this index, but we agree with Pedersen who writes: 'It might be a good idea, therefore, if students of party systems would decide to stick to one measure – namely, F (i.e. Rae's). Instead of inventing new indices of fragmentation, one could instead concentrate on the task of delimiting the contexts in which F can legitimately be used' (Pedersen, 1980: 397). F carries the same information as N, but the advantage of N is that its scores are much more easily interpreted. Finally, a fifth indicator on the number of parties is the aggregation index: the share of the largest party/ the number of parties. An index with this designation was constructed by Mayer (1980: 517). It measures the share of the largest party in relation to the number of parties (we have modified Mayer's original formula).

Another set of indicators expresses the ideological distance within a party system; as a rule the distance on a right–left scale is referred to. Even if one-dimensional measures like the right–left scale are criticized, they catch an essential dimension within the party systems. The starting point is to classify parties on a right–left scale, a problem attended with great difficulties. We have used a scale going from 0 to 10 where the extreme right is given the value 10 and the extreme left the value 0. One indicator, the right–left score, shows the point on the right–left scale that a party system reaches at a certain election, and this value is weighted on the basis of the electoral strength of the parties. Another well-known indicator is the polarization index; here we use the same index as Taylor and Herman (1971) and Sigelman and Yough (1978); a system is polarized maximally when 50 per cent of the electorate is at the respective pole, whereas there is no polarization if all are in the political centre. Our formula for the polarization index is:

$$p = \sum_{i=1}^{n} f_i (x_i - x)^2 \qquad [3]$$

where n is the number of parties, f_i is the share of vote of the respective party, x_i is the right–left score of the respective party and x is the right–left score of the party system. The ranking of a party on the left–right scale is based on the left–right location of the parties as reported on in Table 3.16.

A large number of indicators may be devised that measure the occurrence of social cleavages in the party system. This was the focus of the famous Lipset–Rokkan analysis in their introduction to *Party Systems and Voter Alignments* (1967b). According to them, the modern party systems of Western Europe are the result of a process through which various cleavages in society are transformed into the various voter alignments of the party systems.

The idea of some kind of relationship or correspondence between party system and social cleavages reoccurs among several scholars. Bingham Powell refers to the 'relationship between party systems and societal cleavage structures' (Powell, 1980: 13), and Hans Daalder states that 'European countries reveal considerable differences according to the character and the intensity of the cleavage lines that form the basis for political conflict and political organization' (Daalder, 1966a: 67).

We use the following indicators to cover as much as possible of the idea of the social orientation of party systems. All these indicators are based on a classification of nearly all political parties in ten party types, see Chapter 3. Thus, we have the following indicators: (a) the strength of agrarian, ethnic and religious parties, i.e. the shares of agrarian, ethnic and religious parties; (b) the stregth of class-based parties, i.e. the shares of communist, socialist and left-socialist parties; (c) the strength of non-structural parties, i.e. the shares of conservative and liberal parties.

There are indicators that somehow reveal the dynamics of party systems, i.e. they express changes within a party system. We take one indicator into account: volatility. An indicator on volatility has been suggested by Pedersen (1979: 4) to be calculated according to the following formula:

$$V_t = 1 / 2 * \sum_{i=1}^{n} | \Delta p_{i,t} | \qquad [4]$$

where *n* is the number of parties participating in elections at the time *t* and/or *t-1*, and delta p_i stands for the change in the share of the vote of the party p_i over the two elections. This measure shows net changes for all the parties within a party system between two elections; gross changes are possible to estimate only on the basis of survey data. Pedersen (1979: 4) names this concept volatility, but it has been used by other scholars under other designations (Przeworski, 1975: 53; Dodd, 1976: 88).

Relationships between the indicators

We have arrived at a list of indicators measuring aspects of the organization of parties into party systems. Whether it is useful or not depends

Table 5.1 *Correlation matrix of party system indicators*

	V1	V2	V3	V4	V5	V6	V7	V8	V9	V10	V11	V12	V13	V14	V15
V1	1.00														
V2	.21	1.00													
V3	−.22	−.63	1.00												
V4	−.16	−.58	.85	1.00											
V5	−.19	−.89	.71	.65	1.00										
V6	−.16	−.91	.70	.65	.94	1.00									
V7	.20	.78	−.75	−.84	−.82	−.76	1.00								
V8	−.14	.18	−.14	−.16	−.25	−.12	.28	1.00							
V9	.11	−.15	.10	.13	.13	.10	−.24	−.42	1.00						
V10	.27	.30	−.29	−.08	−.30	−.30	.09	−.25	.04	1.00					
V11	.07	−.36	.27	.19	.39	.30	−.32	−.65	.59	−.40	1.00				
V12	.49	−.25	.17	.17	.15	.19	−.18	−.09	−.11	.17	−.06	1.00			
V13	.33	.06	−.12	.04	−.04	−.10	−.13	−.71	.45	.77	.28	.13	1.00		
V14	−.56	.16	−.08	−.15	−.09	−.09	.21	.46	−.16	−.35	−.11	−.84	−.65	1.00	
V15	−.05	−.11	.17	.13	.20	.19	−.15	.06	.17	−.30	.18	−.16	−.19	.23	1.00

V1 Electoral participation
V2 Strength of largest party
V3 Number of parties in parliament
V4 Number of parties reported in Rose and Mackie
V5 Fractionalization index
V6 Effective number of parties
V7 Aggregation index
V8 Left–Right score
V9 Polarization index
V10 Strength of socialist parties
V11 Strength of parties to the left of socialist parties
V12 Strength of agrarian, ethnic and religious parties
V13 Strength of class-based parties (= V10 + V11)
V14 Strength of non-structural parties (= 100–(V12 + V13))
V15 Volatility

on whether it allows us to make any interesting observations about West European party politics. Let us first inquire into any possible interaction between the indicators. A correlation analysis has been done comprising the preceding indicators (Table 5.1).

The correlations between the various indices on party system properties reported on in Table 5.1 are, generally speaking, not very high, which means that the indicators do not go together. There are some cases of interaction which should be pointed out. The indicators on the number of parties in the party system and the strength of the largest party tend to co-vary considerably, as expected. Thus, the Laakso and Taagepera index on effective number of parties is positively correlated with the Rae fractionalization index and negatively corrrelated with the aggregation index of Mayer. And the number of parties in parliament also co-varies considerably with the other indicators on party system fractionalization. The two measures on party systems distance or ideological spread between the two extremist poles, the left–right score and the polarization index, are not closely related.

On the other hand, there is considerable interaction between the indicators on the social orientation of the party system, simply because some of the indices have been calculated in much the same way. One may also note that volatility does not co-vary with any of the other party system dimensions, which reflects the circumstance that volatility stands for party system instability in general. Let us look at a few of these indicators more closely in order to discuss the famous Lipset and Rokkan hypothesis about the party systems of Western Europe as frozen and highly stable.

How different are the party systems in the major countries in Western Europe? As we set out to search for signs of instability in these party systems it is also vital to note the variation between the countries on a number of indicators. Actually, we may employ the eta-squared statistic to tap whether the total variation on the party system indicators refers to the between-country variation or the within-country variation over time. If it were true that the West European party systems were highly stable, then we expect to find very high eta-squared scores for each party system property as well as low volatility scores for each national party system. Do these predictions meet with empirical support?

Electoral participation

In the democracies in Western Europe the level of participation in elections does not change much from one election to another. But we also note a change as the overall trend seems to be towards less citizen interest in politics, the average rate of participation for all countries included falling below a score of 80 per cent for the first time in the late 1980s. There is a persistent variation between the countries, some scoring above and others below the average value of 82.4 per cent (Table 5.2).

Participation in national elections is consistently high in Austria, Belgium and Italy whereas it is consistently low only in Switzerland, Ireland and the United Kingdom. Less citizen involvement and more political apathy distinguish in particular the developments in Finland, France, the Netherlands and Ireland during the 1980s. The low scores for Switzerland of about 47 per cent in the 1980s indicate a profound citizen indifference towards the Swiss political parties. In the new democracies in southern Europe the rate of participation is also rather low. The rate of participation has changed in Switzerland, the Netherlands and Austria

Table 5.2 *Electoral participation*

	1945 –49	1950 –54	1955 –59	1960 –64	1965 –69	1970 –74	1975 –79	1980 –84	1985 –89	Aver- age
Austria	95.6	95.8	95.1	93.8	93.8	92.1	92.6	92.6	90.4	93.6
Belgium	92.4	92.9	93.6	92.3	90.8	90.5	95.0	94.6	93.5	92.7
Denmark	86.1	81.1	83.7	85.7	89.0	87.5	87.2	85.8	81.3	85.2
FRG	78.5	85.8	87.8	87.7	86.8	91.1	90.7	88.9	84.3	87.0
Finland	76.4	77.3	75.0	85.1	84.9	81.8	74.6	75.7	72.1	77.9
France	79.9	80.2	79.6	68.8	80.5	81.2	83.3	70.9	71.9	77.7
Greece	–	76.3	75.2	82.2	–	79.5	81.1	78.6	83.5	79.4
Ireland	74.2	75.9	71.3	70.6	76.0	76.6	76.3	74.4	70.9	74.1
Italy	90.7	93.9	93.7	92.9	92.8	93.1	91.9	89.0	90.5	91.9
Netherlands	93.4	95.0	95.6	95.1	94.9	81.3	88.0	84.0	82.9	89.1
Norway	79.2	79.3	78.3	79.1	84.6	80.2	82.9	82.0	83.4	81.3
Portugal	–	–	–	–	–	–	88.3	81.2	72.4	81.7
Spain	–	–	–	–	–	–	72.5	79.5	70.4	73.0
Sweden	82.7	79.1	78.5	84.9	89.3	89.6	91.3	91.4	87.9	86.2
Switzerland	71.7	69.8	68.6	64.5	63.8	56.8	50.4	48.9	46.8	60.0
UK	72.7	82.9	77.9	77.2	76.0	74.7	76.3	72.8	75.4	76.6
Average	83.9	82.2	82.1	83.0	84.8	83.1	83.0	80.9	79.0	82.4

Eta-squared by country .78
Eta-squared by time period .03
Note: Electoral participation is measured as total votes cast as a percentage of eligible votes.

where we have a clear decline and in Sweden where there is an increase in participation. Perhaps the changes in the election procedures in Sweden (introduction of post office voting) and the Netherlands (removal of the obligation to vote) may have contributed to these changes.

Fractionalization

A typical feature of West European party systems is the variety of political parties. Two indices may be employed to present a picture of the multi-party nature of the West European party systems, the first of which only takes into account how many political parties reach some kind of national representation (Table 5.3).

The average values inform us that about 6 to 8 parties are represented in the parliaments in Western Europe. This is a high score testifying to the extent of fractionalization in these party systems. At the same time the country differences are pronounced with some distance between Italy and Switzerland with about 11 parties on average, and Austria and the Federal Republic of Germany with a mean of some 4 parties. The indicator on the number of parties in parliament informs us about the existence of many

Table 5.3 *Number of parties in Parliament*

	1945 –49	1950 –54	1955 –59	1960 –64	1965 –69	1970 –74	1975 –79	1980 –84	1985 –89	Aver- age
Austria	3.5	4	3.5	3	3	3	3	3	4	3.3
Belgium	4.5	5	5	7	7.5	8.5	11	12	11.5	8
Denmark	6.5	6.3	7	7	6	8	11	9	8.5	7.8
FRG	11	6	4	3	3	3	3	3.5	4	4.3
Finland	6	6	7	8	8	8	9	9	9	7.6
France	5.7	6	7	8	6.5	10	7	7	6	6.7
Greece	6	6.7	9	4		6	8	3	4.3	5.7
Ireland	6	5	6	6	3.5	3	3	4.3	6	4.7
Italy	10.5	9	12	10	9	8	11	14	14	10.8
Netherlands	7.5	8	7.5	10	11	14	13	11	9	10
Norway	5.5	6	6	6	5.5	8	6	7	6	6.1
Portugal	–	–	–	–	–	–	6.7	7	6	6.6
Spain	–	–	–	–	–	–	12	10	13	12
Sweden	5	5	5	5	5	5	5	5	6	5.1
Switzerland	10	9	9	9	10	10	12.5	13	15	10.8
UK	8	4	3.5	3	4	6.7	8	9	9	5.8
Average	6.6	6.0	6.5	6.1	6.0	7.3	8.4	7.5	7.9	7.0

Eta-squared by country = .61
Eta-squared by time = .09
Note: The number of political parties in parliament simply counts the number of parties represented by at least one seat.

small parties that manage to get national representation, but it tells us nothing about the weight of the small parties. Let us look at a somewhat different indicator, the effective number of parties (Table 5.4).

Judged by this index which takes the strength of the parties into account besides the simple number of parties it appears that the variation between the countries becomes less pronounced. The degree of fractionalization does not vary that much, because the European party systems are typical multi-party systems. There is a set of national party systems that are more fractionalized than others: Finland, the Netherlands, Switzerland and Belgium. Inversely, the set of nations that score low – relatively speaking – consists of Austria, the United Kingdom, Ireland and the Federal Republic of Germany. There are signs of a seminal trend towards more fractionalization in Western Europe during the 1980s as new parties have challenged the old ones in several countries and have reached parliamentary representation with the exception of the Federal Republic of Germany where the introduction of a 5 per cent threshold in 1953 reduced the opportunities for new parties to become represented.

The data on fractionalization in Belgium and Denmark speaks about the major changes that have taken place in these party systems involving a

Table 5.4   *Effective number of parties*

	1945 –49	1950 –54	1955 –59	1960 –64	1965 –69	1970 –74	1975 –79	1980 –84	1985 –89	Aver- age
Austria	2.5	2.7	2.5	2.5	2.4	2.3	2.3	2.4	2.7	2.5
Belgium	3.2	2.8	2.7	3.0	4.1	5.4	6.6	8.9	8.1	5.0
Denmark	4.2	3.9	3.9	3.8	4.4	5.8	5.3	5.5	5.8	4.8
FRG	4.9	3.4	2.8	2.8	2.5	2.4	2.4	2.6	2.9	2.9
Finland	5.0	5.0	5.2	5.9	5.2	6.1	5.8	5.5	6.1	5.5
France	4.6	5.4	6.0	5.3	4.3	5.9	4.9	4.0	3.9	4.8
Greece	2.7	5.0	2.9	2.6	–	2.7	3.7	2.7	2.6	3.2
Ireland	4.1	3.3	3.2	3.2	2.8	2.8	2.8	2.8	3.4	3.1
Italy	3.8	4.2	3.9	4.2	4.0	4.1	3.7	4.5	4.6	4.0
Netherlands	4.8	5.0	4.4	4.8	6.2	7.0	4.0	4.4	3.8	4.9
Norway	3.9	3.5	3.4	3.5	3.7	5.0	3.6	3.9	4.2	3.9
Portugal	–	–	–	–	–	–	3.6	3.3	3.9	3.6
Spain	–	–	–	–	–	–	4.3	3.4	3.9	4.0
Sweden	3.4	3.3	3.3	3.3	3.1	3.5	3.6	3.4	3.8	3.4
Switzerland	5.3	5.1	5.0	5.0	5.6	6.1	5.7	6.0	6.8	5.6
UK	2.7	2.3	2.2	2.5	2.4	2.9	2.9	3.1	3.1	2.7
Average	4.0	3.9	3.7	3.6	3.8	4.4	4.3	4.0	4.3	4.0

Eta-squared by country = .55
Eta-squared by time = .04
Note: The effective number of parties is measured by the Laakso and Taagepera index.

sharp rise in the number of parties. Belgium is the outstanding case of increased fractionalization in the party system, going from some 4 or 5 parties in the late 1940s to roughly 12 parties in the early 1980s. The social conditions for the Belgian developments are the activation of the ethnic cleavages. There is also a noticeable increase in the number of effective parties in Switzerland and the United Kingdom where new parties have been introduced.

Polarization

Polarization or the distribution of the electorate along the classical right–left scale is clearly a relevant property when describing the West European party systems, as much of the politics in several of these countries has taken the form of a confrontation between left-wing and right-wing parties of some sort or other. However, the amount of polarization cannot be described as exceptionally high, because theoretically it is conceivable that party systems reach as high a degree of polarization as 25.0. Generally speaking, an increase seems to have occurred in polarization since the 1960s (Table 5.5).

Table 5.5   *Polarization index*

	1945 –49	1950 –54	1955 –59	1960 –64	1965 –69	1970 –74	1975 –79	1980 –84	1985 –89	Aver- age
Austria	2.7	2.8	2.6	2.4	2.0	2.2	2.2	2.1	2.1	2.4
Belgium	2.2	1.9	1.8	1.8	1.8	2.0	2.3	2.7	2.6	2.1
Denmark	2.6	1.9	1.7	2.0	2.3	2.4	2.6	2.8	3.0	2.4
FRG	4.0	3.4	3.6	3.5	3.7	3.4	3.4	3.7	4.0	3.6
Finland	3.9	3.7	4.0	4.0	3.8	3.8	4.2	3.9	4.0	3.9
France	3.4	5.1	5.1	5.4	5.8	5.8	5.4	5.0	6.7	5.1
Greece	2.1	3.1	4.7	3.4	–	3.4	4.2	4.0	4.2	3.7
Ireland	0.8	0.7	1.2	0.9	0.6	0.8	0.8	1.0	1.3	0.9
Italy	3.2	4.6	3.8	3.7	3.7	4.2	3.9	3.9	3.6	3.7
Netherlands	3.8	3.7	3.4	3.6	3.7	3.9	3.5	3.7	3.2	3.6
Norway	3.0	2.8	2.7	2.8	2.8	3.5	3.2	3.7	4.1	3.2
Portugal	–	–	–	–	–	–	4.7	5.2	4.0	4.7
Spain	–	–	–	–	–	–	3.1	3.6	3.7	3.4
Sweden	3.0	3.0	3.3	3.2	3.0	3.0	3.3	3.8	3.5	3.2
Switzerland	1.8	1.6	1.6	1.6	1.5	1.6	1.7	1.7	1.5	1.6
UK	3.4	3.6	3.7	3.4	3.5	3.2	3.0	2.8	3.0	3.3
Average	3.0	2.8	3.2	3.0	2.9	3.0	3.2	3.2	3.5	3.1

Eta-squared by country = .82
Eta-squared by time = .03
Note: Polarization as measured by the polarization index is sensitive to the ideological distance between the political parties as well as the shares of the extremist parties of the electorate.

The country variation in polarization is striking as it may be pointed out that a few nations tend persistently to have scores twice as high as some others. Polarization is a typical feature of France, Portugal, Finland and Italy. On the other hand, polarization is of no importance in Ireland, Switzerland and of only slight importance in Denmark, Austria and Belgium. It may be noted that the polarization score has risen in France although the French Communist party has declined at the same time as a new right-wing extremist party has scored some electoral success – Front National.

Structural versus non-structural parties

The contents of the various national party systems may be analysed by the employment of the distinction between structural parties and non-structural parties introduced in Chapter 3. The West European party systems include a number of types of parties, some of which have of tradition been orientated towards determinate social groups – the structural parties. Have these parties remained unchanged during

Table 5.6   *Strength of class-based parties*

	1945 –49	1950 –54	1955 –59	1960 –64	1965 –69	1970 –74	1975 –79	1980 –84	1985 –89	Aver- age
Austria	46.9	47.4	47.8	47.0	43.0	50.4	51.8	48.4	43.8	47.9
Belgium	41.1	41.1	38.9	39.8	32.1	30.1	29.0	27.5	31.1	34.3
Denmark	46.1	45.0	42.5	49.1	46.6	43.6	46.1	47.3	47.4	46.1
FRG	34.9	31.0	31.8	38.1	42.0	46.1	42.9	40.8	37.0	38.8
Finland	47.5	48.0	48.1	45.9	51.0	42.6	42.8	40.5	38.0	45.0
France	47.9	41.2	37.9	36.9	42.0	43.9	48.9	55.2	46.1	44.4
Greece	0	10.0	17.3	13.6	–	23.1	37.4	60.3	53.8	25.8
Ireland	8.7	11.8	9.1	12.0	16.2	14.8	13.0	11.9	11.9	12.4
Italy	38.9	39.8	41.5	45.2	45.8	44.5	47.2	46.9	45.6	43.8
Netherlands	36.1	35.2	36.0	33.8	30.1	31.6	36.4	33.5	34.8	34.2
Norway	52.2	51.8	51.7	52.1	50.7	46.5	46.9	42.4	45.5	49.0
Portugal	–	–	–	–	–	–	55.6	52.4	37.9	49.6
Spain	–	–	–	–	–	–	40.5	50.6	49.4	46.0
Sweden	52.4	50.3	49.6	52.4	53.1	49.5	48.2	51.2	49.6	50.4
Switzerland	31.3	28.7	29.4	28.8	26.4	25.8	28.1	26.5	21.1	27.6
UK	48.6	47.7	45.2	44.3	48.2	39.9	37.0	39.3	40.5	43.3
Average	40.7	35.8	37.6	37.1	39.8	39.1	42.3	39.6	40.5	39.3

Eta-squared by country = .72
Eta-squared bt time = .02
Note: The index on class-based parties adds up the proportions of the electorate who vote for socialist and communist parties.

the post-War period as the Lipset and Rokkan hypothesis implies? One important set of structural parties is the socialist and communist parties or class-based parties.

In the set of European party systems, generally, a steady and continuous growth in the electoral strength of left-wing parties has taken place. When the European political systems were democratized in the early decades of the century, the left-wing parties secured hardly one third of the total vote; it seems as if the Second World War had a significant impact on the attractiveness of left-wing parties since during the post-war time intervals they receive roughly 40 per cent of the total vote.

Actually, the extent of variation in the electorate concerning the orientation towards socialist and communist parties (including left-socialist parties) is great. Class-based parties do not figure prominently in Ireland, Switzerland, Belgium and the Netherlands, whereas the contrary is true of the Nordic countries as well as Austria, France, Italy and the UK (Table 5.6).

Due to the existence of one large social democratic party or two smaller socialist parties in several of the West European party systems in combination with a communist party of some size, these party systems have included class-based parties to a considerable but variable extent.

Table 5.7   *Strength of ethnic, religious and agrarian parties*

	1945 –49	1950 –54	1955 –59	1960 –64	1965 –69	1970 –74	1975 –79	1980 –84	1985 –89	Aver- age
Austria	46.9	41.3	45.1	45.4	48.3	43.9	42.4	43.0	41.3	44.3
Belgium	44.2	45.9	48.5	45.8	45.5	50.3	52.5	41.7	39.5	46.1
Denmark	25.7	22.5	25.5	21.4	19.1	14.1	15.9	11.7	11.2	18.3
FRG	38.6	53.8	54.9	45.3	47.0	44.9	48.6	46.7	44.3	47.1
Finland	31.6	31.2	30.0	30.2	27.6	24.1	26.3	25.5	25.8	28.1
France	26.4	12.5	11.2	8.9	11.5	12.5	0.0	0.0	0.0	11.3
Greece	0.0	0.0	0.0	0.0		0.0	0.0	0.0	0.0	0.0
Ireland	5.5	3.0	7.7	4.6	0.0	0.0	0.0	0.8	1.0	2.0
Italy	42.7	40.7	43.0	38.7	39.2	39.3	39.3	34.2	37.0	39.6
Netherlands	55.4	54.7	52.5	52.2	47.4	41.9	37.8	36.7	40.4	46.1
Norway	16.1	19.6	19.5	19.0	19.0	23.3	21.0	16.1	15.0	18.2
Portugal	–	–	–	–	–	–	14.3	22.4	8.0	14.8
Spain	–	–	–	–	–	–	11.1	8.7	10.9	10.5
Sweden	12.4	10.7	11.1	14.5	17.8	25.7	22.5	17.4	13.3	16.6
Switzerland	34.2	36.1	36.4	36.4	34.7	33.8	34.2	33.6	32.9	34.8
UK	0.6	0.5	0.7	0.9	1.2	4.3	3.9	3.5	3.9	2.2
Average	30.2	22.6	25.8	22.2	26.3	25.7	24.4	21.0	17.2	23.8

E^2 by country .93
E^2 by time period .04

This indicates a kind of radical orientation which to some extent reflects the *Zeitgeist*. In Italy and in Greece the amount of radical orientation has increased during the 1980s whereas it has declined in Belgium, Finland, Norway and the UK. At the same time the division of the votes of class-based parties varies considerably from one country to another between the social democrats and the communist parties although the 1980s have been a period of general decline for the latter. Several of the West European communist parties have begun considering a change of their party label as a reaction to the major events in Eastern Europe.

Another indicator on the contents of the party system is the aggregate share for other structural parties besides the class-based parties, i.e. the agrarian, ethnic and religious parties. Table 5.7 shows their combined relevance in West European elections since 1945.

The combined strength of the structural parties that are not class-based has been reduced during the post-Second World War period. This reflects not only the decline of the agrarian parties but it also indicates the reduction in support for religious and ethnic parties in the 1980s in spite of the tendencies towards an ethnic revival as well as a rejuvenation of the religious parties in the 1970s. The West European party systems differ most considerably with regard to the existence of these types of structural parties. In some countries they are virtually non-existent

Table 5.8   *Strength of non-structural parties*

	1945 –49	1950 –54	1955 –59	1960 –64	1965 –69	1970 –74	1975 –79	1980 –84	1985 –89	Aver- age
Austria	6.2	11.3	7.2	7.6	8.7	5.7	5.8	8.6	14.9	7.8
Belgium	14.8	13.1	12.6	14.4	22.5	19.7	18.6	30.8	29.5	19.6
Denmark	28.3	32.5	32.0	29.6	34.4	42.4	38.0	41.1	41.5	35.7
FRG	26.5	15.2	13.3	16.6	11.1	9.0	8.5	12.6	18.7	14.1
Finland	21.0	20.9	21.9	23.9	21.4	33.3	30.9	34.0	36.2	26.9
France	25.7	46.3	51.0	54.2	46.6	43.6	51.1	44.8	53.9	44.3
Greece	100.0	90.0	82.8	86.4	–	76.9	62.6	39.7	46.2	74.2
Ireland	85.8	85.3	83.2	83.4	83.8	85.2	87.0	87.3	87.2	85.6
Italy	18.5	19.5	15.5	16.1	15.0	16.2	13.6	18.9	17.4	16.6
Netherlands	8.6	10.1	11.6	14.0	22.5	26.5	25.8	29.9	24.9	19.7
Norway	31.7	28.6	28.8	28.9	30.4	30.2	32.1	41.5	39.6	32.8
Portugal	–	–	–	–	–	–	30.1	25.3	54.2	35.6
Spain	–	–	–	–	–	–	48.5	40.7	39.8	43.4
Sweden	35.2	39.9	39.3	33.2	29.1	24.9	29.4	31.4	37.2	33.0
Switzerland	34.5	35.2	34.3	34.8	38.9	40.4	37.8	39.9	46.0	37.6
UK	50.8	51.9	54.1	54.8	50.6	55.8	59.1	57.2	55.6	54.4
Average	29.0	41.6	36.6	40.7	33.9	35.2	33.3	39.4	42.3	36.9

Eta-squared by country = .88
Eta-squared by time = .04
Note: The non-structural party index measures the strength of conservative and liberal parties in a party system.

as in the United Kingdom, Ireland, Greece and France whereas in Finland, Norway and Denmark their combined strength is rather low when compared with countries like Switzerland, Austria, the FRG, Belgium and the Netherlands.

Another orientation index shows the overall distribution between structural parties and non-structural ones (Table 5.8). In some party systems political parties that appeal to the voters less in terms of a specific social group profile have a strong position: France, Greece, Ireland, and the UK, whereas in other party systems these kinds of ideologically orientated parties have little footing: Austria, Belgium, the Federal Republic of Germany, Italy and the Netherlands.

This orientation index captures a variation between two kinds of non-socialist alignments: either the voters support traditionally bourgeois parties – conservative or liberal – or they support parties with an orientation towards certain social groups – ethnic, religious parties. The index reveals significant variations in the way the non-leftist vote is distributed between these two blocs. In some nations the traditional bourgeois parties – the conservatives or the liberals – are strong: Greece, France, the UK, and the Nordic countries. Some national party systems are dominated by

Table 5.9   *Volatility*

	1945 –49	1950 –54	1955 –59	1960 –64	1965 –69	1970 –74	1975 –79	1980 –84	1985 –89	Average
Austria	17.1	3.6	4.3	1.7	6.2	4.3	0.9	4.7	6.3	5.8
Belgium	14.9	8.6	4.9	5.3	12.1	7.5	6.7	16.2	8.7	9.5
Denmark	16.6	6.1	3.8	7.1	10.7	19.4	16.2	11.6	7.6	11.4
FRG	64.2	21.2	9.2	14.3	7.1	6.0	3.9	6.5	5.9	13.8
Finland	15.9	3.4	6.4	5.9	8.4	9.4	7.3	10.5	11.1	8.8
France	16.2	21.6	22.6	20.9	7.9	7.7	7.8	13.5	10.5	14.4
Greece	41.3	32.8	10.9	11.7	–	34.7	2.6	27.2	5.7	19.9
Ireland	14.0	10.7	11.2	9.4	6.1	3.3	6.7	5.2	11.7	8.4
Italy	24.3	12.8	7.7	8.4	5.4	6.3	7.5	8.6	9.1	11.1
Netherlands	11.9	6.3	6.4	5.0	10.8	13.0	12.7	9.1	7.7	9.3
Norway	12.6	3.5	2.4	3.5	6.2	19.3	14.5	11.0	9.7	9.3
Portugal	–	–	–	–	–	–	10.4	7.3	22.2	13.3
Spain	–	–	–	–	–	–	7.7	39.0	10.6	17.0
Sweden	9.8	3.8	5.3	3.3	5.6	7.8	4.8	7.9	7.9	6.1
Switzerland	8.8	4.0	1.9	1.6	6.0	7.4	5.5	6.6	7.7	5.2
UK	13.3	7.1	2.7	6.0	4.3	8.0	8.5	12.1	3.9	7.0
Average	18.5	11.5	7.3	7.6	7.7	10.5	8.7	11.0	9.4	10.4

Eta-squared by country = .21
Eta-squared by time = .15
Note: Volatility has been measured by means of the Pedersen volatility index.

the existence of ethnic or religious parties: Austria, Belgium, Italy, the Federal Republic of Germany, and the Netherlands.

Volatility

The maximum and minimum values of volatility are theoretically 100 and 0, respectively. During all the intervals of time we observe the occurrence of net changes in voter support for political parties, but European party systems can hardly be characterized as extremely volatile, as the average value of the index ranges from about 5 to roughly 20. However, there is an interesting variation over time. The Second World War broke normal ways of party functioning, which had the result that the electorate immediately after the war faced some difficult choices like how to realign itself towards old and new parties. Consequently the period 1945–9 has the highest degree of volatility. The 1950s give the impression of firm voter alignments, whereas we observe a clear increase in volatility since 1970. The data indicate that the level of volatility is still high in the 1980s but not that it is still increasing (Table 5.9).

Countries with a high average volatility score include the new democracies in Greece, Spain and Portugal but also France and Denmark. The high average score for the FRG depends very much on the major changes in the 1949 election. The set of nations with a low degree of volatility includes Austria, Sweden, Switzerland, and the United Kingdom.

Party system stability?

A fundamental problem in the study of West European party systems pertains to the extent to which the party systems are characterized by change or stability. Whereas it used to be argued that the West European party systems were frozen in terms of a definitive shape – the Lipset and Rokkan hypothesis – it is now stated that the national party systems have become much more unstable (Pedersen, 1979: 24; Borre, 1980: 162–3; Maguire, 1983; Shamir, 1984; Lawson and Merkl, 1988; Mair and Smith, 1989). The seminal trend towards a higher average score on the volatility index from about 7.5 per cent in the late 1960s to 11 per cent in the early 1980s supports the hypothesis that instability is much more characteristic of West European political parties than what the frozen party system hypothesis implies.

The party system of Belgium has experienced a profound reorganization since 1945; the fractionalization increased while the radical orientation and the polarization decreased, indicating the rise of ethnic alignments as a dominant characteristic of the party system. In the Federal Republic of Germany, the extent of radical orientation increased, whereas the support for traditional bourgeois parties diminished, at the same time as the general level of fractionalization has declined. The movement of the German party system towards a large socialist party and a large religious party besides a small liberal party means a very different kind of party system compared with the remnants of the party systems of the Weimar Republic and the Third Reich still operating in the late 1940s. The change in the Italian case stems largely from the expansion in the electoral support for firstly the Communist Party and then for the Socialist Party, as the scores on both radical orientation and polarization display a positive trend. At the same time the level of volatility declined; it seems as if the electorate became more firmly organized along the left–right dimension. In Denmark we find a significant increase in fractionalization, which is not difficult to interpret. The Glistrup phenomenon has attracted traditionally bourgeois voters at the same time as other new parties were founded.

Concerning the data on the French system, the differences between the Fourth and the Fifth Republic may be noted; the amount of support for traditionally bourgeois parties rose indicating the coming of the Gaullist phenomenon, and the level of polarization increased, because of the rise of the Socialist Party at the expense of centre and left-wing extreme parties. Party-system change in Finland is a function of the increased fractionalization of the party system which results from the rise in electoral support for a number of discontent parties (Vennamo's SMP) belonging to the right wing. In Greece, the party system experienced a decline in the support for traditionally bourgeois parties because the centre union fell apart after the end of the dictatorship, while the amount of radical orientation increased due to the rise of the PASOK. There are actually two different types of party systems in Greece: before the dictatorship the centre of gravity focussed upon the competition between two non-socialist and non-structural parties, the conservatives and the liberals, and after the dictatorship the centre of gravity is the left–right dimension.

In the British party system we find the re-entrance of the Liberal Party as well as the degree of radical orientation declining due to reduction in the electoral support for the Labour Party. The decline of Labour and the introduction of the Liberal-SDP Alliance also meant less of polarization. In the Netherlands, the trend after 1945 is that the Liberal Party increased at the expense of the religious parties. The degree of fractionalization diminished in Ireland, and this measure captures the tendency towards a three-party system in Ireland. In some countries the party systems have become generally more unstable in terms of fractionalization: Belgium, Denmark, West Germany and the Netherlands. Some national party systems do fluctuate in fractionalization over time meaning that new parties are formed or old parties die: Denmark, France, Italy and Greece. There is a fluctuation in the combined strength of traditional bourgeois parties from one election to another in Belgium, France, the Netherlands, and Italy. The extent of polarization varies little from election to election in all party systems with the exception of Germany, Greece, France, Italy and Belgium. The share of the vote for leftist parties varies extensively in Greece and Ireland, whereas there is little fluctuation in radical orientation in countries like Austria, Finland, Switzerland and Sweden.

Conclusion

The party systems of European democracies are different. To account for the differences, one needs more dimensions than the typical one-dimensional models. Thus, we cover fractionalization (the variation in the number and strength of the constituent parts of the party system), polarization (the variation in the ideological distance between the political parties along the right–left scale), radical orientation (the variation in the strength of leftist parties), structural orientation (the variation between class-based parties, traditional bourgeois parties and religious, ethnic and agrarian parties) and volatility (the variation in net mobility between political parties). A party system is a system of elements with relationships. We have identified some party system properties, of which some refer to the elements of party systems, whereas the others refer to relationships (fractionalization, polarization and volatility).

The findings indicate that the widely accepted hypothesis that West European party systems are characterized by stability is not in accordance with the data. Actually, several of the party systems studied have changed since 1945. The Lipset and Rokkan party system stability hypothesis must be qualified, if not rejected. The party systems of the following countries must be described as unstable: Denmark, France, Greece, Portugal and Spain. We have dealt extensively with the political parties in Western Europe and their relationships to social cleavages. Moreover, we have analysed the various national party systems at length. It is time to move to the next level of analysis, the government level.

6

Decision-Making Institutions: Autonomy

Introduction

Government institutions afford mechanisms for the making of collective choice. These mechanisms constitute intervening variables between the structure of society and the decisions and actions of political élites. If political stability is not simply a reflection of the cleavage structure in society or the way the electorate aligns itself behind the various parties in the system, then we must investigate the extent to which mechanisms for conflict resolution are conducive to political stability. In Chapters 6 and 7 we analyse political institutions for social choice. The public organization of society may be analysed along two fundamental axes: autonomy and influence.

Collective action in the form of public policy is considered appropriate in some spheres of action but not in others. Fundamental to a democratic regime is a set of individual liberties, which defines the autonomy of the citizen. These liberties may be negative, stating where collective action is not appropriate in delimiting public decision-making. They may also be positive, opening up new areas of individual action as a result of public intervention. Individual autonomy is a basic aspect of the political systems in Western Europe, the various expressions of which are analysed herein. Besides individual autonomy there is institutional autonomy or the extent to which organizations – private or public – decide about the conditions of their activities. In this chapter let us also look at the distribution of decision-making competence between levels of government in the political body. The idea of a political system implies that autonomy can not be complete, i.e. the state of nature in which no government exists is not a political predicament. The exercise of authority in political systems means that the opposite of autonomy, heteronomy, comes into existence as Harry Eckstein and Ted R. Gurr show in their *Patterns of Authority* (1975). For various reasons collective action becomes a necessity or an opportunity and the scope of individual or private action becomes restricted through the operations of government. There is no magic size of the public as the post-war development of the welfare societies has witnessed.

Collective action in the form of exercise of public authority or as channelled into public-resource allocation does not imply autarchy or authoritarian rule ipso facto. Heteronomy, or 'the making of decisions of governments concerning private individuals and institutions', may be complemented by influence on the part of those governed over government. Typically, political systems define and institutionalize articulate mechanisms for the exercise of influence. These mechanisms include procedures for the election of candidates, the making of choices in real decision-making assemblies and the interpretation of relations among branches of public power: executive, legislative and judicial powers. In Chapter 7 we survey the variation in democratic procedures for the arrival at collective choice in the nations of Western Europe. Here we deal with autonomy.

The political system patterns choice situations and institutionalizes mechanisms for the implementation of the decisions of political bodies. Predictable structures for the making of political decisions are of fundamental importance to political systems, which is reflected in the attempt to solidify mechanisms of public choice by means of a constitution. By the concept of a constitution we refer to the legitimate principles for political decision-making. It is necessary to make a distinction between constitutions in operation and obsolete constitutions. Our analysis of the decision-making mechanisms in the European democracies covers constitutions in operation, following an emphasis on the importance of norms whether written or unwritten for the structuring of political authority (Weber, 1947).

The survey of individual autonomy in Western Europe is based on a few conceptual distinctions. We distinguish between individual and institutional autonomy, focussing first on the legal protection of citizen rights in a constitutional setting. Secondly, as we move to institutional autonomy a distinction between territorial and functional autonomy is suggested. The first feature of institutional autonomy deals with the extent to which public authority is decentralized in space, whereas the second refers to how public authority is exercised over various social functions or areas of activity. We note the occurrence of home rule in particular. The survey of institutional autonomy includes an analysis of the general structure of public authority in the European democracies, including the division of power among levels of government: national, regional and local.

Individual autonomy as constitutional rights

The relationship between the individual and the state is ambiguous in the modern welfare state. One aspect of the role of the individual as citizen in a nation state in Western Europe is the contribution of government to social welfare and individual freedom. The expansion of the public sector since the Second World War has meant that governments at various levels fund and operate programmes that – at least in theory – are supposed to be conducive to an increase in the opportunities for individual action, or what is often referred to as positive liberty.

However, a traditionally salient aspect of the interaction between the individual and the state is the amount of negative liberty that the citizen is able to secure by various legal instruments such as a constitution, the law or custom. A basic trait of the European democracies is the institutionalization of a set of fundamental citizen rights. Perhaps the expansion of the public sector has had the result that most attention on the state–citizen relationship has been diverted towards questions concerning the impacts of taxation and public expenditure. Yet, there has been a sustained and growing interest in defining the state–citizen relationship more clearly in negative terms, i.e. to specify norms that state what governments may not do and to devise mechanisms that guarantee that such rules of conduct are upheld. Citizens are not only interested in what governments may do for them but also deeply concerned with the protection of certain individual rights against infringement from other actors, collectivities or the state. According to traditional democratic theory the state derives much of its legitimacy from its capacity to protect the citizen from attempts to curtail his/her capacity to act in certain areas. The guarantee of such citizen rights also binds the state.

Which are these crucial citizen rights that states promise to protect by means of constitutions? Perhaps the most important individual rights specify various features of the freedom of thought. In a minimal sense the individual wants freedom of conscience, the right to a system of beliefs and values to which the individual adheres of his/her own free will. In a liberty state all citizens have freedom of religion, ideology and science. Individuals are not to be oppressed or harassed because of their beliefs or values. The liberty of the mind is the essence of freedom of thought, but it has to be supplemented by other fundamental individual liberties which make freedom of the mind a reality. Thus, a vital extension of the principle of freedom of thought is the set of rights that constitutes freedom of speech.

Of what value is freedom of mind if there is no guarantee that the citizen is allowed to declare openly what he/she believes or values? Freedom of mind is only a necessary condition for the freedom of thought but it is not sufficient. The citizen also wishes to have clearly defined and secure avenues that permit the public expression of his/her beliefs and values. The state must guarantee that nobody can be prosecuted or jailed because of what he/she states openly. The step to another set of rights contained in the idea of freedom of thought – freedom of the press – is a small one. The borderline between those liberties which define the principle of freedom of the press and those liberties which are part of the concept of political freedom is not a sharp one, as the right to vote to elect representatives and to participate in referendums may be interpreted as extensions of freedom of speech and freedom of the press. The fundamental individual rights contained in the concept of political liberty define the borders of the autonomy of the individual at the same time as they provide a mechanism for the exercise of influence over the state. In essence, the rights to vote, to representation and to participation are at the cross-roads between the two dimensions of public decision-making systems identified: autonomy and influence.

Another important set of rights defines the freedom of the individual to act collectively. To the libertarian state it is not enough to guarantee that the state itself or other collectivities will not prevent the individual from forming or expressing the thought and values to which he/she adheres. The concept of the citizen implies that the individual has certain rights to interact with other fellow citizens. The rights of association include a number of different individual rights from the right to participate in meetings, strikes, and demonstrations to the socially more powerful rights to form organizations and participate in political party action or trade-union activities.

The freedoms of thought and of association broadly defined as sets of clearly specified individual rights are uncontroversial in a constitutional perspective on the modern state. The liberty state is said also to institutionalize the freedoms of property and contract, the interpretation of which has been a contested matter. This is not the place to engage in a lengthy discussion about what the concept of personal freedom really implies in economic life. Suffice it to note that some constitutions include the rights to own and dispose of property as well as to form and dissolve contracts as basic individual rights. When property rights are questioned then it is argued that these rights are not in consonance with the principle of equality. Equality as a source of social rights and duties has been the target of much conflict. One is reminded of the serious contention about the interpretation of equality as the right to equal opportunities or as a right to equal outcomes. The state may take a more neutral route stating that it will protect the principle of equality of treatment or equity. Before the law it is argued each individual is to be treated equally, but there is no assurance that this implies either equal opportunities or, even less, equal outcomes. However, the principle of equal treatment before the law is a socially important mechanism for the protection of various minorities.

In his *Rights and Liberties in the World Today: Constitutional Promise and Reality* (1973) I.D. Duchacek presents an overview of constitutional rights in the present-day world. He separates six categories of rights and liberties which may be related to the concepts introduced above. These categories include: (1) Guarantees of personal liberty, right to privacy, freedom of thought, right to equality, and minority and women's rights;

(2) Right to social progress and happiness; (3) Right to impartial justice; (4) Freedom of expression and right to be informed; (5) Right of access to decision-making through the intermediary of political parties and universal suffrage; (6) Right to formulate specific group demands and form interest groups for this purpose (Duchacek, 1973: 40–2).

Some of these rights and liberties refer to negative freedom whereas others deal with positive freedom; some liberties specify individual autonomy whereas other liberties define mechanisms of influence. It is one thing to specify constitutionally what the state cannot do with regard to the citizen; it is another matter to require that the state legally commit itself to activities that will enhance the freedom of the individual. Our survey of the existing systems of individual rights and liberties focusses primarily upon what the various constitutions of the West European nations say about negative freedom, though we will also note a commitment towards positive freedom. As data source we employ besides various country studies, *Constitutions of the Countries of the World* edited by Albert Blaustein and Gisbert Flanz.

Comparative Perspective

Characteristic of the West European political systems is the strong institutionalization of a set of principles that regulates the relation between the citizens and the state. Although the idea of a body of natural principles concerning freedom of thought and speech and legitimate entitlement to a decent life is given an expression in all present West European democracies there are variations that must be pointed out. The status of individual autonomy in a country reflects the kind of political regime that it houses. The institutionalization of individual autonomy cannot be taken for granted in Western Europe, particularly in those countries where authoritarian regimes have been in power in this century. Regime transition is one thing and regime consolidation another as underlined in *Securing Democracy: Political Parties and Democratic Consolidation in Southern Europe* (Pridham, 1990).

Nations differ as to codification or the extent to which such principles have been entered into written constitutions. Some countries, like West Germany, Italy, Portugal and Spain, pay considerable attention to the problem of identifying a set of constitutional liberties and rights, codified in logically structured formalism. Other nations, like the United Kingdom and France, take a different approach, the first lacking a written constitution and the second resting content with its famous *Declaration of the Rights of Man and Citizen* from 1789. In between stand nations where there is some mention of citizen rights and natural law liberties, the more so the younger the constitution. The search for constitutional safeguards of these liberties was particularly strong after the Second World War, when the United Nations Universal Declaration of Human Rights from

1948 inspired various attempts at constitutional protection.

Let us compare Norway and the Netherlands with the new constitution of Portugal. The 1814 Norwegian constitution expressed the established principles of constitutionalism at that time safeguarding the principles of division of power and equality under the law. As may be expected there is little about human rights in the Norwegian constitution. One paragraph (100) upholds the liberty of the press and the freedom of conscience and speech, as the constitution of Norway deals mainly with the regulation of powers. The constitution of the Kingdom of the Netherlands valid up until 1982 contained no special section on human rights. Citizen rights were regulated here and there in this constitution which was the outcome of decades of constitutional developments and revision since 1815. The first chapter of the constitution introduced equality under the law, freedom of thought, freedom of the press and the right of association, but the wording was short and unambiguous. In other places there were guarantees of the principle of personal liberty and due legal process (articles 163–80) and the principle of religious freedom is specified in a separate section (articles 181–7). In 1983 when there was a complete overhaul of the constitution, a lengthy list of social rights was added to it.

Modern constitutional theory emphasizes the importance of establishing human rights in a special legal form. This trend towards a codification of general principles governing the individual and the state appears in the new constitutions from the 1970s. Not only is the drive towards a constitutional recognition of human rights typical of post-Second World War developments. Equally important is the broadening of the scope of human rights to comprise not only the typical negative freedoms but also a number of positive freedoms obligating the state to do certain things and not just refrain from doing other things. The transition to democracy in Portugal was given a strong constitutional expression, partly under the influence of the marxist orientated Armed Forces Movement.

The Portuguese constitution from 1976 and revised in 1982 is a massive set of principles comprising some three hundred articles. Part 1 deals with Fundamental Rights and Duties – roughly seventy articles – and here we encounter a radical interpretation of the idea of a constitutional recognition of a catalogue of human rights. The constitution of Portugal interpreting citizen rights is very much orientated towards positive liberties. However, we also find a large set of detailed rules directed towards the concept of negative freedom: the principle of equality, the right to life, to personal integrity and to freedom and security, to identity, a good name and privacy. There are the traditional legal principles including an article 31 called 'Habeas Corpus'.

The development of Swedish constitutional theory and practice corroborates the preceding argument that there is a growing interest in the constitutional codification of a set of basic rights and liberties of the individual citizen. This is not to say that the constitutions of the nineteenth century completely neglected citizen rights. In the 1809 Swedish constitution there was the famous paragraph 16 which codified a tradition of citizen rights dating back to the Middle Ages. The King's Oath used to contain a statement of an obligation to protect a set of citizen rights – a statement that was transformed into constitutional documents. When the Swedish government began to work on a new constitution after the Second World War it was considered appropriate to emphasize a set of Fundamental Freedoms and Rights. Thus, Chapter 2 in the 1974 constitution states that every citizen shall be guaranteed a minimum set of personal liberties, which are mainly of the negative kind. The constitution guarantees the freedom of expression, of the press, of communication, of association, of religion, and of movement; moreover, the constitution also presents each citizen with the right to information, to demonstration, and to strike. It has been discussed to introduce into the constitution a concept of positive rights. Into such a catalogue would enter basic principles of public policy in the Swedish welfare state. On the other hand there is the counter-argument that the specification of such liberties is more political symbolism than real commitment that may be tried in court.

The drive for a legalistic definition of citizen autonomy so typical of post-war events is not only orientated towards the traditional negative freedoms but much influenced by the welfare state ideology that liberty also requires that the state assume responsibility for full employment, the protection of the elderly as well as for citizen health and education. Generally, in Western Europe the younger the constitution is the more the concept of positive freedom is underlined. Look at the difference between the constitutions of Austria and Belgium and that of Spain.

General rights of the citizens of the Austrian state are outlined in the so-called Basic Law of the State, which dates back to 1867 though it has been amended a few times. The Basic Law consists of eighteen articles that specify the rights of individual action and the boundaries of collective action. The sphere of the freedom of the citizen to act individually is specified through the enumeration of many liberties, including: freedom of movement, the right to use his/her property inside the state, freedom of residence and domicile, protection of the home, secrecy of the mail, secrecy of long-distance communications, freedom of creed and conscience, freedom of religious practice and freedom to choose vocation.

The constitutional framework in Belgium is the outcome of changes over the years in the 1831 constitution. The Belgian constitution comprises a special section (Heading II) devoted to 'the Belgians and their rights', consisting of twenty articles which regulate the scope for individual action. Firstly, the constitution defines who is a Belgian, that every

Belgian is to be treated equally under the law, and that discrimination is prohibited. Secondly, a few articles define individual liberty as protection against illegal prosecution and unlawful detention. Thirdly, we have the typical negative liberties: the home is inviolable, property is guaranteed, freedom of worship and freedom of manifest personal opinions in every way, religious freedom, freedom of the press, the right to hold peaceful, unarmed meetings, the right to associate and to address petitions, secrecy of letters.

The Spanish constitution, enacted by means of a referendum in 1978, is very much a reaction against the Franco regime. Roughly one third of its articles deal with the rights of the Spanish citizen versus the state, both negatively and positively. The concept of negative freedom is specified in a number of Basic Rights and Duties where we find various individual rights. However, the concept of positive freedom is given much attention in a set of rights included under 'The Guiding Principles of Economic and Social Policy'. Actually, the specification of the positive freedoms is almost as large as that in the constitution of Portugal, but the tone is different. A number of goals of public policy are introduced as if politics could be reduced to the calculation of the best means available to the achievement of objectives, for example protection of the family, the children and the workers abroad, social security, health protection as well as the protection of the environment, access to culture, the right to enjoy decent and adequate housing, to promote the free and effective participation by the young in political, social, economic and cultural development, to implement a policy of prevention, treatment, rehabilitation and integration of the physically, sensorily and mentally handicapped, to defend and foster the consumers and users, to promote the enrichment of the historical, cultural and artistic patrimony of the peoples of Spain.

The strength of the concept of negative liberties is that it has clear action implications, confining the state to respect identifiable expressions of individual action. These rules can be upheld by the courts institutionalizing a number of specific rights. The concept of positive freedom on the other hand has a different status in a practical perspective. Theoretically, lists of positive freedoms may be impressive, but in reality they live a shadow life. It could be pointed out that the framers of the Spanish constitution were well aware of this fact, apparently. Negative freedom rights have a special protection in that the constitution states that they are binding on all public authorities as well as protected by an action with the Constitutional Court – 'recurso de amparo' – which to date, not surprisingly, has been resorted to extensively. There is no such protection as regards positive freedom rights which will be difficult to secure in Spain, especially considering economic conditions, political tradition and bureaucratic inertia and resistance to change. Nevertheless,

Article 53: 3 of the Constitution – the Article securing negative freedom rights being Article 53: 1 – states:

> Recognition, respect and protection of the principles recognized in the Third Chapter shall guide positive legislation, judicial practice and the actions by public authorities. They may also be argued before ordinary jurisdiction through procedures established in the laws affecting them.

Nations differ in the extent that institutional practice corresponds to legal formalism. It is undoubtedly telling that the United Kingdom with its long tradition of recognizing the concept of negative freedom both in legal and political theory traditions has not engaged at all in any constitutional codification efforts, whereas the constitution of Portugal hardly accepts any limits to the possibility of legally identifying liberties of various kinds. The idea of citizen rights is more entrenched in the United Kingdom than in Portugal, Spain, and Greece, where democracy has been fragile for most of the century. This is not to say that the formal recognition of individual autonomy is without political significance. The principles of freedom of mind, rights of property and entitlements are taken for granted in some of these nations simply because they have entered these political systems for a long time. Or, these principles appear as highly visible in other nations because the institutionalization of the idea of basic citizen rights has been a controversial aspect of their political life during the twentieth century. Look at the constitutional development of the Federal Republic of Germany, Italy, and Greece.

The German constitution dates back to the establishment of the German Federal Republic in 1949. The first section of the Basic Law deals with so-called basic rights. In the words of Gisbert Flanz: 'It represents a reaffirmation of essential human values and a rejection of the inhumanities of the National Socialist regime.' (Flanz, 1974: 74–5). The German version of a constitutional codification of individual rights is almost exclusively orientated towards the concept of negative liberty. Most articles approach basic human rights as freedom from the state. A few articles refer to what the state may demand from its citizens. Article 7 proclaims that the state has the right to supervise the entire educational system, Article 12a states a liability to military service and Article 15 admits the possibility of a transfer of private ownership to public ownership. The emphasis on the limits of state power predominates, and the first section of the first paragraph sets the tone: 'The dignity of man shall be inviolable. To respect and protect it shall be the duty of all state authority'. It is often stated that besides the use of the concept 'Sozialstaat' there is little mention in the constitution of the concept of positive freedom (Beyme, 1979: 24).

Similarly, we expect to find a strong commitment to human rights in the constitution of Italy enacted in 1947 following the fall of fascism. Article 2 of the Basic Principles of the constitution states:

The Republic recognizes and guarantees the inviolable rights of man, both as an individual and as a member of the social groups in which his personality finds expression, and imposes the performance of unalterable duties of a political, economic and social nature.

Part one of the constitution – Rights and Duties of Private Citizens – substantiates this commitment in no less than forty-one articles. The Italian version of a human rights catalogue not only is comprehensive but contains a number of policy promises by the state to its citizens. We learn that the Republic has extensive obligations to the family, the children, the sick, the unemployed, the disabled. It appears that the Italian state has constitutionalized several elements of the basic principles of the welfare state. The constitution provides for personal liberty, freedom of thought, religious liberty, fair judicial process, freedom to associate and organize as well as equality under the law. Yet, the most interesting aspect of the Italian constitution is the strong orientation towards a concept of positive individual freedom.

In 1975 the Greek constitution now in force was introduced after the breakdown of the Junta regime. The constitution of Greece contains a large number of articles related to individual and social rights, twenty-one articles divided into two or more subheadings. The Greek version of a catalogue of human rights is mainly orientated towards the concept of negative freedom; its purpose is to bind the state and prohibit encroachments on what is referred to as 'the fundamental and inalienable rights of man'. Article 2 directs the constitution towards the protection of citizen rights stating that 'respect and protection of the value of the human being constitutes the primary obligation of the State'.

A source of variation is the extent to which there exist legal institutions which may be employed for the protection of citizen rights. Typically, no West European nation allows for the possibility of taking the state to court for alleged violation of positive liberties and few give the negative freedoms absolute precedence over state law to be tried in a constitutional court. Look at constitutional practice in Denmark and Finland.

Part 8 in the Danish constitution from 1953 deals with individual rights, most of which delimit what the state may do to the individual in its authority. Most interestingly, the Danish constitution includes an article no. 75 that states that the citizen has a right to expect positive action on the part of the government: 'to advance public welfare effort should be made to afford work to every able-bodied citizen on terms that will secure his existence'. Theoretically, not only is the Danish state committed to one of the chief goals of the welfare state – full employment – as a result of the particular power constellations prevailing in the Folketing but Danish citizens could appeal to a constitutional duty if he/she senses that the government is not doing enough to combat unemployment. In some political systems the government may be prosecuted and tried in court if a citizen is of the opinion that the government does not obey the constitution. In Denmark there is no such constitutional court; consequently, this positive liberty is only a statement of principle.

Chapter 2 in the Finnish constitution refers to equality before the law, the freedom of thought and its various modes and the guarantee of due legal process. Actually, the 1919 Finnish version of the basic human rights catalogue is fairly conventional, besides the obligation of the state to find employment opportunities for every Finnish citizen. A constitutional amendment in 1972 inserted citizen rights that may be employed to raise demands on the state. The Finnish political system does not, however, provide a device for the legal enforcement of such positive liberties.

It is readily seen that the old Swiss constitution from 1874 is mostly concerned with regulating the powers of the confederation to the cantons. The idea of citizen rights is by no means non-existent in the constitution, but it does not play the major role. Interestingly as we move to a draft of a new constitution of Switzerland things become different, although the draft was never finally accepted. It is no exaggeration to state that the idea of a constitutional regulation of the relationship between citizens and state from both negative and positive aspects looms largely in this draft. We find a number of fundamental rights as well as principles of social, economic and cultural policy. These new constitutional aims are specified in a set of negative rights and a set of policy principles, but it is also clear that the latter are different as the implementation of the policy principles cannot be tried in court although there is a constitutional court in the Swiss political system. When revising constitutions most governments are not content with a catalogue of rights, which inform citizens how much individual action they may expect to take without being hindered by another person or the state. It is considered important to express constitutionally the policy ambitions of the state in objectives that call for state action for their effective implementation, yet are without legal implications.

Summing up

After this overview of ways of institutionalizing individual autonomy we try to capture some of the variation by some overall measure. One type of individual autonomy index may be calculated on the basis of various indicators of the position of the individual citizen during the 1970s: the political rights index measures the right to play a part in determining who governs; the civil rights index summarizes the rights of the individual vis-à-vis the states (Gastil, 1979); the political discrimination index states the exclusion of a social group from the opportunity to participate in political activities or to obtain élite positions; the economic discrimination

Table 6.1   *Individual autonomy for the 1970s*

	Political rights index	Civil rights index	Political and economic discrimination	Human rights index	Individual autonomy rescaled
Austria	1.00	1.00	1	1.4	8.15
Belgium	1.00	1.00	0	1.4	9.15
Denmark	1.00	1.00	0	1.0	9.55
FRG	1.00	1.25	1	1.5	7.80
Finland	1.25	1.25	0	1.0	9.05
France	1.00	1.50	1	1.8	7.25
Greece	2.00	2.00	0	2.6	5.95
Ireland	1.00	1.25	0	2.0	8.30
Italy	1.75	1.50	0	1.8	7.50
Netherlands	1.00	1.00	1	1.4	8.15
Norway	1.00	1.00	0	1.3	9.25
Portugal	2.75	2.25	0	2.0	5.55
Spain	3.50	3.25	0	2.8	3.00
Sweden	1.00	1.00	0	1.2	9.35
Switzerland	1.00	1.00	1	1.4	8.15
UK	1.00	1.00	1	1.1	8.45

Note: The various index scores where a higher value means less political rights, civil rights or human rights and more discrimination have been added and transformed into an overall individual autonomy index by rescaling scores so that low values indicates a low degree of autonomy and high values a high degree of autonomy.

index summarizes the exclusion of a social group from desired economic goods or conditions because of the group's ascribed characteristics.

Data for the various country rankings are available for the 1970s in *World Handbook of Political and Social Indicators* (3rd ed., edited by Jodice and Taylor, 1981). We also include a human rights index that captures the prevalence of human rights (Humana, 1983). To compare the extent of individual autonomy across European democracies we have calculated an autonomy index comprising an average of the civil rights scores 1976–9, an average of the political rights scores 1976–9, a political and economic discrimination score for 1975 (0–1) and the human rights index. In Table 6.1 we adjust the scores in these standard indices somewhat. Thus, the low scores for Finland on the political rights and civil rights indices have been modified. Furthermore, the summary index is rescaled so that high values indicate a high degree of individual autonomy and low values indicate a low degree of individual autonomy.

The first autonomy index appears to identify a variation in individual autonomy that is not large but yet significant. As expected Spain, Portugal and Greece score low reflecting the transition from authoritarian rule to fragile democratic institutions. However, even among the traditional democratic nations there are noticeable differences which the

Table 6.2   *Individual autonomy in Western Europe (some estimates)*

	Individual autonomy scores				
	1960	1965	1975	1980	1985
Austria	1	1	1	1	1
Belgium	1	1	1	1	1
Denmark	1	1	1	1	1
FRG	2	2	1	1.5	1.5
Finland	1	1	1	1	1
France	2	2	1.5	1.5	1.5
Greece	2	2.5	2	2	2
Ireland	1.5	1	1.5	1	1
Italy	1	1	1.5	2	1
Netherlands	1	1	1	1	1
Norway	1	1	1	1	1
Portugal	6	6	4	2	1.5
Spain	7	7	5	2	1.5
Sweden	1	1	1	1	1
Switzerland	1	1	1	1	1
UK	1	1	1	1	1

Note: These estimates are our own but in general they follow Gastil (1987), Bollen (1980); the higher the score, the less of individual autonomy.

index captures. It comes as no surprise that Sweden, Denmark, Norway and Belgium display the highest scores reflecting a long tradition of institutionalization of individual rights.

In order to illuminate how individual autonomy has developed over time another overall measure may be employed. Country scores on human rights developed on the basis of data in Gastil (1987) and Bollen (1980) are presented in Table 6.2 in such a way that the higher the score the lower the degree of individual autonomy.

Not unexpectedly, several West European countries are characterized by a consistently large amount of individual autonomy: the Nordic countries, Belgium, the Netherlands, Austria, Switzerland and the United Kingdom. However, a few countries have scores that vary over time as these countries have sometimes taken measures that restrict the amount of individual autonomy: the Federal Republic of Germany, France, Ireland and Italy. The newly institutionalized democracies in southern Europe may be identified as a set on its own, as the transition to democracy involved a sharp increase in individual autonomy. The process of regime consolidation in the 1980s has meant that Portugal, Spain and Greece now display individual autonomy scores that are similar to the other West European countries.

Individual autonomy is an important aspect of political systems.

Although principles of fundamental individual rights identifying a sphere of individual freedom guide the public bodies as to what they may or may not do, any description of decision-making systems in the public sector must also pay attention to institutional autonomy.

Institutional autonomy and decentralization

The modern state has formalized the exercise of political authority (Friedrich, 1963; MacIver, 1947). Its institutionalization means that the political system is governed by a system of rules or norms which specify principles for structural diversification and functional specification. The modern state operates on the basis of organizational behaviour; public authority is exercised by organizations in action making and implementing decisions, setting goals, and evaluating outcomes. However important the individual participants – parliamentarians, political leaders, government officials, bureaucrats, and judges – are to the political process, the fabric of the political system consists of a web of organizations that make and implement governmental decisions.

Public authority is exercised by various kinds of government, the structural and functional division between which is of crucial importance for public operations. Public authority is structured hierarchically between different levels of government on a territorial dimension as national policy makers exercise authority over implementers within some region or locality of the nation. We must recognize that the exercise of such powers may be more or less hierarchical implying either a unitary or a federal state. Federalism may be real or only symbolic. Decisive is the extent to which there is some correspondance between the formal constitutional provisions for power sharing between the federal or central government on the one hand and the regional or state governments on the other hand. There is always the risk that the long-term development of the political life of a country brings about a different real-life division of powers between the centre and the regions than the one formally conceived of in the written constitutional documents. Most often such a divergence works in favour of centralization.

Modern democracies are not only structured from the top downwards in a system of superordination–subordination of state institutions and state officials; the democracies of Western Europe grow from the existence of government structured from bottom upwards as all of them have some system of local government. And systems of local government may differ in terms of the extent to which decision-making discretion is granted the local governments, as emphasized by Edward Page and Michael Goldsmith in *Central and Local Government Relations* (1987). Thus, for each country we must inquire into the extent of regional or local government autonomy. Also federal political systems comprise sub-national levels of government referred to as provinces or communes besides their regional governments (see Appendix 6.1).

Institutional autonomy not only covers the amount of decentralization of the state apparatus in federal political systems or the amount of local government autonomy in unitary political systems but institutional autonomy may take on a special territorial aspect, the granting of self-government to particular regions within a nation (home rule) due to ethnic or cultural reasons. What is decisive for the overall structure of the political system – its degree of centralization or decentralization – is the territorial aspect of country politics which locates public decision and implementation functions at various levels of government (Rhodes and Wright, 1987). Moreover, institutional autonomy has another important mode: functional autonomy.

Political authority may be divided between various levels of government on the basis of territorial criteria and autonomy may be granted various organizations in different fields of activities. In some countries religious organizations have their own system of education and in others ethnic groupings or class-based organizations carry on functions that in other countries are under public authority. Besides the territorial dimension of institutional autonomy or the extent to which various regions or localities may exercise decision-making over their own lives, we must pay attention to the status of functional organizations operating all over a country in relation to the state.

It should be emphasized that the distinction between the two modes of territorial autonomy – decentralization within a unitary state and the extent of federalism in political systems comprising states – is a technical one in legal terminology. In reality the similarities must be underlined as the demand for territorial autonomy may be the same but take on different expressions due to the legal framework of the nation. Institutional autonomy is not greater in a federal state than in a unitary state simply because the first is labelled 'federal' and the second 'unitary'. What matters is the distribution of public authority between different levels of government; conceivably extensive decentralization of a unitary state may result in more territorial autonomy than it would in a federal system heavily dominated by the federal government.

Institutional autonomy may be described as having four modes: federalism, home rule, decentralization within a unitary state as well as functional autonomy. In *Decentralist Trends in Western Democracies* (1979), L.J. Sharpe also identifies the neighbourhood movement as a decentralist tendency. However, it is not dealt with here because the focus is on the basic constitutional principles of the political system.

The rising demand for territorial autonomy has constituted a threat to the principle of national unity entrenched in Europe since 1919. The demand for autonomy changed politics in Western Europe during the 1970s reducing political stability. Countries differ in the extent to which they face a demand for territorial autonomy of special regions; and they differ in the extent to which they have been prepared to supply home rule to some of their constituent parts. Our approach is to survey the trends in the demand for and supply of territorial autonomy at the same time as we describe our nations according to the dimension unitary state – federal state. The purpose is to present information that allows us to rank our sixteen cases according to the degree of institutional autonomy. Measures of institutional autonomy and its various modes – decentralization, federalism, special territorial autonomy (home rule) and functional autonomy – are ordinal, stating whether a nation has a high, medium or low degree of autonomy. Before we present the institutional autonomy index ranking the West European countries according to their score on the dimensions identified here, we describe the modes of institutional autonomy in Western Europe.

Federalism
Three sources of variation in the phenomenon of European federalism may be identified. Firstly, federalism may be a political reality or constitutional symbolism. Secondly, the federalist principles may be based on the distinction between legislation and implementation reserving the former to the federal powers and the latter to the various states. Thirdly, the power of the federal government may be on the increase or on the decrease. Let us exemplify these distinctions.

   The Austrian state has of tradition institutionalized federalism; the federal constitutional law from 1929 states as Article 2 that 'Austria is a federal state', but it is apparent that Austrian federalism is orientated more towards stating what the federal government may do than listing a number of restrictions on national government authority. According to the constitution the federal government has the authority to legislate and implement in the following matters:

> national elections and referendums, foreign affairs, immigration and emigration matters, federal finances and monetary policy, matters of civil law and criminal law like economic association, detention of criminals and protection of the press, maintenance of peace, order and safety, regulation of trade and markets, traffic matters including railroads, air travel and shipping, regulation of mining, forestry and water as well as electrical plants, certain matters of public health, as well as of science and culture, the federal police and the federal army, federal authorities, population policy (Article 10).

   The amount of autonomy of the Länder depends upon how these extensive powers are interpreted over time. Moreover, we must also take into account those functions in which legislation is federal business whereas execution or implementation belongs to the Länder such as housing, poverty matters and health policy, land reform, labour law, composition and organization of the Kollegien of the Länder, the compulsory public schools and of Kindergarten, administrative procedure and execution as well as representation in the typical Austrian chambers or corporations (Articles 11 and 12). However, one has to consider that constitutional provisions can become obsolete by legislation with a two-thirds majority. This is largely the case with the power of the Länder.

The constitution actually states little about what the Länder may do themselves in legislation and implementation; a country expert characterizes the Austrian state system as 'symbolic federalism' and he writes:

> Even if technically the Constitution provides that all matters not delegated to the federation shall be left to the provinces, in effect very few matters have been left to them. Almost all important political matters have in fact been delegated to the Federal Government (Gerlich, 1981: 214–15).

The German version of federalism is formally reminiscent of the Austrian framework as it is based on the distinction between legislation and implementation, but it is more real. The Basic Law provides the federation with extensive legislative powers. Article 70 contains the fundamental proviso that the power of the national government has to be specified in a positive sense, meaning that the Länder may legislate themselves in so far as they do not infringe upon the specific legislative powers provided by the federal government. There are three types of federal legislative powers: exclusive, concurrent and framework legislation.

The exclusive type of legislation contains the typical federal matters. The concurrent type of legislation concerns the remaining kinds of public activities where on the one hand the Länder may legislate to the extent that the federation does not do so. On the other the federation may legislate if a Länder legislation considerably affects other Länder or if Länder legislation is not efficient or if the maintenance of legal or economic unity, especially the maintenance of uniformity of living conditions beyond the territory of any one Land, necessitates such regulation. Moreover, the federation and the Länder may set up organizations for joint tasks and the implications of the principle of fiscal federalism in the Federal Republic have to be recognized. Given these extensive federal legislative prerogatives one may ask what the German version of federalism in effect amounts to. As Gordon Smith points out the emphasis is upon the Länder implementation of the federal laws (Smith, 1979b: 48–51; Smith, 1989). Article 83 in the Basic Law contains the key to German federalism: 'The Länder shall executive federal laws as matters of their own concern in so far as this Basic Law does not otherwise provide or permit'.

Moreover, Article 84 instructs the Länder to establish the 'requisite authorities' and provide for 'the regulation of administrative procedures' to implement the federal laws. The same article also states that the federal government may supervise the Länder implementation involving the right to take legal action against violations of federal law. However, the reliance on federal legislation and Länder implementation has its safeguards in the checks and balances of the system, the legal framework including a federal constitutional court on the one hand, and the bi-cameral system on the other, presenting the Länder with an important mechanism for exercising influence on the federal legislation. The position of the Federal Constitutional Court is a strong one. Article 93 invests the *Bundesverfassungsgericht* with extensive competency as far as the interpretation of the Basic Law is concerned. It is worth quoting Proviso 3 which makes the court the final arbiter of the German version of federalism:

> The Federal Constitutional Court shall decide: in case of differences of opinion of the rights and duties of the Federation and the Länder, particularly in the execution of federal law by the Länder and in the exercise of federal supervision.

If Austrian and German federalism have developed towards centralization, then the Italian version of federalism displays the opposite trend – from symbolism towards reality. During the 1970s the Italian political system took real steps to implement the strong federal elements inherent in the 1948 constitution. In constitutional theory the Italian state is more federal than unitary, but realities so far have not been in accordance with the paragraphs of the constitution. Fully implemented we would have an Italian version of federalism dividing public authority between the national government and the regions, the interaction between which is to be supervised by the Constitutional Court. Five regions are singled out for particular conditions of autonomy stated in laws: Sicily (1946), Sardinia (1948), Valle d'Aosta (1948), Trentino-Alto Adige (1948) and Friuli-Venetia Julia (1963).

In theory Italian federalism implies that the regions have their own regional councils, a giunta as well as a President that engage in legislation and administration in a large number of functions. However, though the regions are political bodies legitimized by direct popular elections they have been confined by 'the laws of the state', which so far has implied that the Italian state has been more unitary than federal. The regions are bound to certain 'fundamental principles' as well as constrained in their financial autonomy by 'the laws of the republic'. Actually, the constitution provides various mechanisms of control for the national government including the right to scrutinize the legitimacy of administrative decisions, to dissolve the regional council, if it seriously violates the laws, and to approve or disapprove laws enacted by the regional council. In the last resort conflicts between the regional council and the central government are to be tried by the constitutional court as a section of the constitution outlines.

The actual constitution will be a function of how political forces interpret these constitutional rules. Following the introduction of regional government in 1970 the regions have begun to legislate on a number important matters: town boundaries and town planning, urban and rural police, health and hospital assistance, education and culture, communications, environmental policies and artisanship. The 1970s witnessed more and more of a federal interpretation of the Italian constitution, particularly since 1976–7, though it cannot be described as federal but regionalized as independent tax-raising does not exist and several other attributes of federalism are not present. One country experts states: 'The regions' weak influence on intergovernmental financial relations serves merely to underline the pervasive presence of central governments in ways quite different from the ordinary forms of control' (Sanantonio, 1987).

Dividing the public powers between various levels of government is to a certain extent a zero-sum game. When the process of regionalization was carried through in Italy it not only involved the transfer of decision functions from the national government to the regional governments. It also meant that the system of local governments which had earlier been under the firm grip of the state now faced a new powerful actor at the regional level (Sanantonio, 1987).

The Swiss version of a federation is still of another kind, not based on the legislation–implementation distinction and a more firm political reality. The Swiss Republic is the oldest example of federalism in Europe, dating back to the first confederation in 1291. Constitutional theory designates the cantons as 'sovereign', but in reality the development of the Swiss political system has strengthened the grip of the federal government, which the ongoing constitutional revision will recognize in all probability. However, it cannot be doubted that the Swiss version of a federalist political system provides the cantons with a considerable scope for autonomous action. The federal principles imply that the cantons have their own legislative power in accordance with separate cantonal constitutions. The confederation is instructed to deal with internal and external peace, the freedom and rights of the cantons and 'common prosperity', which leaves ample space for autonomous cantonal action within the fields of education, health and social care, road construction as well as amenities. Whenever federal and cantonal legislation conflict the federal directives take precedence over the cantonal ones. In addition, the cantons take on various tasks delegated to them in the implementation of federal policies. What distinguishes Swiss federalism from Austrian or German federalism is the emphasis on the legislative function of the canton.

Regionalization

Institutional autonomy in unitary states may differ not only in its actual extent but in how intensively it is demanded. The same applies to the particular version of institutional autonomy – home rule. The drive for decentralization within unitary states has been strong in the 1970s and 1980s. It may be expressed in different forms: regionalization, home rule and local government autonomy. Let us deal first with the drive for regional devolution, then move on to local government discretion and after that exemplify the special mode of institutional autonomy, home rule.

The demand for decentralization within a unitary political system may be strong enough to offset a movement towards some kind of federalism. Belgium and Spain have had to develop in a federalist direction to come to grips with the demand for institutional autonomy. In the Belgian political system constitutional theory and practice has been very much an issue. In some nations constitutions exist for decades without any manifest innovation or reconsideration. In other political systems, on the contrary, the constitutional question lies at the heart of the political process. The Belgian constitution used to designate the country as a unitary state. The provinces were – according to theory – to be governed by legislative authority, 'exercised collectively by the King, the House of Representatives and the Senate'. The idea was that 'all powers stem from the nation', as the 1971 version of the Belgian constitution stated. However, the constitutional revision proposed by a constitutional assembly in 1970 and carried on in the constitution revision and in the Laws of Institutional Reforms passed in 1980 meant that federalist notions were inserted into the Belgian political system.

The Belgian constitution with the amendments made in 1980 and 1981 regards territorial autonomy as a response to the deep seated linguistic conflict between the pillars in Belgian society: the Flemings, the Walloons and the small German-speaking group. Institutional autonomy in the Belgian political system is based upon two concepts: the cultural communities and the linguistic regions. Although Article 3c identifies three language communities – French, Dutch and German – Article 3b talks of four linguistic regions: the French language region, the Dutch, the bilingual region of Brussels, and the German language region. Administratively, regional autonomy is exercised by the councils: the Flemish Council, the Council of the French Community, the Walloon Regional Council and the Council of the German cultural community. The French and Walloon councils overlap considerably (Senelle and Van de Velde, 1981).

The 1980 reform of the state in reality meant that the Belgian politico-administrative system resembles the federal type (Fitzmaurice, 1983). Elected regional councils have been created besides the national Parliament – one in each linguistic region. The regionalization of public authority is extensive, and each council appoints an executive body which elects a president. These regional executives constitute a type of government that in many ways operates as a substitution for the national government. The members of the regional executives are prohibited from being members of the national government, they engage in collegiate decision-making and the executives act on the basis of a specification of regional competence. Besides having their own source of power and legitimacy they also possess independent financial prerogatives. In the words of one observer:

> The regional competences are: urban planning, green protection, land planning, environment, energy, housing, provincial and local administration, water-management, economy, employment and related research. Regions take also the administrative control over the budgets, accounts and manpower of townships, agglomerations and provinces (Van Hassel, 1982: 10).

Actually, it is an open question as to whether the Belgian political system may be characterized as a federal state, because the drive for recognition of the linguistic cleavages more and more takes on the expression of territorial autonomy. To the Belgian the constitutional guarantee of individual rights concerning the languages to be used is not enough as the demand for autonomy has a striking territorial dimension. As the process of devolution has progressed the status of bilingual Brussels within the new Belgian state has become a difficult issue (De Ridder and Fraga, 1986).

A similar development although not as striking is to be found in Spain. The Spanish political system is a unitary state much characterized by the demand for regionalization, decentralization and territorial autonomy. When the employment of force and the national emphasis were no longer adequate to contain the forces searching for more autonomy, there was an attempt to meet the autonomy demand. The Spanish constitution devotes several articles to the territorial organization of the Spanish state. The process of introducing regional autonomy has proceeded on a piecemeal basis, each region negotiating about its own solution.

Steps towards territorial autonomy have to be regional initiatives and various regions may be treated differently. Each autonomous community shall have a special statute that is to be accepted by the Cortes Generale. Regionalism depended for its outcomes on how the various statutes were framed. In 1983 the mainland map of regionally autonomous communities had been drawn after separate negotiation of their powers with each regional government between 1979 and 1982 (Gillespie, 1990). A country expert states:

> At present, after a long and arduous process of negotiation seventeen autonomous regions have been created, covering the entire Spanish territory, each with its own directly elected government (Clegg, 1987).

Although attempts were made to slow down the process of piecemeal decentralization, four regions have acquired regional statutes with a constitutional status: Catalonia, the Basque Country, Galicia and Andalusia.

The Spanish public structure now involves seventeen autonomous regions as well as a local government system of provinces and municipalities – autonomas republicas.

The severe contention that the regional question arouses in the Spanish society is well-reflected in the quasi-contradictory nature of the Spanish constitution. According to the principles of the political system the autonomous communities are to be true institutions of self-government, legislating and administering in a number of areas exercising financial autonomy, but they are also to be controlled by national bodies: the Constitutional Court, the Central Government, and the Court of Accounts. Control by the Central Government can – in theory – be exercised in only two ways.

Firstly, the Central Government can promote control of the constitutionality of autonomic statutes, delegated legislation and by-laws, by lodging an appeal with the Constitutional Court. Secondly, in exceptional conditions, the Central Government can act in default. This control requires a set of conditions, stated in Article 155 of the constitution, these conditions being failure, on the part of the autonomous communities, to perform their duties or action in a way which may gravely attack the national interest. Moreover, the government can only adopt default measures after warning the autonomous community to rectify and – if this warning proves unsuccessful – with notice being previously given and consent received from the upper chamber, the Senado. The outcome may be anything from a semi-federal system to some version of decentralization within a unitary state (Coverdale, 1979; Graham, 1983). Whereas the autonomy granted the municipalities – some 8 500 – or the provinces – 50 – belongs to the traditional element of decentralization in a unitary state, the concept of an autonomous community brings out the strong tensions in the Spanish state as the autonomous communities could imply federalist development in Spain. Article 143 states:

> In the exercise of the right of autonomy recognized in Article 2 of the Constitution, bordering provinces with common historical, cultural and economic characteristics, the island territories and the provinces with a historical regional entity may accede to self-government and constitute themselves into autonomous communities in accordance with the provisions of that Title and the respective Statutes.

It has been proved difficult, to say the least, to arrive at a mutual understanding of the role of regional government and the legitimacy of the Spanish state in the Basque provinces (Liebert, 1990).

The new Portuguese republic is an example of a combination of a unitary state and home rule. Articles 227–30 define on a constitutional basis the so-called autonomous regions of Portugal: the Azores and Madeira. The rights and duties of the regional bodies of these islands are part of the wider framework of decentralization expressed in the system of regional bodies covering the whole nation, but the regional assemblies within the autonomous regions have a stronger position than do the regional bodies on the mainland. The regions are in essence planning areas with assemblies, executive committees and advisory councils. The regions have duties rather than powers, and Article 262 specifies that in each region there shall be a representative of the government, i.e. of the Republic. The implementation of these provisions has been rather dilatory, and until recently only the North had a properly functioning regional organization. In other unitary states the demand for institutional autonomy or decentralization has concerned the status of the local government system. Let us look at the United Kingdom and some Scandinavian countries.

Local government autonomy

The seminal trend towards more decentralization within unitary states has also affected the local government system in the West European countries. The expansion of the welfare state in Western Europe has meant that the local government system in various countries has expanded the tasks it fulfils. At the same time, organizational expansion has constituted the basis for demands for more local autonomy. As a matter of fact, only the United Kingdom appears to have moved in the opposite direction.

The pure type of the Westminster model of governing does not admit the possibility of independent institutional autonomy. Political decision-making is to be exercised by a party in majority facing the institutionalized opposition of the minority on the basis of a real probability that the two (major) parties may alternate in power. The Westminster model is founded upon the idea of the sovereignty of Parliament. Whatever institutional autonomy there may exist has to be based on delegation of the powers of Parliament. Local self-government is an issue in the political life of the United Kingdom. Typical of the local government system in the United Kingdom has been that the local governments operate under the Westminster model meaning that these units have no ultra vires, i.e. they cannot act unless Parliament has laid down directives that they may do so. However, this does not imply that local autonomy is without significance, as the various local governments have enjoyed considerable discretion up until the Thatcher government.

Centre–periphery relations in the United Kingdom came under severe strains under Thatcher as the centre has pushed for changes in the local government system (Danziger, 1978; Sharpe and Newton, 1984; Page and Goldsmith, 1987). Michael Goldsmith and Edward Page describe the English tradition of local self-government as a *dual polity* system existing within the framework of the principle of sovereignty of Parliament. The extent of decentralization was considerable depending on the degree of discretion allowed local authorities in Parliament legislation or mandates, the absence of close national government inspection and auditing as well as on a relatively wide scope for local revenue raising. When the Thatcher government questioned the dual polity system it narrowed down the financial discretion of local government besides abolishing some local authorities like for example the Greater London Council, replacing them with non-elected boards.

In the Swedish political system, known for its unitary nature and its ideology of local government, the assessment of the extent of decentralization is a complex matter. Articles 5 and 6 in the new Swedish constitution state that the national government rules the country, but that local government decision-making is exercised by elected assemblies which have the right to levy taxes to handle their functions. The Swedish local governments possess a general competence to handle their own affairs, the interpretation of which provides the county communes and the municipalities with a certain degree of local discretion. That there is no ultra vires clause does not mean, however, that the national government is not involved in the local government operations. The national government both specifies what functions are obligatory and regulates the functions that are voluntary. The local governments are provided with autonomy as a matter of principle, but the discretion of these bodies is restricted by national government directives, financial initiatives as well as legal rulings restricting the degrees of freedom in local government autonomy (Magnusson and Lane, 1987).

During the 1970s the local government system expanded at a rapid rate as both the municipalities and the county councils became more and more responsible for the provision of public services in the Swedish welfare state. To strengthen the capacity of the municipalities to engage in service production comprehensive amalgamation was resorted to first in 1952 and then in 1969 and 1974. The reduction in the number of municipalities was quite substantial, from roughly 2 000 to about 285. These reforms and the concomitant expansion of the activities of the various local governments resulted in local government units being transformed into large-scale formal organizations with heavy bureaucracies, big budgets and a large number of employees. Also the 23 county councils providing for health care services have experienced a long period of organizational expansion.

Likewise in Norway institutional autonomy is expressed in the decentralization of the unitary state. Besides the national government the political system comprises an elaborate system of local governments, 'fylketing' at the regional level and 'kommuner' at the local level. We note the trend towards less and more of local government so typical of the development of several political systems since 1945. The paradox is that the number of communes has been reduced from about 750 (1950) to roughly 454 (1980) to facilitate homogeneity in the planning of the welfare state among other things, while the demand for increased local government autonomy has grown stronger (Hansen, 1981).

Typical of the Norwegian political system was the close state supervision of the regional and local governments, carried out by means of a strong position for the governor as state official. Not only was the Fylkesman directly involved in the administration of the Fylketing, but the Fylkesman also had the right to approve or disapprove of municipal decisions. During the 1970s significant steps were taken to introduce more decentralization. Thus, the powers of the Fylkesman were reduced and the local governments have become independent of the regional state administrative system. Two country experts state: 'In forty years, local government in Norway has developed from a relatively subordinate institution, with direct responsibility for few tasks, to one with substantial discretion in providing many of the basic public services' (Fevolden and Sörensen, 1987: 44).

Although the Norwegian political system is a typically unitary state heterogeneity and variety are safeguarded in the decentralized state with an emphasis upon local government autonomy. The decentralized trends are contained by various mechanisms that provide the state with actual or potential capacity to supervise what happens at the regional or local level. This is organized decentralization, the regulation of which has not been carried over into constitutional theory as the old Norwegian constitution is heavily focussed upon the structure and functioning of the national government.

Similarly, local government in Denmark is '... big. It spends funds equivalent to one-third of GNP; one of five workers is employed by a local authority' (Bogason, 1987: 50). The amount of local government discretion varies over time as a function of the shifting emphasis on either equality in access to and cost of services on the one hand or on local government variations in the provision of goods and services on the other hand. When equality is emphasized centralized measures are implemented whereas when decentralization is underlined, then more local variation is accepted.

Local government in southern Europe is characterized by less discretion than in the Nordic countries. A strongly centralized unitary state such as France has had to recognize the demand for institutional autonomy. The idea of territorial autonomy may appear to be of little relevance to the French political system, characterized by country specialists like Vincent Wright and Jean Blondel as centralist. However, the widely spread drive towards various modes of autonomy has found expressions in French politics.

The French constitution contains special articles regulating the territorial units outside of France. These areas have assemblies elected on the basis of universal suffrage, and are also represented in the French parliament. These overseas islands have some degree of territorial autonomy. The demand for regional autonomy has increased within France, growing from the first attempts in the late 1950s and the second effort in 1964 up to the more definitive decisions in 1972 and 1973 (Wright, 1983: 257). The first policy of decentralization in France involved the creation of regional bodies that would allow for the coordination of the departments as well as the communes. The emphasis was more on efficiency than on local participation. The design of the office of the regional prefect and the two regional councils implied less of a transfer of power from the capital but rather an even more firm grip of the centre over the periphery (Gourevitch, 1981).

However, the demand for a regionalization of the French political system proved strong enough to effect another administrative reform between 1981 and 1983 (loi Defferre). The office of the prefect was abolished though the prefectoral corps were retained and a new system of departmental and communal autonomy was introduced. Each department is to be governed by a directly elected Conseil Général headed by a chairman, elected by the council. The centre or the ministries in Paris is to be present at the level of the department through a so-called Commissioner de la République who remains the main coordinator of the centre's activities at local level. It is an open question how the relationship between the Conseil Général and the Commissioner de la République will develop, but the real amount of institutional autonomy inserted into the French political system by the reform of 1982 is an outcome of the power balance between these two institutions. The reform appears to have bypassed the earlier difficulties, because this reform did not aim at the regional level above the prefects and the local notables. Instead it favoured the local political bosses abolishing one major French tradition, the office of the prefect (Ashford, 1983). The typical French prefects appointed by the centre have been replaced by executives elected by the local and regional community, but 'it will be seen that, while France remains a centralised country, and the dominance of Paris is incontestible, the form and extent of central control have been modified under the pressure of the periphery' (Mény, 1987: 57).

Local government discretion appears to have grown in France more due to increased organizational complexity than as a result of reform fiat. Due to the creation of regions France now has four levels of government: state, region, department and commune. At the same time as the state still maintains a strong grip on the public sector, the complex interaction between various bodies with different functions and powers has enhanced the discretion of local authorities (Mény, 1987: 105).

Local government in Italy and Spain has changed, it is true, but the degree of local government discretion remains low. The Italian local governments, the province and the commune have increased their functions, but the regionalization of the Italian state since 1970 has not meant any significant increase in local government discretion.

Home Rule

Any description of institutional autonomy and the decentralist drive would be incomplete without mentioning the demand of separate regions for special status. The source of the urge for special territorial autonomy is different from that of the demand for a general decentralization of power, as the drive for home rule originates among cultural minorities or separatist groups. Countries differ not only in the extent that home rule has been granted but in the system relevance of the demand for special territorial autonomy. In some systems home rule has been institutionalized peacefully whereas in others it is a cause of serious contention.

The Scandinavian countries are by tradition unitary states; in these nations a strong central government is balanced by an extensive system of local government. Yet, there are some interesting expressions of special territorial autonomy. With the Danish state the areas with home rule are far larger than those where the unitary state is in full force. Of course, we are considering the autonomous islands in the Danish realm, the Faroe Islands and Greenland. According to law – in 1948 and in 1979 respectively – these parts were entrusted with far-reaching territorial autonomy as both have their own legislative and executive bodies. Morover, Danish minorities in Germany and German minorities in Denmark fight for their own cultural expression in the areas of Schleswig and Holstein. Today the tiny German minority in Schleswig finds certain expressions of its identity: private schools, a daily newspaper and representation in local and regional councils.

Finland is also characterized as a unitary state, but the Finnish political system comprises important elements of institutional autonomy. Home rule is practised at the island of Åland, to which was given autonomy in 1920, reinforced in 1951. The autonomy of Åland involves a parliament with legislative functions as well as an administration responsible to the parliament at Åland. The Finnish version of home rule at Åland is a far-reaching one as the national government only controls functions such as jurisdiction and communication whereas Åland may act autonomously with regard to health policy, education, environmental policy, although the governor is appointed by the president of Finland. The purpose of the territorial autonomy is twofold: to protect and maintain the special culture of the Swedish-speaking population of the island, and to neutralize the island as a source of international conflicts. Since 1921 the island of Åland has been completely demilitarized in accordance with an international convention and the Åland population does not serve in the Finnish army.

There is nothing of territorial autonomy or regionalism in general in Greece, except the autonomy of the Holy Monasteries at the Athos peninsula. Autonomy in the Greek political system has several religious aspects. The regime of Aghion Oros is in effect a Holy Community, a piece of the state being governed by non-secular authority in accordance with ancient traditions. Article 3 in the constitution also guarantees special prerogatives to the Orthodox Church of Greece. At the same time as it is declared the 'prevailing religion in Greece' it is also guaranteed autonomy from the state. Here we have an example of functional autonomy, as the state church is said to be autocephalous and is administered by the Holy Synod of Serving Bishops and the Permanent Holy Synod originating therefrom.

In Italy special territorial autonomy is guaranteed the Vatican City State, governed in accordance with the 1929 concordat that enters the 1948 constitution, as well as San Marino, whose independence, dating from the Middle Ages, was solemnly reaffirmed in 1862 by the newly born Italian state in a treaty renewed several times and guaranteed by other powers. The distinction between a large extent of home rule and national independence is tenuous with regard to the Vatican state and San Marino.

Although the political system of the United Kingdom is a pure type of unitary state, where in theory all public power derives from Parliament, there have been expressions of territorial autonomy in the United Kingdom before the devolution movement beginning in the 1960s. The various adjacent islands (Isle of Man and Channel Islands) have been run by legislative assemblies with special powers granted by Parliament. The Ulster solution implied the establishment of the Stormont parliament, which operated up until the beginning of the Northern Ireland crisis; after 1972 Northern Ireland was governed directly from Westminster. There are decentralized offices for Scotland, Wales and Northern Ireland in their capitals, Edinburgh, Cardiff and Belfast. They do have tiny offices in Whitehall and they are part of the central government in so far as their ministerial heads – the secretaries of state for Scotland, Wales and Northern Ireland – sit in the Cabinet. In the 1970s the demand for autonomy became a real issue. The 1979 referendum was not a rejection of territorial autonomy in Scotland as 52 per cent of those voting voted 'Yes' to the Scotland act, but the act required a positive vote from at least 40 per cent of the electorate and the turnout was insufficiently high for this. In Wales 80 per cent of those who voted said 'No'.

Functional Autonomy

Institutional autonomy and the demand for decentralization does not have to carry a territorial implication. Power may be diffused in society to various institutions by focussing upon functions or activities instead of territorial areas. In some nations there is a strong reliance on letting organizations excercise decision-making concerning functions that in other political systems are administered by public bodies. Let us pinpoint some typical examples of functional autonomy.

It may be noted that the formal institutional rules are not always a reliable guide to the principles actually operating for political decision-making. Not only have the various articles in the constitution been interpreted and applied differently from time to time, but major political decisions forming the basis of functional autonomy may be regarded as constitutional practice. Consociationalism in the Dutch version is an example of this and it is greatly oriented towards institutional autonomy on a functional basis. The 1815 constitution provided for a rather centralized framework; typical of the Dutch political system is the functional autonomy laid down in the consociational model (Daalder, 1966b; Lijphart, 1975; Kruijt, 1974).

Consociationalism or the pillarization of the society as a basis for the political system developed during the nineteenth century as a reaction to the religious cleavage between Calvinists and Catholics on the one hand and the formation of a working-class movement on the other. The principles of Verzuiling include both the social organization of collectives and the public recognition legitimizing the various Zuilen. A famous state decision promoting Verzuiling was the 1916–17 school pact, which opened the way to the private provision of education supported by public subsidies. Hans Daalder states:

> Special interest groups co-operating across sub-cultural lines jointly repre-sented powerful political and social forces. Successive governments found it profitable to share with such interests in the elaboration of new policies, and often to leave them a substantial share of practical execution and daily administration. A pattern, first set in the equal financing of public and religious schools after 1917, was thus extended to many social sectors, including social insurance, health care, and many forms of culture and recreation (Daalder, 1989: 15–16).

Although there was a strong reaction against this mixture of consoc-iationalism, corporatism and functional autonomy in the 1970s and 1980s, 'traditions of accommodation and consultation have traditionally been strong in the Netherlands, and they are easily set aside' (Daalder, 1989: 16). Besides the official recognition of the religious and secular pillars special autonomy has also been provided for the Frisians with the use of their own language and their own culture including a Frisian Academy and Cultural Council (Stephens, 1976).

The Dutch political system may be regarded as the most clear case of functional autonomy in Western Europe. Whereas some nations distribute authority in a federal structure or provide special territorial autonomy for some regions, the Dutch political system distributes considerable authority on the basis of functions. The state accepts that various organizations provide for services that are usually classified as public or semi-public. Thus, the pillars have been given autonomy in managing not only churches but also economic associations, hospitals and leisure associations. During the last decade signs appeared that consociationalism was losing its grip on the Dutch political system. The isolation between the pillars has declined and élite cooperation has become more fragile – 'depillarization' (Thung et al., 1982).

As a matter of fact, it is not easy to find another West European nation that has institutionalized functional autonomy to a similar extent. We have to remain content with finding a few examples of functional autonomy. There is an element of functional autonomy in the Austrian framework as the famous state treaty of 1955 reestablishing the independence of the Austrian state contains articles that guarantee the 'rights of Slovene and Croat minorities in the Länder of Carinthia, Burgenland and Styria'. They are treated on equal terms with other Austrians by means of various elements of functional autonomy: right to elementary instruction in the Slovene or Croat language and to a proportional number of their own secondary schools, the acceptance of the Slovene or Croat language as an official language in addition to German, and topographical terminology and inscriptions in all three languages.

In Italy, the special position of the Catholic Church has been recognized besides the territorial autonomy provided by the Lateran pacts as the church enjoys a considerable degree of functional autonomy; the state is not the principal of the church within the Italian nation. Article 7 states: 'The State and the Catholic Church are, each within its own ambit, independent and sovereign'. Something similar to functional autonomy may be identified in the Irish state, referring to the rights of the Catholic Church and the Gaelic Community. The constitution safeguards a certain amount of autonomy for religious denominations. Furthermore, the constitution obliges the government to fund the schools operated by religious denominations. The Irish language has been given a special position with the result that there is a recognition of organizations engaged in the revival of Gaelic in the region of Gaeltacht. In a sense the combined state and voluntary efforts have provided some of these pressure groups with a semi-public status as autonomous bodies within the nation, for example the Gaelic League (O'Donnell, 1974).

Summing up

A number of distinctions concerning institutional autonomy have been exemplified with the West European political systems. However, it is difficult to devise an overall measure that describes the country differences more systematically. Two indices may be suggested that attempt to measure institutional autonomy, although it must be admitted that they are not based on existing indices.

The first overall measure has been calculated on the basis of ordinal characterizations of the European democracies concerning the following properties: the extent of federalism (0–2), the occurrence of home rule or special territorial autonomy (0–1), the existence of various degrees of functional autonomy (0–2) and the amount of financial autonomy typical of the local government system (0–2). Financial autonomy refers to the proportion of resources allocated by the central government in relation to regional or local governments. The characterization of the European democracies in these properties must be somewhat crude given the judgemental nature of the indices, but together they capture a country variation in institutional autonomy that pertains to the 1980s. Thus, the scores for Spain and Italy take into account the ambition to introduce a far-reaching regionalization of the political system. Likewise, the score for Belgium recognizes the 1980 revision of the state. Table 6.3 has the scores.

There is more variation in institutional autonomy than in individual autonomy in Western Europe. Not only is there a striking difference between the extremes – Switzerland with its high degree of decentralization and centralized countries like Greece, Ireland and France – but there is also a number of differences in between these nations with a mixture of centralization and decentralization. Belgium and the Federal Republic of Germany are characterized by much institutional autonomy. It appears that a federal constitution is not a necessary condition for the existence of a substantial amount of institutional autonomy. Actually, a few unitary states display considerable autonomy although in general they have a lower degree of institutional autonomy than federal ones.

Another overall measure of institutional autonomy could be an index that measures the allocative size of the central government, i.e. proportion of central government expenditures on goods and services in relation to total public sector outlays for the provision of goods and services. Table 6.4 presents a variation that is rather close to that contained in Table 6.3.

It must be pointed out that control over the public purse is by no means the crucial indicator on the autonomy–heteronomy relationship between various levels of government in a country. Sometimes a central government may provide the regional or local governments with financial resources that they may spend with much discretion on their own part. However, we do find that the federal political systems rely to a considerably lesser extent on central government spending. And in southern Europe where a model of centralized government has prevailed the central government spends far more than the regional and local governments with regard to the provision of goods and services in the public sector. The extent of political decentralization in West European

Table 6.3   *Institutional autonomy index*

	Federalism (0–2)	Special territorial autonomy (0–1)	Regional and Local government discretion (0–2)	Functional autonomy (0–2)	Institutional autonomy summary score
Austria	1	0	1	1	3
Belgium	1	0	1	2	4
Denmark	0	1	2	0	3
F R Germany	2	0	2	0	4
Finland	0	1	1	0	2
France	0	0	1	0	1
Greece	0	0	0	0	0
Ireland	0	0	0	0	0
Italy	0	0	1	0	1
Netherlands	0	0	1	2	3
Norway	0	0	2	0	2
Portugal	0	1	0	0	1
Spain	0	0	1	0	1
Sweden	0	0	2	0	2
Switzerland	2	0	2	1	5
United Kingdom	0	1	1	0	2

Note: The overall institutional autonomy score adds up the scores for the four dimensions. The index takes into account the extent of reforms in the 1980s in increasing regional autonomy in Belgium, Spain, Italy and France or decreasing local autonomy in, for example, the United Kingdom. Local government discretion is higher the greater the degree of freedom they have when making decisions (see Humes and Martin, 1969; Goldsmith, 1986). The scores for Spain, Portugal and Greece refer only to the period of democratic rule.

countries depends crucially on whether the state is or has been organized according to the prefectorial system in its French version as introduced by Napoleon. When the state has been or remains organized in accordance with a system of prefects spread over the country but acting as the agent of the state as principal, then the notion of local government and its basic idea of public discretion for representatives elected *von unten* has had difficulties in competing with the principle of state authority or the legitimacy of power *von oben*.

Conclusion

Political systems in Western Europe handle autonomy differently. Some nations institutionalize a high degree of both institutional and individual autonomy, in particular Switzerland, whereas a few nations have scored low on both dimensions, viz. Spain, Portugal and Greece before the regime transition in the mid 1970s. Typical of several nations is that

Table 6.4 *Regional and local financial autonomy*

	1950	1960	1970	1980
Austria	53	49	46	35
Belgium	76	78	77	74
Denmark	[50]	46	[40]	31
F R Germany	30	30	25	19
Finland	[50]	44	40	33
France	[80]	77	76	72
Greece	83	79	78	74
Ireland	57	58	51	46
Italy	73	68	58	55
Netherlands	55	47	48	45
Norway	56	51	46	40
Portugal	87	87	88	87
Spain	[80]	77	78	68
Sweden	59	45	37	30
Switzerland	[30]	27	28	23
United Kingdom	71	67	59	59

Note: This index measures the proportion of central government final consumption in relation to general government final consumption; a high proportion indicates a strong position for central government. Figures in brackets [ ] are crude estimates.
Source: OECD: National accounts (various years).

they institutionalize a higher degree of individual autonomy than of institutional autonomy: France, the United Kingdom, Ireland and Italy. The political systems of Belgium and the Federal Republic of Germany, however, are characterized by the combination of a high degree of individual autonomy and considerable institutional autonomy.

Autonomy is a fundamental aspect of the political organization of societies, and it has two basic modes: individual autonomy and institutional autonomy. Political systems in European democracies differ in their institutionalization of autonomy, in particular institutional autonomy. The degree of institutional autonomy in the political system is a function of the degree of centralization of political power in the polity. Typical of the political systems that adhere to the Westminster model of government is a low degree of institutional autonomy, emphasizing the sovereignty of Parliament. Characteristic of the consensus model of government is a high degree of institutional autonomy underlining power dispersion to various levels of government. In actual realities, the countries in Western Europe are to be placed somewhere in between these two pure types. The variation in institutional autonomy is a basic aspect of the public structure of decision-making. Another aspect of the political system is the influence dimension or the system of mechanisms for the exercise of influence by citizens and organizations on public policy, to the analysis of which we now turn.

7

Decision-Making Systems: Influence

Introduction

Political systems have an impact upon their environments in the consequences of decisions taken and actions implemented. Citizens and organizations are affected by the activities of governments at various levels within the political system. Since the capacity of individuals and organizations to exercise influence over the making and implementation of policy is crucial in democratic polities the structuring of the decision-making process to institutionalize the exercise of influence becomes of principal importance. Various modes of citizen influence are conceivable, and it is an open question whether various decision-making mechanisms have different effects on policies and political system properties. One of the most well-known political science laws – the Duverger hypothesis about the outcome of electoral systems – states that the choice of election rules has consequences for the party system as well as for political stability where proportional representation schemas would be conducive to fractionalization and political instability. There is a large amount of literature discussing modes of structuring citizen participation in the political process as the analysis of influence mechanisms covers more than electoral systems. We discuss some topics in so far as they relate to our main concern.

In most systems political parties face competition from other influence mechanisms, either the referendum institution or interest organization involvement in policy-making. It seems crucial to be alert to the country variation in the extent to which influence is exercised in direct participation by means of referendum or in indirect participation via political parties or interest organizations. One may distinguish between one *direct* influence mechanism, the referendum, and a number of *indirect* influence mechanisms such as election systems offering political party representation, patterns of government formation, type of parliamentarism, corporatist patterns of interest intermediation and consultation as well as so-called consociational devices. These indirect influence mechanisms provide channels for political parties and interest organizations to have an impact on the making and implementation of public policies. And these influence mechanisms may be structured differently from one country to another. This is the variation we set out to describe in this chapter.

Political party influence is far from a proportional function of electoral support. Citizen influence is not simply a function of the alignment of the electorate along party lines but is very dependent upon prevailing patterns of government formation, in particular the building of coalitions. Political systems differ not only in the rules of electing parliamentarians but in the principles adopted for the creation of governments. As we deal with the country variation in electoral systems and patterns of government formation, it is a natural question to inquire into the relationship between the two. Finally, let us try to identify whether the types of influence mechanism tend to co-vary.

Modes of citizen influence

Citizens may influence the decisions of the political system by direct participation, i.e. through the referendum institution. Many political systems contain some type of referendum, but only a few nations give a major role to the referendum as a standard procedure for the making of political decisions. It is possible to identify a country variation in the reliance on direct participation as some nations employ the referendum in an obligatory fashion whereas in others the verdict of the voters is handled only as a recommendation. More common no doubt are various forms for indirect participation as modes of citizen influence. Typical of political systems is the mediation role of political parties looking for the vote of the citizen in exchange for a position in the decision-making institutions from which it may influence policy-making. What matters are the rules that govern the choice of representatives in legislative assemblies, mainly the national parliament.

Although there is much literature about electoral systems it is possible to focus the analysis upon a few major properties: the size of constituencies, the extent of proportionality and the degree to which separate candidates or party lists are voted on (Rae, 1971; Lakeman, 1974; Newland, 1982). Vernon Bogdanor (1983) presents a neat classification of the major types of electoral system, which we reproduce for our set of nations (Figure 7.1).

In citizen influence the employment of a plurality or a proportionate system has different effects. Whereas a plurality system is conducive to effectiveness in the responsiveness of government to major changes in public opinion, a proportionate system is superior when it comes to the representation of a variety of citizen opinions. Thus, representativity is maximized in proportional electoral systems where the whole nation is one constituency and there are no electoral limits to the size of the group to be represented. The extent to which proportional systems also manage to create stable governments that serve as an effective mechanism for the

Figure 7.1   *Typology of election systems (Bogdanor, 1983: 17)*

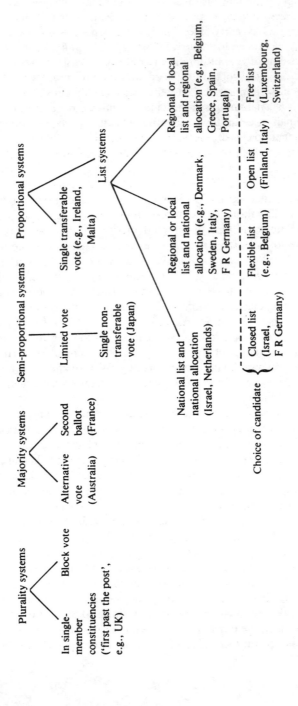

expression of citizen preferences has been much discussed.

It is often stated that an election system based on simple majority in one-man constituencies results in more durable governments than a proportional election formula because such a system favours the creation of single majority governments. That political stability, government formation pattern and election rules hang together has been adduced by several scholars (Duverger, 1954; Blondel, 1968; Sanders and Herman, 1977). The counter-argument is that the plurality formulas may not be conducive to other aspects of political stability like social order (Powell, 1982) and that durable governments may exist in multi-party systems characterized by proportional election systems (Dodd, 1976).

The principles controlling government formation are of crucial importance in determining which citizen groups may have a say over the making of public policy. Some political systems lean towards single majority government, whereas others rely on the creation of coalitions. A variety of types of coalition may be identified: minority governments based on ad hoc coalitions in parliament, minimum-winning coalitions, minimum-distance coalitions and various over-sized coalitions (Riker, 1962; Axelrod, 1970; De Swaan, 1973; Strom, 1984; Luebbert, 1984; Strom, 1985).

The well-known size hypothesis predicts on the basis of game-theoretical deliberations that societies will tend to produce governments that just barely pass the majority number. However, the minimum-winning as well as minimum-sized coalition models have been criticized for their lack of institutional assumptions. It may matter very much if the party system is highly fractionalized or highly polarized; the suggestion is that the size hypothesis may operate in decision-making systems where there are few large groups that are not ideologically constrained. In other institutional environments the coalition pattern may be different as parties may try to find ideologically close partners minimizing policy distance or remain content with a minority government. Moreover, cabinet formation is not simply a function of the ambition to maximize the divisible gains for each potential partner, but coalition behaviour may take system considerations into account.

Consociational theorists have pointed to the choice of over-sized coalitions as a decision mechanism for the reduction of the consequences of social cleavages to promote political stability. It is hardly likely that the large variation in patterns of government formation in West European democracies since the Second World War is reducible to a simple typology or model. Looking at the variation in government coalition structures we need to take into account not only the size of the coalition but also the composition of the government. It seems pertinent to inquire into the extent to which governments deviate from the minimum-winning ideal type and whether the pattern of coalition typically follows ideological distinctions on a right–left scale or some other dimension.

Nations are not ruled by just a popular elected assembly and its parliamentary government; some countries recognize a position for a president or allow for an indirectly elected legislative chamber. Not only may the procedure for electing a president or a second chamber vary, but the powers of such bodies may also differ. Presidential power or an influential second chamber enter the analysis of influence mechanisms. Citizens may be able to affect public policies via their influence on the choice of president much more effectively than via their participation in parliamentary elections. And the existence of a second chamber may allow for the recognition of interests that are not visible in the national elections. In federal systems the various states may have a profound impact upon the central government in their participation in the national policy process in the form of representation in a second chamber. What counts is not only autonomy but also access.

We must recognize the importance of the bureaucracy in the policy process (Peters, 1978; Hogwood and Peters, 1983). Citizens and organizations have to deal with civil servants at various levels of government, and their image of whatever influence they are able to exercise on the political system is affected by the way the bureaucracy operates (Dogan, 1975). Bureaucracies may appear far removed from society, devoted to the neutral pursuit of technical tasks; sometimes such bureaucracies are recruited from the élite strata of society which further enhances the impression of separateness and remoteness. However, modern bureaucracies may be structured in a manner that is more responsive to citizen demand. Some nations may even take steps to secure that various social groups are entitled to recruit parts of the bureaucracy (Proporz). And in some countries there may exist an emphasis that entrance into the bureaucracy should be open to each and everyone, and that the bureaucracy should be orientated towards service to the citizens.

Political parties used to be considered the legitimate representatives of public opinion and the development of corporatist patterns of policy-making has been regarded as a threat to traditional democratic decision-mechanisms. However, as S.E. Finer points out in *Comparative Government*:

> Thus it is that in all liberal democracies there exist, not one but two channels of popular representation. Political parties and the electoral process are one; pressure groups provide the other (Finer, 1970: 152).

The concept of pressure group includes the major interest organizations in a country as well as the more numerous and smaller promotional groups. Finer (1970: 153) states that collectivities that pursue 'a function or economic good' belong to interest groups (trade unions, churches and universities), whereas collectivities 'whose purpose is propagandist' are promotional groups (societies for the protection of wild birds, children or animals).

Any analysis of social choice in a public setting must take into account the influence of organized interests of various kinds. However, it is an open question how and to what extent interest mediation and interest consultation enhance citizen influence. Although there is the risk that the growing role of organized interests in government policy-making may be more conducive to the furthering of organizational power than citizen interests, it seems clear that interest mediation and consultation may provide an alternative route for the exercise of influence of major citizen groups (Schmitter, 1983). The institutionalization of corporatist patterns of decision-making varies from one country to another (Schmitter and Lehmbruch, 1979; Lehmbruch and Schmitter, 1982).

Following the concept formation suggested by Philippe Schmitter we distinguish between three models of organized interest participation. *Pluralism* is distinguished by the following: multiple, voluntarily, competitive and non-hierarchically ordered organizations, self-determination, non-licensed, non-recognized, non-subsidized, no representational monopoly. *Societal corporatism* means: limited number of organizations as a result of associational development and arrangement, quasi-compulsory as a result of organizational power and pressure, non-competitive as a result of interorganizational policy, hierarchically ordered as the outcome of internal organizational processes, state recognition and state subsidies without conferring public status, representational monopoly as the outcome of membership density. *State corporatism* stands for: limited number of organizations by means of state authoritarization and state recognition, compulsory membership defined by law, hierarchically ordered in a public structure, functionally differentiated by state-defined vocational categories, representational status in state assemblies (Schmitter, 1979: 7–52).

It is not only the development from the pluralist model to the societal corporatist model that is of interest in the interpretation of interest policy-making in post-war Western Europe. We must also look for traces of state corporatism, either as a remnant from the past or as a possible future development of the emergent forms of political participation of organized interests. According to one argument corporatist patterns of decision-making are at odds with the principles of representative democracy which relies heavily upon political parties as the main vehicle of public opinion. However, there is the counter-argument that corporatism may enter into a beneficial cooperation with party government which enhances political stability (Lehner, 1983; Olsen, 1983). We must take into account a country variation in the pattern of corporatist arrangements, as no doubt corporatist arrangements constitute a new element in the policy-making mechanisms:

With its hierarchical coordination, state recognition, policy concertation, and developed authority, it has separated more effectively than before the interaction between interest associations and public authorities from the vagaries of electoral success and legislative choice (Schmitter, 1983: 913).

The pluralist model of public decision-making and citizen involvement in politics has been questioned also by the so-called consociational theory (McRae, 1974). Sometimes the consociational theme and corporatist theory are mixed in a model of influence mechanisms that emphasize the narrowness of the pluralist model of two-partism, single majority party government and cabinet parliamentarianism (Lehmbruch, 1982). The theory of consociationalism maintains that we must recognize different types of modern democracy (Lijphart, 1984a; Lijphart et al., 1988). A number of pure models of democracy have been proposed as a distinction between Madisonian, populist and polyarchical models of democracy have also been suggested (Dahl, 1956). The growth of corporatization has resulted in suggestions to the effect that we must also recognize a new model of democracy, corporatist democracy (Schmitter, 1984; Streeck and Schmitter, 1985) or organized democracy (Olsen, 1983). We wish to emphasize the variety of institutional mechanisms for the exercise of citizen and organized interest group influence in Western Europe. To what extent is there a co-variation between these mechanisms? Recognizing the mixture of the elements of various pure decision models may help us to account for the impact on political stability of political institutions designed to make citizen and group influence possible.

Empirically we face a variation countrywise in a number of mechanisms for the exercise of citizen and organization influence on policy-making and policy-implementation. Political systems adhering to democratic rules may differ as to the extent of direct versus indirect democracy, the degree of proportionality of its election rules, the structure of its parliamentary system, the nature of its cabinet, the pattern of government formation as well as the extent of consociationalism or corporatism. The nature of these influence mechanisms is discussed. The description is not comprehensive as the purpose is only to exemplify distinctions between various modes of influence mechanisms.

The Referendum

The place of the referendum in the political system is not a prominent one among European democracies with the exception of Switzerland. Most political systems pay homage to the principle of direct citizen rule in their constitutions, but few practise referendum on a regular basis.

The element of direct democracy is not very prominent in Austria: if 200 000 citizens so demand a law proposal has to be submitted by the national government to the Nationalrat, which may decide to call a referendum. The referendum institution has been employed only once so far, in the 1978 Zwentendorf-vote concerning nuclear power. Instead citizen influence focusses on the election of party representatives to the Nationalrat. Similarly, the referendum institution is unimportant in the Belgian context; it has been employed once, in 1950 concerning the royal question. And the role of the referendum is insignificant in Finnish politics as there has been only one, in 1931. There is a referendum institution in the Greek political system (Article 44). When the military junta resigned power in 1974 the constitution of 1952 was reinstated and some months later a referendum confirmed the introduction of a new constitution. It is no exaggeration to state that the Storting is the most important mechanism for the exercise of citizen influence in the Norwegian parliamentary democracy. Since there is only a weak referendum institution the way to express public opinion to have an impact on the course of the nation is to influence the political parties.

In some systems the referendum institution is employed infrequently but on important issues. A conspicuous feature of the Danish political system is the referendum mechanism for the exercise of direct citizen influence. Firstly, the constitution cannot be changed without popular acceptance in a referendum in which at least 40 per cent of those eligible say 'Yes'. The referendum institution also provides for the possibility of legislative initiative calling for a popular vote on an adopted bill in parliament. If one third of the members of parliament ask for such a referendum, then it must be held on all kinds of legislation except finance, budgeting and international law. If a majority in the referendum rejects parliament legislation on the assumption that those voting 'No' constitute 30 per cent of those eligible, then the vote is decisive. The referendum mechanism is also to be employed on two special occasions: the change of the age for participating in elections and the transfer of national powers to international bodies. If proposals concerning sovereignty transfers do not carry a five-sixths majority, then they may be up for referendum (Fitzmaurice, 1981; Worre, 1982). The referendum mechanism is not political formalism, as it has actually been employed in Denmark in about ten referendums since 1916, among others the 1953 constitutional referendum, the entry to EEC in 1972 and six referendums about the voting age.

The constitution of the Fourth Republic recognized the possibility of a referendum following parliament initiative. Actually, four referendums were held during the Fourth Republic, but power essentially resided within the Assemblée nationale in its elaborate system of senate and chamber standing committees. In the political system of the Fifth Republic the referendum is one of the techniques of presidential power, meaning that popular opinion has had a direct channel to political power making the president vulnerable to changes in mass opinion, as De Gaulle experienced in the 1969 referendum. The referendum institution has been

Table 7.1   *The referendum institution since 1945 (nationwide)*

	Constitutional recognition	Number of referendums	Importance of referendums
Austria	Art. 46	1	0
Belgium	–	1	0
Denmark	Art. 42, 88	8 (12)	1
F R Germany	Art. 29, 118	0	0
Finland	–	0	0
France	Art. 11	9 (10)	2
Greece	Art. 44	4	1
Ireland	Art. 47	8 (11)	1
Italy	Art. 75	5 (10)	1
Netherlands	–	0	0
Norway	–	1	0
Portugal	–	0	0
Spain	–	5	1
Sweden	Chap. 8: Art. 4	3	1
Switzerland	Arts.: 89, 120, 121, 123	ca 250	3
United Kingdom	–	1	0

Note: The scale measuring the importance of the referendum institution ranges from 0 to 3 and is based on both the number of and the political consequences of referendums; the number of issues dealt with in the referendums is presented in parenthesis.

Sources: Blaustein and Flanz, 1972; Butler and Ranney, 1978; Austen et al., 1987.

employed frequently, particularly after the war and in connection with the introduction of the Fifth Republic. The Italian constitution also recognizes the direct form for citizen influence. If 500 000 voters or five out of twenty regional councils so demand, there has to be a referendum about a law proposal. The referendum institution has been employed on some spectacular occasions: ending the Monarchy (1946), on divorce (1974), state financing of parties (1978) and on abortion (1981). In Sweden the referendum institution (optional and consultative) has not been employed on a frequent basis but it carried weight in deciding a few major decisions that the Riksdag had difficulties in handling: liquor prohibition (1922), right-hand traffic (1955), the supplementary pensions question (1957) and nuclear power (1980). Table 7.1 identifies a cross-country variation in the formal recognition, the frequency and the importance of the referendum institution.

Only Switzerland has institutionalized the referendum as a regular feature of national policy-making. The Swiss political system provides mechanisms for the exercise of both direct and indirect citizen influence (Schumann, 1971); in addition there is a dose of corporatism (Lehner, 1983). Duverger (1959) called Switzerland a 'démocratie semi-directe' referring to the strong institutionalization of the referendum at both the federal and cantonal levels. The federal referendum mechanism involves three elements: 'Volksinitiative', obligatory referendum, and facultative referendum. The rule of Volksinitiative includes the right to demand constitutional changes to be approved of in a referendum if 100 000 citizens so wish. On the other hand, there must be a referendum if a constitutional change is suggested by the federal government. This means that whatever the source of the proposal for a constitutional change may be, it must be accepted by the Swiss people in a referendum. Moreover, 50 000 citizens may also demand a referendum on special laws concerning international matters or matters relating to human rights. It should be pointed out that the principle of Volksinitiative is interpreted in a broad sense meaning that a number of issues may be brought to a referendum – Switzerland as 'Referendums-demokratie'. In the post-war period there were no less than roughly five federal referendums per year.

In several of the cantons the referendum institution is more comprehensive than at the federal level: the right to propose laws, obligatory law and finance referendums. At the cantonal level the referendum has been employed most frequently. To quote a country expert:

> Hence, more people participate in communal (69 per cent) or cantonal (69 per cent) politics than federal politics (60 per cent).... Contrary to what common opinion suggests, popular initiatives are not used exclusively by large and wealthy interest organizations capable of marshalling the required logistical and financial means; 40 per cent of all popular initiatives are launched by either small non-government parties (54 per cent) or small ad-hoc interest groups (46 per cent) (Kreuzer, 1990: 26).

The referendum restricts the space for partisan conflict opening up the possibility of considerable citizen influence on the actions of political parties, if practised as in Switzerland. When employed infrequently but in issues that the political parties have difficulties resolving, the referendum takes on a different meaning. Issues that political parties face difficulties in handling may be put directly to the voters to break a deadlock or relieve the parties of severe strain. When the referendum is used on infrequent but divisive issues it is often that the parties are internally divided. Thus, the referendum institution may not only substitute party government but also complement it.

Election Systems
Party government is the basic mode of democracy in the major European democracies, allowing for the exception of Swiss direct democracy and the strong element of presidentialism in France, Portugal and Finland. The source of party government is parliamentarism exercised on the basis of a popularly elected national assembly. The variety of election formula used appears in Table 7.2. Although a number of different election formulas

are conceivable most of the political systems in Western Europe employ some type of proportional election system, mainly the d'Hondt method or the modified Sainte-Laguë technique (Hand et al., 1979; Carstairs, 1980). Let us give a few examples.

The members of the Norwegian Storting are elected for a four-year period by means of a proportional method, the Sainte-Laguë technique. Proportionality is also highly valued in Denmark, as the Sainte-Laguë technique is combined with a number of equalization mandates (40) which corrects for the outcomes in the regional districts to secure as much proportionality as practical. The 2 per cent limit on entry to the Folketing has hardly acted as a major brake on the continuing fractionalization of the Danish party system though it did exclude some minor parties in the elections of the early 1980s. In Sweden citizen preferences are translated into parliamentary opinions by means of an election formula that is more orientated towards strict proportionality, with the exception of a 4 per cent threshold (or 12 per cent in a single constituency) that eliminates

Table 7.2   *Properties of election systems*

	Electoral formula	Electoral district magnitude	Proportionality index
Austria	PR: Hare (d'Hondt)	20.3	99
Belgium	PR: Hare (d'Hondt)	7.1	91
Denmark	PR: Sainte Laguë (largest remainder)	9.7	97
FRG	Plurality and PR: d'Hondt	2.0	98
Finland	PR: d'Hondt	13.3	95
France	Majority and Plurality (PR: 1945–1956, 1986)	1.0	79
Greece	PR: Hagenbach (d'Hondt)	5.4	88
Ireland	PR: STV	4.0	96
Italy	PR: imperiali quota (largest remainder)	20.3	95
Netherlands	PR: d'Hondt	150.0	96
Norway	PR: Sainte Laguë	8.2	91
Portugal	PR: d'Hondt	12.5	94
Spain	PR: d'Hondt	6.7	83
Sweden	PR: Sainte Laguë (largest remainder)	12.1	98
Switzerland	PR: Hagenbach	7.7	96
UK	Plurality	1.0	85

Note: The electoral district magnitude measures the number of seats to the number of constituencies. The proportionality index measures the extent of deviation from strict proportionality focussing upon electoral outcomes instead of formalities.
Source: Mackie and Rose, 1982.

small parties from the Riksdag. Since 1952 the modified Sainte-Laguë method is practised instead of the earlier d'Hondt method, and in 1970 a system including a number of nationally proportional mandates (39) was introduced, contributing to strict proportionality.

The Dutch political system consists of three levels of government, which citizens may influence by means of the election of proportionally composed assemblies. Proportionality is interpreted in a very strict sense and there has as yet been no majority support for the introduction of limits, excluding minor parties. Besides there is only one constituency for the whole of the Netherlands. Since the Netherlands is a unitary state, citizen influence on public activities is first and foremost channelled through the Staten-Generaal, which is the basis of a parliamentary democracy (Daalder and Irwin, 1989).

Similarly, the election procedure adopted in Austria puts a high premium on proportionality; the seats in the Nationalrat are allotted to the parties by means of a two-stage procedure to enhance a close relation between vote and seat. The same emphasis on proportionality reappears in the composition of the Bundesrat; its members are elected by the various Länder in proportion to their population by the main political body in these regional governments, the Landtag. This representative body is in its turn elected by means of a similar proportional technique; the Landestag appoints a Landesregierung, which in most Länder is composed of representatives of the various parties of the Landestag on a proportional basis. Finally, there are representative assemblies at the local government level, Gemeinderat, which is elected by means of a proportional procedure. It appoints an executive and a Bürgermeister. Basically Irish political power is to be exercised on the basis of the political composition of the Dáil, the lower chamber of the Irish parliament. The Dáil is elected for a five-year term by means of a special election procedure, the single transferable vote (STV). The 166 members of the Dáil are elected in a manner that is conducive to a high level of proportionality, although the STV favours large parties to some extent (O'Leary, 1979). The 212 members of the Belgian lower chamber are elected using d'Hondt's proportional system. The Finnish Parliament is composed of 200 members elected in proportional elections for a four-year term by the d'Hondt method.

Some political systems combine proportional and plurality techniques. The lower chamber in the Italian political system is composed of 630 members, who are elected by a proportional method for five years. There is a limit inherent in the fact that a party has to make a quorum in at least one constituency but this does not mean much as in 1987 four parties with less than 1 per cent of the vote won seats in the Chamber and another with less than 2 per cent of the vote won eight seats. The senate with its 315 members is directly elected by a combination of a majority rule and a proportional system; if a candidate receives at least 65 per cent of the vote the candidate is elected, and, if not, then senators are elected by a proportional method from party lists in each region. Whilst technically the senate electoral law is a mixed system, in practice it is a proportional representation system, because the threshold of 65 per cent is so high that very few candidates are elected at this stage. The Portuguese parliament consists of one chamber with 250 members on a four-year term, elected by means of d'Hondt's method.

The construction of the Spanish election system in 1977 reflects the ambition to use electoral rules for political purposes. The elections to the upper chamber were to employ the simple majority principle but in a special Spanish version each voter has three votes and the candidates who receive most votes are elected. Each province elects four senators – 208 in all. The elections to the lower house are based on a special framing of proportional rules, combining a minimum allotment of three seats to each constituency, a restriction of at least 3 per cent of the overall vote to get representation and the use of d'Hondt's method. These election rules no doubt favoured some parties more than others, the rules of the lower chamber resulting in an over-representation of the large number of small constituencies in country areas, whereas the rules of the senate helped large parties.

West German citizens are directly represented in the Bundestag by means of an election system that combines majority and proportional election rules. Fifty per cent of the candidates are to be elected in 'first past the post' constituencies and another 50 per cent are elected by means of a proportional rule from lists made up on a Länder basis in such a way as to ensure that the overall result in the Land, i.e. taking into account also the first 50 per cent elected from single-member districts, is true to the d'Hondt principle. There is a 5 per cent limit, in effect from the 1957 election, which prevents fractionalization as well as the representation of anti-system parties. At the Länder level there is a similar system mixing majority and proportional rules. It is generally considered that the election system to the Bundestag favours the large parties, but that it is also a fairly representative system – 'personalized proportional representation' (Johnson, 1983; Smith, 1989).

The French legislative assembly has two chambers: the national assembly with 491 members and the senate with 305 members. The national assembly of the Fifth Republic used to be recruited every fifth year by means of a special election technique, the two-ballot system up until 1985 when a proportional system based on the d'Hondt formula was introduced (Knapp, 1985); it was, however, only employed once in the 1986 election, after which they returned to the second ballot system (Cole and Campbell, 1989). In the single member constituencies the winner has to score more than 50 per cent of the vote in the first round; if nobody scores a majority, then there is another election two weeks later in which those candidates participate which receive at least 12.5 per cent of the electorate (about 20 per cent of the votes cast) in the first round; the winner is chosen by means of the plurality rule. It is well-known that this technique favours the very big parties in the centre of the political spectrum and disfavours small- and medium-sized parties on the wings, like the French Communist Party. What is gained in the effectiveness to produce majoritarian government is lost in representativeness.

The subordinate body of the senate comprising 305 members for a period of nine years is indirectly elected by a large electoral body consisting of the national assembly, 3 000 electors from the Départements and 100 000 electors from the local governments. The two-ballot system technique is employed to elect the president. The electoral system of the Fourth Republic was basically a proportional one, though there were deviations from strict proportionality; in 1945 and 1946 elections were straightforward d'Hondt. For the 1951 and 1956 elections the rules were altered to reduce the representation of anti-system communists and Gaullists. This did favour the smaller centrist parties, but it was not an 'anti-big party' strategy, but rather an 'anti-anti-system party' strategy.

There is one strict plurality system, the United Kingdom. There are 630 members of the lower chamber of the United Kingdom, elected in single-member constituencies for at most five years; the British version of a majoritarian election procedure vastly distorts the relation between votes and seats because the constituencies are not equally large. In the 1987 election Thatcher managed to capture 57.8 per cent of the seats with a 42.3 per cent share of the vote because of the distribution of votes among the three major parties or alliances which gave Conservative candidates a majority or a plurality in most constituencies. The party with the largest share of the vote is not always most benefited by the election system; the Labour Party in 1951 actually had a plurality in the electorate but still could not control Parliament. Yet, the tendency of this electoral system to disfavour small parties, except very regional ones, is obvious.

The country difference in the proportionality of party representation in the legislative assembly or parliament is closely tied to the distinction between proportional techniques and plurality methods. However, the fit is not perfect as the deviant case of Spain attests to. And we may not conclude that the Sainte-Laguë method invariably results in a better proportionality than the d'Hondt method. Other factors like the size of the electoral district and the extent to which the electoral districts are of the same weight enter the equation.

Andre Blais has suggested a simple classification system identifying the basic properties that may vary from one election system to another (Figure 7.2). In Western Europe there is, as a matter of fact, a large variation with regard to these properties of an election system. It remains to be seen whether the choice of election system makes a difference. As

Figure 7.2   *Properties of election systems*

A. The Rules
  1. The ballot structure
     A. the object of the vote (list/individuals)
     B. the procedure: (a) number of votes; (b) type of vote (nominal/
        ordinal/numerical)

  2. The constituency structure
     A. its nature (whole constituency/districts)
     B. its magnitude

  3. The formula (majority/plurality/proportionality)
B. The Outcome: degree of disparity

Source: Blais, 1988.

shown in *French Electoral Systems and Elections Since 1789* politicians sometimes change the election system in order to manipulate the election outcomes in the firm belief that such changes have an impact on party fortunes in elections and in government formation (Cole and Campbell, 1989).

Government formation pattern

Several aspects of government institutions tend to be durable over time, but the composition of governments is a reflection of temporary forces. A few distinctions may be made concerning types of government. A minimum-winning coalition is a coalition that would not be in majority if one of its participants left the coalition (Riker, 1962: 40). Other types of government involve minority, grand coalition and oversized coalition governments. Whereas an oversized coalition government would be a majority government that is not a minimum winning coalition, a grand coalition has more than a 75 per cent suppport from Parliament. A government is identified by means of its prime minister and the participating parties; the maximum length of time of a government is one standard election period. If there is a change in either of these there is a new government. Table 7.3 shows how the size of governments has varied since 1945.

There is a considerable variation between as well as within nations in the types of government formed during the post-war period. Minimum-winning coalition governments are by no means typical of the cabinets in Western Europe during the post-war period (Strom, 1989). It is true that the minimum-winning coalition is most often the type of government in systems such as Austria, Belgium, the Federal Republic of Germany, Ireland and the United Kingdom. But we also find several systems where other types of coalition pattern prevail. Minority governments are to

Table 7.3　Types of government: size

	Minimum-winning					Grand coalition				
	1950	1960	1970	1980	1985	1950	1960	1970	1980	1985
Austria	53	100	84	100	100	100	100	13	0	60
Belgium	92	96	86	55	77	31	43	13	23	0
Denmark	0	35	37	0	0	4	0	0	0	0
FRG	75	32	100	100	100	0	0	28	0	0
Finland	3	32	37	4	0	33	0	40	17	0
France	28	10	18	16	0	28	39	31	0	0
Greece	65	90	29	100	95	50	11	21	0	5
Ireland	37	67	55	85	43	0	0	0	0	0
Italy	0	13	18	0	0	12	0	0	0	0
Netherlands	25	4	61	59	33	75	39	0	0	0
Norway	100	68	54	16	15	0	0	0	0	0
Portugal	–	–	–	22	57	–	–	–	13	0
Spain	–	–	–	28	97	–	–	–	0	0
Sweden	67	28	20	36	0	0	0	0	0	0
Switzerland	0	40	0	0	0	88	53	100	100	100
UK	100	100	94	100	100	0	0	0	0	0

	Over-sized coaliton					Minority				
	1950	1960	1970	1980	1985	1950	1960	1970	1980	1985
Austria	47	0	0	0	0	0	0	16	0	0
Belgium	7	0	13	45	33	1	4	2	0	0
Denmark	4	0	0	0	0	96	65	63	100	100
FRG	25	68	0	0	0	0	0	0	0	0
Finland	63	16	53	81	100	34	53	11	15	0
France	52	50	48	84	23	21	40	35	0	77
Greece	27	0	53	0	5	8	10	18	0	0
Ireland	0	0	0	0	0	63	33	45	15	57
Italy	82	11	67	44	95	18	76	16	56	5
Netherlands	75	96	35	41	0	0	0	4	0	67
Norway	0	0	0	0	0	0	32	46	84	85
Portugal	–	–	–	39	0	–	–	–	39	43
Spain	–	–	–	0	0	–	–	–	72	3
Sweden	0	0	0	0	0	33	72	80	64	100
Switzerland	100	60	100	100	100	0	0	0	0	0
UK	0	0	0	0	0	0	0	6	0	0

Note: The data measure the proportion of time of each type of government. In our definition the maximum length of time possible for a government is one normal election period. The time periods covered include: 1946–54 (1950), 1955–64 (1960), 1965–74 (1970), 1975–85 (1980) and 1985–89 (1985). Miminum winning = if one party leaves the coalition it loses its majority; grand coalitions = a majority in excess of 75 per cent of the seats; minority = a cabinet without a majority; over-sized = a majority coalition but not minimum-winning.

be found in Denmark, Italy, Norway and Sweden whereas over-sized coalitions characterize governments in Switzerland, the Netherlands and Finland. Frequently we find over-sized cabinets, indicating that we must also look at the party composition of these governments. Grand coalitions occur around the end of the Second World War, but they are less frequent in normal peace time periods with the exception of Austria. One finding here is that minority governments occur more frequently in the 1980s than in the 1970s indicating less government cohesion in Western Europe.

Ideology in the classical left–right dimension is a relevant consideration in the formation of governments in Western Europe as governments tend to be either bourgeois or socialist. Table 7.4 shows how the ideological composition of governments has varied since 1945.

There are only five countries where the two camps, socialists and non-socialists, participate in governments on an equal basis: Austria, Belgium, Italy, Finland and the Netherlands. Such a pattern in Austria is to be found only during the 1950s and the 1960s. Only in three nations – Ireland, Italy and Switzerland – is bourgeois dominance very common whereas socialist dominance may be found at times in Sweden and the Federal Republic of Germany. The most frequent pattern is bourgeoisie hegemony or socialist hegemony, the first pattern occurring more often than the second. Shifts between bourgeois hegemony and socialist hegemony may be found in a number of nations: Denmark, West Germany, France, Norway, Sweden and the United Kingdom. Only Switzerland and Finland are characterized by the adherence to one pattern of government formation. Let us exemplify.

Typical of Finnish and Swiss government formations is the coalition. Since 1945 there have been no fewer than thirty-seven governments in Finland of which almost all were coalitions. In 1945–8, 1966–8, 1976 and 1977 there were grand coalition governments. The federal executive in the Swiss system is a special institution. It consists of seven members elected for a fixed, four years participating in the government for about ten years. The Bundespräsident is elected for a one-year term among the members of the Bundesregierung being a rotating office. This type of government operates as a collegial executive in which the major parties participate in a grand coalition on a permanent basis.

In Denmark up until the late 1960s it was possible to create majority coalition governments of various kinds, but the erosion of the party system since the 1973 election has made it more difficult to create strong and durable governments. Typical of the Danish government formation is the rather weak position of the Social Democrats, who were in power for certain periods: 1947–50, 1953–68, and 1975–82 in various combinations, including explicit cooperation with non-socialist parties and tacit support from the Socialistisk Folkeparti. Since 1945 there have been no fewer than twenty-six governments, thirteen of which belong to the period

Table 7.4   *Types of government: ideological composition*

	Bourgeois hegemony					Bourgeois dominance				
	1950	1960	1970	1980	1985	1950	1960	1970	1980	1985
Austria	0	0	40	0	0	0	0	0	0	0
Belgium	49	28	30	55	67	0	0	0	23	0
Denmark	51	0	48	23	100	0	0	0	0	0
FRG	100	100	19	23	100	0	0	0	0	0
Finland	12	58	13	7	0	0	4	0	0	0
France	41	71	100	63	43	31	11	0	0	0
Greece	100	100	100	67	0	0	0	0	0	7
Ireland	62	78	82	77	57	38	22	18	23	43
Italy	30	47	16	42	5	60	43	11	19	0
Netherlands	0	61	49	59	97	0	0	18	0	0
Norway	0	1	64	33	32	0	0	0	0	0
Portugal	–	–	–	35	84	–	–	–	0	0
Spain	–	–	–	72	0	–	–	–	0	0
Sweden	0	0	0	60	0	0	0	0	0	0
Switzerland	13	48	0	0	0	87	52	100	100	100
UK	34	97	38	57	100	0	0	0	0	0

	Even					Socialist dominance				
	1950	1960	1970	1980	1985	1950	1960	1970	1980	1985
Austria	100	100	13	0	60	0	0	0	17	40
Belgium	32	38	70	23	23	18	34	0	0	0
Denmark	4	0	0	0	0	0	73	0	12	0
FRG	0	0	28	0	0	0	0	53	77	0
Finland	47	38	41	93	100	24	0	40	0	0
France	18	18	0	0	0	9	0	0	0	0
Greece	0	0	0	0	5	0	0	0	0	0
Ireland	0	0	0	0	0	0	0	0	0	0
Italy	10	11	73	39	95	0	0	0	0	0
Netherlands	100	39	33	41	3	0	0	0	0	0
Norway	0	0	0	0	0	0	0	0	0	0
Portugal	–	–	–	30	8	–	–	–	19	0
Spain	–	–	–	0	0	–	–	–	0	0
Sweden	0	0	0	0	0	33	28	0	0	0
Switzerland	0	0	0	0	0	0	0	0	0	0
UK	0	0	0	0	0	0	0	0	0	0

Table 7.4   *continued*

	Socialist hegemony				
	1950	1960	1970	1980	1985
Austria	0	0	47	83	0
Belgium	1	0	0	0	0
Denmark	44	27	52	65	0
F R Germany	0	0	0	0	0
Finland	17	0	6	0	0
France	1	0	0	37	57
Greece	0	0	0	33	88
Ireland	0	0	0	0	0
Italy	0	0	0	0	0
Netherlands	0	0	0	0	0
Norway	100	99	36	67	68
Portugal	–	–	–	15	8
Spain	–	–	–	28	100
Sweden	67	72	100	40	100
Switzerland	0	0	0	0	0
United Kingdom	66	3	62	43	0

Note: Bourgeois hegemony refers to a coalition where all the participating parties are bourgeois; bourgeois dominance means that there are also some socialist party in the coalition but the bourgeoise parties are in a majority; the same applies to socialist hegemony and socialist dominance. The time periods covered are given in Table 7.3.

1968–89. Minority governments have been typical, twenty-two out of the twenty-six; of the remaining four, three were minimum-winning whereas one was a large over-sized coalition.

In some nations there are both minimum-sized and grand coalitions. Portugal has had about a dozen governments since 1974, the first ones over-sized, followed by minority governments and minimum-winning governments (PS and PSD). There has been a mixture ranging from hegemonic socialist to evenly distributed and hegemonic bourgeoisie governments. The effort to maximize representation has meant that a multi-party system is characteristic of Dutch politics and the large number of parties has been conducive to a large number of governments. No fewer than some twenty cabinets have been formed since 1945; with the exception of a minimum-winning coalition between 1946–48 the early post-war period saw over-sized governments in accordance with the principles of consociationalism. Since the major change in Dutch politics in 1966–67 almost all cabinets have been minimum-winning, which indicates more adversarial politics in the Netherlands (Lijphart, 1989: 53).

Likewise a number of parties have participated in Belgian governments. Among the thirty governments in the post-war period only two can be considered minority governments. Government formation has mostly been minimum-winning, but there are also cases of consociational government formation, meaning over-sized majority governments, all seven being large coalitions. Cabinet participation has come more and more to recognize the language division. Not only have the major political parties accepted the new language parties as legitimate partners in government formations or that these parties themselves have split into separate linguistic parties with separate party labels and varying levels of formal/informal institutional linkage, but since 1970 the formal composition of the government reflects the language cleavage. In a kind of Proporz system it was required constitutionally that there be as many Flemish as Francophone ministers. Besides, some informal kind of Proporz is applied to recruitment to the civil service meaning that over time each major social group will have a proportionate share of the state offices (MacMullen, 1979: 222). Also since 1945 Italy has had several either over-sized or minority governments – forty-three cabinets in all. All governments have been dominated by the bourgeoisie parties since the DC has been represented in all of them and it is only from 1981 that the party has not persistently held the post of the premier.

The Westminster model has left its imprint on the political systems of several European democracies meaning that we may expect to find minimum-sized cabinets or cabinets close to this ideal. Basically two types of government have ruled Ireland since 1945: either single-party governments with Fianna Fail or coalition governments including Fine Gael and Labour. Although parliamentarism has been practised in Sweden since 1917 the relationship between the government and the Riksdag has hovered between cabinet dominance and committee parliamentarism. Since the end of the Second World War the cabinet has clearly advanced its positions at the expense of the Riksdag, not least due to the long period in power for the Social Democratic Party: majority coalition 1936–9 (with the Agrarians), grand coalition during 1939–45, majority government from 1945–8, minority government 1948–51, minimum-winning coalition 1951–7 (with the agrarians), minority government 1957–68, majority government, 1968–70, minority government 1971–6, minority government 1982–. The exceptionally long and stable Erlander era created the impression of a highly stable political system orientated towards piecemeal engineering and rational social reform. The 1970s witnessed not only the novelty of four bourgeois governments – 1976–78 (Fälldin I), 1978–79 (Ullsten), 1979–81 (Fälldin II), 1981–82 (Fälldin III) – but also mounting difficulties in applying the Swedish decision-making style (Ruin, 1982).

Similarly, in Norway since 1945 there have been twenty-two cabinets with minimum-winning cabinets up to the 1961 election, followed by mostly minority governments, although the Borten government between 1965 and 1971 was minimum-winning. Looking at the whole post-war period we find that there have been socialist governments most of the time. Generally, in Greece there is a political tradition of étatism, of removing political matters from citizen influence. There has been a strong influence of the bureaucracy on policy-making, compensating for the difficulties in creating durable government. Between 1945 and 1967 there were no fewer than thirty governments either minimum-winning or minority governments. In comparison there have been nine governments from 1974, six of which may be characterized as minimum-sized. The emergence of the new socialist party, the PASOK, has no doubt brought more stability to government formation. Since the introduction of a democratic polity in Spain there have been only three prime ministers: Suarez (UCD, minority), Calvo Sotelo (UCD, minority) and Gonzales (PSOE, majority).

Types of chamber system

The source of party government is parliament. And parliaments consist of either one or two chambers. A distinction may be made not simply between one-cameralism and two-cameralism but also between two types of two-cameralism; in some systems with two chambers the upper house carries the same weight as the lower house, both having the same or almost equal powers whereas in other systems the upper house is dominated by the lower house meaning that its function is to act only as a moderator on the lower house. Let us exemplify these distinctions.

The Belgian Parliament has two chambers, the Chamber of Representatives and the Senate. Up until the reform of the state this bi-cameral system was modelled on the image of one lower directly elected chamber and one upper indirectly elected chamber, the upper chamber exercising a more conservative restraint upon the more popular lower chamber. The reform of state in 1980 implies that the Senate was given a different role as the guardian of regional and language community interests. The election procedure for the Senate is complicated as there are three categories of Senators: 106 directly elected, 50 elected by the provincial councils, and 25 co-opted Senators. Although the Senate differs from the Chamber of Representatives both in political composition and to some extent in the type of politicians it attracts, its role was scarcely similar to that of the British House of Lords, as it has been more active and, in particular, a more politicized body. Except for some minor details, the two chambers have formally the same function in legislation and budget-making. Although the Senate was not as important as the Chamber of Representatives, as it operated more as a reviewing or blocking chamber, the reform of state implied a more important role as it is now to guard the interests of the regions. The Senators will also constitute the two separate regional assemblies – the Flemish and the Walloon assemblies – with important regional decision-making functions in a federal perspective (Fitzmaurice, 1983: 111–43).

It is not true that the British upper house – 'this strange and antique body' (Finer, 1970) – has no real power any longer; its constitutional powers of delay and its political powers of publicity have forced governments to modify their policies over important questions. The House of Lords consists of some thousand people: hereditary peers, prelates and life peers. This bi-cameral system is of the traditional non-federative kind: the upper chamber is to moderate the decisions and actions of the lower chamber to safeguard constitutional development and wise decision making. Similarly, the Senate of the Irish Parliament consists of 60 members and it operates as a conservative moderating force on the popularly elected Dáil. The prime minister appoints 11 senators, 6 are elected by university graduates and 43 are elected from vocational lists by an electoral college comprising Dail deputies, outgoing senators and local councillors.

Perhaps the Italian bi-cameral system is less the federal kind than the British type where the upper chamber is to act as a restraining and conservative force on the lower directly elected chamber. The term of office is five years. To the senate also belongs some prominent people, for example the former presidents of the Republic who stay in the senate for life time service. The two chambers are of equal powers and their assent to the legislative proposals of the government is necessary. Concerning the relation between the two chambers of the French Parliament it may be stated that the senate has a weak position in relation to the national assembly. Although the senate participates in the legislative work the national assembly makes the final decision if the two chambers have different opinions that remain after the obligatory mediation procedure. The Dutch Staten-Generaal consists of two chambers; its lower chamber has 150 members, which are elected each fourth year on country wide lists. The upper chamber only houses 75 members, elected by an indirect method by the eleven provincial assemblies This bi-cameral system is not a federally inspired one, as the role of the upper chamber is not so much to represent the interests of the provinces as to constitute a general balance to the lower chamber. Initiative rests with the lower chamber, but all legislation has to be approved of in both chambers.

Looking at the federal type the German Bundesrat consists of forty-one members appointed by the Länder in a way that to some extent recognizes the substantial differences in the number of inhabitants in the various Länder. The rule of Länder representation presents the large states – those with more than 6 million people – with five representatives each:

North Rhine Westphalia (17 million), Bavaria (10.8 million), Baden Würtemberg (9.1 million), Lower Saxony (7.2 million); the medium-sized Länder have four representatives: Hesse: (5.6 million), Rhineland-Pfalz (3.6 million) and Schleswig-Holstein (2.6 million); those Länder that comprise less than 2 million people have been given three representatives: Hamburg (1.7 million), Bremen (0.7 million) and the Saarland (1.1 million). In addition West Berlin sends four representatives though they are without voting rights. From the relationship between number of seats and size of the Länder it appears that the Bundesrat is less orientated towards the representation of the citizens in the Länder as the Bundesrat is a mechanism of influence for Länder interests. The Bundesrat is definitely not a parliamentary chamber. It is a 'federal organ' with legislative and administrative functions (Smith, 1989).

Austria and Switzerland are different: The Austrian Federal Council and the Swiss Ständerrat represent the Austrian or Swiss nation, as the representative lower chambers do. The members of the Bundesrat are representatives of the governments of the Länder. Furthermore, they vote according to directives of the Länder – governments 'en bloc' (3, 4 or 5 votes), i.e. they are not allowed to split votes. The constitution ascribes an important role to the Bundesrat or the Länder representatives in federal legislation. Actually, the constitution assigns a number of functions to the Bundesrat in legislation, but it is only with the so-called 'zustimmungsbedürfige Gesetze' that the Bundesrat possesses the veto power, i.e. federal laws that involve the Länder; this is most typical of federal government activity that must be based on the acceptance of the Länder. Other types of law may be changed or rejected by the Bundesrat but the Bundestag may over-ride the decision of the Bundesrat with an equivalent vote; the exception refers to constitutional amendments which require a two-thirds majority in both chambers. Besides, the Bundesrat is expected to look into government directives issued as statutory instruments as a consequence of law-making which requires the consent of the Bundesrat. This legal requirement more than the others has had the consequence that the Bundesrat is really involved in federal policy-making and that the federal government has to devise both strategy and tactics to come to grips with the opinion of the Bundesrat (Johnson, 1983: 118–68).

Citizen influence in Switzerland is not only to be exercised by various forms of referendums; the Swiss political system includes elected assemblies at both the federal and the cantonal levels where citizens may express their public opinion by voting for political parties. The federal parliament comprises two chambers: the Nationalrat and the Ständerrat. This bi-cameral system is of the federal kind, as the Ständerrat represents the cantons. Both chambers have equal powers. The Nationalrat is composed of 200 members elected in a proportional election for a

Table 7.5   *Types of parliamentary chamber systems*

	1950	1960	1970	1980
Austria	1	1	1	1
Belgium	1	1	1	1
Denmark	1	0	0	0
F R Germany	2	2	2	2
Finland	0	0	0	0
France	1	1	1	1
Greece	0	0	0	0
Ireland	1	1	1	1
Italy	1	1	1	1
Netherlands	1	1	1	1
Norway	0	0	0	0
Portugal	–	–		0
Spain	–	–	–	1
Sweden	1	1	0	0
Switzerland	2	2	2	2
United Kingdom	1	1	1	1

Note: 0 = Uni-cameralism; 1 = Weak bi-cameralism; 2 = Strong bi-cameralism

four-year term; it is the chamber representing the Swiss people. The Ständerat is smaller, comprising forty-six members that are appointed by the cantons in majority elections. Since both chambers are equal in competence, sometimes rather elaborate procedures must be relied upon to arrive at the same decision in both chambers (Schumann, 1971).

The weak version of bi-cameralism is often called the English type or the conservative version whereas strong bi-cameralism is often tied to federalism. It must be pointed out that the association between strong bi-cameralism and federalism is not invariant and that the weak version of two-cameralism does not presuppose the English type of a conservatively recruited upper house. Table 7.5 shows the variation.

Austria is an example of a federalism combined with weak bi-cameralism (Nassmacher, 1968). The Nationalrat constitutes the lower chamber of the Austrian Parliament, consisting of 183 deputies elected for a four-year term; it is the main legislative body and the cabinet must have its confidence, at least tacitly. Although the Austrian political system is a federal one and includes a popularly elected president it is principally a parliamentary democracy. Its lower chamber is far more important than the upper chamber – Bundesrat – which represents the interests of the provinces (Länder). The federal government – Bundesregierung – is responsible only to the Nationalrat, though it is appointed formally by the Bundespräsident. The president is elected for a six-year term, but his functions are 'mostly ceremonial' (Gerlich, 1981).

Table 7.6   *Presidentialism versus parliamentarianism*

	1950	1960	1970	1980
Austria	1	1	1	1
Belgium	1	1	1	1
Denmark	1	1	1	1
F R Germany	1	1	1	1
Finland	0	0	0	0
France	2	0	0	0
Greece	1	1	1	1
Ireland	1	1	1	1
Italy	2	2	2	2
Netherlands	1	1	1	1
Norway	1	1	1	1
Portugal	–	–	–	0
Spain	–	–	–	1
Sweden	1	1	1	1
Switzerland	1	1	1	1
United Kingdom	1	1	1	1

Note: 0 = Presidentialism; 1 = Cabinet parliamentarianism; 2 = Committee parliamentarianism

Types of regime

Party government implies parliamentarism, that the survival and existence of the cabinet depends on the trust of the parliament, tacitly or actively. Presidentialism is based on a different principle of government in that the executive is more independent of the legislature; it tends to be focussed more on a single politician than a party programme or party ideology. Various combinations are possible, but there are limits to the combination of parliamentarism and presidentialism meaning that the institutionalization of both principles must bring about government strain. Two types of parliamentarism may be identified: cabinet and committee depending on which of the two poles – the cabinet and the parliament – is the stronger one. Table 7.6 shows that all three types are to be found in post-war government structures. We present some examples.

The political system of the United Kingdom is often regarded as a model system for liberal-democratic government. Samuel E. Finer states that it is an 'outstanding example' because of its stability, organic growth and administrative capacity and authority (Finer, 1970: 131); others argue that the Westminster model of government is superior because of its capacity to reflect public opinion and the institutionalization of political opposition in uniform principles of government deriving from parliamentary sovereignty. Whether the British system of political decision-making is to be regarded as a normative model may be contested (Lijphart, 1984a), but it can be looked upon as a cognitive model of what an extreme influence system looks like.

Typical of the British style of government is the almost complete focus on national government decision-making:

> In law the government of the United Kingdom is vested in a composite body styled the Crown-in-Parliament. This consists of the Sovereign, nominally the supreme executive, in whose name ministers carry out the duties with which they have been charged – either by custom and precedent (the 'prerogative powers') or by statute; of the House of Lords; and of the House of Commons (Finer, 1970: 149).

Whatever public authority is exercised must be derived from some parliamentary decision, whether it be powers exercised by the administration, the public corporations or by local government (the ultra vires principle).

The British model recognizes neither a division of power between independent public bodies nor any constitutional limits to the power of parliament. The British government is not separate from parliament, as the cabinet is simply a very special group within parliament. The judicial system is not to judge the laws and decisions of parliament by any higher standard, passing judgement on the constitutionality of what parliament decides. The system of government with its extreme centralization of political power is unique in the role that is afforded one institution, parliament, although it must at once be admitted that parliament may admit far-reaching decentralization to the bodies upon which it vests the task of exercising public authority; it may be worth noting that the British model is different from the other European systems in its focus on central government as the source of political power.

This British model is entrenched in a large number of legal or quasi-legal sources; whether the term constitution is or is not applicable to these norms is a matter of contention, which to some extent depends on what one means by a constitution – see Ivor Jennings' *Cabinet Government* (1951) and *Parliament* (1961). In any case there is a body of documents that besides practice lay down strict rules for how the Crown-in-Parliament is to operate. The cabinet is part of parliament and conducts the work of parliament. It is collectively responsible for the policies of the ministries, directing the work of the administration. The British model of government implies that the cabinet dominates the parliament and yet stays within the latter's basic control as no cabinet can survive if the parliament takes a vote of no confidence. This is cabinet parliamentarism:

> In brief, the actual 'Westminster model' is that of authoritarian single-party governments in a House of Commons dominated by the Prime Minister and composed largely of disciplined parties with most votes in the House of Commons being highly predictable... (Wolf-Philips, 1983: 282–3).

Citizen influence is to be transmitted into government policy-making by means of the creation of strong and stable governments for long periods of time while the institutionalization of political opposition implies that today's majority may become the minority of tomorrow. The 'shadow cabinet' is part of parliament.

Reminiscent of the Westminster model in the Federal Republic of Germany is the strong position of the chancellor – 'chancellor government' (Ridley, 1966). The cabinet is the government of the chancellor as the chancellor is the only one within the cabinet who is responsible to the Bundetag. Let us quote from Articles 63 and 64 of the constitution:

> (1) The Federal Chancellor shall be elected, without debate, by the Bundestag upon the proposal of the Federal President. (2) The person obtaining the votes of the majority of the members of the Bundestag shall be elected. The person elected must be appointed by the Federal President... (1) The Federal Ministers shall be appointed and dismissed by the Federal President upon the proposal of the Federal Chancellor.

The political system of West Germany combines federative and parliamentary aspects along with a presidency. The principles of the German chancellorship imply cabinet parliamentarianism: the chancellor nominates the ministers, identifies the main policy outlines and sets the tone in foreign policy. It is an open question how the extensive formal powers attributed to the chancellor under the constitution fare in practical politics where a number of constraints derive from different sources. Although the chancellors thus far have differed in the way of conducting the business of the chancellor, it is clear that the German chancellor is an institution that can be employed for policy-making that is sensitive to public opinion. While the constitution explicitly asserts that the office of the chancellor is not to be a vehicle for party dissension and governmental instability, Article 67 requires the Bundestag to appoint a new chancellor if there is a vote of non-confidence:

> (1) The Bundestag can express its lack of confidence in the Federal Chancellor only by electing a successor with the majority of its members and by requesting the Federal President to dismiss the Federal Chancellor. The Federal President must comply with the request and appoint the person elected. (2) Forty-eight hours must elapse between the motion and the election.

It seems as if the constitution contributes to governmental stability as there have been fifteen governments since 1949, all majority coalition governments, and most of them minimum-winning. Most conspicuous may be the Grosse Koalition between 1966 and 1969. Thus, although the chancellor institution very much reflects the Westminster model there is in addition an attempt to place the chancellor above the Bundestag as the Bundestag may not do as it wishes in declaring no confidence. As a matter of fact, the decision-making system includes other traits that are not in agreement with the Westminster model; besides the general federative structure we must also take the corporatist pattern into account.

Denmark is a typical Scandinavian parliamentary democracy where periods of cabinet parliamentarism have alternated with times of committee parliamentarism, back and forth. The overall trend towards a growing weakness of the cabinet in relation to the Folketing, which has often been dissolved to accomplish a re-election, has meant that parliamentary negotiations have become more and more important for the fate of the government and various policies.

To give an example of the two other types of government we turn to France. Scholars interpreting the French political system employ a distinction between France IV and France V to separate the decision-making system of the Fourth Republic (1946–58) from that of the Fifth Republic (1959–). The 1958 constitution is often regarded as a radical break with a political tradition dating back to the Third Republic (1875–1940), introducing a quite different system of political decision-making as a French type of presidentialism replaced a French version of parliamentarianism.

The constitution enacted in 1946 was based on the principles inherent in the Third Republic (Wright, 1950; Thompson, 1969). Two major changes were introduced in 1946: a weakening of the second chamber of parliament in relation to the first chamber and the abolition of the possibility of the government to issue certain laws without the approval of the parliament, so-called décrets-lois. Political decision-making at the national level in France between 1946 and 1958 was interpreted by its opponents as an archetype of political instability: gouvernement d'assemblée, a habit of débrouillage and immobilisme. Actually, the political system of the Fourth Republic implemented a particular version of parliamentarianism based on the dominance of parliament compared with the executive.

Committee parliamentarianism implies that government bills could be transformed radically by changes here and there, the chamber standing committees subtracting from and adding to the original proposals in contradistinction to cabinet parliamentarianism where the government dominates the parliament. The national assembly had possession of powerful instruments to make the government dependent on its confidence. Besides the approval of the president's proposal for a premier it could at any time question the confidence in the government by the ordre du jour institution. To check the position of the president not only did the parliament appoint the president, but each and every major action of the president had to be countersigned by a minister. Ministers were collectively responsible to the chambers for the general policy of the government as well as individually responsible for their personal actions. The strong adherence to committee parliamentarianism meant that political parties became the principal actors in the Fourth Republic; the shape of the French party system further increased the centrifugal forces of the constitution.

Political instability characterized the Fourth Republic; no less than twenty-seven governments held office of which twelve can be characterized as over-sized majority governments. Various other combinations were also tried – nine minority coalitions. The amount of political instability was exaggerated as several ministers participated in more than one government securing some kind of continuity in government work over time (Siegfried, 1956). In addition the profound place of the French bureaucracy must be taken into account; its élitist orientation constituted a balancing force to committee parliamentarianism and government instability. The French governments between 1946 and 1958 were far from all being ineffective; at crucial moments some governments proved capable of action, but la question algérienne proved too difficult to solve.

The constitution of the Fifth Republic, framed by de Gaulle and Debré as long-standing critiques of the constitutional tradition, was less a systematic innovation than a sharp reaction to the practices of the Fourth Republic. Its actual content was just as much determined by the evolution of events and the interpretation by the chief actors of its final wording in 1958. The basic change of the Fourth Republic by the Constitution was to reduce the powers of the national assembly.

The constitution of the Fifth Republic singles out the president as the leading central authority. Since 1962 the president has been directly elected by the people, a source of immense legitimacy. The French president is the head of the state, not only carrying out a number of symbolic and representative functions but very much involved in the government, appointing the premier, participating in government decision-making, appointing the important civil servants. What further strengthens the position of the president is the possession of a number of prerogatives like the capacity to dissolve the national assembly as well as call a referendum. If these rights are not enough, the president may fall back on Article 16:

> When the institutions of the Republic, the independence of the nation, the integrity of its territory or the fulfillment of its international commitments are threatened in a grave and immediate manner and when the regular functioning of the constitutional government authorities is interrupted, the President of the Republic shall take the measures commanded by these circumstances, after official consultation with the Premier, the Presidents of the assemblies and the Constitutional Council.

There can be no doubt that the French presidents have made use of the large potential power inherent in the Gaullist constitution. The French political system combines presidentialism with parliamentarianism in a special mixture. Although the prime minister dominates the work of the government and the president is elected directly, the ministers including the premier must have the confidence of the national assembly. The potential conflict between the president and the premier is typical of national decision-making in France, although the regime survived the 'co-habitation' of a socialist president (Mitterand) and a non-socialist premier (Chirac) for a few years in the late 1980s.

According to the constitution the premier is to direct the work of the ministers and the premier also possesses prerogatives in relation to the national assembly such as the right to call a meeting and to propose legislation. There have been eighteen governments since 1959, some were minimal-winning majorities and some over-sized while five were minority governments. The functions of the legislative assembly refer mainly to the passing of legislation and the control of government. In both respects, French presidentialism implies that the national assembly and the senate carry on their work within restrictions that benefit the government and the president. A number of rights and duties were devised to counteract the power of the French legislative assembly in force during the Fourth Republic: the right of the government to call a vote on the totality of a proposal prohibiting a vote on particular pieces within the proposal, to demand from the assembly the right to issue government directives to be ratified by the assembly, and the right to call a vote of special confidence in some decision to be taken by the assembly. Moreover, a vote of no confidence has to be backed by an absolute majority (Wright, 1983).

The role of the president has come to dominate much of the debate on the Finnish political system (Hidén and Saraviita, 1978; Anckar, 1984b). The emergence of strong presidentialism implies that the meaning of parliamentary democracy in the Finnish context has been questioned. Reform proposals were put forward that either would limit presidential power or make the president more accountable to public opinion. According to the 1919 constitution the executive function rests with the president, who is to govern the country with the cabinet and the administration. The president also has a part in the legislative function, as the president may place a temporary veto on bills passed in the parliament. Moreover, the president is also the commander-in-chief of the defence. Dag Anckar states that the list of presidential powers in Finland is truly impressive (Anckar, 1984a).

Before 1987 the president was elected for a six-year term by an indirect procedure. A direct procedure was introduced in 1988 meaning that a candidate is elected president if he/she receives more than 50 per cent of the votes in a direct election; if not, the indirect procedure is resorted to. Re-election is possible without limit. There are 301 electors chosen by the Finnish people in proportional elections using the same technique as that employed for parliamentary elections; balloting is secret. Due to special circumstances the presidents were appointed by the Finnish parliament in 1919, 1944, 1946 and 1973 by means of a special law. The combination of strong presidentialism and the lack of a direct mechanism for the election of a president creates a strain on Finnish democracy, accountability not matching power, resulting in a call for a new procedure of electing the president. The president may dissolve the parliament and ask for re-elections. The cabinet must have the confidence of the parliament to govern the country, but presidential decisions in the cabinet must not be approved by the president.

Similarly, Portuguese policy-making is heavily concentrated in the parliament and the president, as the elements of direct democracy are weak. The government stands somewhere in between the parliament and the president, as both may dissolve the government. Since 1976, when the first constitutional government took office, there have been tensions between president and parliament over the control of governments – which explains a key aspect of the 1982 constitutional revision. In practice, however, the president has had to accept that parliamentary factors dictate the shape and operation of governments. The 1982 revision of the constitution involved a restriction of the powers of the president to dissolve the Assembly, dismiss the prime minister and veto legislation and the abolition of the military Council of the Revolution (Gladdish, 1990).

According to the constitutional formula Greece is a 'republican parliamentary democracy'. The Greek parliament consists of one chamber with 300 members, elected for a four-year term in proportional elections. Legislative power rests with parliament, which also exercises some means of control over the cabinet. However, the Greek government is to be characterized as a parliamentary system rather than as a quasi-presidential system. The cabinet needs the tacit approval of both the parliament and the president. The president is supposed to appoint the premier from the largest party in the parliament, but it remains to be emphasized that the president appoints the cabinet. The Greek parliament may express a vote of no confidence if an absolute majority supports such a proposal, but it is the president who discharges the premier. However, the intent is clearly that the premier is to govern the country with the cabinet. And constitutional practice has not falsified that with respect to day-to-day business the government, not the president, of the republic is to rule.

Up until 1986 the president of the Greek republic had a number of prerogatives in a political system that consists of a unitary state with a strongly centralized bureaucracy. The president is the head of the Greek state, concentrating on various honorific duties. Article 48 in the constitution admitted the possibility of presidentialism entrusting the president with far-reaching emergency powers if there is an external or internal threat to the Greek state. However, the delineation of Greek presidentialism to emergency states implies that the powers of the president were more circumscribed than was the case in the 1952 constitution. On the other hand, there was an attempt in the new constitution to strengthen the position of the cabinet and the premier in relation to the parliament. The constitution comprises a number of provisions which enhance the position of the premier, meaning that the executive is strengthened at the expense of the parliament. However, up until the 1986 constitutional downgrading of Greek presidentialism initiated by premier Papandreou against President Karamanlis circumstances decided the power relation between the president and the prime minister:

> The distribution of powers between the president and the prime minister that is laid down in the constitution is such that political primacy could rest with either, depending on the particular political circumstances of the day and of the personalities involved (Kohler, 1982: 149).

It may be claimed that cabinet parliamentarianism is a typical mode of government in Western Europe. A majority of the European democracies adhere to this principle of party government although we find both presidentialism (France, Finland, Portugal) as well as committee parliamentarianism. Typical of the Fourth Republic was the strong position of the parliament committees over the cabinet and the executive; and policy-making in Italy has been somewhat similar to this mode of government. A direct election procedure of the president is conducive to the existence of strong presidentialism as in Portugal and France, but a direct procedure is not a sufficient condition with Austria and Finland as examples. The political system in West Germany may be regarded as a blend of various constitutional elements.

Consociationalism and corporatism

Party government may be limited by various checks and balances in a constitutional structure – the Madisonian model of democracy – or it may be unrestrained in the expression of the popular will except by the internal behaviour rules adhered to by those in power – the Populist model of democracy (Dahl, 1956). Which model of democracy is to be preferred? Unlimited party government may result in the oppression of the minority by the majority. But, is a constitutional fabric of divided powers, special majorities and extensive veto opportunities really a necessary or sufficient condition for majority rule to respect the rights of minorities? The normative problem of recommending a model of democracy is a tricky one. The empirical analysis of European democracies suggests that party government may be restrained in various ways.

The extent to which consociational devices have been institutionalized matters as does the degree of corporatization. Whereas consociational

Table 7.7   *Consociationalism and corporatism*

	Consociationalism	Corporatism
Austria	1	2
Belgium	1	1
Denmark	0	2
F R Germany	0	1
Finland	0	2
France	0	0
Greece	0	0
Ireland	0	0
Italy	0	1
Netherlands	1	1
Norway	0	2
Portugal	0	1
Spain	0	1
Sweden	0	2
Switzerland	1	1
United Kingdom	0	0

Note: These two scales order countries according to the extent to which they are characterized by consociationalism (after Lijphart, 1979) and corporatism (after Schmitter, 1981).

devices may include the kind of consociational checks and balances conceived of in the Madisonian model of democracy, the corporatist challenge to party government lacks such formal recognition and legitimacy (Schmitter, 1984). Table 7.7 shows that party government may be restrained by a combination of consociational devices and corporatism.

Corporatism is more widespread than consociationalism, as only three countries have weak corporatist arrangements: the United Kingdom, Ireland and Greece. Interest mediation and interest articulation are particularly conspicuous in Austria and the Scandinavian countries, whereas consociationalism is to be found in societies with ethnic or religious cleavages: the Netherlands, Belgium, Austria and Switzerland. Over time a difference between consociationalism and corporatism may be noted as corporatism has clearly advanced since the end of the Second World War whereas consociational practices declined in importance in some of its typical nations – the Netherlands and Austria. Let us look a little more closely at a few nations.

The Austrian political system is well-known for its informal constitution, its consociationalism and its corporatism. By means of Grosse Koalition, Proporz and corporatist interest mediation the system tried to present major groups with stable channels for the exercise of influence on policy-making. If the formal constitution presents the citizens of Austria with access to government decision-making, then the informal constitution recognizes the importance of the participation of collectivities and organizations in the policy process. Austria used to be characterized as consociational due to the existence of a grand coalition between 1945 and 1966. Consequently, the end of the period of the Grosse Koalition should imply that Austria should be characterized as less consociational during the 1970s and the early 1980s. The government between 1945 and 1966 had broad parliamentary support as the two major parties controlled roughly 90 per cent of the seats in the Nationalrat. After 1966 there were both single-party minority governments (1970–71), single-party majority governments (1966–70, 1971–83) and two-party majority coalitions (1983–). However, Austrian consociationalism involves far more than large coalitions (Pulzer, 1974).

The phenomenon of the Grosse Koalition was based on a series of coalition pacts between the different Lager which was also expressed in the phenomena of Proporz and Sozialpartnerschaft. According to Proporz the relative strength of the main parties as revealed in the recent election should have institutional implications for the recruitment to the bureaucracy at various levels, within the ministries as well as within public corporations, the armed forces, the police and the universities. The Proporz principle opened up participation within the state to the broad bulk of Austrian society, the three Lager. Élite cooperation in large coalitions in no way reduced the social relevance of the Lager division:

> ... Lager-based traditionalism is widespread, but what was once a millenarian vision has become a set of routinized dogmatic attitudes. The Lager have not disintegrated. They have merely colluded in letting their ammunition rust. The character of the parties has not changed beyond recognition. What has happened is that those wings of the parties which favour peaceful co-existence have gained strength compared with the inter-war period (Pulzer, 1974: 171).

The return to party competition and the formation of Westminster model governments have taken place within the strong confines of Austrian corporatism, which is intimately associated with consociationalism.

The corporatist elements have formal as well as informal sides; a country expert states:

> In general this is referred to as Sozialpartnerschaft (social partnership), a term which strongly underlines the consensual and cooperative aspects. Since 1948, unions and business had collaborated intermittently to restrain wages and prices. This collaboration was turned into a more formal and permanent one in 1957 ... (Lehmbruch, 1979: 158).

Formal Austrian corporatism includes the so-called chambers, which are statutory public corporations with compulsory membership; there is a large number of such chambers at both federal and provincial level. The most important ones are those of labour, agriculture and business. These interest corporations are involved in all kinds of matters pertaining to wages and prices; in addition they are heard on matters relating to legislation (Begutachtungsrecht). Informal Austrian corporatism refers to the mutual trust and pattern of cooperation built up between the major interest organizations including the Österreichische Gewerkschaftsbund (ÖGB) for labour. Organized interests have conducted interest mediation in various decision fora: the so-called Paritary Commission for Questions of Price and Wage Regulation, the Advisory Council for Economic and Social Problems and the governing council of the Nationalbank. The Sozialpartnerschaft is based on 'paritärische' participation and the attempt to control interest conflict by means of voluntary agreement. It opens up a large amount of group influence to major social organizations. Austrian corporatism includes both independent unions (ÖGB), the system of public chambers and occupational leagues. Each Lager has its own party, chambers, league or union and these economic organizations are very closely tied to its Lager and its party (Ucakar, 1982; Matzner, 1982).

The Dutch political system used to be considered as one of the few ideal examples of the institutionalization of consociational practices, besides Belgium, Switzerland and Austria. In 1966 Hans Daalder stated:

> At least three distinct subcultures coexist: an orthodox Protestant one (comprising some 20–25 per cent of the nation); a Catholic one (numbering over a third); and a 'general' one. The latter comprises less than half of the population and, being composed mainly of Dutchmen who are neither orthodox Protestant nor Catholic, it tends to assume a rather special place on the political continuum (Daalder, 1966b: 213).

The Verzuiling of the Dutch society had a counterpart in the party system where a number of parties represented each major pillar. The strong centrifugal forces inherent in the segmentation of the population into various Zuilen were accommodated by means of élite cooperation at the national government level, including a number of influence mechanisms designed to give each pillar a voice in policy-making, including the formation of over-sized coalitions, the representation of a variety of legitimate interests on various boards, and the resort to bargaining between élites to enhance consensus. The developments since the introduction of 'new politics' in the Netherlands in 1966–67 have meant that the consociational model of policy-making lost in relevance (Lepszy, 1979; Scholten, 1980; Van Schendelen, 1984). There has been a movement towards an open model of policy-making with the parties competing for the support of a more volatile electorate presenting the government with more autonomy in relation to the established organizations when choosing policies (Irwin and van Holsteyn, 1989; Wolinetz, 1988).

Generally speaking, the decline in relevance of consociationalism has often been more than balanced by an increase in corporatism. The emphasis on direct forms for citizen influence in the interpretations of the Swiss political system neglects the existence of encompassing structures and elements which over-arch the high autonomy and pluralism typical of Switzerland and leads to political results one otherwise hardly could expect. Lehner points out that organized interests have grown strong in Switzerland as they have institutionalized access to policy-making, particularly at the federal level. Lehner states that Switzerland is a typical case of 'liberal corporatism':

> Swiss consociational democracy is institutionalized through an elaborate system of hearing and bargaining procedures, an extensive system of committees, and a large amount of formal and informal consultation. This system allows for much participation of interest groups, parties, and cantons in national policy-making (Lehner, 1983: 207).

Corporatization constitutes a general phenomenon all over Western Europe, but this process has been particularly strong in countries where the structure of organized interests has been encompassing and peaked. In Norway the 1970s witnessed a transfer of influence from the cabinet to the Storting, but at the same time the interest organizations enhanced their position vis-à-vis politicians and administrators in national policy-making. In his *Organized Democracy* (1983) Johan P. Olsen employs the concept of integrated participation to denote a variety of characteristics in the inter-penetration of state and interest groups in the stages of the policy cycle.

Integrated participation characterizes the Norwegian system, but it is not formally laid down as a general technique for handling decisions. Instead integrated participation is resorted to when the issues are more material than symbolic, when the number of participants is small rather than large and when the implementation outcome can be predicted. Integrated participation is widely employed in Norway but its status is controversial. It fits well with the emergence of a large administration at the national level. The Norwegian bureaucrat plays an influential role in the government process as he/she is protected by tenure, enjoys considerable discretion and may work up support from stable coalition partners among politicians, organized interests, in particular Landsorganisationen (LO) and Norsk Arbeidsgiverforening (NAF).

The Norwegian policy-making style is neither that of ministerial hierarchy nor that of power dispersion and ungovernability. Olsen summarizes:

> Today, executives are more often in a bargaining situation both within the governmental apparatus and with organized interests in society, and the main tendency is toward specialization. The major response to the problems of capacity, understanding, and authority has been a political-administrative division of labor. And administrative sectorization has increased because the various ministries, departments, and divisions have developed specialized external patterns of contacts and support. The result is a segmented structure with stable, nonhierarchical functional coalitions (Olsen, 1983: 116).

It must be recognized that corporatism looms large in the mixed economies in the Scandinavian democracies interpreted as a negotiation economy run by iron triangles (Hernes, 1978). And the growing strength of the system of integrated participation evoked a citizen reaction in Norway in the 1970s asking for more local citizen influence – participatory democracy. It even came to harsh expressions of civil disobedience as environmentalist groups rejected the decision of the Storting concerning the Alta River. However, local government is a viable mechanism for the exercise of citizen influence via the political parties. Elected assemblies appoint executives in the various municipalities and fylken; the election procedure is the same as the one practised at the national level.

Influence on Swedish government policy-making is exercised in the forms of referendums, parliamentary elections and corporatism. The basic form is still the expression of citizen preferences for political parties competing for seats in the Riksdag although corporatist elements have grown stronger, particularly in the 1970s and the early 1980s. It has been argued that consensus politics has become increasingly difficult between the various political parties (Ruin, 1982) and that the Swedish version of corporatism and interest mediation has turned against the system resulting in more and more institutional sclerosis, decision inertia as well as power of distributional coalitions. The strong position of the Social Democratic Party in state and society opened the way for the participation of organized interests in policy-making, exercising influence at the various stages of the policy process. The major interest organizations include: the LO (Landsorganisationen), the TCO (White Collar Workers), the SACO-SR (Academics), the SAF (Employers' Association) and the LRF (Farmers' Association).

The Swedish version of corporatism is a mixture of societal and state corporatism; the background is the mobilization of organized interests in accordance with the societal model, but the 1970s saw a strong dose of state corporatism: state subsidies as well as public recognition, transfer of public functions, monopoly of representation. Corporatism no doubt contributed to the ease with which many social reforms could be enacted and implemented; however, it seems as if the growth in the power of interest organizations has become increasingly difficult to accommodate within the decision-making system. Not only has power been transferred from the Riksdag to the Cabinet, but public power appears to have become more diffused among several different groups of actors, among which may be mentioned various bureaucracies that have grown from the exceptional expansion of the Swedish public sector, different organized interests, regional and local groups of actors. The constitution singles out the Riksdag as the main institution of power:

> Article 3. The Riksdag is the principal representative of the people. The Riksdag enacts the laws, decides on taxes and determines how public funds shall be used.

However, the uni-cameral Riksdag (the bi-cameral Riksdag of 1866 was abolished in 1970) seems to have become less and less capable of taking strong action in various fields.

The Finnish political system has attracted international interest not only because of its somewhat curious type of presidentialism but also because of the clear development of a new type of relationship between the organizations and the state, neo-corporatism. In their *Consultation and Political Culture* (1983) Voitto Helander and Dag Anckar show that events since the end of the Second World War exemplify a transition from a pluralist to a neo-corporatist conception of the place of organized interests in society, particularly with major interest organizations. They show that structural corporatism – i.e. the organized participation of interest organization in state policy-making in preparatory, consultative, bargaining and decision stages – has increased since the 1960s at the time of the advent of an incomes policy. They state:

> This kind of consultation and cooperation seems to have brought with it an ever-increasing number of differently named joint-organs, in which the participating organizations have in general equal representation (Helander and Anckar, 1983: 24–5).

Besides consultation there are also other highly conspicuous elements of corporatism: the use of indirect state administration in which the organizations assume functions of a public character as well as the formal right of organizations to appoint members of state lay boards. Again we quote:

> Advisory councils established for certain central bureaus and increased sittings have indeed created in practice very good opportunities for the interest-organizations to involve themselves directly in authoritative decision-making (Helander and Anckar, 1983: 26).

The coming of strong corporatism in combination with the strong presidentialism already described has no doubt decreased the power of the political parties and eroded some of the basis for parliamentary democracy in Finland.

Corporatism is omnipresent in Western Europe. Organized interests have become legitimate participants in the policy process entering in various ways into policy networks. It may be argued that such policy styles may compensate for the implementation gap or control deficit typical of national government action in an increasingly complex society (Hanf and Scharpf, 1978; Richardson and Jordan, 1979; Dunleavy, 1985; Sharpe, 1985). The organizations of interest groups in post-war Germany began shortly after the fall of the Nazi regime resulting in high organization of employers and employees: for example Deutsche Gewerkschaftsbund, Deutsche Beamtenbund and Bundesvereinigung der Deutschen Arbeitsgeberverbände. The corporatist pattern of interest mediation has had to compete with a strong liberal ideology emphasizing the rule of markets and the limits of state intervention in the interaction between the organized interests. In the 1960s the so-called Konzertierte Aktion was inaugurated, a kind of societal corporatism including income policy and coordination of various business activities with regard to macro-economic objectives. The German version of neo-corporatism has been orientated more towards developing trust and collaboration than towards entrusting the interest organizations with public functions (Lehmbruch, 1979: 147–83).

Corporatist patterns of policy-making loom large in the Italian political system. The Italian structure of organized interests consists of a large number of interest organizations; the fragmentation between competing groups in the trade union movement is considerable and there are a few giant institutions on the employers' side. Three large trade-union organizations compete with each other: the CGIL (Communist-dominated), the CISL (gathering Catholic workers, but far from entirely ranked with the DC) and the UIL (Socialists, Social Democrats and Republicans). The Socialists have a bare majority in the UIL, but retain a vocal minority in the CGIL and even in the CISL. On the employers' side there is the huge Confindustria that represents some 100 000 firms. Catholic Action must also be mentioned as it represents several important Catholic associations. Besides there are two large agricultural organizations. One may separate between two types of pattern: the *clientela* and the *parentela*. The first refers to a close cooperation between private institutions and public authorities, whereas the second stands for a close interaction between interest organization and political party, based on ideological ties including Catholicism. The combination of these two patterns of corporatist interaction has resulted in the so-called il sottogoverno, or the undergovernment. There have been ties between the *Confindustria* and some ministries as well as between Catholic Action and the DC, and the CGIL and the PCI.

Conclusion

The political systems of the major European democracies vary in several aspects in a set of mechanisms of influence for citizens and organized interests. It may be argued that some of the distinct influence mechanisms dealt with in this chapter are more or less substitutes, i.e. they have similar functions. Citizen and collectivities search for influence in democratic polities to have an impact on the policies of governments. One type of influence would be mass influence, or the capacity of citizens to influence policies or policy-makers – the referendum institution and the degree of proportionality in election formulas. Another indicator of influence would be élite influence on policy-making – consociationalism and corporatism.

Table 7.8   *Central government influence index*

	Mass influence	Elite	Party Government efficacy	Influence mechanism index
Austria	3	2	2	7
Belgium	1	1	2	4
Denmark	4	2	0	6
F R Germany	3	1	2	6
Finland	2	2	0	4
France	2	0	2	4
Greece	1	0	2	3
Ireland	3	0	2	5
Italy	3	1	0	4
Netherlands	2	2	2	6
Norway	3	2	2	7
Portugal	1	1	1	3
Spain	1	1	1	3
Sweden	3	2	1	6
Switzerland	4	2	0	6
United Kingdom	0	0	4	4

Note: The tentative influence scores have been computed on the basis of ordinal classifications: mass influence = referendum and proportionality (0-4); élite influence = corporatism and consociationalism (0-2); party government efficacy = frequency of minimum-winning cabinets (0-4).

We also want to identify government formation as a kind of influence – the effectiveness of influence. It may be argued that the existence of minimum-winning cabinets would be conducive to effective translation of citizen preferences into policies, all other things equal. Let us tentatively rank the West European democracies in these three influence types as well as introduce an overall index of influence mechanism (Table 7.8).

There is a variation in these three types of political influence structures. Some nations emphasize mass influence in the form of either a system of frequent referendums or an election system that makes party representation in terms of seats allocated to the party in the Parliament highly proportional to the number of votes received. Sone countries employ élite influence techniques like consociational devices or corporatist patterns of policy-making variously expressed in accommodation and consultation politics. A few political systems display the combined practice of both influence methods. However, a few nations employ a very different influence technique: minimum winning cabinets as a proper technique for effective influence of party government on the making and implementation of public policies. The crux of this influence technique is that the minimum winning coalitions that form an effective government are also minimum sized in the sense that the minimum winning coalition has

Figure 7.4   *Westminster and consensus model political systems*

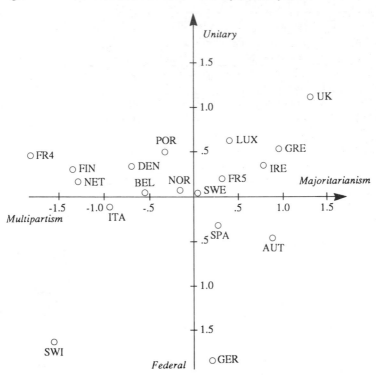

Note: AUT = Austria; FR4 = French Fourth Republic; FR5 = French Fifth Republic. The federal–unitary dimension comprises governmental centralization, unicameralism–bicameralism and constitutional flexibility. The majoritarianism–multipartism dimension covers minimum winning cabinets, cabinet durability, effective number of parties, number of issue dimensions and electoral disproportionality.
Sources: Lijphart et al., 1988: 12.

the smallest possible majority and that the opposition today may be the government of tomorrow.

The consensus model of the political system underlines the first two influence methods: referendum, proportional representation and élite accommodation. The Westminster model of government emphasizes the third influence technique: the open contestation between the government and its opposition where the winner takes all and the political parties alternate between government and opposition roles. However, one has to recognize that the institutional variation in West European political systems is not easily reduced to a dichotomous distinction such as for example the Westminster model and the consensus model. Figure 7.4 shows that the West European political systems cannot be classified as belonging either to the Westminster model or the consensus model.

Adding the dimension of institutional autonomy to the influence dimension one sees that only the United Kingdom and Switzerland may be neatly classified as pure examples of a Westminster model regime and a consensus model regime, respectively. Most political systems in Western Europe consist of some combination of properties of these two Weberian ideal types.

The overall orientation of the political system towards these various techniques for the exercise of influence on political decision-making is of profound importance for the structure of the polity. It may also be expected to have an impact on political stability. Having analysed the institutions of autonomy and the mechanisms for exerting political influence, we proceed to look at the very subject-matter of politics: issues.

8

Issues

Introduction

Societal problems must be politicized before they can affect the institutions of the system; and the politicization of problems to be handled by the public may constitute a viable method for the peaceful settlement of profound social cleavages. Actually, issue-making and issue-resolving may constitute a method for the reduction of tensions in society. How could there be conflict management without a continuous process of politicization? How could there be political stability without issue-making and issue-resolving? Yet, issue-making may also threaten political stability and even result in system destruction.

General theories concerning the political system approach these types of social system as action systems. The Eastonian systems analysis models the political system as an input–output organization processing demands and support, converting these into the production of decisions and activities (Easton, 1965). In a similar fashion Almond and Powell identify six action aspects: interest articulation, interest aggregation, rule formulation, rule application, rule adjustment and communication – relating demand and support to outputs (Almond and Powell, 1966). A systems approach may be transformed into a communication approach placing the same emphasis on decision-making and the processing of inputs into outputs as the Deutsch model shows (Deutsch, 1963). Ongoing decision-making processes in political systems focus upon so-called issues. Theories of political behaviour and collective choice identify issues as of crucial importance in shaping electoral choice, party outcomes and decision-making processes in legislative assemblies (Budge and Farlie, 1977; 1978; Tufte, 1978; Whiteley, 1980; Alt and Chrystal, 1983). Roll-call analysis identifies issues as the substance of legislative decision-making to be handled by means of decision rules in accordance with the preferences of the actors to arrive at a collective outcome (Riker and Ordeshook, 1973; Brams, 1975; Riker, 1982; Moulin, 1983).

Empirically it is interesting to study the appearance of the issue-making process cross-nationally. We face a variation in the political relevance of various problems both cross-sectionally and longitudinally as well as a variation in how issues are handled. Which issues have the West European countries struggled with and how? We wish to relate the analysis of the occurrence of political issues to the overall theme of institutionalism versus a political sociology approach. A basic problem in understanding how political systems handle issues is the extent to which the politicization of problems is a function of the environment. Is it possible to evaluate the claims of a political sociology approach and of institutionalism in relation to how problems become issues with data about West European societies? The analysis of issue-making in the context of European democracies covers the time period after the Second World War.

The concept of an issue

The basic problem with the concept of an issue is to specify those properties that out of the raw materials of politics distil a set of problems that are politically highly salient. What properties define a problem as politically salient enough for it to be labelled an issue? Actually, there is no standard definition of issue in the literature. In his *Party Strategies in a Multiparty System* (1968) Gunnar Sjöblom states:

> ... 'issue' in this context refers to a matter of dispute between the parties in the electoral arena. Normally, one also reads into the concept that an 'issue' must not be a too insignificant matter of dispute, which only appears sporadically or incidentally in the election debate (Sjöblom, 1968: 123).

Sjöblom singles out three properties: target of conflict, politicization and significance for the political system. In voting studies issues refer to 'statements that allege differences between the contending parties or candidates' (Berelson et al., 1954: 182) and Easton follows this usage: 'Of necessity, these will be the demands that have become the subject of greatest controversy and, following standard usage, I shall call them issues' (Easton, 1965: 140). Evidently, what is typical of an issue is that it is either an object of different and conflicting orientations of the political parties or a problem of systemic importance. Finding operational criteria for these properties is a difficult problem: What is a significant matter? Could there be issues of systemic importance although they are not the object of conflicts between the established political parties? How can one separate issues from non-issues if some types of systemic social problems never become politicized? How can one distinguish between various degrees of 'issueness'?

The problem of presenting a definition of the concept of issue that comprises a set of necessary or sufficient conditions for the application of the concept was debated at length in the famous struggle concerning the concept of power (Dahl, 1961; Bachrach and Baratz, 1963; Polsby, 1963).

There is a risk that a non-issue and a non-existent issue will be seen as identical thus making the distinction between issues and non-issues barren (Wolfinger, 1971).

To avoid the problem of separating issues and non-issues Kenneth Janda in *Political Parties: A Cross-national Survey* (1980) starts from the assumption that issues are what politics is all about; the problem then becomes to single out a set of important issues interesting enough to warrant a cross-national study. Janda states:

> We further narrow the universe by also requiring that the issues be pervasive enough to elicit conflicting positions by parties in more than two countries – insisting, in fact, that the issues must either cut across countries in different cultural-geographical areas or that they be common to most of the party systems within a single area... (Janda, 1980: 53).

Each and every selection of relevant issues in a country implies that some issues are regarded as more important than others – a judgement which may be contested. The crux of the matter is whether one has selected the important ones, i.e. important for the understanding of the politics of the country in question. Janda maintains:

> The issues that we selected constitute a 'sample' of the universe only to the extent that we have not included all the issues that might be included in a cross-national analysis. We hope that we have selected the important ones, but we certainly have not exhausted the universe of possibilities (Janda, 1980: 53).

The Janda criterion on issue importance – 'elicit conflicting positions by parties in more than two countries' – parallels the Sjöblom definition though it introduces a narrower concept because of the cross-national requirement.

Again, stating operational criteria is problematic: What criteria could make us confident that the 'important ones' have been identified in various countries? No doubt the concept of an issue is widely employed in comparative politics to sort out questions that somehow pertain to conflict in a manifest or latent fashion. The following quotation may serve as a typical statement about the function of issues in political systems:

> Dutch politics is a politics of accommodation. That is the secret of its success. The term accommodation is here used in the sense of settlement of divisive issues and conflicts where only a minimal consensus exists (Lijphart, 1975: 103).

The theory of the issue cycle identifies the various steps in the process of handling political matters in so far as they have 'issueness': politicization of a problem, decision-making finding alternatives and a solution, and depoliticization of the problem. However, how do we identify these phases? When have issues been settled? How much consensus must have prevailed for how long before an issue can be said to be depoliticized? Suffice it here to establish that the operational criteria are as important as the theoretical properties and that the operational criteria refer somehow to political conflict or to problems that are important to the political system as a system, systemic impact.

Observation and classification of issues

Issues constitute a subset within the social problems of a country in contrast to the private problems of the citizens. Operational criteria that are each sufficient for designating a social problem as an issue include:

1 *Target for parliamentary action*: An analysis of parliamentary decisions may contribute to the identification of the set of issues in a nation which simultaneously displays the pattern of conflict surrounding an issue.

2 *Target for public opinion activities*: An analysis of the major newspapers may present an overview of the problems that have become politicized which complement the parliamentary analysis.

These criteria – parliamentary decision activity and/or public opinion attention – may be unnecessary for the identification of issues in general, but they are probably sufficient for describing political issues in Western Europe. Below we solve the problem of finding the major issues by employing the two techniques previously discussed. On the one hand *Keesings* Contemporary Archives have been used to check what various national newspapers have focussed on; on the other hand we identify those decisions in parliament that have or could have been the cause of shifts in government or in coalition patterns according to various national specialists.

Issues have a few salient dimensions: intensity of conflict, duration in time, number of participants involved and frequency of occurrence. These properties capture the 'issueness' of a social problem. If they were easily operationalized, a scale measuring issueness could be derived simply by adding the scores of an issue on the dimensions above. Unfortunately, these properties of issues are difficult to identify empirically. It is a truism that there is a set of major issues in all countries but it is anything but clear how such a set is to be identified and what values on the dimensions of issueness constitute necessary or sufficient conditions for singling out an issue as a major one.

A basic problem in the study of political decision-making is the categorization of issues once the identification problem has been solved. Classifying issues requires a typology which may be based on various considerations. Janda suggests that thirteen categories cover the various types of issue: government ownership of means of production, government role in economic planning, redistribution of wealth, social welfare, secularization of society, support of the military, alignment with East/West blocks, anti-colonialism, supra-national integration, national integration, electoral participation, protection of civil rights, and interference with civil liberties (Janda, 1980: 55). A similar list of issue types is suggested by Thomas (1975). It may be argued that the Janda list is too detailed, and broader categories have been proposed by Lijphart, who speaks of a few ideological dimensions typical of the politics of the 1970s: socio-economic, religious, cultural-ethnic, urban–rural, regime support, foreign policy and post-materialism (Lijphart, 1981: 28–9). As the comprehensiveness of the categories is expanded the risk of losing valuable distinctions increases.

Compared to the Lijphart typology Janda may pinpoint important distinctions between types of socio-economic issues like government ownership of the means of production versus government role in economic planning. On the other hand a detailed list such as Janda's may result in double classifications: How is one, for example, to distinguish between redistribution of wealth and social welfare? A detailed list of types of issue also runs the risk of being not detailed enough. If, for example, electoral participation constitutes an issue type what about environmental issues? If social welfare is an important issue type, how about property rights and workers' participation?

Issues also appear in party manifestos. *Ideology, Strategy and Party Change: Spatial Analyses of Post-War Election Programmes in 19 Democracies* (Budge et al., 1987) is a cross-national inquiry into the extent to which electoral programmes contain a unified ideology. To what extent do the same issues show up in the party manifestos of various political parties in different countries? The tool for understanding a variety of information about party platforms is factor analysis based on an intricate system of coding the information. The interpretation of party programmes relied on 7 domains with 54 categories, where the scores on these categories were subjected to factor analyses. The analyses identify two fundamental dimensions in the party platform data for each country, one of which is the traditional left–right dimensions whereas the second dimension may differ according to the national party system studied. In their conclusion Budge and Robertson find that the left–right dimension is the most basic cleavage dimension in these party ideologies although not in each and every system studied.

A typology of issues must take into consideration the theoretical problems to be elucidated. Since our focus when surveying the major issues in West European democracies is to test the hypothesis that issue occurrence depends on the environment our typology is based on a distinction between structural and non-structural issues. Figure 8.1 shows the classification scheme. It is hardly to be expected that our classification schema covers each and every issue; moreover, some

Figure 8.1   *Types of issues*

Structural issue types

Class: Industrial relations: nationalizations, strikes, industrial democracy, participatory democracy. Income distribution: distributional policies, equality, taxes, unemployment, concentration of wealth.

Religion: State–church relations. Moral questions: abortion, divorce, alcohol policies.

Regional: Cultural relations: language problems, ethnic relations. Status of minorities: immigration. Regional economic development. Agriculture: prices, land reform

Non-structural issue types

Foreign policy and defence:
Multi-lateral relations and orientations: EC, OECD, UN, East–West bi lateral relations and orientations. Third world relations and orientations: decolonization. National forces: nuclear weapons, role of the military, rearmament and disarmament. Military cooperation, NATO

Political system:
Constitution: rights, liberties, institutions, levels of government. Governmental style: devices, corruption. Internal order: war criminals, terrorism.

Public sector:
Economic policies, public-sector development, inflation, social security, education and health policies.

Ecology:
Nuclear power, pollution, zero-growth politics

---

issues can be classified under more than one issue type; for example the distinction between class-orientated issue types and issues related to economic strategies is a tenuous one, which also applies to the separation between social security issues and class-based issues. Any classification scheme has to struggle with the problem of issue identification – What is to be left out? – and the problem of parsimony – How much is to be included in various issue types?

The occurrence of various kinds of issue is measured by an ordinal scale which also takes into account the intensity of the issue process. It must be admitted that the assignment of issue scores is based on judgements which may not meet with unanimous acceptance. However, a comparison with a similar classification in *Explaining and Predicting Elections* (1983) by Budge and Farlie presents an opportunity to check the reliability of the coding. Budge and Farlie employ a rather detailed classification scheme covering some fourteen issue types in order to measure the occurrence of these issues in twenty-three countries, and they take into account the frequency distribution cross-nationally as well as longitudinally. It appears that the differences between their scores and our scores are not substantial, but the identification of class-based issues or what Budge and Farlie refer to as socio-economic issues differs. According to Budge and Farlie there are few occurrences of these kinds of issue in France during the whole time period studied as well as in Italy during the period 1945–65 which is not in agreement with our observations; also, Budge and Farlie observe more public-sector related issues in the Netherlands and the United Kingdom during the period 1945–65.

One type of issue – gender politics – has become more and more salient in Western Europe. It is actually a complex mixture of issues, some of which have received extensive as well as intensive national political attention like for example abortion. It is difficult to measure the occurrence of woman questions as well as their intensity. However, it is true that:

> The modern women's movement has exerted a profound influence upon contemporary political thought, research, and action in Western Europe. Despite important differences within the ideological and political orientations of modern feminism, the overall impact of this movement has been pronounced, albeit largely unrecognised and unexplored within the Western European and especially European politics fields (Bashevkin, 1985: 1).

Some aspects of gender politics will be covered in the overview on the following pages when for example abortion has been politicized in a country. Feminism or the Women's Liberation Movement (WLM) has brought woman issues onto the political agenda, especially in the 1980s. However, the politicization of woman questions has not taken place by means of the channels of party government. Instead there has been a recognition of woman interests in various kinds of legislation, including equal opportunity, anti-discrimination and the establishment of equality agencies. Moreover, more women have been recruited to political positions within government and the establishment (Lovenduski, 1990).

Theories of issues

The concept of an issue is employed to theorize about political problem-solving, its nature, conditions and implications. Political systems may be conceived of as a set of decision-mechanisms responding to citizen demands by the making and implementation of policies. Political problem management is a function of both the nature of the problem encountered and the problem solving capacity of political institutions. The political management of problems may involve problems being removed from the arena (depoliticized) although there is no solution in the proper sense of the word. It may also involve the identification of non-issues, the making of pseudo-policies and the employment of delays and redefinition of the problems involved. The impact of issues upon political institutions has been emphasized in political economy and voting studies (the political popularity function), but it must be recognized that the 'issueness' of a social problem depends upon the response of political institutions. The behaviour of institutions in the political system affects which problems become issues as when the government changes the economy to improve its political prospects (the political business cycle).

Following a popular theme in political sociology we discuss if and how issues depend on social cleavages in a West European context. The data set has to be assembled in such a manner that it permits a wide representation of the occurrence of various kinds of issue as well as includes a number of dimensions of social structure. Starting from the preceding questions the basic distinction is between structural and non-structural issues. We arrive at measures of issue occurrence that describe both the cross-sectional variation in political issues between European democratic systems as well as the longitudinal variation in political issues in each West European nation. The emphasis in our analysis is thus on issue variation, its origins and effects. Let us begin with an overview of the occurrence of different types of issue in the various West European political systems, alerting one to the presence and significance of mechanisms that govern the definition, the politicization and the resolution of issues. Some types of issues tend to occur in each of the West European countries at different points of time whereas other types of issue characterize the politics of a particular country. The *Zeitgeist* matters, meaning that some issues tend to occur in most countries at a certain time.

Mixture of issues

Some nations focus upon structural issues, whereas other nations concentrate upon non-structural issues. Still other political systems are confronted with a mixture of these two issue types. The predominance of structural or non-structural issues may vary over time, but in some systems both have occurred simultaneously in a kind of mixture.

In Italy we find a balance between two fundamental types of issue. After the fall of Italian fascism the political system faced a serious constitutional problem that formed a potential threat to civil order: republic or monarchy. This issue divided Italy into two camps, but the adherents of a republic won the issue in a referendum 1946 (54.3 per cent versus 45.7 per cent). The outcomes were accepted by an overwhelming majority, though monarchism has attracted minor groups in the post-war period. The two basic conflict dimensions in the Italian polity refer to the contest between labour and capital on the one hand and religion versus secularization on the other. These two conflict dimensions are partly expressed in the struggle between the Catholic Party and the Communist Party. It must be emphasized, however, that both conflict dimensions are far broader than the contest between the DC and the PCI. Besides the class conflict and the religious contest we also find ethnic and regional issues, particularly since the mid-1970s.

Ethnicity as a source of conflict is to be found in the very north of Italy, in the Alto Adige (South Tyrolia) and the Aosta Valley where German- and French-speaking groups demand autonomy because they constitute a majority of the population. The more general regional conflict dimensions include both the tension between urban and rural areas and the contrast between northern and southern Italy. The Italian political system has not persisted for a longer period of time and it is often considered to be a highly unstable one, but when one examines the decision-making in major issues all is not failure. We find a capacity on the part of the system to handle several issues that are tied to deep seated conflicts between various groups (Allum, 1973; Penniman, 1977; Ruscoe, 1982; Clark, 1984; LaPalombara, 1987). A country expert states:

> The Italian parties did, however, succeed in establishing an exceptionally strong form of party state, built upon two pillars. The first was the close links between the parties and the major social actors – links which had the additional advantage of preventing a high degree of representational (as opposed to ideological) polarization, since both major parties assembled broad alliances of interests within their army of supporting organizations. The second, strengthening consistently over the post-war period, was the strong control established by the parties over the institutions of the state (Hine, 1990: 79–80).

Political issues in France are of several types; we find both structural and non-structural issue types, and the level of politicization has been very high for issues belonging to each type. As we know colonial problems brought down the Fourth Republic in 1958. It is unclear how structural and non-structural issues are to be separated in French politics; there seems to be a close association between the two, sometimes structural conflicts resulting in political system problems, sometimes governmental instability causing structural issues. There were two main types of non-structural issue, the politicization of decolonization problems and the constitutional problem. Various kinds of structural problem, class conflicts and autonomist movements among the ethnic minorities remained latent during the 1950s with the exception of the sudden outburst of Poujadism. In 1968 these forces turned manifest.

Some of the forces of the spring upheaval carried over into the 1970s, but in the 1980s the intensity of class issues has declined whereas the demand for regional and local autonomy has partly faded due to the sweeping decentralization reform initiated by *Loi Deferre* in 1982 (Ashford, 1983). The class conflict between left and right is an ongoing concern, but the struggle for workers' participation (*autogestion*) and nationalization was stronger in the 1970s than in the 1980s. Confronted with the increase in relevance of market values and monetarist economic policy principles left-wing militancy has mellowed in France, although the privatization policy of the Chirac government between 1986–88 met with resistance from the left. In the 1970s and the 1980s we also find the ecology conflict with ecologists trying to mobilize support for their resistance against nuclear power plants (Ehrmann, 1976; Wright, 1983; Wright, 1984).

Danish politics is a similar mixture of structural and non-structural issues. The party system includes parties that have strong social links, and these have politicized some problems that are crucial to their special adherents. However, there are also parties that attract diffuse social support, and these have concentrated on problems that concern a wider group of citizens. Foreign policy issues, defence issues and political system issues were handled during the years following the armistice. Left-wing groups became the main opponents to Danish entry into the Common Market when this problem was politicized again in the early 1970s. Although the issue was handled by means of a referendum which caused intense debate and mobilization of pro- and counter-groups within several of the political parties, the issue was successfully resolved. Denmark is now strongly attached to the EEC. Danish governments have been less successful when it comes to another major type of non-structural issue: problems of economic strategy. A number of governments have tried with varying degrees of success to come to grips with huge deficits in external balance and in the public sector. There have been a couple of structural issues in the Danish political system. As a matter of fact, we find all four structural issue types represented (Miller, 1968; Fitzmaurice, 1981; Haue et al., 1981).

Political systems may handle various types of issue; there may even be a politicization of both structural and non-structural problems. However, political systems cannot deal with all types at the same time. The distinction between latent and manifest issues is an instrumental one as it points out that only one or two problems come up for political decision-making at a time. The development of political problem-solving in Belgium is an example of this rule. After the Second World War politics focussed upon the re-establishing of the Belgian state. The political parties had to deal with both the internal problem about what to do with the royal family (Question Royale) and how to handle the external initiatives concerning a rearmament of Western Europe (the NATO question).

Belgium inherited a major political problem because of its colonial past, the Belgian Congo. Although the Congo problem was a severe one Belgian political parties did manage to handle the problems that concerned its constitutional affairs and its foreign relation affairs; these so-called non-structural issues were mainly managed during the 1950s. It turned out that the Belgian political system was to do much worse when it was faced with structural problems in the 1960s and the 1970s. It is true that the system managed to handle the religious problem with the 1958 decision (pacte scolaire) concerning the principles governing the funding of the school system. The structural issue that has had a most profound effect on all aspects of the Belgian political system is, however, the language problem (Weil, 1970; Fitzmaurice, 1983).

Preponderance of non-structural issues

Some political systems concentrate on the politicization and resolving of social problems; these systems produce decisions that may change social life creating new opportunities and new patterns of behaviour. Other political systems are preoccupied with the principles of the system itself. They face continuous debate or conflict concerning how the country is to be ruled. In such systems political conflict does not deal with how society is to be changed providing the state with an active role in social forces; these systems deal with the very existence of the political system itself. In such systems where persistence of the system itself is the main issue we are bound to find a preponderance of non-structural issue types. Greece belongs to this category.

In Greece political conflict has resulted in not only political instability but the disruption of the political system. The basic issue in Greek politics has for a long time been the political system itself. The conflict over how the country is to be governed was inherited from the period before the Second World War (the Metaxas regime) and resulted in a civil war between 1946 and 1949. The issue has several aspects as the political system problem comprises several issues. Besides the issue of a constitutional monarchy in Greece there was the systemic problem of how to handle groups at the far end of the left–right spectrum.

A third aspect of the political system issue is the problem of the frontiers of Greece. Various groups nurtured an irredentist idea covering not only Greece but also traditional Greek settlements in Asia Minor and the island of Cyprus (Enosis); these groups include the military though conservative groups were not generally irredentist. The conservative tradition in Greece based on the old territories and consisting of the pre-war people's party and the post-war parties lead by Papagos and Karamanlis were anti-irredentist whereas the Liberal Party of Venizelos and its successors – eventually the Centre Union of the elder Papandreou – were orginally pro-expansionist. These ambitions have been activated to and fro, from the 1921 defeat in Asia Minor to the 1974 debacle on Cyprus, each causing the downfall of a Greek regime. The Papandreou PASOK government has pursued an active foreign policy resulting in the

Greek entrance into the EEC and a tense relation to Turkey to and fro. The development of a major socialist party (PASOK) that was accepted in government between 1981 and 1989 was conducive to the institutionalization of the 1974–75 solution of the difficult political system issue in Greece. A referendum voted against the King's return in 1974 and the new constitution with its bias for presidential power was enacted in 1975. However, in 1986 the Papandreou government abolished the presidential powers that Karamanlis had favoured. It also appears that foreign policy issues have been depoliticized (Legg, 1969; Kousoulas, 1974; Clogg, 1979; 1983; Penniman, 1981; Kohler, 1982; Mavrogordatos, 1983). The constitutional revision reducing the extensive presidential powers indicated a consolidation of the new Greek republic and its orientation to parliamentary democracy that the disclosures of corruption and maladministration in the late 1980s was somewhat overshadowed (Featherstone, 1990a; 1990b).

Issue-making in the Finnish political systems tends to be strongly concentrated on two types of non-structural issue: constitutional principles, concerning mainly the presidency, and foreign policy. This issue-orientation was the outcome of the Finnish decision to join the war effort of the Nazi regime against the USSR. Actually, the consequences of the participation in the so-called continuation war for the Finnish polity can hardly be exaggerated. It has focussed political conflict lines upon problems concerning how to define the relationship between Finland and the Soviet Union, which has meant that other social problems have not been politicized to the same extent as in other European democracies. There is a strong dose of accommodation politics in Finland where oversized majority governments in combination with presidentialism mitigate the centrifugal forces in the fractionalized party system. In the 1980s policy-making was reorientated towards the right as the major conservative party was finally accepted in government replacing the earlier influential agrarian Centre Party.

Conflicts between the major political parties concern the following areas of domestic policy: economic strategies, income distribution, ethnicity and religion. The questions relating to the Swedish-speaking minority or moral questions concerning for example abortion flare up from time to time, though these problems have not been strongly politicized on any occasion. Economic conflicts are salient in the Finnish political system. They comprise class conflicts between employers and employees as well as between workers and farmers, but there is also a regional dimension: the poor North versus the rich South. In 1956 class conflicts burst out in a general strike (Wahlbäck, 1967; Klockare, 1971; Nousiainen, 1971; Allardt and Starck, 1981; Elder et al., 1982; Anckar, 1984a).

Typical of the issue-making in West Germany is the heavy dominance of non-structural issue types. Recalling the clear social links of the political parties in the German political system we find this astonishing. There is a disproportionate occurrence of political system issues reflecting the precarious status of the new republic. Foreign policy issues as well as defence issues are also numerous. The restructuring of the German political system after the downfall of the Nazi regime was to characterize the politicization of questions during the 1940s and the 1950s. Structural issues have not been as visible as issues like the Spiegel-affair or the Ost-Politik, but none the less they have been there all the time. However, when the question of a reunited Germany appeared somewhat unexpectedly in 1989 with the drastic disintegration of the German Democratic Republic, there was basically agreement between right and left about how to proceed. The so-called *Genscherism*, i.e. the unorthodox policies of the FDP foreign minister, has reduced the distance between the Kohl government and the SPD opposition with its adherence to Brandt's *Ostpolitik* (Smith, 1989).

The basic policy cleavage between the CDU/CSU and the SPD appears in issues related to industrial relations and income distribution. The social links of these two parties are reflected in the conflict between labour and capital, the SPD favouring ideas of industrial democracy, participatory democracy and distributional policies. No doubt, the SPD has been more active towards expanding social security programmes and promoting the welfare state in general, though we have to remember that there has been a social ambition in the CDU/CSU as a heritage of social Catholicism. The occurrence of ethnic cleavages must be mentioned. There are two types of cultural issue, on the one hand the old problem of the Vertriebene after the downfall of the Third Reich, and on the other the recently developed unrest due to the immigration of Gastarbeiter from the Mediterranean area (Edinger, 1977; Beyme, 1979; Smith, 1979b; Johnson, 1983) as well as the heavy influx of Germans in the wake of the collapse of East Germany.

The Green Party entering the Federal Parliament in 1983 has mobilized post-materialist sentiments in the Inglehart conception. Its focus is not only environmental problems in a wide sense but includes also a general rejection of German statism. According to one country expert:

> The Greens have built on student protests of the late 1960s, the anti-Berufsverbot campaigns and the citizens' initiatives of the 1970s, and the peace movement of the early 1980s. They are now struggling to articulate a conception of politics that, as Wolf-Dieter Narr has suggested, is 'not focused on the state, but rather on the interests of citizens'(Kvistad, 1987: 225).

Issue-making is not independent of the shape of the political system; when a political system breaks down and is replaced by a new polity this occurrence of system failure is bound to affect issue-making. Whereas system persistence tends to be conducive to a concentration on kinds of issue other than political system issues, the opposite obtains when a political system breaks down. In autocratic Portugal the fundamental issue was the political system issue whether Salazar or Caetano would manage to mobilize enough support to keep the regime intact. The basic test of the capacity to sustain the autocracy came with the process of decolonization in the African provinces.

Since the fall of authoritarian rule political debate and conflict focussed upon political system issues predominantly. There have been a number of crucial constitutional problems, which the system has had great problems in resolving, pertaining to the role of the military and the division of power between the presidency and the prime ministry. The constitutional revisions in 1982 and 1986 abolishing the military Revolutionary Council as well as restricting the strong presidential powers have contributed to the consolidation of the new Portuguese democracy (Gallagher, 1988).

These constitutional problems have been politicized in the midst of sharp class conflict. Class conflict has not been clearly polarized between the socialists and the rest. Indeed class conflict is not really polarized, at least in the classic sense, because the disadvantaged mass is split three ways – poor rural smallholders, rural workers and urban workers. Although the political system issues have been the more spectacular ones the new political system has not been paralysed, but has introduced a considerable number of reform bills, nationalization or denationalization of private industry and banks, the introduction of land reforms as well as the annulment of such reforms. The reform measures have been extremely mixed in both aims and performance. A great deal of the policy of all governments has been dictated by the requirements of the IMF. The political system issues have tended to coincide with the structural issues, although the memory of the autocracy has constrained the contending parties into accepting the basic features of the new political system (Robinson, 1979; Graham and Makler, 1979; Gallagher, 1982; Graham and Wheeler, 1983; Bruneau, 1984; Gladdish, 1990).

Spanish issue-making is similar to the politicization of problems in Portugal. The concentration on political system issues follows naturally from the breakdown of the Franco autocracy, but as in Portugal other kinds of issue cropped up once the restraints on political opinion and political demands were removed. Spain is somewhat different from Portugal in so far as political conflict has focussed more on structural issues, mainly the regional problems, than on the matters relating to the systems persistence of the democratic regime. At the same time there was actually a serious more real attempt at a coup d'état in Spain in 1981, because there was a strong right-wing group that had not given up autocracy. Yet, we do not find the persistent preoccupation with constitutional problems that characterize Portuguese issue-making.

The basic structural issue in the Spanish political system concerns the relationship between the centralized government in Madrid and some of the larger old regions – the Basque provinces, Catalonia, and Galicia – which nurture cultures that are different from the main Spanish one. It not only involves the matter of language but includes old historical demands difficult to accept for the major non-socialist parties, to which a united Spain is very important. Although a number of small regional parties have attracted voter support during the 1980s, the regionalization of the Spanish nation-state was carried through in Catalonia, the Basque Country, Galicia and Andalusia between 1979 and 1981 in a manner that has eased but certainly not resolved the regional issue (Liebert, 1990).

The fall of the Franco autocracy brought forward both class conflict and the clash between Catholicism and secularization. The class conflict has been mitigated by a concern on the part of leading groups within the socialist and non-socialist camps to safeguard the democratic constitution. After the disintegration of the Suarez UCD in 1981, the various non-socialist groups have not been able to gather in a common front against the Gonzáles' PSOE which has pursued a centre orientated policy (Gillespie, 1990). The regime has also been successful in solving foreign policy issues, like for example the entrance into the EEC and the decolonization of the Spanish Sahara.

The emergence of the strongly supported Gonzales social democratic government has consolidated the new Spanish democracy around moderate centre orientated policy-making. Spain will remain a member of the Western alliances even though strong leftist forces have opposed Spanish participation in NATO; the 1986 referendum was in favour of Spanish NATO participation. Serious conflict arises from time to time in connection with issues involving cultural, religious and ideological beliefs, for example issues referring to divorce, education and abortion have been discussed (Carr and Fusi, 1979; Coverdale, 1979; Graham, 1983; Bell, 1983; Lancaster and Prévost, 1985; Gillespie, 1990).

Issue resolution

Issue-making in Sweden used to belong to the type where there is a concentration on specific problems to be solved presumably by state action of some kind. Although a new constitution was introduced in the early 1970s political system issues have never been politicized to such an extent that they have resulted in political instability. Political issues tend to focus upon the size of the public sector, where the socialist parties have been more in favour of public-sector expansion as well as increased public administration of social life than the non-socialist parties. This basic confrontation line has been activated on two major issues: the fight over the supplementary pensions plan in the 1950s and the creation of a system of public funds owning a substantial portion of the capital in business companies suggested by the social democratic party in the 1970s. Both issues caused deep-seated conflicts and the question of the supplementary pensions programme had to be resolved through a referendum in 1957. Actually, the referendum technique has been employed most skilfully by the political parties fearing that the issues involved would result in internal party schisms. The ecology issue has been heavily politicized since the mid-1970s, as a reaction to a rapid build up of nuclear power plants and the disclosure of extensive pollution.

Sweden used to be famous for its homogeneity as was emphasized in the early Rustow analysis (Rustow, 1955). However, political systems change and no doubt there has been an increase in heterogeneity due to the extensive immigration from Finland and the Mediterranean areas. Moreover, we also find a regional issue dimension relating to the uneven regional development of Sweden since the early 1960s. Striking in the political development in Sweden is the large amount of consensus among the political parties. Such a consensus orientated system that is mainly preoccupied with more or less technical issues handles conflict in two widely different ways: it suppresses conflict on a day-to-day basis only to concentrate on a single major issue within every decade.

It is argued that the Swedish model of policy-making has lost much of its vitality (Ruin, 1982), though the process of politicization, decision-making and depoliticization has been strongly institutionalized in the political system. Even if the level of conflict may have been high between the various blocks there has been a tradition of accepting the outcome of the decision-making process. The first major deviation from this pattern concerns the fund decision in 1983 which the non-socialist parties agree to undo if they are returned to power (Birgersson et al., 1984; Lewin, 1984). The technical orientation of Swedish politics towards finding and implementing public solutions to social and economic problems has run into more and more problems as the workings of the large Swedish welfare state have been called into question. It has also proved more and more difficult to find stable solutions to important problems, for example the dismantling of nuclear power, particularly so after the strong advance of the Swedish Green Party in the 1988 election (5.5 per cent of the votes).

The non-occurrence of political system issues may be interpreted as a sign of system persistence; it may still be difficult to create stable governments and the occurrence of other kinds of issue may trigger civil disorder actions as in Norway. Up until the emergence of Carl I. Hagen's discontent party with its questioning of the Norwegian welfare state the Norwegian political system was widely accepted among all political groupings. Actually, there has been little debate on political system issues since the Norwegian Social Democratic Party accepted parliamentary democracy in the 1920s. If there is little conflict concerning the political system, this provides the decision-makers with an opportunity to concentrate on other problems. This is also what we find in Norway where the state is heavily involved in various activities. The dominant position of DNA in government up until the 1980s meant an extensive build up of the public sector, which mainly the conservative party contested. The state is also engaged in the oil industry where the carefully built up state involvement is generally accepted though the conservative party had opted for more private initiatives.

If one looks for more fiercely contested issues, one should turn to spectacular conflicts like the Common Market referendum in 1972 and the demonstrations concerning the Alta river. The occurrence of conflict over the Norwegian entrance into the Common Market was not accidental. Foreign policy issues as well as defence policy issues tend to swing to and fro because a considerable leftist group within DNA is unhappy with the Western orientation inherent in Norwegian foreign policy and the defence system. The entrance into NATO was not unanimously accepted and leftist political groups have since the 1950s demanded that nuclear weapons of any kind should not be stored in Norway. The course of events in the EEC issue where extra-parliamentary groups managed to defeat the proposal of the two major parties – DNA and Höyre acting in unison – testifies to the fact that an issue may require extraordinary decision techniques and cause a rise in political instability, even though the system persistently operates.

Besides the occurrence of class-based issues in the confrontation about public sector issues between the DNA on the one hand and the non-socialist parties on the other hand, there are also two structural issues that are politically relevant because two parties have made these issues their prime concern. Kristelig Folkeparti keeps the problem of abortion politicized whereas the Venstre used to be a strong adherent to the new Norwegian language opposing the classical Norwegian language. More recently ecology problems have become more salient than the language question (Bergh et al, 1977; Heidar, 1983; Olsen, 1983).

Time-span of issues

Issues vary in their life-span; some issues are short, being politicized almost over night and resolved in the political process or dismissed by the political process. Other issues stay after being introduced into the political system and they may have a force of their own making it possible for the issue to remain salient over generations of policy-makers. These long-term issues need not be always the most prominent ones as short-term issues may be explosive in character.

Issue-making in the Netherlands used to be characterized by the predominance of long-term issues with high or low saliency, which were handled by means of the classical decision-making mechanism, the politics of accommodation. We find, however, that when we take a broader look at issue-making since the Second World War the consociational model has lost most of its applicability, because a change seems to have occurred in the pattern of issue-making since the 1960s. Now the type of issue that predominates is different. There are a few short-term highly intensive issues that the Dutch political system has been confronted with since 1945; decolonization issues, the South Moluccan protests in the 1970s, and scandals caused by the royal family (the Lockheed affair). We still find traces of the old long-term issues that used to characterize the conflict between the so-called zuilen; yet, we also find new issues, viz., the problem of regional development, questions relating to the participation of the Netherlands in NATO (nuclear weapons, i.e. the Pershing rockets) as well as ecological matters.

These new issues tend to replace the classical confrontation lines between the zuilen, but they are hardly salient enough to create a political system issue. These ongoing concerns in the political system also include the confrontation between leftist parties and conservative parties about the overall size and shape of the public sector (Lijphart, 1975; Lepszy, 1979; Bakvis, 1981; Van Schendelen, 1984). The overall trend is the depillarization of Dutch issues and the emergence of 'new politics' less preoccupied with accommodation and consultation and more concerned with post-materialist values, decentralization and citizen participation (Daalder and Irwin, 1989).

Some issues are confined to limited periods of time; they go through a process of politicization, conflict and depoliticization ending in some sort of solution. Other political issues are less instrumental and more symbolic in nature; they acquire a life of their own sustaining a political tradition. Issues may be created and may die, but issues may also enter into the political tradition being reflected in the party system. Irish politics is a mixture of instrumental issues and symbolic ones. The latter was predominant after the creation of the Irish Free State under the terms of the Anglo-Irish Treaty of 1921 but the development of the Irish polity since the Second World War has implied that more tension has focussed upon instrumental issues. The over-riding problem in Irish politics used to be the relationship to the United Kingdom and Northern Ireland. This issue was politicized into the party system on a more permanent basis by the contest between Fianna Fail – the anti treaty party – and Fine Gael – the pro treaty party. In 1949 the nationalist ambitions were rewarded in the creation of an Irish republic outside of the Commonwealth. This is as far as the problem of a united Ireland separate from the United Kingdom has got.

How Ireland Voted: The Irish General Election 1987 (Laver et al.,

1987) shows that the policy issues are no different in Ireland than elsewhere in Western Europe. The distinctions between, on the one hand, conservative corporatism versus social democratism and, on the other, between welfare versus markets seem to capture the realities of Irish politics much more than the myth of the civil war cleavage.

The examination of the electoral outcome shows that the new Dail derives its freshness from its radically different political composition, not because of any major change in its social composition. To make a comparison with the 1987 net volatility we must go to the Danish 1973 earthquake election. The choice of the voter seems to express more discontent with established practice than a real understanding of the issues involved or an attachment to party leaders. That Irish politics is different is less true after 1987 than before, but it is not incomprehensible, comparatively speaking.

The idea of uniting Ireland is more symbolism than Realpolitik, though Irish politicians now and then express some sympathy for Catholic political organizations in Northern Ireland. Perhaps the Irish republic has shown more sympathy and understanding towards nationalist movements in Northern Ireland than in the Irish republic, particularly so when Fianna Fail has been in government. After the Second World War issue-making tended to concentrate more on instrumental issues; there are a number of structural issues that have been handled by the political system. Issues in Irish politics have tended to become more similar to issues in other West European countries, particularly after the 1987 earthquake election (Mair, 1989).

The question of the Irish language relates to the problem of Irish identity, and programmes for the support of the Irish (Gaelic) language are supported more strongly by the nationalists in the Fianna Fail, though no major group actively opposes this policy. There is a continuing problem of church–state relations, despite the removal in 1972 of a clause in the Irish constitution referring to the 'special position' of the Catholic church as the church of the majority. The slow process of secularization in Ireland was reflected in the results of the referendum in 1983 which amended the constitution to prohibit any legislation that might make provision for abortion and the 1986 referendum on divorce (Penniman, 1978; Chubb, 1982; Peillon, 1982; Gallagher, 1985).

In Austria a major number of political issues have referred to either internal or external aspects of the political system. The predominance of non-structural issues in a society with such a heterogeneous culture as Austria's reflects the peculiar position of Austria at the end of the Second World War. The occupation created much uncertainty as to the constitutional status of the country, which appears in a number of issues. One set of such issues focussed upon the constitutional rules concerning the relation to the powers of occupation as well as the settlement with the remnants of the Nazi period. Problems dealing with the overall governing of the nation keep cropping up. The issue over the status of the Austrian state was resolved in the state treaty of 1955 in which sovereignty was recognized in exchange for neutrality. However, the province of Tyrol, or Alto Adige, has presented the Austrian government with a problem that has been politicized at various times. The ÖVP in particular has been sensitive to the position of the German-speaking majority in the northern Italian province, though Austria has never demanded any territorial changes. It seems as if the issue was resolved in 1972, when Austria and Italy arrived at an agreement.

We do not find a level of structural conflicts corresponding to the cleavages in the social structure. Religious problems were salient in 1945 and 1962. The religious issue has had two aspects, the first dealing with the nature of religious instruction in state schools, and the other referring to the position of confessional schools. The nationalization problem has been politicized to and fro during the whole time period because there has been disagreement on how the nationalized sector was to be governed. Among the SPÖ there has been substantial sympathy for a more planned economy, but there have been no new demands for more nationalization. There was one new spectacular issue in the late 1970s, the referendum in 1978 on the Zwentendorf nuclear reactor. The issue stirred up much animosity within the SPÖ. It contained elements not only of environmentalism but also of a general revolt against the established order.

Austrian political decision-making has faced a few serious problems which have been more the outcome of the political situation of the country due to its Anschluss with Nazi Germany in 1938 than a reflection of its inherited social structure. The Waldheim issue proved to be a very delicate one where system inertia was decisive: despite much criticism from abroad as well as from domestic groups Waldheim was elected president in two rounds (49.6 per cent and 53.9 per cent in the second round). However, the general impression is that Austrian politics in the Second Republic is very different from its politics in the First Republic, characterized by sharp political cleavages along the Lager boundaries (Steiner, 1972; 1981; Weinzerl and Skalnik, 1972; Fischer, 1982; Nick and Pelinka, 1983).

Partisan nature of issues

A distinction between two types of conflict pattern that characterize political systems can be introduced. Conflicts may tend to be issue orientated, meaning that issues dominate over political party orientation, or conflict may be predominantly partisan in character, meaning that the basic conflicts between the political parties look for issues as outlets.

Typical of the latter type is the occurrence of profound party conflicts, though it is not always the case that highly divisive issues may be identified. The former type is very much substantiated in the Swiss polity, where each issue tends to be decided upon on its own merit having its own decision-making process. It follows that it is not difficult to identify issues in the Swiss political system, because of their extensive use of referendum as a decision-making mechanism.

The Swiss referendum is employed to handle both structural and non-structural issues. Among these two types we find both trivial and non-trivial ones. Though issue-making is specific, issues may be long term as the adherents of a proposal in a referendum do not have to abide by a negative outcome but may reintroduce the issue. The most spectacular political system issue is the question of a female franchise in federal elections. In 1959 the proposal of female franchise was rejected, but in 1971 time was ripe as a considerable majority (65.7 per cent) accepted the constitutional change. Among the smaller political system issues we may identify the Mirage affair in 1963 and the critique of the typical Swiss way of governing (élite cooperation). To the set of non-structural issues belongs depoliticization of the question of atomic energy. The Swiss manner of handling the atomic energy problem is typical of the Swiss model of government. In 1957 the people decided to accept the introduction of nuclear power plants, and in 1979 the people rejected a proposal to tie the employment of nuclear power to stringent criteria. What was accomplished by means of two simple decisions causing little contention between the ruling political parties has been the subject of endless political confrontation in other countries where the political parties have politicized the questions concerning nuclear power along conflict lines between the parties.

However, the ecological issues were far more difficult to tackle for the Swiss political system in the 1980s. Two environmental parties, the moderate GPS (Grune Partei der Schweiz) and the radical GAS (Grune Alternative Schweiz), rose from an insignificant 1 per cent in electoral support in the 1979 election to a substantial 9 per cent in 1987. The support for the Swiss Greens and the heavy politicization of environmental problems reflect more of a specific issue orientation than a general commitment to post-materialist values, i.e. opposition to centralization of power and the affluent society. The background of the Swiss Green Parties is in this respect different from that of the German or Austrian Green Parties (Kreuzer, 1990). At the same time, '... although environmental issues are not yet dominant in Swiss politics they are becoming far more divisive than consociationalists might have imagined' (Church, 1989).

We find two main structural problems that the Swiss political system has had difficulties in managing over a long time. Repeated referendums have been resorted to in order to come to grips with the popular resentments against foreign workers as with the consistent demand from the French-speaking majority in Jura for a separate canton (Steiner, 1974; Steinberg, 1980; McRae, 1983; Schmidt, 1985).

The political system of the United Kingdom is the opposite to that of Switzerland in so far as decision-making mechanisms are concerned. Issue-making in the United Kingdom hinges on the political parties, which means that it is impossible to separate political issues from party conflict. The only issue which has been initiated without the backing of the major political parties is the ethnic problems occurring in Scotland, Northern Ireland and in Wales. The breakthrough of these new problems into the political arena has also implied a change of the British party system together with the rise of a new party, the SDP. The regional demands have met with some sympathy on the part of the Labour Party and the Liberal Party, speaking about the need for devolution. Yet, the seminal trend of the 1980s was the revitalization of the Westminster model of centralized government, as local government discretion was reduced by the Thatcher government (Page and Goldsmith, 1987).

Two types of issue dominate conflicts in the British political system: questions of economic policy and class relations on the one hand and foreign policy matters on the other. The initiative in both areas came from the Labour Party after the Second World War. The idea to expand the public sector and create social security programmes came out of Labour Party ideology, which is also true of the idea of decolonization. A shift in power with the Conservatives replacing Labour meant simply that the Labour policies were reversed, denationalization replacing nationalization as well as a slower process of decolonization instead of a faster one. The advent of Thatcherism and its version of a supply-side economic policy in the 1980s intensified class-based issues.

New kinds of issues cropped up in the 1960s when the relationship to the Common Market became a difficult problem to handle for the political parties. Actually, the political parties had to deviate from the traditional principle of the sovereignty of Parliament to have the issue decided. A referendum in 1975 confirmed a parliamentary decision to enter the EEC. It seems as if the employment of an un-British principle of decision-making coincided with forces that have resulted in a major transformation of the British party system. However, these new trends have also been affected by the declining performance of the British economy, which is an issue that the political system has had great problems in managing.

The successful policy in utilizing the oil resources outside of Scotland has presented temporary alleviation to the major parties, but it must be emphasized that the utilization of the oil resources has been politicized along traditional partisan cleavages, the Conservative government conducting a policy of privatization of the oil industry (Rose, 1974a; Sked and Cock, 1979; Rose and McAllister, 1982; Budge et al., 1983). The privatization issue became highly salient during the 1980s as it involved the traditional right–left clash between the Conservatives and Labour and because the privatization policy was pursued on such a large scale by the Thatcher government. According to one country expert:

> Until 1979, the United Kingdom possessed one of the largest public enterprise sectors in Europe. By the end of three terms of Thatcher government (i.e. 1992), it is scheduled to be extinct (Heald, 1988: 36).

However, not only the extent of the privatization plans proved difficult for the left to accept, but also the consistency with which they were carried through:

> Political events in the United Kingdom in the 1980s have been shaped by the absence of constitutional protections and the willingness of the Thatcher government to assert centralised power and to override so-called 'vested interests'. In this sense, there are common features between the privatisation of nationalised industries and the emasculation of local government (Heald, 1988: 46).

The sharp edge of Thatcherism showed that political ideology had hardly lost its potential for creating intense confrontation. The 'end of ideology'-theme, propagated in relation to the coming of a post-industrial society, oversimplifies too much. Although the attraction of extremist ideologies is gone, the debate about the future of the West European welfare state will most probably involve a confrontation between laissez-faire inspired belief-systems and a traditional socialist welfare ideology.

Comparative analysis of issues

After this overview nationwise we make an attempt at some comparative generalization based on a tentative coding of the occurrence of some major types of issues in the sixteen countries. The classification scheme concerning issue-making contains seven categories, and we map the occurrence of these in the properties of issues – intensity, extension, number and frequency – along an ordinal scale from one to five. The time period since the Second World War is divided into two: 1945–65 and 1966–89. The validity and reliability in the application of the issue categories to empirical data are problematic. The analysis covers sixteen nations at two periods of time; since Portugal and Spain have had democratic governments for a limited period of time we end up with thirty cases. The classification of issue occurrences is given in Table 8.1.

Cross-sectionally speaking issue-making varies more within the nations than between them. When we concentrate upon the occurrence and saliency of seven issue types – class, religion, region, ecology, political system, foreign policy and public sector – and map these issue types for

Table 8.1   *Classification of issue occurrence in Western Europe:*
1945–64 (I) and 1965–89 (II)

	Public sector		Class		Religion		Region		Ecology		Political system		Foreign policy	
	I	II	I	II	I	II	I	II	I	II	I	II	I	II
Austria	4	2	3	1	1	2	1	4	4	1	4	1	1	3
Belgium	4	3	4	2	3	5	1	3	4	5	4	2	2	4
Denmark	3	2	1	2	2	2	1	3	2	1	2	4	2	5
FRG	3	2	2	1	2	2	1	4	4	4	5	4	1	2
Finland	4	3	1	2	2	3	1	1	3	4	5	4	1	2
France	4	5	2	1	2	4	1	3	5	3	5	3	2	3
Greece	5	3	2	2	1	1	1	1	5	5	3	4	1	2
Ireland	1	1	3	3	2	3	1	2	2	2	2	4	1	2
Italy	4	4	4	5	4	2	1	3	4	4	2	2	2	4
Netherlands	2	2	2	2	1	2	1	3	1	1	3	1	1	3
Norway	3	2	2	3	2	1	1	4	1	1	2	4	2	3
Portugal	–	5	–	2	–	1	–	1	–	5	–	3	–	3
Spain	–	4	–	3	–	5	–	3	–	5	–	2	–	3
Sweden	2	2	1	2	1	2	1	5	1	1	2	2	2	3
Switzerland	1	1	2	2	4	4	1	4	1	1	1	1	1	2
UK	4	4	2	2	2	5	1	3	1	4	4	3	2	4

Note: The scale of issue occurrence ranges from 1 to 5 meaning that the more intense, the more frequent and the more durable the issue the higher the score.

the two time periods the finding is that the various types of issue tend to occur in most nations and that several nations concentrate upon certain issue types to the exclusion of others over time.

Longitudinally speaking issue-making tends to be constant meaning that the within time differences in issue-making over time are greater than the between time differences. Thus, we do not find great differences in the types of problem politicized in European democracies before and after 1965. The only trace of the emergence of new politics is found in the rise in the scores for ecology and public sector issue-making.

Aggregating the various issue scores into an overall country measure of issue-making for each of the two time periods we find that nations differ in the extent to which problems are politicized. The finding is that the inter-nation differences in overall issue-making during the two periods studied are much larger than the intra-nation differences over time. We rank the nations in the following way on the basis of their overall issue score: Spain, Belgium, Italy, France, the United Kingdom, Portugal, Federal Republic of Germany, Finland, Greece, Austria, Denmark, Norway, Ireland, Sweden, Switzerland, and the Netherlands.

The occurrence of issues displays few interdependencies. The finding is that in the politics of the post-war period the occurrence of political system issues is closely related to class issues and weakly related to religious issues. We also find that political system issues and foreign policy issues go together with ecological issues. The overall picture is, however, that issue types are not a function of each other.

Issue-making displays a few clear relationships with the social structure though certainly properties or dimensions of the social structure of a nation do not strictly determine the occurrence of issues. Obviously, it is hardly a daring guess that the extent to which a country is fragmented ethnically or religiously has a bearing on the politicization of certain kinds of problem, but the difficult part of the equation is to show how strong the social implications for issue-making are; more specifically, between what social structure dimensions and which kinds of issues is there this type of relationship?

Although recognizing the shortcomings of the analysis it is clear that there is at least some truth to the old saying that 'politics is a reflection of society'; the emphasis here is not on 'truth' but on 'some'. The occurrence of issues – intensity, extension, frequency and saliency – has social roots, but the set of such social sources is a limited one and the strength of the associations varies. Most interestingly, we find some specific relationships between the occurrence of issues and properties of the social structure. Ethnic politicization is clearly affected by the ethno-linguistic structure as countries like Belgium, Spain, Switzerland and the United Kingdom are characterized by a heterogeneous ethnic structure and tend to have highly salient ethnic issues.

Correspondingly, the proportion of Catholics in the population affects the occurrence of a politicization of religious problems, which is particularly true of Italy. A large Catholic population is also conducive to the politicization of political system issues because of the tension between church and state. The saliency of political system issues depends somewhat upon the wealth of a nation as we find this type of politicization in Greece, Spain, Portugal and Italy. However, poverty is not a necessary condition for the occurrence of political system issues, as Belgium, France and the United Kingdom testify. Whereas an unequal distribution of incomes seems to be conducive to the occurrence of class-based issues, the politicization of public sector problems as well as ecology problems tends to occur the more affluent the society is. This is as far as the social structure is relevant for the determination of issue-making. Obviously, issue-making in political structures is not simply a reflection of divisions in society, but it is also not the case that issue-making has no social connections.

Conclusion

Issue-making may be approached as a link between social structure and social cleavages on the one hand and government on the other. The politicization of social problems is not a strict function of the divisions in the social structure, the behaviour of political parties simply reflecting cleavages between social groups. At the same time it must be emphasized that issue-occurrence is not random. There is a finite set of issue types that tend to occur in a set of political systems like the West European ones. There is no country specific pattern in so far as the occurrence of certain types of issue is concerned; and there is no time specific pattern in the occurrence of various kinds of issue with the exception of the emergence of post-materialist issues including the ecology problems in the late 1970s and 1980s.

Moreover, neither is the occurrence of issues entirely separated from the structure of society nor is issue-resolving mechanical. The capacity to handle social problems that have been politicized varies between nations as well as over time. Structural issues are more salient in societies that are heterogeneous in ethnicity, religion and class, but it is not generally true that the occurrence of political system issues depends upon the occurrence of structural issues (Greece and Finland). It seems that some nations keep concentrating on political system issues for long periods of time whereas other systems display a capacity to take on various issue types and to resolve them efficiently; to some extent at least, it seems as if this differential is related to the affluence of the society in which the political system is embedded. The capacity to resolve issues is relevant to the understanding of political stability which we turn to next.

9

Political Stability

Introduction

The concept of stability as applied to political systems belongs to that set of concepts which appear to function well in discourse as long as one does not ask what the concept really refers to or means. It seems that some political systems are more unstable than others, and that political systems may change from more to less stability; yet, once such statements begin to be questioned, it is not at all clear how they are to be tested, or what matters of fact would falsify such assertions. Scholars do not adhere to one standard definition of the concept from which follow the necessary and sufficient conditions for the application to data. Thus, a description of the variation in stability between political systems in Western Europe has to be based on conceptual commitments, or on methodological decisions as to how the concept of stability is to be handled with the phenomena investigated. Firstly, we outline the semantics of 'political stability' identifying various conceptions. Secondly, we proceed from a few distinctions derived from the conceptual analysis to describe the country differences in political stability and finally we end by suggesting some explanatory factors that may account for the country similarities and differences. The problem is, as usual, whether social factors explain better than institutional ones.

Ambiguity

There are different approaches to the concept of stability (Dowding and Kimber, 1983; 1985; 1987; Bealey, 1987). The concept may simply be regarded as explicitly multi-dimensional due to the unfortunate employment of an ambiguous term. Lijphart states that the concept of political stability is 'multi-dimensional' referring to system maintenance, civil order, legitimacy, and effectiveness (Lijphart, 1977a: 4), assuming that the property of stability may be predicated on democratic regimes in the sense that democracies may be more or less stable. However, it is not quite clear whether the property of stability is to be predicated about democracy or about the regime. To some scholars a stable democratic regime is a political system whose democracy is stable, though it is conceivable that the expression 'a stable democratic regime' could refer to a political system that is stable but also democratic. The problem is that stability may be a property of both democracy and the political system. It seems important to emphasize the conceptual distinction between being stable and being democratic.

The combination of an unstable but democratic regime should not be mixed up with a regime whose democracy is unstable. Actually, both may occur simultaneously, but not necessarily. Lijphart hypothesizes that the two properties of political stability and democratic effectiveness go together (Lijphart, 1977a: 4). This is an empirical argument to be tested against a body of data; it is logically possible that a system may have a high probability of remaining democratic and yet show a high level of civil violence (or government turnover) at times (Barry, 1970).

Multi-dimensionality may also be the unintended outcome of a variety of uni-dimensional approaches to the concept of political stability. Semantic investigations have come up with a list of various dimensions which cover the somewhat different properties identified with 'political stability' by various scholars. Leon Hurwitz states:

> The differing views and approaches to political stability are seen to be (a) the absence of violence; (b) governmental longevity/duration; (c) the existence of a legitimate constitutional regime; (d) the absence of structural change; and (e) a multifaceted societal attribute (Hurwitz, 1973: 449).

It is not difficult to find studies of political stability that employ one or two of Hurwitz's properties. Gerhard Loewenberg (1971: 181–2) describes the semantical predicament in very much the same way: the concept of political stability appears to cover such phenomena as (1) absence of political violence (Rummel, 1971; Feierabend and Feierabend, 1971); (2) system maintenance or system persistence (Easton, 1965); (3) typologies of regimes (Rose, 1969); and (4) governmental performance (Eckstein, 1971). In a similar vein David Sanders and Valentine Herman point out the variety of the denotation of the concept: continuation of a set of constitutional norms, continuity in governmental offices, social stability (meaning absence of violence), political effectiveness (referring to policies or outputs) (Sanders and Herman, 1977: 346).

Ambiguity or multi-dimensionality may be handled in two ways. On the one hand such a semantic predicament may be accepted, and the effort may be concentrated upon the identification of a set of relevant dimensions by means of reducing the various properties to make them conceptually independent. Huntington and Dominguez suggest that basically the concept of political stability contains two elements: order and continuity. They state:

> The first involves the relative absence of violence, force, coercion, and

disruption from the political system. The second identifies stability with a relative absence of change in the critical components of the political system, a lack of discontinuity in political evolution, the absence from the society of significant social forces and political movements that wish to bring about fundamental changes in the political system (Huntington and Dominguez, 1975: 7).

Perhaps, this identification could be criticized as it does not seem obvious that order and continuity are conceptually distinct. If there exist 'significant social forces and political movements that wish to bring about fundamental changes in the political system', then one may hardly expect an 'absence of violence, force, coercion and disruption from the political system'.

On the other hand, ambiguity may be rejected by fiat, denouncing such a semantic predicament in favour of an explication procedure which introduces a 'better' concept. According to Ian Budge and Dennis Farlie 'political stability' means, or should mean, regime continuity:

> The continuity of basic features of a regime seems to form the only viable and truly general definition of stability, while their non-continuance constitutes regime change (Budge and Farlie, 1981: 335).

The plausibility of an explication has to be judged on the basis of a number of considerations. One such consideration is the fit of the proposed definition with commonsense. The Budge and Farlie definition implies that a political system is unstable if and only if its basic regime features are changed or endangered. Obviously, this is considered a sufficient condition for the application of the concept of political stability. But is change of basic regime features also a necessary condition for political instability? It seems that the definition states a sufficient condition for political instability only as it seems to be that political systems may undergo periods of more or less instability even if their regimes do not change.

Similar in tone is the explication suggested by Ted Robert Gurr (1974b). Gurr speaks of the 'durability' or the 'persistence' of the political system and equates political stability with the persistence of political institutions. He states: 'A "stable" political system, on this premise, is one whose authority patterns remain similar over a long period of time' (Gurr, 1974: 1484).

The premise referred to in the quotation is the Eckstein and Gurr theory that political institutions are authority structures (Eckstein and Gurr, 1975). If we wish to observe political instability in European democracies, we should focus upon changes in properties of authority structures like openness of executive recruitment, decision constraints on the chief executive, extent of political participation, scope of governmental control, and complexity of governmental structures (Gurr,

1974b: 1485; Lichbach, 1982). The Gurr definition may contain a necessary condition for the application of 'stability' to the political system, but it may not be a sufficient condition. Is it not conceivable that a political system is considered unstable due to an extensive and iterative replacement of its government even when the authority structure remains the same during the period of time studied? To us, system persistence, however important, is not conceptually identical with political stability, although there are important reciprocities between these two entities.

Another explication – regularity – has been suggested by Claude Ake:

> A political system is stable insofar as political actors proceed as usual – that is, confine their choice of political behavior to the general limits imposed by the role expectations of political interaction (Ake, 1974: 586–7).

The problem with this definition is not that it appears to be arbitrary and uni-dimensional – as previously stated, other scholars approach the concept uni-dimensionally with a necessary and sufficient condition for the application of the concept. The difficulty stems from the definition itself because its terms are too general to possess discriminatory power: When is there 'a regularity in the flow of political exchanges'? Whereas a multi-dimensional approach may render the concept unclear, the uni-dimensional approach runs the risk of conceptual vagueness.

A complete definition is a statement of the necessary and sufficient conditions for the application of a term. Although operational criteria are only part of these conditions, they certainly cannot be neglected. It is questionable if the various theoretical definitions of 'political stability' have any strict relationship to indicators commonly used in the concept of political stability. Moreover, they often contain paradoxes, like for example a nation may be characterized by high levels of social disorder, governmental instability and inflation as typical features of its political system, and thus these properties could be said to belong to the 'regularity of the flow of political exchanges'. This means that one would have to classify such a country as politically stable, which seems counter-intuitive.

In David Sanders' overview, there is a similar theoretical argument, although Sanders pins it down to indicators and measures it with an elaborate time series analysis. The general definition reads:

> The extent to which a political system may be characterized as 'unstable' at any given point in time varies in direct proportion to the extent to which the occurrence or non-occurrence of changes in and challenges to the government, regime or community deviates from the previous system specific 'normal' pattern of regime/government/ community changes or challenges; a pattern which will itself vary over time (Sanders, 1981: 66).

Sanders offers an operationalization of this definition (deviation from a previous normal pattern), identifying instability with the residuals in time series estimations, which allows for both linear and non-linear trends (Sanders, 1981: 77–89). However, there is a serious counter-argument: If the developmental pattern of political stability in a country displays a regular sine function hovering between low and high values, then that pattern would have to be classified as one of political stability, though the premises include the observation of both political stability and instability.

Semantic predicament

Various semantic inquiries into the meaning and reference of 'political stability' show that the expression is predicated on different kinds of entities, that its employment presupposes some minimal kind of ordering of these entities both cross-sectionally and longitudinally, and that the ordering is done on the basis of a variety of properties. From the literature on political stability it appears that stability is predicated on four different objects: regime, cabinet, party system, and society. It may also be established that the properties referred to in different uses of 'political stability' vary as a function of the object to which the term is applied. A semantic table may summarize the nature and variety of properties employed (Table 9.1).

The defining properties are of different sorts, as they vary in both abstraction and discriminatory power. The time requirement in the formal statement is met differently by the various definitions: some imply precise quantitative time measurements, whereas in others it seems to be difficult to pin down a time dimension. In such a semantic predicament – the term predicated on different objects and its meaning including different properties and states of affairs – the search for a definition is a premature task. A more promising route is to identify a set of conceptually relevant properties by means of which the concept of political stability may be handled with regard to a specified set of phenomena.

The time requirement contained in several definitions of 'political stability' may receive a variety of interpretations. On the one hand, there is Sanders' interpretation, which employs very short time periods – monthly data; on the other hand, there is the Budge and Farlie interpretation which would require the use of much longer time periods to identify a change in basic regime features. If political instability is defined as a property of the basic features of a political system, the best strategy is to allow for considerable time periods. If, however, political instability is used to denote a phenomenon that 'may not last longer than a week' (Sanders, 1981: 67), then a quite different strategy has to be followed.

We have no argument with these two contrary strategies. It seems

Table 9.1 *The semantics of 'political stability'*

Regime:
Uninterrupted continuation of political democracy, absence of a major political movement opposed to the democratic rules of the game (Lipset, 1959: 48); persistence of pattern, decision effectiveness, authenticity (Eckstein, 1966: 225); system's ability to survive intact (Lijphart, 1986: 8); existence of viable consensus (Tsurutani, 1968: 918); the probability at any given moment of an abrupt change in the institutional structure of governments and the norms of politics (Loewenberg, 1971: 182); longevity, legitimacy, effectiveness (Hurwitz, 1971); the regular flow of political exchanges (Ake, 1974: 586); the continued operation of specific patterns of political behaviour (Lustick, 1979: 325); the continuity of basic features of a regime (Budge and Farlie, 1981: 335).

Cabinet:
Instability of personnel (Russett, 1964: 447); duration of government in days (Taylor and Herman, 1971: 29); (coalition) cabinet exists as long as there is no change in the parties that compose the cabinet (Dodd, 1976: 122); the survival of governments (Sanders and Herman, 1977: 357); cabinet duration (Warwick, 1979: 468); extraordinary changes in government, change in composition of the government (Mitra, 1980: 249–50).

Party system:
Continuity of party alternatives over time (Lipset and Rokkan, 1967b: 50); change in electoral strength of political parties over time (Rose and Urwin, 1970: 295); continuity over time in the identity and relative strength of parliamentary parties (Dodd, 1976: 88); stability of party systems (Pedersen, 1979: 24); electoral instability (Borre, 1980: 145).

Society:
Dimensions of domestic conflict behaviour: turmoil, revolutionary and subversive dimensions (Rummel, 1971: 39); manifestations of political violence (Feierabend and Feierabend, 1971: 155); collective protest, internal war, power transfers (Yough and Sigelman, 1976: 225).

---

obvious that we have to distinguish between a long-run and a short-run perspective on political stability. The first approach focusses on regime change or regime longevity. What does it mean to our set of countries, the European democracies?

Long-run perspective

What is regime stability? The concept of political regime is not clear-cut and it may be somewhat arbitrary to spell out which changes should count as regime instability. Political systems may be changed in several aspects and regime longevity may accommodate some transformation but not all. Speaking of the European democracies it seems natural to tie the concept of regime stability to the persistence of a democractic polity, i.e. the institutionalization of individual rights and liberties as well as the existence of a set of mechanisms that guarantee political influence to the citizens of a country.

Table 9.2   *Regimes in Western Europe*

	Time for democratization		Time for institutionalization		Authoritarian experience		
	Male suffrage	Female suffrage	Modernized leadership	Institutional sclerosis	Begins	Ends	Constitution
Austria	1907	1918	1918	35.95	1934	1945	1929/1955
Belgium	1919	1948	1848	61.19	1940	1945	1980
Denmark	1915/1918	1918	1866	57.60	1940	1945	1953
F R Germany	1869/1871	1919	1871	46.07	1933	1945	1949
Finland	1906	1906	1919	40.26	–	–	1919
France	1848	1946	1848	43.56	1940	1945	1958
Greece	1877	1952	1918	28.69	1967	1974	1975
Ireland	1918/1922	1918/1922	1922	37.34	–	–	1937/1949
Italy	1912/1918	1946	1871	43.60	1922	1945	1946
Netherlands	1917	1919	1848	63.21	1940	1945	1983
Norway	1897	1913	1905	56.94	1940	1945	1814
Portugal	1911	1974	1910	39.20	1926	1974	1976/1982
Spain	1869/1907	1869/1931	1909	25.78	1939	1975	1978
Sweden	1909	1921	1905	59.90	–	–	1974
Switzerland	1848/1879	1971	1848	63.24	–	–	1874
UK	1918	1928	1832	90.08	–	–	1215/1832

Note: These indicators capture regime changes that are related to democratic principles of structuring the political system. The concept of modernized leadership is discussed in Taylor and Hudson (1972). The index of institutional sclerosis measures the extent to which durable political institutions have been established; it is a composite index taken from Choi (1983).

It may be established that regime longevity in the sense of the continued operation of a democratic system of government is not striking in the West European context. Democratic polities were created around the First World War as measured by the year of introduction of male suffrage (Table 9.2). The inter-war experience put hard pressure on these democratic systems as it proved that democratic stability was fragile. In several West European systems the democratic regimes were replaced by authoritarian systems: Italy (1922), Portugal (1926), Germany (1933), Austria (1934), Greece (1936) and Spain (1939). And what was left of democracy was almost totally smashed by the Nazi expansion, except for the United Kingdom, Ireland, Sweden and Switzerland.

After the Second World War democracy proved far more vital in Western Europe. Not only were democratic regimes successfully restored in most West European nations, but the authoritarian systems in Spain and Portugal did not manage to suppress the striving for democracy. Moreover, in Greece an authoritarian regime was defeated and replaced by a democratic one. Characteristic of West European politics during the post-war period is the continued operation of democratic principles of government. The conspicuous examples of regime change refer to Spain, Portugal and Greece. The process of regime transition was not a peaceful one in these countries, but the developments towards democratic consolidation have not resulted in civil war.

Regime transition and regime consolidation are interwoven, yet the forces that are conducive to or oppose regime transition may not be equally relevant when the period of regime consolidation sets in. That processes of regime consolidation have a different logic from that of regime transition appears clearly in the case of democracy (Pridham, 1990). A democractic political system may arise out of very *different genetic conditions*: from slow processes of social change and their emergent implications or rapid constitutional developments following the employment of political violence. The firm institutionalization of a new democratic regime requires the very *same persistence conditions*: a well-functioning system of party government. How well a process of regime consolidation fares depends on the party system and the relationships of the parties to the state and society.

Party government may be modelled by the ideal-types of Westminster government versus consensus government, but if one takes an inductive approach to party government all that is revealed about party operations does not appear ideal. It is true that democratic consolidation requires the successful operation of party government according to one model or another, but the non-ideal practices of party government may mean obstacles in the process of democratic consolidation. The careful empirical examination of the regime changes in southern Europe shows that the realities of party government may be neither Westminsterian or consociational. Thus, Italian and Greek *clientelism* involves that the resources of the democratic regime serve the special interests of the parties in power. And Portuguese and Spanish *personalismo* as well as Greek *patrimonialismo* result in party penetration of the democratic state as well as a lack of stable relations between the democratic institutions on the one hand and major groups in the social structure on the other hand.

Viable and stable party government is a necessary condition for the consolidation of a representative democracy, but party government may be neither efficient in the Westminster model sense nor lead to power sharing in the consensus model sense. Party government may tumble in a succession of short-lived governments (Portugal) or suffer from *protagonismo* between similar but competing parties (Spain) or end up in *partitocrazia* (Italy, Greece) meaning that the state is penetrated to enhance the interests of some party(ies) to the exclusion of others, a major party subjecting the state to its interests and not the other way around.

Some nations have changed their constitutions within the framework of a democratic polity. The most far-reaching constitutional revisions were made in France (1958) and Belgium (1980) whereas the new constitutions in Denmark (1953) and Sweden (1974) were not as extensive in actual practices. Taking a long-run perspective on political stability in Western Europe the post-Second World War period appears exceptionally stable, but regime longevity is not the sole aspect of political stability. Let us look at the short-run perspective.

Short-run perspective

If the objective is to describe a cross-sectional and longitudinal variation in political stability among European democracies in a short-term perspective, then the semantic inquiry above implies that a list of indicators measuring the occurrence of periods of political instability must include two subsets of indicators. Obviously, political indicators referring to changes in the cabinet or the government are relevant. The second subset would comprise indicators mapping the occurrence of disorderly phenomena in a broader aspect of the society, from political strikes to deaths from domestic violence.

Thus, the political indicators would capture that aspect of instability that somehow pertains to government. The relevant indicator measures governmental transformation which may be constructed in various ways depending on how executive transfers, number of governments and governmental change is identified. Firstly, a government has to be identified so that the occurrence of government change can be measured. Here we focus on the party composition of the government as well as its leader; should these things change we have a new government. Secondly, the maximum length of time of a government would be the normal time period between two ordinary elections, i.e. usually three, four or five years. Thirdly, the actual time period of a government would be the number of months that it has been in power meaning that we may derive an index of governmental stability in a country by dividing the actual number of months with the maximum possible length of government according to the normal rules of that country. The index on government stability ranges from 8 to 100.

The indicators on the occurrence of societal stability or social order would cover two types of factors. One factor would cover deaths from domestic violence, armed attacks and assassinations to be separated from another factor constituted by political strikes, riots and protest demonstrations. We denote these two dimensions by 'violence' and 'protest' respectively. It should be emphasized that both may be interpreted as referring to social disorder. They may be measured by means of standard indicators in the literature (see Appendix 9.1).

Table 9.3   *Correlation matrix of the instability dimensions*

	Government stability	Protest	Violence
Government stability	1.00		
Protest	−.20	1.00	
Violence	−.16	.50	1.00

Arguments may be adduced in favour of the recognition of a third subset of indicators referring to instability in the political economy of a country. Although such indicators as unemployment and public debt are seldom recognized in political sociology, they are certainly employed as measures of instability by political economists. Indicators on the state of the political economy of a nation may indeed be considered relevant to a judgement of the state of the political system, since the performance of governments is evaluated partly in the outcomes of their economic policies. On the other hand, there is the counter-argument that such economic variables may properly be understood as potential causes of political instability. However, this depends on what is regarded as system and as environment. One may approach political stability either way, placing the political economy indicators inside or outside the system.

Here we choose to include only the indicator on governmental stability as well as the indicators on the occurrence of internal disorder or societal instability. Since our focus is not primarily on constitutional legitimacy, we confine the political indicators to those aspects of the political system which may vary in stability at the same time as the regime remains unchanged. Thus, only democratic political systems enter the analysis meaning that Spain, Portugal and Greece are included only when democratic rules of governing are recognized.

Since our indicators include measures of governmental instability and social disorder, we use yearly data. From a theoretical point of view it also seems that yearly data afford a proper perspective on political instability, at least if the purpose is to conduct cross-national comparisons for the post-war period. Thus, we arrive at the selection of one-year time periods as our basic measurement unit. A simple correlation matrix comprising the operationalization of these three dimensions shows that they are really distinct (Table 9.3).

The two dimensions of government instability and social disorder appear to be independent to such an extent that they each require separate treatment. The interpretation is that governmental instability does not necessarily imply social instability or vice versa. This finding is clearly relevant to various theories of political stability as it implies that we explicitly state to what dimension of political stability we are referring when we take a short-term perspective. The concept of political stability must be handled with care as it is necessary to be clear about whether one is talking about government stability or social order.

Patterns of variation

If one were to draw an outline of how political stability has developed over time in the West European countries, then we wish to know if there is a pattern emerging. Since political stability may vary both between countries and over time we may employ the eta-squared statistic in order to see whether the between-country variation is larger than the intra-country variation over time.

The index of government stability may be measured for the entire time period, i.e. 1945–89. Table 9.4 indicates neither strong between-country differences nor a large and stable over time variation. Thus, government durability in many countries goes up and down and this in a way that is not systematically related to certain time intervals.

It appears from Table 9.4 that Switzerland is outstanding when it comes to government durability, which reflects the constitutional provision for

Table 9.4   *Stability: government durability scores*

	1945 –49	1950 –54	1955 –59	1960 –64	1965 –69	1970 –74	1975 –79	1980 –84	1985 –89	Aver- age
Austria	44.4	83.0	74.4	41.0	87.6	79.8	93.2	92.4	82.2	75.3
Belgium	36.0	52.0	83.2	90.0	65.2	57.6	49.0	66.8	72.6	63.6
Denmark	53.6	49.2	63.4	44.0	59.4	50.2	41.2	50.8	77.2	54.3
FRG	100.0	100.0	100.0	67.6	58.6	64.6	86.6	72.6	100.0	81.7
Finland	45.0	28.6	30.6	41.2	48.0	45.8	30.8	66.4	100.0	48.5
France	14.2	13.0	27.8	67.2	55.2	44.0	47.6	39.6	38.6	38.6
Greece	22.8	47.0	52.0	39.0	21.3	28.0	69.4	73.8	88.2	53.4
Ireland	90.2	76.0	61.8	77.6	61.0	95.0	79.6	58.2	76.6	75.1
Italy	13.5	29.0	25.6	38.8	65.4	19.8	38.2	33.4	46.6	35.0
Netherlands	63.8	100.0	72.6	78.8	70.8	73.6	97.4	78.8	86.0	80.6
Norway	97.6	45.2	83.0	64.8	89.2	39.8	64.0	52.6	70.4	67.4
Portugal	–	–	–	–	–	–	21.4	66.4	67.0	51.6
Spain	–	–	–	–	–	–	37.3	63.6	83.2	63.1
Sweden	49.2	76.6	59.4	94.2	87.4	92.8	71.0	73.4	84.4	76.5
Switzerland	100.0	67.6	92.6	100.0	100.0	100.0	100.0	100.0	100.0	95.6
UK	92.0	58.0	39.0	65.6	69.8	65.8	56.6	81.4	90.4	68.7
Average	57.3	58.9	61.8	65.0	68.4	63.2	61.8	66.9	79.0	65.0

Eta-squared by country = .33
Eta-squared by time period = .05
Note: The government stability index measures the length of actual time for a government in power in relation to its maximum time period.

Table 9.5   *Stability: protest scores*

	1948 –49	1950 –54	1955 –59	1960 –64	1965 –69	1970 –74	1975 –77	Aver- age
Austria	0.68	3.46	0.80	0.88	0.52	0.52	1.30	1.20
Belgium	3.51	2.73	1.53	3.60	1.68	0.57	0.54	1.97
Denmark	0.87	2.30	0.23	1.41	0.67	1.08	0.36	1.04
FRG	1.52	2.91	0.45	0.56	2.34	1.08	0.91	1.41
Finland	8.78	0.36	0.24	0.46	0.00	0.23	0.55	0.85
France	2.94	2.10	3.06	2.21	1.71	2.91	2.67	2.46
Greece	0.00	1.79	0.32	1.06	4.57	6.83	4.81	2.12
Ireland	2.17	0.59	0.30	0.00	2.81	3.98	4.19	1.84
Italy	5.44	3.51	1.08	1.91	2.08	2.91	2.52	2.53
Netherlands	0.70	0.43	0.13	0.00	0.62	0.66	1.16	0.47
Norway	1.40	0.28	0.00	0.38	0.94	0.51	0.83	0.53
Portugal	–	–	–	–	–	9.92	7.35	8.00
Spain	–	–	–	–	–	–	7.59	7.59
Sweden	0.00	0.42	0.00	0.00	1.06	1.43	1.06	0.59
Switzerland	0.58	0.00	0.43	0.41	0.55	1.41	1.37	0.64
UK	0.43	0.89	1.05	1.78	2.45	5.82	3.65	2.39
Average	2.07	1.56	0.69	1.05	1.48	1.97	2.56	1.53

Eta-squared by country = .33
Eta-squared by time period = .09
Note: The protest score measures the occurrence of various types of protest phenomena.

power sharing in Switzerland. In addition, there is a high degree of government stability in a few other countries: the Federal Republic of Germany, the Netherlands, Sweden and Austria. On the other hand, political stability tends to be low in Italy, France during the Fourth Republic and Finland. One of the difficulties in the process of democratic regime consolidation in Portugal has been to arrive at governments that last their entire period (Gladdish, 1990; Liebert, 1990). Although there is no seminal development trend over time in the five-year average data, we may note that political stability in general is higher in the 1980s than after the Second World War.

Civil disorder is measured by two different indicators: one referring to violence and the other to protest. Data on these two indicators are only available for the time period 1948–1977. The variation in the two phenomena of social disorder is larger between the countries than with regard to different time periods. At the same time the overall picture with regard to the occurrence of protest as well as violence phenomena is very much the same as that of government instability as the variation between the countries is not very stable over time. Table 9.5 presents an analysis of variance with regard to protest phenomena.

The new democracies in the Mediterranean, in particular Portugal and

Table 9.6   *Stability: violence scores*

	1948 −49	1950 −54	1955 −59	1960 −64	1965 −69	1970 −74	1975 −77	Aver- age
Austria	2.40	1.87	0.00	0.77	0.43	0.17	1.00	0.80
Belgium	0.00	1.37	0.00	1.49	0.29	1.42	0.84	0.84
Denmark	0.00	1.36	0.24	0.00	0.00	0.00	0.36	0.30
FRG	0.56	1.30	0.26	0.30	0.92	1.04	1.12	0.79
Finland	1.26	0.25	0.00	0.64	0.00	0.00	0.00	0.23
France	1.12	0.93	1.52	2.80	0.57	1.91	3.37	1.70
Greece	14.90	1.47	0.90	0.85	2.35	1.92	3.43	2.71
Ireland	0.73	1.00	2.68	0.98	1.66	5.10	6.11	2.56
Italy	3.44	1.70	0.98	1.97	1.25	2.79	3.79	2.06
Netherlands	0.00	0.00	0.13	0.00	0.78	0.49	2.07	0.44
Norway	0.00	0.28	0.27	0.00	0.26	0.50	0.00	0.22
Portugal	–	–	–	–	–	4.03	5.06	4.80
Spain	–	–	–	–	–	–	5.55	5.55
Sweden	0.00	0.18	0.00	0.00	0.16	0.89	0.86	0.29
Switzerland	0.58	0.00	0.75	0.20	0.19	0.66	0.63	0.40
UK	0.00	0.54	0.34	0.17	1.33	8.15	7.52	2.51
Average	1.78	0.87	0.58	0.73	0.68	1.81	2.61	1.18

Eta-squared by country = .26
Eta-squared by time period = .11
Note: The violence scores measure the occurrence of various types of violence phenomena.

Spain but also Greece in the 1970s, appear to be vulnerable to various kinds of protest phenomena such as demonstrations and political strikes (Pridham, 1984). This reflects the slow process of regime consolidation in these countries (Pridham, 1990). The high score for Spain points out the regional problem in consolidating democracy after the fall of authoritarianism, in particular the anti-system opposition of the pro-ETA Herri Batasuna alliance in the Basque provinces (Gillespie, 1990). At times severe protest has occurred in other countries as well: Italy in the late 1940s and the United Kingdom in the early 1970s. However, as Joseph LaPalombara argues in *Democracy, Italian Style* (1987), the sharp conflicts have contributed to the consolidation of the democratic regime in Italy.

The new democracies in southern Europe also face severe difficulties in containing violent phenomena like armed attacks and deaths from domestic violence. High violence scores are also to be found for the UK and Ireland which reflects the conflict in Northern Ireland. Table 9.6 contains an analysis of variance of data on the occurrence of various types of social violence.

It should be pointed out that Greece and Ireland have an overall high measure on one of the social disorder dimensions (violence) whereas they

score low on the other social disorder dimension (protest). The opposite
is true of France (Table 9.6). However, there is an overall association
between the two dimensions of social disorder when they are measured
by yearly scores ($r = .50$) as shown in Table 9.3.

It is well known that the basic features of West European politics
changed on at least two occasions since the end of the Second World
War. In the standard idiom, the end of the 1940s constituted a period
of unrest and political realignment, whereas the 1950s were characterized
as a decade of depoliticization and increasing stability. The 1960s, and
in particular the later part of the decade, became famous for growing
tensions and the saliency of civil disobedience. This period of uproar
against established patterns of authority and of legitimate voice against
the inherited order was followed by a decade of tranquility and increased
emphasis on standard operating procedures. The end of the 1970s and the
early 1980s have been described as a new period of increasing instability
due to the difficulties of big government. Now, do the indices on political
instability confirm these sweeping statements?

Less variation over time is to be found when the overall development of
governmental stability is investigated. Probably, the country variation is
stronger than the time variation. Yet it clearly appears that the 1960s have,
on the whole, been a somewhat more stable period than the early 1950s
and the 1970s. The impression of depoliticization is confirmed in the data
for the late 1950s and early 1960s. Moreover, the data indicate that there
is no uniform trend towards an increase in governmental instability during
the 1970s. The level of social disorder, measured in violence and protest,
depends on the spirit of the times.

The indices single out the late 1960s as the starting point of something
new. Quite naturally, the late 1940s displayed some of the phenomena of
social disorder, particularly political strikes and protest demonstrations.
But there is a uniform reduction in the violence dimension as well as
in the protest dimension during the 1950s and the early 1960s. The
rise in social disorder culminates in the mid-1970s, when the violence
dimension in particular displays high values. These measures capture the
overall picture, showing that the concept of political stability bears a time
and space aspect. A state or a nation is more or less unstable during a
definite period of time; the dynamic aspect of political systems becoming
more or less stable is basic to the concept of political stability.

Ekkart Zimmermann also identifies two dimensions of political conflict: collective protest and internal war. Looking at the 1970s and early
1980s he identifies three types of nation-groups:

'noisy-participatory' states such as the United Kingdom, France, Italy, and
more recently Spain and Portugal – and Greece if taken on per capita
base. The group of rather 'quiet' democracies consists of the Scandinavian
countries, Switzerland and Luxembourg, with the remaining countries forming

the middle, less clearly delineated group (Zimmermann, 1989: 179).

Explaining political stability

It is difficult to account for the occurrence of the manifestations of political instability by means of some causal theory. We may look for necessary or sufficient conditions as well as contributory conditions among two alternative sets of factors: social forces or institutional variables. Which are the main contending theories? One hypothesis singles out the two-party systems with a homogeneous culture as politically stable in Western Europe (Almond, 1956; Lipset, 1959). Another hypothesis designates the countries with a multi-party system and a heterogeneous culture governed by means of consociational devices as the politically stable systems (Lehmbruch, 1967; Lijphart, 1968; Steiner, 1974).

The findings in our analysis imply that the picture is not all that clear. Multi-party systems may be both stable or unstable. It is not true that a homogeneous culture always results in political stability. The two-party systems included do not score higher on the dimensions of political stability than a number of multi-party systems do, even though it may be argued that the high value on social disorder for the United Kingdom simply reflects that the political system includes a highly heterogeneous culture within one separate part of the country (Northern Ireland). It is true that nations with a multi-party system and a homogeneous culture tend to belong to the set of politically stable nations, but their stability varies over time as for example in Denmark.

Not all multi-party systems with a heterogeneous culture are stable if they employ consociational devices. The consociational model operates with various degrees of success in both space and time. Austria and Switzerland are the jewels in consociationalism, but the Lorwin (1974) example of Belgium is a failure for several periods of time. Not all multi-party systems with a heterogeneous culture are stable only if they employ consociational devices, as the development of government stability in West Germany testifies. Indeed, Austria appears to be the most stable political system during the 1970s, a period when it employed consociationalism to a far lesser extent. Which factors, then, account for the variation in political stability? What is the impact of the factors discussed in earlier chapters? The analysis focusses on government instability and the two types of social disorder, viz. protest and violence phenomena.

The political organization of society comprises a variety of institutions for the making and implementation of public policy. Not only are there government structures of various kinds and at different levels, but the political system involves political parties, interest organizations and citizen groups. Although it is far from clear what a 'democratic' political system really stands for we have identified among West European nations a set of sixteen democracies for the purpose of analysing the problem(s) of political stability. The set includes the major political systems of Western Europe – Ireland, Luxembourg and the tiny states of Andorra, San Marino and Monaco excluded – because in these nations political structures are institutionalized which are related to concepts of democracy. Among such institutions we count basic individual rights, the freedom of the press, constitutional government based on free elections and referendums, parliamentarianism or presidentialism based on popular vote. In most of the European democracies these political structures have been firmly institutionalized during the post Second World War period, but we also know how precarious the status of these institutions has been in Spain, Portugal and Greece.

It is readily admitted that these structures may not be sufficient for designating a political system a 'democracy'. There are several concepts of democracy (Naess et al., 1956) and a variety of normative models of democracy (Lively, 1975). And these concepts or models pertain in no way only to the political system. Democracy is a property or bundle of properties that are relevant to other kinds of organization (Pateman, 1970; Abrahamsson, 1977). To some democracy is basically an ideal of which there is no real life example (Walker, 1966; Lewin, 1970; Dahl, 1971). To others the concept of democracy may be employed as a descriptive concept for real world political systems which have institutionalized certain clear-cut procedures for the making and implementation of public policy (Tingsten, 1955; Lijphart, 1984a). Not denying the importance and relevance of a normative approach to democracy we employ the term here in a basically descriptive context to single out a set of real life political systems. These sixteen West European nations are identified as democracies because they uphold political institutions that organize autonomy and influence in these societies. By recognizing a considerable amount of autonomy of citizens and collectivities from the state as well as a substantial degree of influence of citizens and organizations on public policy-making these political systems differ from dictatorial or authoritarian political systems. These democracies vary in political stability, some in terms of a long-run perspective involving constitutional change and all in a short-run perspective focussing on government durability and social disorder phenomena.

The concept of political stability cannot be equated with the general notion of continuity or lack of change. A definition of political instability such as change in general would be far too broad. It is necessary to tie the concept to some specific properties. The descriptive problem of political stability focusses on the existence of relative differences between political systems. How are we to identify and map such differences in a comparative approach to European democracies? Or to understand the country differences in political stability? Let us evaluate a few hypotheses about the conditions for political stability in the light of one dominating mode of approaching political stability: multipartism.

Theme of multipartism

A basic hypothesis in the literature about political stability in West European politics states in one version or another that political instability reflects social forces, in particular the nature and severity of social cleavages. For lack of a more appropriate expression we designate this political sociology hypothesis or set of hypotheses the theory of multipartism, because implicit is a set of hypotheses of how social cleavages are translated into a fragmented party system of a multi-party nature which in its turn is conducive to political instability.

Multipartism cannot be approached as the sole cause of political instability, merely mirroring extensive social cleavages. Such a model would seriously neglect the institutional context of the party system as an entity in the overall political system. Theoretically, a multi-party system may be identified as an instrument for the exercise of citizen influence on government policy-making. By voting for a variety of parties citizens express their preferences about policies. The number of effective parties enters into a system of institutions for collective choice. A broad model of the relationships between various determinants of political instability may be outlined on the basis of distinctions discussed and described empirically in earlier chapters (Figure 9.1).

The framework outlined in Figure 9.1 approaches political instability as a function of several conditions, bypassing the mono-causal hypothesis that social heterogeneity produces a fractionalized multi-party system which automatically translates into political instability. The shape of the party system is one intervening variable between the cleavage structure in society and political instability. Other relevant institutional factors include: election rules, coalition patterns and governmental structures. It is difficult to spell out exact causal relations between the entities in the model.

The data employed to estimate models of political stability in a general framework cover the post-war period for sixteen nations in so far as they have adhered to democratic procedures. Summarizing much of what is dealt with in earlier chapters we include the following variables:

Social heterogeneity: If it is true that multipartism is a natural reaction to the structure of society, then one would expect to find relationships between multipartism and social fragmentation. To test such propositions we employ a number of indices concerning social heterogeneity: socio-economic structure indices (affluence) as well as indices that measure

Figure 9.1 *Framework for analysis*

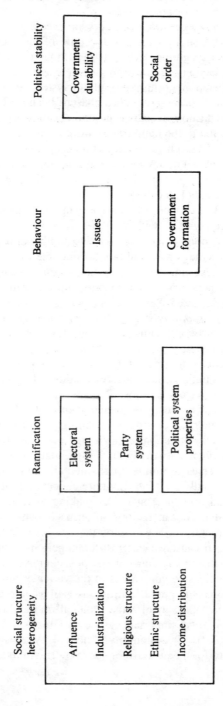

religious, ethnic and class-based cleavages (Tables 2.1, 2.4, 2.9, 2.10, 2.28 and 2.31).

Electoral system: Standard indicators on electoral formalities have been used, one indicator measuring the type of electoral formula and the other electoral magnitude (Rae, 1971; Lijphart, 1985). Although a large variety of election procedures exists we classify them according to the following schema: majoritarian or plural systems versus proportional systems (d'Hondt, Sainte-Laguë, Hagenbasch-Bischoff, Hare and STV). The magnitude indicator measures the number of seats in the National Assembly in relation to the number of constituencies. The description of the formal side of the election system is often supplemented by an indicator measuring the extent of deviation from strict proportionality focussing upon electoral outcomes instead of formalities. Such a proportionality index is also included (Table 7.2).

Multipartism: The concept of multipartism is complex as it refers to properties of party systems which do not co-vary. Multipartism is here approached as a combination of the effective number of parties, the extent of conflict between the parties and how volatile the party system tends to be. We measure these dimensions by means of three separate indices: the Laakso and Taagepera index, a polarization index and the volatility index (Tables 5.2, 5.4, 5.5 and 5.9).

Political system properties: (a) Direct democracy: The referendum institution has a different status in various European democracies. An indicator on its function in the political system may be derived by mapping the number of times it has been employed (Table 7.1). (b) Representative institutions: The variety of indirect democratic procedures is mapped by several distinctions. Perhaps the most basic differences concern uni-cameralism versus bi-cameralism (Table 7.5). (c) Regimes: The concept of a political regime is an ambiguous one; we employ it to refer to some crucial distinctions concerning how power is exercised in an overall sense: parliamentarism versus presidentialism, as well as cabinet parliamentarism versus committee parliamentarism (Table 7.6). (d) Corporatism: In the rapidly growing literature concerning interest mediation and organizational influence on policy-making there are a few indices ranking the West European nations in terms of what Schmitter refers to as societal corporatism. We employ the Schmitter index although we make adjustments because we cover different periods of time (Table 7.7). (e) Consociationalism: The concept of consociationalism is a summary concept as it combines certain values of the variables already introduced like representationalism, grand coalition as well as élite cooperation and proporz. However, a measure of consociationalism should enter the analysis due to its theoretical importance. The variable is in effect a dummy variable (Table 7.7). (f) Autonomy: Political systems institutionalize certain boundaries for the exercise of state power. An index of individual autonomy measures the distribution of citizen rights and an index of institutional autonomy taps the division of power between different levels of government (Tables 6.2 and 6.4); both indices are scaled in such a manner that a higher score means less individual autonomy or institutional autonomy.

Issues: If multipartism implies political instability, then multipartism must have implications for the nature of conflict between political parties. We measure the occurrence of issues by means of an index that recognizes both the type of issue involved as well as the intensity of conflict. This permits us to test hypotheses about relationships between multipartism, the politicization of social problems and political instability (Table 8.1).

Patterns of government formation: It is pertinent to distinguish between the formal structure of the coalition – whether it includes one, two or more parties – and the political colour of the coalition in the ideology to which the participating parties adhere. Thus, we separate between different types of government according to the nature of the coalition: minimum-winning coalitions including one-party majority governments, large coalitions, minority governments and over-sized coalitions (Table 7.3). Moreover, the various governments are classified according to their predominant ideological appearance: bourgeoisie hegemony, bourgeoisie dominance, even, socialist dominance and socialist hegemony (Table 7.4).

Political stability: In the argument that multipartism is conducive to political instability the focus is upon government instability. We use the index that measures government durability discussed earlier in this Chapter (Table 9.4) However, we have also entered separate indices that tap other independent dimensions of political stability; one index measures the occurrence of social violence in society, another the occurrence of organized protest (Tables 9.5 and 9.6).

To test models about the sources of multipartism as well as its implications we will pool the data previously described according to a division of the post-war period into roughly four separate intervals: 1945–54, 1955–64, 1965–74 and 1975–84. Thus, we have some sixty cases. The justification for the use of a pooled data set is simply that average values for such a long time period would eliminate a substantial amount of the variation in the data which has theoretical import. It should be pointed out that the following findings are tentative as there is instability in the estimated coefficients due to the low number of cases, among other things. We only employ simple measures of association, i.e. Pearson's correlation coefficient, in order to evaluate whether social forces or institutional factors are most important as conditions for political instability. To test for robustness we use two data sets, one pooled set with $N=58$ and one set covering the 1980s with $N=16$.

Table 9.7   *Multi-party system properties as a function of social structure*

		Effective number of parties	Polarization	Volatility
Affluence	[N=58]	.31*	.05	−.10
	[N=16]	.39	−.12	−.30
Religious awareness				
Weekly	[N=58]	−.16	−.45**	−.03
	[N=16]	−.11	−.34	−.04
Ethnic structure				
Fragmentation	[N=58]	.31*	−.20	.01
	[N=16]	.58*	−.26	.42
Dominating				
	[N=58]	−.42**	.26	−.01
	[N=16]	−.76**	.23	−.37
Class structure				
Quintile				
	[N=58]	−.23	.56**	.33*
	[N=16]	−.45	.65 *	.06
Narrow heterogeneity index				
	[N=16]	.41	−.27	.12
Broad heterogeneity index				
	[N=16]	.20	.08	−.02

Note: The statistical associations reported on are Pearson's correlations. The asterisk means statistical significance at the .01 level (*) or at the .001 level (**).

Testing models of political stability

Firstly, the theme of multipartism claims that social structure determines the basic shape of the party system, heterogeneity resulting in a high degree of fractionalization, polarization and volatility. Is this true? Table 9.7 reports on correlations between social structure properties and party system dimensions.

The findings in Table 9.7 do not support the first claims of multipartism that social heterogeneity translates into the party system. The party system of a country does not mirror the social structure of society. Yet, the opposite hypothesis that society has no implications whatsoever for the shape of the party system is equally unfounded. Thus, the sharper the class structure measured in terms of income inequality, the higher the level of polarization. On the other, a strong religious awareness may dampen the

Table 9.8   *Multi-party system properties as a function of the electoral system*

		Effective number of parties	Polarization	Volatility
Number of referendums	[*N*=58]	.32*	−.27	−.02
	[*N*=16]	.21	−.43	−.10
Electoral formula	[*N*=58]	−.19	.42*	.11
	[*N*=16]	−.27	.22	−.09
District magnitude	[*N*=58]	.33*	.03	−.14
	[*N*=16]	.16	−.01	−.17
Proportionality	[*N*=58]	−.01	−.45	−.60**
	[*N*=16]	.02	−.38	−.66*

Note: Table 9.8 reports Pearson's correlations. The asterisk means statistical significance at the .01 level (*) or at the .001 level (**).

extent of polarization within the party system. It is also evident that ethnic cleavages have an impact on the fractionalization of the party system.

The political sociology model that relates party system properties to the structure of society may be contrasted with an institutionalist model searching for determinants of party system variables in for example the election system. Table 9.8 indicates that institutional factors matter, but that they do not explain everything.

The extent of deviation from strict proportionality between votes received in elections and seats allocated in parliament is not such a crucial determinant of the number of effective parties as is often believed. Actually, there is hardly any relationship at all between proportionality in the election system and fractionalization whereas proportionality is relevant for polarization and volatility. A more proportional voting system tends to lessen the ideological distance within the party system as well as contribute to the stabilization of the party borders reducing electoral volatility.

Secondly, multipartism argues that the shape of the party system has a considerable impact on political stability. The basic hypothesis is that more fractionalization, polarization and volatility means less political stability. Table 9.9 tests some models that are relevant for the theory that multi-party system properties determine political instability.

Again, the finding is that the clear association between multi-party system properties and political instability that multipartism conceives of is not confirmed. Government instability and social disorder is not caused by properties of the party system such as fractionalization, polarization and volatility. The theme of multipartism is simply not true of Western Europe. Although a high level of party system fractionalization,

Table 9.9   *Political stability as a function of multi-party system properties*

| | | Government stability | Social disorder | |
			Protest	Violence
Electoral				
participation	[N=58]	−.20	−.06	−.1
	[N=16]	−.26	−.18	−.19
Effective number				
of parties	[N=58]	−.11	−.32*	−.26
	[N=16]	−.07	−.43	−.43
Polarization	[N=58]	−.42**	.19	.07
	[N=16]	−.43	.27	.03
Volatility	[N=58]	−.24	.45*	.21
	[N=16]	−.12	.54	.29

Note: the table reports Pearson's correlations. The asterisk means statistical significance at the .01 level (*) or at the .001 level (**).

Table 9.10   *Political stability as a function of political institutions*

| | | Government stability | Social disorder | |
			Protest	Violence
Individual				
autonomy	[N=58]	−.23	.46**	.29
	[N=16]	−.35	.72**	.44
Institutional				
autonomy	[N=58]	−.41**	.47**	.33*
	[N=16]	−.31	.69*	.59*
Chamber				
system	[N=58]	.43**	−.05	.06
	[N=16]	.31	−.10	.10
Presidentialism	[N=58]	−.13	.04	.03
	[N=16]	−.04	−.17	.03
Consociationalism	[N=58]	.44**	−.22	−.24
	[N=16]	.60*	−.37	−.36
Corporatism	[N=58]	.03	−.42**	−.51**
	[N=16]	.08	−.51	−.74**

Note: the table reports on Pearson's correlations. The asterisk means statistical significance at the .01 level (*) or at the .001 level (**).

Table 9.11 *Political stability as a function of government formations*

| | | Government stability | Social disorder | |
			Protest	Violence
Minimum-winning	[*N*=58]	.17	.04	.16
	[*N*=16]	.44	.11	.32
Grand coalition	[*N*=58]	.21	−.10	−.22
	[*N*=16]	.50	−.15	−.27
Minority	[*N*=58]	−.20	.01	−.03
	[*N*=16]	−.50	.07	−.13
Oversized	[*N*=58]	−.01	−.06	−.15
	[*N*=16]	−.00	−.19	−.23

Note: the table reports Pearson's correlations. The asterisk means statistical significance at the .01 level (*) or at the .001 level (**).

polarization and volatility is not completely irrelevant for high levels of political instability – note the association between polarization and government instability for example, or between volatility and social protest phenomena – the strict theme of multipartism fails. Let us move to an institutionalist model of political instability (Table 9.10).

Here we note that institutionalist variables display stronger associations with political instability phenomena than the multipartism model of social heterogeneity causing party system instability which is conducive to political instability. The following institutional factors matter: individual as well as institutional autonomy, consociationalism and corporatism. Both individual and institutional autonomy have an impact on government durability and social disorder increasing the first while reducing the second phenomenon. An interesting finding is the significant association between individual autonomy and protest as well as between institutional autonomy and both government durability and the two expressions of social order. This finding is in accordance with the basic message of the new institutionalism that the framing of political institutions for the making of social choice involves a number of degrees of freedom where picking one institutional set up and not another has implications for the entire polity.

Another important theory about political stability focusses on the pattern of government formation. It has often been stated that a minimum winning coalition is crucial for government durability in particular. Table 9.11 reports on some findings in relation to this model.

It appears that a minimum winning coalition is neither a necessary nor a sufficient condition for government stability. There is an association, but

Table 9.12   *Political stability as a function of issues*

		Government stability	Social disorder	
			Protest	Violence
Class	[N=58]	−.56**	.40**	.28
	[N=16]	−.43	.55	.49
Religious	[N=58]	−.21	.27	.26
	[N=16]	−.50	.22	.27
Regional	[N=58]	.07	.20	.40*
	[N=16]	.12	.09	.31
Ecology	[N=58]	.17	−.03	.13
	[N=16]	.19	−.49	−.37
Political system	[N=58]	−.39*	.52**	.42**
	[N=16]	−.20	.56	.46
Foreign policy	[N=58]	−.30	.15	.06
	[N=16]	−.44	.06	.07
Number of issues	[N=58]	−.41**	.53**	.57**
	[N=16]	−.50	.37	.49
Class and political system	[N=58]	−.47**	.53**	.42**
	[N=16]	−.29	.55	.69*

Note: the table reports on Pearson's correlations. The asterisk means statistical significance at the .01 level (*) or at the .001 level (**).

it is not as prominent as predicted in standard coalition models. What, then, about issues?

The occurrence of class issues as well as of political system issues does affect political stability, because they tend to be intense, long-lived and divisive between various political and social groups.

Political stability whether in the form of government durability or social disorder is not simply a by-product of social cleavages. A political sociology model reducing political instability to deep-seated social cleavages does not work in the West European context, because the politics of these highly complex countries is not that simple. So far the institutionalist criticism of the political sociology approach is correct. However, against the kind of indeterminism that the new institutionalism propagates we wish to raise a word of warning. Political institutions have an impact on political stability but they do not explain everything. And there is some truth to some political sociology models that social cleavages are relevant to the understanding of political instability (Table 9.13).

Table 9.13   *Political stability as a function of social structure*

		Government stability	Social disorder	
			Protest	Violence
Affluence	[N=58]	.21	−.18	−.01
	[N=16]	.04	−.83**	−.65*
Religious structure				
Fragmentation	[N=58]	.50**	−.24	−.11
	[N=16]	.44	−.38	−.12
Catholics	[N=58]	−.09	.44*	.34*
	[N=16]	−.12	.58*	.44
Religious awareness				
Weekly	[N=58]	.25	.25	.39*
	[N=16]	.02	.51	.51
Monthly	[N=58]	.08	.34*	.31*
	[N=16]	.08	.65*	.47
Ethnic structure				
Fragmentation	[N=58]	.26	.05	.07
	[N=16]	.33	.00	.05
Class structure				
Quintile	[N=58]	−.37*	.47**	.34
	[N=16]	−.33	.61*	.43

Note: the table reports on Pearson's correlations. The asterisk means statistical significance at the .01 level (*) or at the .001 level (**).

The long-run perspective

Political stability is a multi-dimensional phenomenon. Different facts may be adduced as indicating political instability: rapid government change, frequent occurrences of violence and protest phenomena. These various factors do not go together meaning that it is necessary to be precise about which political stability dimension one is talking. In the short-run perspective there is considerable variation over time in these aspects of political stability. Political stability may also be approached in a long-run perspective. The long-run perspective on political stability employs data based on averages covering the entire post-war period.

Taking into account regime changes as well as the average values of government instability and social disorder one may rank the democracies in Western Europe on the basis of overall political instability in the long-run perspective (Table 9.14).

We may identify a distinct difference between the Latin countries and the North of Europe. Portugal, Spain and Greece come out as highly unstable because of the transition to democratic rule and the concomitant

Table 9.14 *The long-run perspective on political stability*
1945-1989

	Average government stability score	Average protest score	Average violence score	Regime change score	Summary instability
Austria	75.3	1.20	0.80	1	20.95
Belgium	63.6	1.97	0.84	2	25.69
Denmark	54.3	1.04	0.30	0	21.12
FRG	81.7	1.41	0.79	0	18.13
Finland	48.5	0.85	0.23	0	21.69
France	38.6	2.46	1.70	2	31.30
Greece	53.4	2.12	2.71	3	32.29
Ireland	75.1	1.84	2.56	0	22.28
Italy	35.0	2.53	2.06	1	30.40
Netherlands	80.6	0.47	0.44	0	16.74
Norway	67.4	0.53	0.22	0	18.47
Portugal	51.6	8.00	4.80	3	42.14
Spain	63.1	7.59	5.35	3	41.09
Sweden	76.5	0.59	0.29	0	17.27
Switzerland	95.6	0.64	0.40	0	14.60
UK	68.7	2.39	2.51	1	25.84

Note: The scores on government stability and social disorder (protest, violence) follow Tables 9.4–9.6. The regime-change score ranges from 0-3 in relation to the extent of changes in the political regime. The summary score has been reached through transforming the values of the scores to *T*-scores and then adding the instability scores and subtracting the government stability score, all divided by four; i.e. the lower the value on the summary score, the more political stability.

problems of social disorder. A high degree of political instability also characterizes France due to its government instability and the Gaullist constitutional revision. Italy also scores high. Why are some nations more unstable than others over time? Can we explain these country differences by means of some systemic variables?

Political instability depends upon the extent of conflict as well as the existence of conflict-resolution mechanisms. Thus, we predict that the more pronounced the social cleavages are, the less stable is the political system, all other factors being the same. And we predict that the more the system has institutionalized mechanisms for the resolution of conflict the more stable it appears to be, all other things equal. We focus in particular on the distribution of influence and autonomy in the system (Table 9.15).

Overall political instability depends on two countervailing forces. Social cleavages in the form of religion and class are conducive to a process which results in political instability. A decision-making system

Table 9.15   *Political instability: the long-run perspective*
(correlation analysis)

	Average government stability score	Average protest score	Average violence score	Regime change score	Summary instability score
Proportion Catholics	−.13	.55	.52	.45	.49
Income distribution (top quintile)	−.56	.57	.57	.61*	.69*
Institutional autonomy	−.63*	.65*	.67*	.87**	.84**
Individual autonomy	−.42	.73**	.77**	.78**	.81**
Influence index	.61*	−.69*	−.74**	−.78**	−.84**

Note: The variable indicators in the correlation analysis are taken from Tables 2.4, 2.28, 6.4, 6.2, 7.8; *N*=16; ** indicates significance at .001 level, * indicates significance at .01 level.

that allows for autonomy and influence works the other way around. The net result will depend on how structures for influence and autonomy may restrain the impact of religious and class cleavages. The findings reported on in Table 9.15 support a basic model of political stability that focusses on individual autonomy, institutional autonomy and the pattern of exercising influence on the national government. Actually, the statistical associations presented are significant and confirm a theory of political stability as a function of the combined distribution of autonomy and influence in the political system. Let us, finally, develop this theme somewhat further.

Conclusion

The literature on political stability has come up with several hypotheses about which factors are conducive to political instability. A classical doctrine – multipartism – argues that political instability mirrors deeper social cleavages in a fragmented society through the party system. Looking at data covering the post-war period based on a framework that places multipartism in a system of variables leads to a negative finding. Multipartism is not a major cause of political instability in the form of either government durability or protest phenomena. This is not to deny that fractionalization and polarization have instability conducive effects, raising the issueness of politics and lowering the probability of minimum-winning cabinets. The link between social structure fragmentation, multipartism and political instability is far weaker than envisaged in the traditional interpretation of the interaction among society, political parties and government institutions.

Political stability in the long-run perspective is related on the one hand to social cleavages and their conflict implications and on the other to the decision-making system, in particular to the distribution of influence and autonomy between major groups within a society. We have a set of theoretical entities, cleavages, demand and supply of autonomy and influence, and political stability. A simple model of their interaction may be suggested. The cleavage structure affects but does not determine basic parameters of political systems: political party support and issue-making. Political stability will be more difficult to reach in societies characterized by profound cleavages, but political instability is not a strict function of the cleavage structure. Social problems must be politicized before they can work out their consequences on the political scene and issue-making depends on factors other than the cleavage structure. The structure of the decision-making system is as relevant, in particular the overall distribution of autonomy and influence.

Demands for increased autonomy crop up in many political systems. Sometimes these demands concern institutional autonomy, a demand for decentralization or regional semi-independence or a demand for less interference in the life of organizations. Sometimes these demands orientate towards individual autonomy, a distrust in big government and government regulation – in particular in systems where democratic institutions have been fragile or non-existent. People and organizations demand both increased institutional autonomy and increased individual autonomy. The demand for autonomy is related to the distribution of influence. Citizens and organizations demand autonomy when they experience government as unresponsive and inefficient. When influence does not work citizens look for more autonomy. On the other hand the demand for influence is a function of the distribution of autonomy. If people and organizations find that their activities in an area are no longer autonomous or at least have no longer the same degree of autonomy they will try to influence the government setting the directives that govern their lives. When people begin to experience that they cannot handle vital problems by themselves, they tend to ask for governmental action (Figure 9.2).

We have plotted the relationships between demand for autonomy and supply of influence and between demand for influence and supply of autonomy on top of each other. If a society with profound social cleavages offers a low degree of influence as well as a low degree of autonomy to its various organizations and citizens, an unstable situation results.

If a society finds itself at the point (x_I, y_I) we see that the demand

Figure 9.2   *Political instability, autonomy and influence on national government*

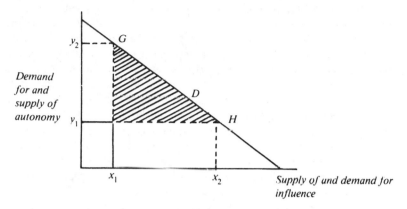

Note: The shaded area represents the possibilities.

for influence (x_2, y_2) as well as for autonomy is high (x_1, y_2). This situation is unstable and there will be a movement towards the line D inside the shadowed region. For example, suppose that the Basque provinces in Spain during the 1970s were able to exert the influence x_1 through participation and representation in legitimate ways. They would then demand a certain amount of autonomy, y_2, considering their view of their separate culture. However, the Spanish government did not allow this amount of autonomy. Only y_1 was available and the provinces faced the choice: demanding more influence (x_2, y_1) or more autonomy (x_1, y_2). Since the provinces are only a minority in Spanish society the Basques could not hope for more influence. Consequently, the choice was the drive for increased institutional autonomy, which proved effective during the 1980s when a successful regionalization reduced political instability in Spain.

Societies that lack a balance between autonomy and influence tend to be politically unstable. Organizations and individuals will demand increased autonomy or increased influence or both. Even before Northern Ireland was governed directly from Westminster, the polity did not provide its various parts with much institutional autonomy (y_1). However, the Protestant group used to have a much larger amount of influence on governmental decisions than the Catholic group had, which implies that the Catholic group was at a non-equilibrium point. It did not command enough autonomy to compensate for the small amount of influence (x_1) and it lacked the influence necessary (x_2) to compensate for the small autonomy. Political stability will not be forthcoming until the influence and/or autonomy of the Catholic group is increased.

Both Sweden and the Netherlands tend to be stable political systems.

A classical explanation focussing on the cleavage structure would point out that the Netherlands is a fragmented system which overcomes its inherent tendencies towards instability by means of the adherence of the élite to consociational devices (Lijphart, 1968). Sweden, however, is a homogeneous country and thus the probability that it is stable would be high, following the Lipset emphasis on the stability conducive implications of social homogeneity (Lipset, 1959). Thus, there would be two different cases or two different sets of conditions for stability. But, let the diagonal line in Figure 9.2 denote points where the demand for and the supply of autonomy are matched by the supply of and demand for influence respectively in such a way that there is a balance.

The Swedish political system may be placed at point H, giving a smaller amount of institutional autonomy to its rather homogeneous groups but on the other hand providing a kind of compensation in influence on extensive national policy-making by means of various devices including corporatism. Dutch society may be placed at point G, on the one hand permitting more autonomy to its basic groups in a divided society but on the other hand requiring less policy concertation at the national level of government. Accordingly, these political systems would be stable for the very same reason: because the important social groups control their own activities, although in somewhat different ways. The availability of these decision-making mechanisms – various combinations of autonomy from the national government and influence over the national government – are conducive to the management of any kind of social cleavages that have conflict implications, be these class-based cleavages in homogeneous societies or mutually reinforcing cleavages of a religious, an ethnic or class-based import in divided societies. In political systems where there is a low degree of both autonomy and influence, there are bound to arise political instability phenomena.

Appendix 9.1 *Political stability indicators*

Indicator	Note
Protest demonstrations Riots	*Source*: Jodice and Taylor, 1981; these events data have been both per-capitalized and logarithmically transformed.
Governmental instability Armed attacks Assassinations Political strikes Death from domestic violence	It is important to state the criteria used when observing a change in government. As long as the prime minister is in office and as long as the set of parties represented in government remains the same, there is no change in government. Change occurs when there is a change of prime minister and/or change in the set of parties represented in government.

10
The Tax and Welfare State

Introduction

The West European countries not only harbour a democratic regime that appeals to wide segments of their population as a set of legitimate political institutions. They also operate big government for broad social welfare purposes. One major question in relation to the West European welfare state concerns the variation between the countries in the programme structure of the public sector as well as the variation in types of income. The West European welfare state is not one and the same in all the major countries in Western Europe. The basic structure of income categories and public policies in each country has its special history and orientation. How can we identify the similarities and the differences?

In the extensive debate about the West European welfare state there has been a search for so-called determinants or explanatory factors of the country variation in the public policies that appear in the public sector. Few themes have aroused so much interest and contention in the analysis of West European politics as the identification of a set of *independent* variables accounting for the cross-country variation in income categories as well as in public expenditure items as the *dependent* variables. The literature on West European public policies and the West European tax state deals with how inputs and outputs of the public household as well as budgetary balance differ between the major countries in Western Europe. This involves a twofold question, as one is interested not only in the problem of why the size of the public sector differs between one country and another but also in accounting for the process of public sector growth that has taken place during the post-war period (Tarschys, 1975; Larkey et al., 1981; Wildavsky, 1986; Lybeck and Henrekson, 1988; Swank, 1988; O'Connor, 1988; Hicks et al., 1989; Schmidt, 1989; Korpi, 1989; Pampel and Williamson, 1988; O'Connor and Brym, 1988; Alber, 1988).

Here, we outline how the public sector varies between our sixteen West European countries and illuminate some of the policy hypotheses used to explain the variation between the countries on a number of financial items. The concept of the public sector is a complex one, to say the least.

It involves a number of distinctions on both the input and output sides as well as between various levels of government. Let us first look at the growth in government in Western Europe.

Public sector growth

A major trend in the development of the politico-economic regimes in the so-called Western world is the growth of the state, particularly since 1945. In all so-called market regimes or advanced capitalist countries there is a major process of government budget expansion measured in terms of resources mobilized by the public sector as a percentage of GDP. The growth of the welfare state has been particularly strong in the major West European countries. Table 10.1 presents data about the growth of the West European tax state from the input side measured in terms of revenues raised by means of taxes and charges.

Focussing on current receipts it may be stated that the public sector

Table 10.1   *General government: current receipts as a percentage of GDP*

	1950	1955	1960	1965	1970	1975	1980	1985
Austria	27.9	29.5	31.4	36.1	39.7	42.9	46.0	47.7
Belgium	24.2	24.0	26.7	30.7	35.2	40.4	43.2	46.5
Denmark	21.7	25.7	27.6	31.4	41.7	46.2	52.2	57.0
Finland	30.3	30.2	31.6	33.5	34.9	38.8	37.8	40.5
France	32.6	33.0	34.1	37.7	39.0	40.3	45.6	48.5
GFR	31.6	34.7	36.0	36.2	38.5	42.7	44.6	45.4
Greece	15.5	18.2	20.4	23.4	26.8	27.4	30.5	34.9
Ireland	23.4	23.8	24.6	28.0	35.3	35.2	41.7	44.3
Italy	21.0	26.2	29.8	31.6	30.4	31.2	37.4	37.5
Netherlands	33.0	28.9	33.4	36.8	44.5	53.2	55.0	54.4
Norway	29.6	30.8	34.5	37.7	43.5	49.6	54.0	56.1
Portugal	20.0	19.1	17.6	20.4	24.3	24.8	31.5	35.9
Spain	–	–	18.1	19.3	22.5	24.4	30.0	33.2
Sweden	26.2	32.7	35.0	42.0	47.0	50.7	56.7	59.4
Switzerland	25.5	24.0	25.4	25.4	26.5	32.1	32.8	34.4
UK	33.5	30.4	29.6	32.8	40.7	40.8	40.9	43.7

Sources: 1950–1965: OECD (1968) *National accounts 1950–1968*; OECD (1979)
National accounts 1960–1977; 1970–1980: OECD (1983) *National accounts 1964–1981*;
1985: OECD (1987) *National accounts 1973–1985*.
Note: Current receipts consist mainly of direct and indirect taxes, and social security contributions paid by employers and employees. General government consists of all departments, offices, organization and other bodies which are agents or instruments of the central, state or local public authorities.

in Western Europe has grown from a level of about 25 per cent of the GDP at the end of the Second World War to roughly 45 per cent or more in some countries in 1985, when the exceptional public sector growth process was brought to a halt. The arrival of a steady-state at such a high level of the total economic resources of a country is rather astonishing as the West European countries have experienced a period of exceptional growth in their economies since the Second World War involving a more than doubling of total output or GDP. Measured as a percentage of the GDP public sector growth in countries like Denmark, Sweden, Belgium, Austria and Norway is conspicuous, but measured in terms of absolute figures the expansion of the tax state in the midst of an economy based on capitalist institutions is staggering. Why would the public budget drive out the market as a mechanism for the allocation of resources and the distribution of income and wealth in countries with strong private ownership institutions?

There are two problems involved in the theories explaining public sector expansion in the West European countries. On the one hand, we have the *longitudinal problem* of the long run growth process in Western Europe: why is there this general growth in the tax state in the rich advanced capitalist countries? On the other hand, we face the *cross-sectional problem* of the country differences in the size of the public sector: why has the public sector grown in such a different manner in various countries? Whereas the tax state has expanded from 26 per cent to 60 per cent in Sweden, the increase in the tax state in Switzerland is only from 25 per cent to 34 per cent. Or look at the Danish public sector growth from 21 per cent of the GDP in 1950 to 57 per cent in 1985 and compare these figures with the corresponding data about the expansion of the Finnish public sector, from 30 per cent in 1950 to 40 per cent in 1985. Although the public sector has expanded both absolutely and in relative terms in each West European country it is still the case that there are substantial size differences between the countries. Why?

Turning to the output side we note a corresponding growth in public sector expenditures. Often the expansion on the expenditure side is even more pronounced as several countries have engaged in deficit spending, the difference between current disbursements and current receipts being either negative or positive financial savings in the consolidated public sector. 'Current disbursements' is a technical concept that covers all types of public expenditures or the costs of running various public policies. However, the basic fact about big government in Western Europe is the heavy commitments in the public budget towards welfare state type of expenditures, i.e. money allocated to education, health and social welfare or the redistribution of money from one group of people to another. Table

Table 10.2   *General government: current disbursements as a percentage of GDP*

	1950	1955	1960	1965	1970	1975	1980	1985
Austria	21.2	23.0	25.4	28.9	33.1	38.6	42.7	45.2
Belgium	25.5	23.8	27.8	29.8	33.0	41.2	48.1	52.3
Denmark	18.0	21.4	21.7	25.9	34.6	43.5	52.2	56.7
Finland	19.7	20.7	21.9	25.8	28.9	32.2	34.3	37.7
France	26.7	29.8	30.2	32.9	34.7	39.2	43.1	49.4
GFR	28.3	27.0	28.2	30.4	32.6	43.4	42.8	43.4
Greece	19.6	16.3	17.8	21.3	22.4	26.7	30.4	45.3
Ireland	22.9	23.4	24.5	27.6	34.2	42.0	48.3	50.4
Italy	20.7	24.6	26.6	30.9	30.2	38.3	41.4	44.1
Netherlands	23.9	25.5	28.0	33.0	40.2	51.1	54.2	55.2
Norway	21.9	24.4	28.0	31.9	36.5	41.8	45.1	44.0
Portugal	16.3	15.9	15.2	17.7	19.5	27.2	33.8	39.4
Spain	–	–	13.7	15.8	18.8	21.2	29.4	34.7
Sweden	23.5	26.4	28.7	31.9	37.2	44.9	57.1	60.8
Switzerland	19.4	18.5	19.1	21.3	21.3	28.8	29.3	30.9
UK	30.1	28.8	29.3	30.5	33.2	41.0	42.3	44.9

Sources: 1950–1965: OECD (1968) *National accounts 1950–1968*, OECD (1979) *National accounts 1960–1977*, 1970–1980: OECD (1983) *National accounts 1964–1981*, 1985: OECD (1987) *National accounts 1973–1985*.
Note: Current disbursements consist of final consumption expenditure, interest on the public debt, subsidies and social security transfers to households. General government consists of all departments, offices, organizations and other bodies which are agents or instruments of the central, state or local public authorities.

10.2 shows the expansion of the West European welfare state.

Now, in several West European countries the consolidated public sector spends roughly 50 per cent of the GDP. Actually, in most countries most of the time current disbursements are somewhat lower than current receipts. There is an ambition to collect a certain total public sector surplus in order to guarantee necessary public capital expenditures. In order to understand the process of public sector growth as well as the country differences in the amounts of money raised on the income side and spent on the output side the public sector has to be disaggregated into a number of income and expenditure categories. How much is welfare spending in a proper sense and how much is traditional public goods allocation? Whereas the first type of expenditure concerns the provision of divisible goods and services, the second type of expenditure covers the costs of indivisible goods or services like defence, law and order.

As a matter of fact, there is much more to be said about the major trend of the expansion in the tax state as well as the welfare state in Western Europe. Firstly, we have to separate out various items of expenditure, where a basic distinction is that between final government consumption in order to produce goods and services more or less free of charge and social transfer payments through money taken from some citizens and given to other citizens. Countries may vary with regard to the overall orientation of big government, some countries underlining the allocation function whereas others emphasize the income redistribution function. Secondly, there is in addition a variation within the consolidated public sector with regard to the relative size of central government versus that of local and regional governments. Finally, we have to look at the way in which governments in West European countries balance their income and expenditure sides of the public household. Before we survey the major theoretical approaches to the problem of accounting for public sector growth we will take a closer look at the variation in public policies in more detail from a *public finance* perspective. There are several interesting country differences that may be pointed out on both sides of the public household as well as with regard to the overall balance between income and expenditure.

Table 10.3 *General government: total tax revenues as a percentage of GDP*

	1955	1960	1965	1970	1975	1980	1985
Austria	30.0	30.6	34.7	35.7	38.7	41.3	42.9
Belgium	24.0	26.5	31.2	35.8	41.8	44.7	46.6
Denmark	23.4	25.4	29.9	40.4	41.4	45.5	48.7
Finland	26.8	27.7	30.1	32.2	36.2	35.3	36.8
France	–	–	35.0	35.6	37.4	42.5	44.5
GFR	30.8	31.3	31.6	32.9	36.0	37.8	37.9
Greece	–	–	20.6	24.3	24.6	28.6	35.2
Ireland	22.5	21.9	26.0	31.2	32.1	35.9	39.0
Italy	30.5	34.4	27.3	27.9	29.0	33.2	34.7
Netherlands	26.3	30.1	33.7	37.9	43.6	45.7	45.1
Norway	28.3	31.2	33.2	39.2	44.8	47.1	47.4
Portugal	15.4	16.3	18.5	23.1	24.8	29.3	31.5
Spain	–	–	14.7	17.2	19.6	24.1	28.8
Sweden	25.5	27.2	35.8	40.2	43.9	49.4	50.6
Switzerland	19.2	21.3	20.7	23.8	29.6	30.8	32.0
UK	29.8	28.5	30.6	37.3	35.7	36.0	38.1

Sources: OECD (1984) *Revenue statistics 1965–1983*. OECD (1988) *Revenue statistics 1965–1987*.

Note: Total tax revenues includes taxes on income, profits and capital gains; social security contributions; taxes on payroll and workforce; taxes on property; taxes on goods and services; and other taxes. General government consists of all departments, offices, organizations and other bodies which are agents or instruments of the central, state or local public authorities.

Policy variation: the income side

The public sector may be financed in three ways: taxes, charges or loans. The distinction between taxes and charges is anything but clear, as social security contributions are often called charges but they belong more properly to the set of taxes, because they are mandatory and cannot be pinned down to a special service offered at the same time as the charge is paid. Table 10.3 shows the rapid expansion in the tax state in Western Europe. The tax state has been on the advance in both rich and poor countries. The chief difference between the two sets of countries in this respect is the level from which the tax state expansion begins. At the same time there are considerable country differences both when the growth process starts after the Second World War and when it reaches some kind of steady state in the 1980s. A few countries support a tax state of about 30 per cent of total resources – Spain, Portugal and Switzerland – whereas others pay almost 50 per cent of their GDP to the tax state – Sweden, Denmark and Norway.

Table 10.4   *General government: taxes on income and profits as a percentage of total tax revenue*

	1955	1960	1965	1970	1975	1980	1985
Austria	23.8	23.5	25.7	25.2	26.2	26.7	26.4
Belgium	31.1	29.9	27.6	31.4	39.3	41.0	40.6
Denmark	47.5	44.8	45.9	51.2	59.0	55.0	56.8
Finland	42.8	41.1	44.0	47.6	52.3	49.1	51.0
France	–	–	15.9	18.3	17.6	18.0	17.6
GFR	22.0	31.9	33.8	32.3	34.5	35.3	34.8
Greece	–	–	9.8	12.3	13.7	19.3	17.4
Ireland	23.8	21.3	25.7	27.1	30.0	36.5	34.5
Italy	12.7	15.7	17.8	17.4	21.5	32.1	36.8
Netherlands	39.6	39.4	35.6	33.4	34.8	32.9	26.4
Norway	46.5	44.2	43.5	38.4	34.4	41.3	39.3
Portugal	27.7	27.8	24.6	23.7	17.4	19.7	25.9
Spain	–	–	24.5	20.2	22.0	26.0	28.0
Sweden	66.9	61.3	54.9	54.2	50.5	43.5	42.0
Switzerland	34.9	35.5	38.2	40.8	43.8	41.4	40.9
UK	40.6	37.5	36.8	40.4	44.4	37.7	38.7

Sources: OECD (1984) *Revenue statistics 1965–1983*. OECD (1988) *Revenue statistics 1965–1987*.

Note: Taxes on income, profits and capital gains cover taxes levied on the net income or profits of individuals and enterprises. Also covered are taxes levied on the capital gains of individuals and enterprises, and gains from gambling. General government consists of all departments, offices, organizations and other bodies which are agents or instruments of the central, state or local public authorities.

In terms of what is sometimes called the tax ratio or the relationship between income generated by all kinds of taxation including obligatory social security charges, several West European countries have a tax ratio of about 45 per cent. In several countries the income generated by means of social security charges has risen considerably. In 1950 social security charges played a major role in financing welfare expenditures only in France and the Federal Republic of Germany. Thirty-five years later the social security charges mobilize more than 10 per cent of the GDP as income to the tax state with a high 20 per cent score in the Netherlands and France. At the same time the country variation has increased as some countries like Denmark, Finland, Greece, Portugal and the United Kingdom rely on this income category to a much lesser extent than the other countries (Table 10.4).

There is a most considerable income variation between direct and indirect taxation that should be pointed out as some countries lean more on the visible taxes on income and profits whereas others favour invisible taxation like indirect taxes and social security contributions.

Visible taxation is employed in particular in Denmark and Finland whereas invisible taxation is resorted to in France and Austria besides Southern Europe. It has been argued that the employment of invisible taxes fosters public sector growth to a higher extent than direct taxation. However, there is not such a manifest connection in the data above. A country like Denmark which hardly employs social security contributions and the Netherlands which uses these extensively both engage in big government spending.

Policy variation: public consumption

It is a classic theory in the public finance tradition (Musgrave and Musgrave, 1980) that the provision of a minimal level of public goods is a necessary condition for social order and the peaceful operation of exchange in various markets. The implication is that we should not expect any extensive variation in one indicator – final government consumption between the nations studied – at least during the first decade covered. However, the expansion of the welfare state means, in a public finance conceptual framework, that the public sector has moved into the provision of semi-public goods or merit goods such as education and health care. The implication is then the opposite, i.e. we may expect a growing variation between our nations as we move into the next few decades, because preferences may vary considerably as regards merit goods and semi-public goods. Table 10.5 shows that the country variation in the allocation function of the public sector has not grown smaller during the last two decades.

Table 10.5   *General government: government final consumption as a percentage of GDP*

	1950	1955	1960	1965	1970	1975	1980	1985
Austria	11.2	11.8	12.9	13.5	14.7	17.2	17.8	18.7
Belgium	12.6	11.4	12.6	13.1	13.7	16.8	18.5	17.7
Denmark	10.2	12.9	12.7	15.4	19.8	24.6	26.7	25.4
Finland	11.6	11.5	12.6	14.5	14.7	17.5	18.6	20.3
France	12.8	13.0	12.9	12.6	13.4	14.4	15.2	16.3
GFR	14.3	13.2	13.6	15.4	15.8	20.5	20.2	19.9
Greece	11.6	11.0	11.4	11.8	12.6	15.2	16.3	20.3
Ireland	11.8	12.2	12.2	13.4	14.7	19.0	21.5	19.2
Italy	11.6	11.8	12.1	14.1	13.8	15.4	16.4	16.6
Netherlands	12.5	14.6	13.5	15.5	16.3	18.2	18.0	16.3
Norway	11.1	12.7	14.0	16.1	16.9	19.3	18.9	18.6
Portugal	11.2	11.7	10.9	12.3	14.2	15.4	14.7	15.5
Spain	–	–	8.8	7.4	8.5	9.2	11.6	13.7
Sweden	14.0	16.8	17.1	18.7	21.6	23.8	28.9	27.4
Switzerland	11.4	10.5	10.2	11.6	10.5	12.6	12.7	13.2
UK	16.4	17.1	16.8	17.2	17.7	22.0	21.5	21.1

Sources: 1950–1965: OECD (1968) *National accounts 1950–1968*, OECD (1979) *National accounts 1960–1977*, 1970–1980: OECD (1983) *National accounts 1964–1981*, 1985: OECD (1987) *National accounts 1973–1985*.

Note: Government final consumption consists of expenditures on goods and services for public administration, defence, health and education. It excludes all transfer payments. General government consists of all departments, offices, organizations and other bodies which are agents or instruments of the central, state or local public authorities.

The allocation function is often considered the most proper part of the public sector, as it covers the government provision of goods and services. The country differences in the size of the allocation state remain large with a distance between about 10 per cent for Denmark and 16 per cent for the United Kingdom in 1950 and 13 per cent for Switzerland and 27 per cent for Sweden in 1985. How about the country variation in less aggregated functions?

As to the nature of the budget variation in major categories of expenditures, some have argued in favour of the *convergence hypothesis* that the variation between nations with a mixed economy is decreasing. Others have denied any such trend (Castles, 1982). One hypothesis states that the country variation will tend to increase as the government increasingly allocates semi-public and merit goods; the second, the convergence hypothesis, argues that country differences in preferences for allocation patterns will decrease over time as all nations tend to regard the provision of certain goods as citizens' rights, the richer a nation becomes and the more visible the welfare state in any one nation becomes for all the other nations. The convergence hypothesis is based on a variety of assumptions

Table 10.6 *General government: health expenditure as a percentage of GDP*

	1960	1965	1970	1975	1980
Austria	2.9	3.0	3.4	4.1	4.5
Belgium	2.1	2.9	3.5	4.5	5.5
Denmark	3.2	4.2	5.2	5.9	5.8
Finland	2.3	3.2	4.1	4.9	5.0
France	2.5	3.6	4.3	5.5	6.1
GFR	3.2	3.6	4.2	6.6	6.5
Greece	1.7	2.2	2.2	2.5	3.5
Ireland	3.0	3.3	4.3	6.3	8.1
Italy	3.2	4.1	4.8	5.8	6.0
Netherlands	1.3	3.0	5.1	5.9	6.5
Norway	2.6	3.2	4.6	6.4	6.7
Portugal	0.9	1.2	1.9	3.8	4.2
Spain	–	1.4	2.3	3.6	4.3
Sweden	3.4	4.5	6.2	7.2	8.8
Switzerland	–	2.3	–	4.7	4.7
UK	3.4	3.6	3.9	5.0	5.2

Source: OECD (1985) *Measuring Health Care 1960–1983*, Table 2.
Note: Public expenditure on health care equals current general government expenditure on health care. By general government is meant central government, state or provincial government, local government and social security funds.

about the development patterns of the post-industrial state (Galbraith, 1967; Bell, 1973). Let us look at various major expenditure items to see which hypothesis is closer to the data, beginning with health expenditures (Table 10.6).

In 1980 several countries spent about 6 per cent of their GDP on health. The country variation is hardly less at that point than in the 1950s before the West European states became heavily involved in the provision of basic health care service to its citizens. Actually, countries differ most considerably in how much they trust public health organizations, Sweden allocating about twice as much of their GDP to public health as several other countries, relatively speaking. Matters are only slightly different with regard to educational expenditures (Table 10.7).

There is considerable variation in public spending on primary, secondary and tertiary education not only around 1950 but also at 1960. The variation in public effort hardly diminishes with time. Most countries spend about 6 per cent of their GDP on various educational programmes at various levels of the system of basic and higher education. Not only has welfare spending in the fields of health and education not converged, but the same is true of a kind of public goods spending, military effort (Table 10.8).

The country variation is striking, from a low 1.6 per cent in Ireland to

Table 10.7   *General government: educational expenditure as a percentage of GDP*

	1960	1965	1970	1975	1980
Austria	2.0	2.2	2.7	3.5	3.8
Belgium	4.5	5.3	6.0	7.8	8.0
Denmark	–	–	7.1	8.1	7.7
Finland	6.6	6.6	6.3	6.6	6.2
France	–	–	–	5.8	5.7
GFR	2.4	3.5	4.0	5.4	5.1
Greece	1.6	1.9	1.9	1.9	2.4
Ireland	3.0	4.3	5.2	6.1	6.5
Italy	3.7	4.0	4.5	5.0	5.6
Netherlands	4.5	5.9	6.7	7.6	7.2
Norway	3.9	5.7	6.4	6.7	6.3
Portugal	–	–	–	–	–
Spain	–	–	–	–	–
Sweden	4.6	5.4	6.2	5.6	6.5
Switzerland	3.1	3.5	4.1	5.6	5.5
UK	3.6	4.5	5.3	6.8	5.6

Source: OECD (1985) *Social expenditure 1960–1990*. Annex C.
Notes: By general government is meant central government, state or provincial government, local government and social security funds. Education includes expenditure on pre-primary, primary, secondary, tertiary, education affairs and services, and subsidary services to education.

a high 7 per cent in Greece in 1985. Most countries have pushed back the relative size of their military spending, but there is still a large country variation as was true of 1950.

Policy variation: transfer payments

The size of public transfers expresses equity considerations according to public finance theory. National ambition in this field of public expenditure is bound to vary as a function of the prevailing political preference function. In nations where equality has a firm basis in the political machinery we would expect high levels of transfer payments as a percentage of GDP. Naturally we expect to find higher levels of redistribution effort as the welfare state matures over time (Table 10.9).

The West European welfare state appears in three shapes. One version is strongly orientated towards social transfer payments as in the Netherlands. Another version emphasizes the public provision of goods and services at subsidized prices playing down the importance of the redistribution function of the public sector as in Finland. A third version attempts both big scale transfer payments and comprehensive public allocation of goods and services as in Sweden.

Table 10.8 *General government: military expenditure as a percentage of GDP*

	1950	1955	1960	1965	1970	1975	1980	1985
Austria	0.7	0.2	1.2	1.2	1.1	1.2	1.2	1.3
Belgium	–	3.8	3.6	3.2	2.9	3.1	3.3	3.0
Denmark	1.7	3.2	2.7	2.8	2.4	2.4	2.4	2.2
Finland	1.8	1.6	1.7	1.7	1.4	1.4	1.9	2.0
France	5.5	6.4	6.5	5.2	4.2	3.8	4.0	4.0
GFR	4.4	4.1	4.0	4.3	3.3	3.6	3.3	3.2
Greece	6.0	5.1	4.9	3.5	4.8	6.5	5.7	7.0
Ireland	1.3	1.6	1.6	1.4	1.3	1.8	1.9	1.6
Italy	4.3	3.7	3.3	3.3	2.7	2.5	2.1	2.3
Netherlands	4.8	5.7	4.1	4.0	3.5	3.4	3.1	3.1
Norway	2.4	3.9	2.9	3.4	3.5	3.2	2.9	3.1
Portugal	3.8	4.2	4.2	6.2	7.1	5.3	3.5	3.2
Spain	–	2.2	2.2	1.8	1.6	1.7	3.1	3.3
Sweden	3.5	4.5	4.0	4.1	3.6	3.4	2.9	2.5
Switzerland	2.6	2.8	2.5	2.7	2.2	2.0	1.9	1.9
UK	6.6	8.2	6.5	5.9	4.8	5.0	4.9	5.3

Sources: SIPRI (1980) *World Armaments and Disarmament*, Tab 1A.4. SIPRI (1988); *World Armaments and Disarmament*, Tab 6A.3.

Note: General government consists of all departments, offices, organizations and other bodies which are agents or instruments of the central, state or local public authorities.

Policy variation: deficit spending

It is a well-known fact that the effect of the development in the world economy during the 1970s was that nations faced growing difficulties in matching expenditure with revenues. The data concerning the budgetary balance may refer to either the total public sector or to the central government. It is often claimed that a deficit in the overall consolidated public sector is much more difficult to handle than a deficit on the central government budget. Yet, several countries have persistent large deficits within their consolidated public sector: Belgium, Italy and the United Kingdom. There is a high co-variation between deficit spending in general and huge national state deficit spending. Here we present data about central government deficits, as they tend to be more politically conspicuous than general government deficits (Table 10.10).

Level of government

So far we have looked at the overall structure of the public sector in Western Europe. There is an additional very important source of variation

Table 10.9   *General government: social security transfers as a percentage of GDP*

	1950	1955	1960	1965	1970	1975	1980	1985
Austria	7.8	9.4	10.0	12.3	15.4	16.9	19.2	20.1
Belgium	9.7	9.0	10.9	12.4	14.1	18.8	21.2	22.0
Denmark	5.8	6.7	7.3	8.3	11.6	13.9	16.8	16.5
Finland	4.5	5.0	5.8	7.0	8.3	9.6	9.9	11.6
France	11.2	13.1	12.9	16.1	17.2	20.6	23.3	26.6
GFR	12.3	11.4	12.6	13.0	13.4	18.4	17.3	16.6
Greece	5.7	4.9	5.8	7.5	8.0	7.4	9.3	15.0
Ireland	4.7	5.6	6.2	6.9	10.8	14.9	15.8	18.2
Italy	6.3	9.4	10.7	13.4	12.7	16.0	16.1	16.9
Netherlands	6.7	7.2	10.3	14.0	18.4	25.6	27.4	28.5
Norway	4.8	6.4	8.3	9.7	12.3	13.6	14.7	14.8
Portugal	2.5	2.6	3.0	3.4	3.1	8.5	10.7	10.9
Spain	–	–	2.3	5.7	7.5	9.3	13.8	16.0
Sweden	6.3	7.4	8.2	10.0	11.6	15.1	18.9	19.3
Switzerland	4.9	5.3	6.2	7.3	6.3	10.1	10.3	13.7
UK	5.4	5.4	6.2	7.4	9.4	10.9	12.5	14.6

Sources: 1950–1965: OECD (1968) *National accounts 1950–1968*, OECD (1979) *National accounts 1960–1977*, 1970–1980: OECD (1983) *National accounts 1964–1981*, 1985: OECD (1987) *National accounts 1973–1985*.

Note: Social security transfers consist of social security benefits, social assistance grants, unfunded employee pension and welfare benefits, and transfers to private non-profit institutions serving households. General government consists of all departments, offices, organizations and other bodies which are agents or instruments of the central, state or local public authorities.

between these countries: the division of tasks between the various levels of government. In some countries the central government has a much larger role in mobilizing income and making spending decisions than in decentralized countries. Although public finance data do not tap the centralization–decentralization dimension in an adequate manner, the division of the public purse between various levels of government is interesting. The degree of fiscal decentralization in a country depends upon other instruments that the state may wish to employ, in particular the use of laws and directives in order to control lower levels of government.

How about the variation in central government final consumption? Table 10.11 informs about how active the central government is in allocating resources in order to itself provide more or less freely goods and services to its citizens.

Most interestingly, the allocation budget of the central government has not expanded as much as the overall public sector. In relative terms the central government as producer of goods and services is only slightly

Table 10.10   *Central government: deficit as a percentage of GDP*

	1950	1955	1960	1965	1970	1975	1980	1985
Austria	0.9	4.0	3.2	3.2	2.3	-0.5	-0.0	-0.7
Belgium	-1.3	-0.2	-2.0	-0.3	0.8	-1.6	-3.9	-6.7
Denmark	-	-	4.7	4.3	6.0	0.2	-2.7	-1.7
Finland	-	-	6.8	4.8	5.1	3.3	1.5	1.7
France	-	-	2.8	3.7	2.9	-0.2	0.9	-2.2
GFR	0.8	3.9	2.9	2.0	2.9	-0.6	0.4	0.6
Greece	-5.6	0.7	1.3	0.3	1.8	-2.1	-2.1	-8.3
Ireland	0.3	0.5	-0.1	0.5	1.5	-5.6	-5.6	-5.5
Italy	-0.2	0.6	2.7	0.5	0.4	-2.6	-4.7	-7.5
Netherlands	-	2.3	4.1	3.4	3.5	2.0	0.7	-1.6
Norway	5.8	4.3	4.5	3.8	4.5	5.9	7.6	-2.3
Portugal	1.8	1.2	1.2	1.2	2.1	-2.5	-2.6	4.8
Spain	-	-	-	3.1	2.6	2.3	0.3	-2.2
Sweden	2.1	3.3	5.1	4.2	3.9	1.5	-5.3	-4.5
Switzerland	-	-	3.3	2.6	1.7	0.7	0.5	0.5
UK	2.3	1.6	0.1	2.1	7.4	-1.3	-1.3	-1.2

Sources: 1950–1965: OECD (1970) *National accounts 1950–1968*. OECD (1979) *National accounts 1960–1977*. 1970–1980: OECD (1981) *National accounts 1964–1981*. 1985: OECD (1987) *National accounts 1973–1985*.

Note: The deficit is current receipts minus current disbursements. Central government consists of all departments, offices, organizations and other bodies classified under general government which are agencies or instruments of the central authority of a country, except separately organized social security funds.

larger in the 1980s than in the 1950s. This means that its share in providing public sector provision of goods and services must have gone down as other levels of government have become more important in the supply of especially the type of semi-public goods and services that make up a large part of the welfare state.

The allocative functions of central government have been reduced in relation to the total allocative functions in the overall public sector. There is a clear tendency to decentralize the provision of goods and services within the West European welfare state to lower levels of government.

However, the finding of a decrease in the importance of the central government in allocating resources does not imply that the overall fiscal role of central government has declined. Besides the allocative functions there are substantial redistributive tasks involving transfer payments of various kinds, not to mention the overall planning functions. Some countries rely on a decentralized structure for the operation of their entire public households. In the following countries less than 50 per cent of the public sector disbursements are decided by the central government: Switzerland, Germany, Austria and Norden. What may

Table 10.11 *Central government: government final consumption as a percentage of GDP*

	1950	1955	1960	1965	1970	1975	1980	1985
Austria	5.9	5.5	6.3	6.4	6.8	6.4	6.3	7.0
Belgium	9.6	8.1	9.8	10.1	10.6	12.9	13.7	13.0
Denmark	–	–	5.8	7.0	–	–	8.3	7.9
Finland	–	–	5.5	6.4	5.9	6.3	6.1	6.2
France	–	–	10.0	9.5	10.2	10.6	10.9	11.4
GFR	4.3	4.3	4.1	5.0	3.9	4.3	3.9	3.8
Greece	9.7	9.3	9.0	9.0	9.8	12.4	12.1	14.4
Ireland	6.7	6.8	7.0	7.8	7.4	9.3	9.9	9.5
Italy	8.4	8.3	8.2	9.7	7.9	8.5	9.0	8.8
Netherlands	–	8.0	6.3	6.5	7.8	8.2	8.1	7.5
Norway	6.2	7.1	7.2	8.0	7.9	8.2	7.5	7.0
Portugal	9.8	10.4	9.5	11.1	12.5	12.2	12.8	13.6
Spain	–	–	–	5.8	6.6	6.5	7.8	6.9
Sweden	8.2	8.9	7.8	9.2	8.1	8.1	8.7	7.2
Switzerland	–	–	2.8	3.2	2.9	2.9	3.0	3.3
UK	11.6	12.3	11.3	10.8	10.5	12.4	12.7	12.9

Sources: 1950–1965: OECD (1968) *National accounts 1950–1968*, OECD (1979) *National accounts 1960–1977*, 1970–1980: OECD (1983) *National accounts 1964–1981*, 1985: OECD (1987) *National accounts 1973–1985*.

Note: Government final consumption consists of goods and services for public administration, defence, health and education. It excludes all transfer payments. Central government consists of all departments, offices, organizations and other bodies classified under general government which are agencies or instruments of the central authority of a country, except separately organized social security funds.

be lost in fiscal decentralization may be regained by administrative centralization as the example of Sweden testifies. In some countries the central government directly spends more than 50 per cent: Belgium, France, Greece and the United Kingdom.

The distribution of the resources of the central government onto various items of expenditure is shown in Table 10.12 for one selected point of time, in which the total expenditure by function comprises current expenditure and capital expenditure. Defence consists of expenditure intended mainly for military purposes whereas education is the provision and support of pre-primary, primary, and secondary schools, universities and colleges, and technical, vocational, and other training institutions. Health expenditures relate to hospitals, medical and dental centres and clinics with a major medical component as well as the provision of national health and medical insurance schemes. Social security and welfare consists of expenditures to compensate for temporary loss of income of the sick and temporarily disabled.

Table 10.12   *Central government: expenditure by function as a
percentage of its total expenditure, 1975*

	Defence	Education	Health	Social security	Housing	Economic	Other services
Austria	3.3	10.6	12.3	45.5	3.3	12.7	12.4
Belgium	6.3	16.2	1.6	43.7	1.6	15.1	15.4
Denmark	7.0	11.5	3.5	43.5	2.0	10.5	22.0
Finland	5.2	14.8	10.7	27.1	1.4	30.8	11.2
France	7.6	9.9	15.0	40.8	3.2	9.5	14.0
GFR	10.6	1.2	19.8	49.4	0.2	8.8	11.0
Greece	20.0	8.4	7.9	26.7	2.0	20.0	14.2
Ireland	–	–	–	–	–	–	–
Italy	5.0	12.6	16.8	33.5	2.1	18.8	3.5
Netherlands	6.4	14.9	11.9	36.4	2.1	9.3	9.0
Norway	9.4	9.7	13.4	32.8	5.8	21.5	11.6
Portugal	13.3	10.7	4.4	26.8	3.7	10.9	22.5
Spain	5.8	7.8	0.9	51.6	1.7	14.0	18.1
Sweden	10.2	11.9	3.0	44.2	1.3	10.2	19.1
Switzerland	10.8	4.1	10.4	48.1	1.3	14.8	10.7
UK	13.7	2.6	12.9	21.7	3.5	12.4	33.3

Source: World Bank (1984) *World Tables*. 3rd ed. Vol. 1 Economic data. Economic
data sheet 2.

Notes: The central government covers all government departments, offices, establishments,
and other bodies that are agencies or instruments of the central authority of a country
and includes decentralized agencies, departmental enterprises, and relevant nonprofit
institutions attached to the central authority. Also included are social security funds,
if operating nationally.

It also covers payments to the elderly, the permanently disabled, and
the unemployed. Housing and community amenities consists of expenditure on housing, such as income-related schemes. Economic services
includes expenditure for: agriculture; industry; electricity, gas and water;
transport and communications; other economic services like tourism
etc. 'Other' comprises expenditure on the general administration of
government etc.

It is readily seen that the provision of public goods is no longer the
major concern of the central governments in Western Europe. On the
contrary, they are more heavily involved in the provision of divisible
than in the indivisible goods. In particular, the central governments in
Austria, Belgium, Denmark, France, the Federal Republic of Germany,
Spain, Sweden and Switzerland are redistributive governments engaged
in the promotion of social justice by income redistribution from various
groups to other groups. With regard to the task of allocating resources for
the production of welfare services in education and health there are most
considerable country differences.

Approaches to and explanations of public sector growth

In the literature on policy determinants it is often asked whether politics matter for policies. In *Politics, Economics and the Public* (1966) Thomas Dye raised the issue of the role of politics as a cause of public policy or public finance spending asking 'Does Politics Matter'? It used to be believed that political parties were the main intermediators between a democratic citizenry and the outputs of governmental activity meaning that it made a difference which political party was in power. However, Dye argued that broad environmental factors such as affluence, urbanization and industrialization meant much more for the structure of the public sector. The environmental hypothesis has been tested in research on the policy variation between local and regional governments where the findings do not support the hypothesis that politics is without importance (Danziger, 1978; Sharpe and Newton, 1984). Are there any significant relationships between environmental factors and indicators on the size of the West European tax state? Is it true that politics does not matter for the variation in national public policies?

The confrontation between environmental and political models when accounting for public sector growth or the variety in size of the welfare state does not exhaust the number of hypotheses that are relevant to consider when one sets out to explain the variation over time as well as between countries in a number of public sector properties. When the public sector is described in terms of monetary categories, then public finance data is employed in the analysis of the growth of the tax state at both the input and output sides. A more general distinction may be made between demand-side approaches and supply-side approaches.

Firstly, when attempting to account for the tremendous public sector growth in rich countries one can focus on *demand* theories which suggest that the expansion of public programmes of various kinds has been wanted by large groups of the citizenry for various reasons. The well-known demand-side hypotheses claim inter alia that socio-economic development of necessity requires public resource allocation (Wagner's law), that increasing affluence implies larger bugets (Wilensky's first law), that the dominance of the left in society or government means budget expansion replacing market mechanisms (Schmidt's law), that a strong position for the right in government is a negative determinant (Castles' law), that collectivist ideologies promote public sector expansion (Wilensky's second law), that sudden social shocks necessitate budgetary shift-points towards much higher levels of public spending (Peacock's and Wiseman's law). Moreover, the demand theories state that technological development pushes industrial societies more towards the public sector to balance the private sector (Galbraith's law), that welfare spending by the neighbouring state may imply a demand for welfare programmes at home (Tarschys' law), that the increasing openness of the economies of the rich countries of the world creates a demand for budgetary stabilization of the erratic fluctuations of markets (Cameron's law) and that all political systems whether capitalist or socialist face the same policy demands for public programmes (Pryor's law).

It has not been possible to evaluate these alternative theories arriving at an unambiguous finding that one hypothesis is the superior one. The overall finding when testing different demand-side hypotheses is that each and every one does not work generally but has some explanatory power in some countries.

Secondly, there is a set of public sector growth hypotheses that argue that *supply-side* factors are more important than demand-side factors, because here the intention and direction of organized actors is clear-cut. Here we find the hypothesis that budget-making must mean oversupply (Niskanen's law), that public spending involves bureaucratic waste (Tullock's law), that public sector growth is a function of bureau size maximization (Downs' law), that public sector productivity is negative, claiming more resources every year for the 'same' output (Baumol's law), that budget-making rests upon fiscal illusions about the relation between cost and benefit (Oates' law), that budget-making is asymmetrical meaning that those benefiting from public sector expansion are strategically stronger than those that have to pay (Kristensen's law), that the amount of institutional sclerosis matters as a prolonged period of uninterrupted policy-making leads to intensive corporatist interest consultation and policy concertation favouring the narrow interests of distributional coalitions at the expense of the public interest (Olson's law), that public officials whether politicians or bureaucrats are motivated by a private interest function tied to the size of the budget (Breton' law), and that it is difficult to close the gap between individual benefit and cost in the public sector (Wicksell's law).

Although research in the various social sciences has been interested in identifying the sources of variation in welfare spending for quite some time, there is as yet no agreement as to which determinants explain the growth of the tax state (Lybeck and Henrekson, 1988). Some scholars point to the role of demographic factors and affluence (Wilensky, 1975), whereas others mention more specific economic variables like openness of the economy (Cameron, 1978). An incremental approach, last year's expenditure determining this year's outlay, has been propounded (Alt and Chrystal, 1983), but it has also been suggested that culture is a determinant (Wildavsky, 1986). Our interest here is tied up with the argument that political factors somehow play a significant role in shaping patterns of expenditure (Wilensky, 1976; Whiteley, 1980; Hibbs and Fassbender, 1981, Castles, 1982; Schmidt, 1982). Is it possible to confirm the hypothesis that politics matter for the understanding of the public sector in Western Europe?

The test of public policy hypotheses concerning the causes of public sector expansion has not resulted in any specific and valid findings. It is believed that the lack of any true general comparative results about the forces that lead to the growth of the state implies that we should resort to a more *institutional approach* focussing on country specific factors (Anckar and Ståhlberg, 1980; Lybeck and Henrekson, 1988; March and Olsen, 1989). No doubt it is important to analyse the expansion of the public sector in each country – conditions, decisions, implementation – but this does not exclude efforts at a comparative understanding of similarities and differences. Let us take a more close look at some of the more well-known policy hypotheses.

Testing public policy hypotheses

Public policies may be analysed with alternative languages. On the one hand, one may focus on a quantitative description employing for example public finance data. On the other hand, one may confine oneself to a qualitative description of the policy looking at its ends and means as well as its programme structure. Both languages have their pros and cons. The limitation of the public finance data is that aggregate spending categories may conceal much interesting information about policies. Thus, two countries may spend a similar aggregated amount of their GDP on public expenditures, but they may do this in very different ways, for example one country favouring final government consumption at the expense of transfer payments whereas the other country has the opposite profile on its public sector. The use of only hard data makes the analysis of country differences simple but rather barren. However, to engage in minute and detailed descriptions of each and every policy in a country is impossible and hardly relevant if the overall differences are to be focussed upon. Some mixed strategy is to be preferred.

In a public finance perspective, public policy or public expenditure belongs, of course, to the public household. The set of public expenditure items is potentially very large depending on the aggregation level chosen; the public budget has a set of variables which may be approached in terms of a simple input–output model of the political budgeting process. National patterns of public spending are typically described by means of some monetary indicator adjusted according to the size of the population of the country. Other indicators for public policies sometimes supplement per capita measures or percentage indices of GDP, but we will use only monetary indices.

A distinction may be made between input–output items and properties that refer to internal transactions within the public finance systems, like fiscal centralization and the transfer of grants. We will look at the distribution of the expenditure 'cake' between various levels of government. With regard to the input categories a vital distinction concerns how income is generated in various income categories like taxes and social security contributions. On the output side, one may distinguish between consumption and transfer payments.

This is all about the problems of identifying and measuring in a proper sense the so-called dependent variable in the policy determinant literature. When we turn to the other side of the coin looking for so-called independent variables that may help us understand why there is a country variation in public policies, then several factors should be included in the analysis following the set of policy hypotheses listed above. Here, we focus on the variables that enter the debate about whether environmental factors or political factors matter most for the variation in the West European tax and welfare state. Let us shed some empirical light on a few of the public policy hypotheses within the large policy determinant literature employing only a simple measure of statistical association, the Pearson's correlation following the methodology employed in Chapter 9.

Institutional factors: One could focus on either the place of the left in society or the power of the right in government. Some crucial measures of conservative strength would include the partisan character of government and parliament (Castles, 1982). The power of the left in a society is not only a matter of the political position of socialist and communist parties; of equal importance is the access to power of the trade-union movement which is partly a function of its organizational density. It appears that measures of the position of the trade-union movement and the position of the socialist parties tend to go together and constitute a dimension of left-wing strength that is separate from that of the position of the conservative camp in a society (Schmidt, 1982).

Environmental factors: Affluence measured in terms of real GDP per capita and GDP growth are chosen in relation to the theme of Wagner's law as the economic dimension. It is often argued that economic affluence is a necessary and sufficient condition for welfare state spending (Wilensky, 1975), but it has also been argued that a rapid growth process in the economy is not likely to go together with big government spending. Besides the level of GDP per capita and the rate of growth in GDP per capita there may be other economic variables that have an impact on public expenditures. A high level of unemployment may be conducive to large budget deficits and a high level of inflation may also characterize periods of budgetary imbalances.

Openness of the economy is another environmental factor to be measured by an index on economic interaction between nations. It seems as if the extent of openness in an economy depends on how large a nation is in terms of population. The larger the nation the less open is the economy, which implies that we may expect to find an extensive openness of the economy among the small European democracies (Cameron, 1978). The set of relevant environmental factors includes more than strictly economic ones. From Chapter 2 we know that the social structure in Western Europe differs from one country to another: does social heterogeneity matter for the size of the public sector? Or perhaps a certain level of social homogeneity is conducive to big government spending as it would reduce highly divisive cleavages creating social agreement on welfare state expenditures?

Can we find any support for these models when we look at the West European tax state? Let us concentrate on a few overall measures of the size of the public sector and relate these to the determinants identified in the public sector hypotheses listed above. In a more refined analysis of the public sector differences between countries and over time one would use stronger methodological tools than those reported on here.

Empirical findings

Table 10.13 reports on simple correlations between various measures of the size of the public sector on the one hand and political and environmental factors on the other hand.

Recognizing that the methodology employed to investigate into determinants of the size of the public sector is crude, we may note a few interesting findings in Table 10.13. There is indeed support for some of the well-known public policy models even when one only looks upon surface associations, not holding any of the other relevant factors constant. Thus, the data partly confirm Wagner's law or the idea that the level of affluence has policy implications increasing the demand for public programmes. Equally true, the model of a negative relationship between the rate of change in the economy and the size of public expenditures receives some confirmation. However, it may be pointed out that also some of the political models meet with some degree of confirmation, in particular the strength of the trade unions in society. Actually, the extent of unionization and corporatism appears to be more important than the party colour of the government. The data do not allow us to come up with some sort of a resolution between the environmental and the political models. We simply note that it is not true that neither environmental nor political factors are irrelevant.

Politics seems to be more relevant for some kinds of policies or expenditures than others. Whereas all countries need so-called public goods like defence and internal peace, law and order, the decisions about welfare programmes may be very much influenced by party political ideology. Thus, the political orientation of the government would make a difference in relation to some special expenditure aggregates like health care programmes and educational programmes whereas it would not matter in relation to military expenditures. Is there support for these implications of the major policy determinant models? Table 10.14 has some relevant data.

We have a somewhat similar finding when we disaggregate the total expenditures into various subsets of expenditure types. Both the environmental and the political models receive some degree of confirmation but there are no strong associations as predicted by the models, taken separately.

The large literature on the growth in the tax state in Western Europe as well as on the considerable country differences in public expenditures has not as yet come up with anything like a conclusive and definitive

Table 10.13   *Determinants of public sector size*

		Current receipts	Total taxes	Social security contributions	Government final consumption	Social security expenditures	Current disbursements
Environmental factors							
Affluence	[N=58]	.77**	.56**	.54**	.60**	.66**	.72**
	[N=16]	.64*	.51	.25	.26	.43	.41
Economic growth	[N=58]	−.43**	−.27	−.31*	−.40**	−.40**	−.53**
	[N=16]	.50	.74**	−.37	.62*	−.13	.32
Religious structure							
Catholics	[N=58]	−.32*	−.54**	.29	−.35*	.18	−.09
	[N=16]	−.58*	−.70*	.29	−.61*	.05	−.37
Class structure							
Gini	[N=58]	−.37*	−.54**	.11	−.36	−.04	−.26
	[N=16]	−.61*	−.54	−.07	−.50	−.32	−.54
Unionization	[N=58]	.47**	.67**	−.13	.62**	.18	.43**
	[N=16]	.47	.75**	−.44	.73**	.04	.52
Political factors							
Class-based parties	[N=58]	.30	.25	.17	.22	.14	.15
	[N=16]	−.09	−.20	.12	−.08	−.12	−.23
Corporatism	[N=58]	.24	.37*	−.14	.16	−.01	.04
	[N=16]	.44	.51	−.14	.34	.04	.25
Socialist dominance in government	[N=58]	.00	.02	−.02	.06	−.00	−.02
	[N=16]	.05	−.01	.16	.10	.04	.01
Socialist hegemony in government	[N=58]	.34*	.51**	−.15	.37*	.00	.20
	[N=16]	.37	.45	−.15	.29	.03	.18

Note: the table reports Pearson's correlations. The asterisk means statistical significance at the 0.01 level (*) or at the 0.001 level (**). N = 58 is pooled; N = 16 covers the 1980s.

Table 10.14   *Public expenditure determinants*

		Health expenditures	Educational expenditures	Military expenditures
Affluence	[N=58]	.71**	.63**	−.18
	[N=16]	.33	.47	−.26
Economic growth	[N=58]	−.66**	−.47*	.13
	[N=16]	.35	.24	−.33
Religious structure Catholics	[N=58]	−.20	−.45*	.01
	[N=16]	−.37	−.37	.08
Class structure Gini	[N=58]	−.25	−.48*	.16
	[N=16]	−.56	−.57	.24
Unionization	[N=58]	.37*	.54*	−.33*
	[N=16]	.35	.54	−.36
Corporatism	[N=58]	.14	.31	−.57**
	[N=16]	.13	.28	−.61*
Socialist dominance	[N=58]	−.01	.01	−.08
	[N=16]	.03	−.18	−.02
Socialist hegemony	[N=58]	.20	.15	−.01
	[N=16]	−.08	−.22	.03

Note: the table reports Pearson's correlation. The asterisk means statistical significance at the 0.01 level (*) or at the 0.001 level (**).

theory. Here we have reported on some factors that have been proposed as determinants of the variation in space and time of income and expenditure categories. It seems as if unionization matters for the welfare state, as a high rate of trade union membership goes together with large welfare state expenditures. How does trade union strength vary? Table 10.15 gives an indication.

Judged by this indicator on trade union strength – relative size of membership – strong trade unions are to be found in the Scandinavian countries as well as in Austria. These countries have strong welfare states. Deficit spending may be related to unemployment. What is the variation in unemployment? Table 10.16 has the data.

Although the relationship between central government budgetary deficits and the unemployment rates is far from a strong linear association, there is a connection as both the unemployment rates and the extent of deficit spending rise in the wake of the economic crisis in the 1970s. Actually, unemployment is a highly sensitive issue in the making of public policy in most West European countries calling for different kinds of government action (Taylor, 1990; Grant, 1990). Countries that have a

Table 10.15 *Estimates of percentage of workforce unionized*
1950–1980

	1950	1955	1960	1965	1970	1975	1980
Austria	62	63	63	63	62	59	58
Belgium	52	53	57	55	61	66	71
Denmark	53	59	62	62	67	67	–
Finland	33	31	32	36	57	75	–
France	32	25	22	21	23	25	–
GFR	33	34	33	32	32	33	33
Greece		–	–	–	–	–	–
Ireland	–	–	–	–	–	–	–
Italy	34	–	–	32	41	47	–
Netherlands	40	38	39	37	39	40	38
Norway	52	54	63	64	64	61	65
Portugal	–	–	–	–	–	–	–
Spain	–	–	–	–	–	–	–
Sweden	67	68	68	71	73	82	85
Switzerland	–	–	–	–	–	–	–
UK	44	44	44	43	47	51	54

Source: Kjellberg (1983); Matheson (1979) for Finland.

Table 10.16 *Unemployment as a percentage of total labour*
force: average

	1950–54	1955–59	1960–64	1965–69	1970–74	1975–79	1980–84
Austria	5.2	3.6	2.1	1.9	1.3	1.7	2.9
Belgium	4.9	3.2	2.2	2.2	2.1	6.2	11.1
Denmark	4.4	4.4	1.8	1.7	1.9	6.6	9.5
Finland	1.4	1.9	1.4	2.5	2.2	5.0	5.1
France	1.3	1.1	1.2	1.6	2.1	4.9	8.0
GFR	6.7	3.1	0.7	0.9	1.1	3.8	6.2
Greece	–	–	–	5.2	2.7	1.9	5.7
Ireland	6.1	5.9	5.0	4.9	5.9	8.1	11.6
Italy	7.4	6.9	3.1	3.6	3.2	6.8	8.6
Netherlands	2.4	1.5	0.9	1.4	2.1	5.3	9.9
Norway	0.8	1.2	1.1	0.9	0.8	1.9	2.5
Portugal	–	–	–	2.5	2.3	6.8	7.9
Spain	1.2	0.8	1.2	1.6	2.5	5.9	15.6
Sweden	2.3	2.1	1.3	1.6	1.8	1.9	2.9
Switzerland	–	–	–	–	–	0.4	0.6
UK	1.2	1.2	1.5	1.7	2.5	4.6	9.5

Source: 1950–74: Madsen and Paldam (1978); 1975–84: OECD (1988) *Labour Force Statistics*.

considerable part of their population unemployed tend also to have large central government budget deficits.

Summing up

When the various systems of public finance are analysed in terms of three dimensions – final government consumption, transfer payments and budgetary balance – we may establish that there is a variation that calls for a search for determinants of various kinds. Transfer payments vary more extensively between the nations than public resource allocation, and variation in budgetary balance is much less stable countrywise than the variation in the other two dimensions. The data do not confirm the convergence hypothesis predicting that country differences in the structure of the tax state in Western Europe will become smaller as the welfare state matures. If there is a pattern of variation in the levels of these public finance dimensions that is stable over time in terms of between-nation differences, then we ask if there are political, economic or institutional traits in these nations that explain the pattern derived.

We cannot here confirm any one single policy determinant model. The analysis aimed at here is much too simplified for any strict model testing. However, we note that both the affluence hypothesis – Wagner's law – and the political party hypothesis meet with some support. The West European welfare state has its sources in the strong economies of these countries which open up the possibility of comprehensive public policy-making. But what is a possibility does not have to be a necessity. Social welfare is not the same thing as a welfare state. Some countries trust the public budget-making mechanism in order to secure a level of social welfare whereas other countries also rely on private sector solutions. This choice between *state* and *market* and the public versus the private sector is influenced by political party ideology, the stronger the left in government or society the more budget-making will be resorted to.

In the 1980s the West European tax and welfare state has met with more hesitance than earlier (Parry, 1990). In several countries there have been made attempts at trimming the structure of welfare programmes. With regard to public consumption the notions of effectiveness and efficiency have gained in policy relevance whereas the transfer programmes have been seen as too generous. Privatization plans have been initiated in some countries with varying thrust (Vickers and Wright, 1988). It may be predicted that the country variation in the size of the West European state will decrease as countries with an already established welfare state reassess several of their government activities while countries where the welfare state is a recent phenomenon expand their public programme structure.

How the policy variation in the West European tax and welfare state will develop in the future will also be affected by the trend towards European integration that has become more relevant in the 1980s. Is there any likelihood that the drive towards economic, social and political unification will be strong enough to wipe out the policy differences between the various West European welfare states? Let us look somewhat more closely at the process of West European integration. How far has it come as of now?

11

European Integration

Introduction

In the earlier chapters we have focussed very much on the variation in political phenomena in West European countries as they appear during the post-Second World War period. Striking as these differences in social structure, party system, government institutions and public policy are, a major development in Western Europe is the strong integration movement in spite of all the severe historical conflicts between these countries (Pryce, 1987; Urwin and Paterson, 1990). Are we witnessing the coming of a united states in Western Europe? Or perhaps a future united states in Europe would also include East European countries, as the fall of the communist model of governing in 1989 and 1990 opens up a number of new possibilities. The movement towards integration in Europe involves much more than politics. The economies of the various West European countries, in particular, has become more and more internationalized. In any case, the creation of common West European institutions has set limits to the operation of the various nation-states in Western Europe. Which are these institutions?

Development of the EC

In 1957 the Treaty of Rome was agreed between France, the Federal Republic of Germany, Italy, the Netherlands, Belgium and Luxembourg which resulted in the formation of the European Economic Community in 1958 (EC). The aim of the new inter-state organization involved both short-run and long-term objectives, both economic and political goals. Building on the coal- and steel-union (ECSC) initiated in 1950 between the Benelux-countries and France, Italy and the Federal Republic of Germany, the members of the EC would dismantle the tolls and other barriers to trade in relation to each other while enforcing the same system of tolls against other nations. In the long-run perspective the EC would develop towards an economic and political federation involving the creation of a sort of federal state above the various member states.

The creation of the Community led to a reaction from other West European countries, forming the European Free Trade Association (EFTA) as an alternative to the EC. The EFTA was already from the start conceived of as a free trade association with no political ambitions to create super-national bodies. As long as it involved a considerable number of countries, the EFTA contributed to the overall economic integration process in Western Europe by lowering trade barriers between its member countries as well as in relation to the countries that had entered the Community. At the peak of its influence the EFTA comprised the four Nordic countries, the United Kingdom, Portugal, Austria and Switzerland. However, since some countries have left the EFTA in order to become members of the EC, it now only covers some 30 million people.

The vision of a united states of Europe with integrated markets for labour and capital as well as with a coordinated foreign policy in relation to the super powers was there already in the Rome Treaty. It took some thirty years to implement the parts and pieces of this new image for Western Europe. The enlargement of the EC to cover more than the six original country members in combination with the collapse of East European communism means that the 1990s may very well see some version of a large European federation come true.

The development of the EC has proceeded along two lines. Firstly, more and more member countries have been brought in. The United Kingdom, Ireland and Denmark entered in 1973; Greece was accepted as a member in 1981 and Spain and Portugal entered in 1986; Cyprus, Malta and Turkey have a special status as associated countries. At present the EC with its 12 member states includes some 320 million people which means that a European federation would be larger than the United States, the Soviet Union or Japan in terms of population. It is apparent that the process of European integration has changed the power balance in the world between the various continents. This became more pronounced with the reunification of Germany in 1990.

Secondly, very arduous work on creating real-life intra-nation institutions had to be put in in order to pin down the lofty blueprints of a united states in Europe into actual outcomes. By 1968 the tolls within the EC had been abolished; in 1973 the European currency union was introduced while in 1977 similar rules for indirect taxation were accepted among the member nations leading to a harmonization of the VAT, the value added tax. The ECU – European Currency Unit – introduced in 1979 constituted a kind of new common money unit. In 1985 a European passport was realized. The next major step is the introduction from the year of 1993 of an integrated market in which the movement of the factors of production would be entirely free.

The creation of the internal market is widely considered as the most important step towards a united Europe. It was launched in 1985 by the

Commission President, Jacques Delors, as a method for counteracting the so-called Eurosclerosis or the trend in Europe towards a decline in competitiveness in relation to other continents, mainly the US and South East Asia. The White Paper on Completing the Internal Market stated that some 300 decisions had to be taken by the Community in order to remove various types of barriers to trade and finance between the member countries. The objective to create an integrated market for all kinds of goods and services not only in the private sector but also within the public sector requires a far-reaching harmonization of laws, taxes and public expenditures in all the member countries. Besides these major steps towards breaking the barriers between the nation-states in Western Europe work has been done on a common system of product standards which would replace the various systems of national standards and it has been tried to coordinate the environmental policies of the member countries in terms of a new directorate implementing the environmental action programmes of the Commission.

The single major policy failure of the EC is to be found in the agricultural sector. Much work, money and strife has gone into the the Common Agricultural Policy (the CAP). It has proved difficult to significantly reduce the EC budgetary support to an oversized and inefficient agricultural production system in the West European countries. Actually, at times almost two-thirds of the Community Budget has been allocated to the CAP. And at times the search for a common agricultural policy has almost split the EC: Britain with its tiny, but modernized agricultural sector rejecting the CAP in confrontation with France and the Federal Republic of Germany.

Already from the outset the integration movement in Western Europe had a political aspect, as it was hoped that nation-state integration would prevent war on the European continent, at least between France and Germany. European Political Co-operation (EPC) has, however, always been a source of conflicts and rivalry when it came down to the crucial question of how much authority was to be given to the supra-national bodies of the Community. The institutional framework of the EC is the outcome of years of negotiations and clashes with structures and functions emerging more out of various compromises than as the implementation of some rationally conceived organizational blue-print. It is no exaggeration to state that France and the Federal Republic of Germany have been more willing to accept the transfer of nation-state powers to the EC than Britain. By means of a strong participation and representation in the various bodies of the EC the Germans were provided with an important international arena to make their voice heard in spite of all the difficulties following as consequences of the defeat of German imperialism in 1945 (Paterson, 1990).

Community institutions

A growing number of persons are involved in the running of a few major EC institutions in Brussels, Strasbourg and Luxembourg. In 1985 the budget of the EC amounted to some 35 billion US dollars which constituted almost 1 per cent of the total GDP of all the EC countries. According to the 1984 Draft Treaty establishing the European Union (EUT) and the Single European Act (SEA) that went into force on 1 July 1987 the EC comprises a number of bodies with a composition and set of functions outlined below. The institutions of the EC involve: the European parliament, the council of ministers, the EC commission, the court and a court of revision, the economic and social committee, the European council and the committee of continuous representatives.

It is possible to make a distinction between institutions representing the member national governments on the one hand and institutions that are European on the other hand. Table 11.1 outlines a few of the dominant institutions.

The European Council: it consists of the French president, the remaining eleven premiers assisted by their foreign ministers, the president of the EC commission and one more member of the commission. It meets

Table 11.1   *Outline of some institutions of the European Economic Community*

Country	Council of ministers		The Commission	Parliament	Court and advocates	Economic and social commission
	N	Votes				
Belgium	1	5	1	24	1	12
Denmark	1	3	1	16	1	9
Germany FR	1	10	2	81	1	24
Greece	1	5	1	24	1	9
France	1	10	2	81	1	24
Ireland	1	3	1	15	1	6
Italy	1	10	2	81	1	24
Luxembourg	1	2	1	6	1	6
Netherlands	1	5	1	25	1	12
Portugal	1	5	1	24	1	12
Spain	1	5	2	60	1	21
UK	1	10	2	81	1	24
Total	12	76	17	518	13*	189

Note: *One extra member from the larger countries.
Source: Archer, 1990.

at least twice yearly and may be considered as the supreme body of the European Economic Community.

The Council of Ministers: its composition varies from issue to issue, each member government sending the minister that heads the ministry to which the issue belongs. It is looked upon as the legislative body of the EC. The number of votes cast being distributed between the member countries in relation to their populations, decisions in the council are being taken by majority vote, qualified majorities and unanimity. 54 YES votes are most often required from a total of 76 votes, if a motion is accepted, meaning that the four large countries cannot overrule all the other countries. It used to be the case that unanimity was required in the council of ministers, but the unanimity rule was changed into a rule of qualified majority decision. However, majority voting does not apply to all questions that the Council deals with, because the country veto is retained on taxation, environmental policy, health controls and the rights of employees.

The Council President: the presidency of the council is rotated among the member countries on a half year basis in accordance with the same rule which designates one member country as the chairmanship country. The president of the council is assisted by a staff which together with the president plays a major role in coordinating the ongoing activities involving the council, the commission and a body referred to as COREPER, which consists of the ambassadors of the various EC countries and which prepares the meetings of the council by negotiating issues where there is disagreement between member nations.

The Commission: it comprises 17 members, elected for a term of four years which may be renewed. Its president stays for two-year terms which are also renewable. The Commission (earlier High Authority) represents the EC as a community and not the national governments that appoint its members. Its decisions are taken by majority vote which is then regarded as a unanimous decision with the minority always supporting the majority. The Commission operates as the chief planning body of the EC. It supervises the implementation of the decisions of the Council as well as looks into how the statutes of the EC are respected and it may suggest new measures to be taken by the Council. The Commission heads a large bureaucracy involving a number of bureaux for various EC activities which is placed in Brussels and the core of which is some 8 000 'Eurocrats', i.e. civil servants involved with various inquiries and planning work.

The EC parliament: it is officially called the 'European Parliament' and it is elected by means of general proportional elections in the various member countries (Great Britain employs majority elections in single member constituencies). Its 518 parliamentarians have five year terms and they are divided into political groups that cut across the national

Table 11.2   *Turnout in European parliament elections*

	1979/81	1984/87	1989
Belgium	80.0	82.0	83.1
Denmark	46.7	51.6	45.6
F R Germany	65.1	55.9	61.6
France	57.5	54.7	47.3
Greece	87.3	79.8	83.4
Ireland	61.2	46.4	66.5
Italy	82.9	79.1	74.4
Luxembourg	80.3	80.6	79.6
Netherlands	57.8	50.5	47.1
Portugal	–	70.3	49.5
Spain	–	67.2	53.6
Great Britain	32.1	32.1	36.6
Northern Ireland	55.6	64.4	48.4

Note: Turnout equals valid votes as a percentage of the total electorate in each country.
Source: Curtice (1989: 218)

identities. The first European elections were held in 1979. Tables 11.2 and 11.3 show the electoral participation in the European elections as well as the electoral outcomes.

However, the functions of the European Parliament have been narrow, restricted to chiefly a role of consultation and public opinion-making. It cannot introduce binding decisions on the member nations, because the more important decision functions rest with the Council. The Parliament, placed at Strasbourg with a secretariat in Luxembourg, is very much involved in the policy-making process of the Community, acting in a consultative role in relation to the Council and the Commission on items of legislation and on budgetary matters. The Parliament operates twelve standing committees preparing statements about the policies of the EC in various areas. And it conducts open debates about the ends and means of the various policies of the Community.

The Court: introduced already in 1952 it supervises the implementation of the EEC legal documents which cover both the various intra-state treaties and the common decisions of the EC bodies over the years. The court is a true supranational institution whose decisions are binding on the member states. Besides one representative from each member state plus one more representative from one of the four large states – 13 all in all – there are six general advocates who consult the judges on the basis of their own expertise, but the judges make their own decisions by a voting procedure.

The court is crucial to the entire EC system of institutions as it clarifies the supranational framework of laws and rules that bind the member states together. It is placed in Luxembourg with a substantial secretariat with

Table 11.3   *Number of seats in the European parliament 1979,
1984 and 1989 in terms of party groups*

		COMM	SOC	GREEN	CHR DEM	EDA	LIB	CON	FAR RIGHT	REG/ NAT	OTH	TOT
BEL	79	0	7	0	10	0	4	0	0	3	0	24
	84	0	9	2	6	0	5	0	0	2	0	24
	89	0	8	3	7	0	4	0	1	1	0	24
DEN	79	1	4	0	0	1	4	2	0	0	4	16
	84	1	4	0	0	0	3	4	0	0	4	16
	89	1	4	0	0	0	5	2	0	0	4	16
FRG	79	0	35	0	42	0	4	0	0	0	0	81
	84	0	33	7	41	0	0	0	0	0	0	81
	89	0	31	8	32	0	4	0	6	0	0	81
FRA	79	19	21	0	9	15	17	0	0	0	0	81
	84	10	20	0	8	20	13	0	10	0	0	81
	89	7	22	9	7	13	13	0	10	0	0	81
GRE	81	4	10	0	8	0	0	0	1	0	1	24
	84	4	10	0	9	0	0	0	1	0	0	24
	89	4	9	0	10	1	0	0	0	0	0	24
IRE	79	0	4	0	4	5	1	0	0	0	1	15
	84	0	0	0	6	8	1	0	0	0	0	15
	89	1	1	0	4	6	2	0	0	0	1	15
ITA	79	24	13	0	30	0	5	0	4	1	4	81
	84	27	12	0	27	0	5	0	5	2	3	81
	89	22	14	5	27	0	4	0	4	3	2	81
LUX	79	0	1	0	3	0	2	0	0	0	0	6
	84	0	2	0	3	0	1	0	0	0	0	6
	89	0	2	0	3	0	1	0	0	0	0	6
NET	79	0	9	0	10	0	4	0	0	0	2	25
	84	0	9	2	8	0	5	0	0	0	1	25
	89	0	8	2	10	0	3	0	0	0	2	25
POR	79	–	–	–	–	–	–	–	–	–	–	–
	87	3	7	0	4	0	10	0	0	0	0	24
	89	3	8	1	3	0	9	0	0	0	0	24
SPA	79	–	–	–	–	–	–	–	–	–	–	–
	87	3	28	1	0	0	2	18	0	0	8	60
	89	4	27	3	0	0	1	17	0	0	8	60
UK	79	0	18	0	0	0	0	61	0	1	1	81
	84	0	33	0	0	0	0	45	0	1	1	81
	89	0	46	0	0	0	0	32	0	1	1	81
TOT	79	48	122	0	116	21	41	63	5	5	13	434
	84	48	167	12	112	28	45	67	17	5	17	518
	89	42	190	31	103	20	46	51	22	5	18	518

Sources: *Electoral Studies* 1984: 3; *Electoral Studies* 1989: 3.

a steadily increasing work load. Besides, there is a special body for the review of the EC budget and the finances of the EC: the review body.

The relationships between the various institutions of the Community change over time as a response to the evolving nature of the overall organization in terms of membership and functions. The role of the EP has been strengthened, partly because of the attention that the European elections attract. In the EP the major parties group more according to ideology than country. The largest group within the EP presently is the socialists with roughly 35 per cent of the seats. Another sizeable group is the Christian Democrats, having 19 per cent of the seats. The EDA stands for European Democratic Alliance which includes the French Gaullists, the Fianna Fail and the Danish discontent party.

Under the impact of the EUT and the SEA the relationships between the major policy-making bodies of the community – the Council of Ministers, the Commission and the EP – will change (Lodge, 1990). The position of the EP as well as that of the Commission will probably be enhanced at the expense of the powers of the Council of Ministers.

New institutional procedures – the so-called co-operation procedure – have been introduced in order to make it possible for the EP to exercise more influence on the policy-making of the Community. The co-operation procedure provides for two readings in the EP of the proposals submitted to it by the Commission. It remains the case that the approval of the Council of Ministers is decisive in order for legislation to be enacted. However, if the EP on the second reading rejects the proposal submitted to it by the Council after the first reading, then there has to be unanimity in the Council in order to override the negative decision of the EP.

The new co-operation procedure will call forth more interaction and interdependence between the Council, the Commission and the EP. In combination with the increasing visibility of European elections, these reciprocities between the EP and the other two main actors, the Council and the Commission, may pave the way towards a more powerful European parliament.

The institutional web of the EC also involves a number of committees which are part of the decision operations of the EEC, preparing new initiatives and commenting on investigations and proposals. Perhaps the best known committee is the economic and social commission which consists of representatives from broad occupational groups. There is also the 113th committee counselling on trade matters. This expansive institutional web also covers a number of interest groups which although not formally part of the EC framework are present in Bruxelles on a permanent basis. Here one may mention inter alia COPA or Comité des Organisations Professionelles Agricoles de la Communauté Européenne, UNICE or Union des Industries de la C.E. and CES or Confédération Européenne des Syndicats.

Conclusion

Although the EC has at times been close to collapse due to severe disagreement about the nature of the common framework or institutions, the EC has displayed a remarkable vitality and relevance. Considering the fact that the idea of West European integration meets with more and more sympathy, it is not too daring a prediction that some kind of federal system, however loose, is in the making. At the same time there is immense uncertainty about which of the alternative routes the future may take in Europe. The collapse of East European communism opens up the prospect of even wider European integration, though the problems to be overcome in achieving such a far-reaching political integration are immense.

12

Conclusion

Introduction

Due to the accelerating process of integration in Western Europe and the sudden but remarkable transformation of the East European communist systems the international attention to European affairs is on the rise. The notion of some kind of a united states of Europe is not, for the first time in a European history of numerous conflicts and war, entirely without foundation. This makes it all the more important to understand the logic of West European politics which appears to be a model of considerable practical importance for the emerging democracies in Eastern Europe. It may be expected that the substantial country variation in political behaviour and political institutions between the major countries in Western Europe will persist during the process of integration that is now taking place. How are we to approach the problem of interpreting West European politics? The analysis in the preceding chapters of various aspects of political life in Western Europe has been structured in terms of a fundamental paradigm choice between political sociology models or institutionalist models. Although a number of findings have been reported on in each chapter we wish to emphasize a few major points in relation to this crucial model distinction.

The political sociology approach

The strength of models stemming from a political sociology approach is that they search for the sources of various political phenomena in society. It would be truly astonishing if politics were entirely disconnected from the structure and dynamics of society. The major West European countries display considerable social differences which appear to be relevant when accounting for political behaviour. Even if it is adequate to designate the sixteen countries that enter this study as rich countries with affluent societies it remains a basic fact that they differ on a number of social dimensions like ethnicity, religion and class but also with regard to levels of affluence.

The weakness of the political sociology perspective is the reductionist bias. Not only social forces matter for the occurrence of political phenomena. Social structure and social dynamics create opportunities for political action but society does not determine political behaviour and institutions. When testing various sociological models of politics we find all the time this latitude in the relationship between social variables and political properties which shows that politics possesses certain degrees of freedom vis-à-vis society.

Social homogeneity and heterogeneity differ in the various West European countries. There is a variation with regard to so-called *objective* social circumstances like ethnic or religious fragmentation and class-based or income differences. And there is in addition a variation in how these social cleavages are experienced, or so-called *subjective* social circumstances. Thus, ethnic and religious consciousness differ as well as class consciousness and the variation in subjective attitudes does not mirror the variation in objective circumstances – again a reminder of the latitude in the connections between various social phenomena, including politics.

The test of a number of models relating various political phenomena to social entities corroborates this confined theory about the social bases of politics. Social heterogeneity constitutes a frame of action possibilities for political parties, but the actual outcome depends as much on the choice of a strategy on the part of the political party. Divided societies tend to have fractionalized party systems whereas homogeneous societies tend towards a smaller number of effective political parties. However, the interaction between social diversity and the party system is not one way, meaning that we can predict the party system components and their size from a knowledge of the structure of social groups. Similarly, social heterogeneity has an impact on political stability and its various manifestations, but the link is intermediated by a number of other factors, mainly institutional ones, which implies that the social environment cannot determine, only condition, political stability. Affluence affects public policy-making, but, again, it is not a question of a necessary and sufficient condition. A high level of economic affluence creates the possibility for large welfare state expenditures but there is no automatic link. On the contrary, the position of the left in society in general is conducive to the expansion of the tax state, because what matters is the actual willingness to use the opportunity for big government spending that a high level of affluence creates.

The institutionalist framework

The institutionalist paradigm has grown stronger in the 1980s. Its revival has been described as an adequate reaction to various reductionist perspectives that attempt to explain how political organizations work by means of non-political factors. Institutions in general and political ones in particular have a logic of their own, the understanding of which requires approaches that are different from the behavioural persuasion or the public choice paradigm.

How do we single out the political institutions in the general set of institutions? Political institutions constitute the political order. However, there are several mechanisms for conflict resolution and steering in a society. Is each and every one part of the political order? One may regard the revival of state theory as an institutionalist trend, but how do we identify the state institutions? The traditional approach to the state emphasizes very much that what is special about the state − sovereignty, centralization, force − is not the fact that it is composed of institutions in general, but that state institutions are very particular. We need to know what institutions are, because we must ask: is an institution a set of behaviour or a set of rules or perhaps both? And would any set of behaviour or rules qualify as an institution? It seems as if institutions are organizations: collective action, legitimacy and symbolism. Focussing on political institutions in Western Europe it is not possible to include only the governmental organizations. Besides state institutions in these countries we must attempt to understand the party system and its institutions as well as the emergence of international institutions above the nation states in Western Europe. How are we to interpret a broad set of political institutions involving not only the typical paraphernalia of the West European state but also political parties, trade unions and the welfare state programmes?

The new institutionalism implies a rejection of two prevailing modes for the explanation of organizational phenomena, the contextual framework and the actor approach. A number of approaches is done away with by the negative argument: behaviouralism, political sociology and rational and social choice, because they share the erroneous assumption that political phenomena like public institutions may be accounted for by means of non-political factors. This negative argument, it must be pointed out, is based on an empirical proposition that is open to confirmation or falsification. It means that there cannot be a theory about political institutions that achieve a high degree of explained variance by relating institutional properties to for example social factors. It may very well be the case that some contextual framework will work well in relation to the explanation of politics in Western Europe.

As a matter of fact, West European politics displays links with the societies in the various countries. The findings reported on in the separate chapters confirm the political sociology idea that politics has social sources, but they also imply a rejection of the deterministic claims of the political sociology approach. The institutionalist framework is highly suitable to a statement of the range and scope of variation in institutional arrangements in Western Europe, but there is no confirmation of the kind of indeterminism characteristic of much of the new institutionalism. There is much to be said in favour of taking a middle road in between the social reductionism of political sociology and the indeterminism of the new institutionalism.

West European political institutions

Political institutions are not primarily norms, belief-systems or symbolism, they are action phenomena meaning that collective activity takes place and leads to social outcomes. What matters in social life is primarily what institutions are up to and that cannot be identified without the action aspect. Human action may be fundamentally affected by formalism, norms and symbolic phenomena – true, but how far this is true is an open question that cannot be resolved by a priori deliberations.

Institutional dynamics or organizational change is a contested process involving accidental outcomes and random activity meaning that results cannot be predicted and change cannot be controlled by fiat. Organizational change involving sluggishness, resistance to change, randomness, surprise and unintentionality seems characteristic of the West European welfare state and its politics. The sustained process of public sector growth since the end of the Second World War has meant that the segmented negotiation state has become the prevalent model in Western Europe. The era of big government is the time of weak government, the segmentation of power and authority onto several quasi-independent public and private organizations. The state was no longer autonomous, centralized or separated from other organizations. The borders between the system of public bureaus and the private interest organizations became difficult to demarcate and coordination based on majority rule became difficult to accomplish even in countries adhering to the Westminster model of government. Corporatist institutions were provided legitimacy although they were never regulated in terms of democratic norms.

The 1980s mean a reappraisal of the state models, their pros and cons. And the established segmented state is criticized by those that adhere to the other models. The adherents of the sovereignty model want to see more democratic decision-making in representative assemblies as well as more political leadership; those that speak for the guardian state wish to replace budget allocation with market allocation; and the believers in the community model look for morally attractive ways of life which promote individual rights and ecological balance. The political outcomes in the 1990s will result from the contestation between the alternative models of the state, because what is at stake is not more or less but the kind of institutions people would choose had they been in a constitutional choice. And the movement towards intragovernmental bodies in Western Europe operates as a constraint on the degree of freedom in choosing political institutions at home (Lodge, 1990).

References

Aardal, B. and Valen, H. (1989) *Velgere, Partier og Politisk Avstand*. Oslo: Statistisk Sentralbyrå.

Abrahamsson, B. (1977) *Bureaucracy or Participation: The Logic of Organization*. Beverly Hills: Sage.

Ahluwalia, M.S. (1976) 'Inequality, Poverty and Development.' *Journal of Development Economics*, 3, pp. 307–42.

Ake, C. (1974) 'Modernization and Political Instability: A Theoretical Exploration.' *World Politics*, 26, pp. 576–91.

Alber, J. (1988) 'Is There a Crisis of the Welfare State?: Cross-national Evidence from Europe, North America and Japan.' *European Sociological Review*, 4, pp. 181–203.

Alford, R.R. (1963) *Party and Society: The Anglo-American Democracies*. Chicago: Rand McNally.

Allardt, E. (1979) *Implications of the Ethnic Revival in Modern Industrialized Society: A Comparative Study of the Linguistic Minorities in Western Europe*. Helsinki: Societas Scientiarum Fennica.

Allardt, E. and Miemois, K.J. (1979) *Roots Both in the Centre and the Periphery: The Swedish Speaking Population in Finland*. University of Helsinki: Research Group for Comparative Sociology.

Allardt, E. and Rokkan, S. (eds) (1970) *Mass Politics: Studies in Political Sociology*. New York: Free Press.

Allardt, E. and Starck, C. (1981) *Språkgränser och Samhällsstruktur: Finlandssvenskarna i ett jämförande perspektiv*. Stockholm: Almqvist and Wiksell.

Allison, P.D. (1978) 'Measures of Inequality.' *American Sociological Review*, 6, pp. 79–105.

Allum, P.A. (1973) *Italy: Republic without Government?* London: Weidenfeld and Nicolson.

Allum, P.A. (1979) 'Italy', in Henig, S. (ed.) *Political Parties in the European Community*. London: Allen and Unwin, pp. 135–69.

Almanach der Schweiz (1978) *Daten und Kommentare zur Bevölkerung, Gesellschaft und Politik*. Bern: Peter Lang.

Almond, G.A. (1956) 'Comparative Political Systems.' *Journal of Politics*, 18, pp. 391–409.

Almond, G.A. (1988) 'The Return to the State.' *American Political Science Review*, 82, pp. 853–74.

Almond, G.A. and Powell, G.B. (1966) *Comparative Politics*. Boston: Little, Brown and Company.

Almond, G.A. and Verba, S. (1965) *The Civic Culture*. Boston: Little, Brown and Company.

Almond, G.A. and Verba, S. (eds) (1989) *The Civic Culture Revisited*. New ed. Newbury Park: Sage.

Alt, J. and Chrystal, A.K. (1983) *Political Economics*. Berkeley: The University of

California Press.

Anckar, D. (1984a) *Folket och Presidenten: En författningspolitisk politisk studie*. Helsingfors: Finska Vetenskaps-Societeten.

Anckar, D. (1984b) 'Presidential Elections in Finland: A Plea for Approval Voting.' *Electoral Studies*, 3, pp. 125–38.

Anderson, M. (1978) 'The Renaissance of Territorial Minorities in Western Europe.' *West European Politics*, 1, pp. 128–43.

Anuario estadistico de España. Madrid: Instituo nacional de estadistica, annually.

Anuário estatistica. Lisboa: Instituto nacional de estatistica, annually.

Archer, C. (1990) *Organizing Western Europe*. London: Edward Arnold.

Armingeon, K. (1989) 'Arbeitsbeziehungen und Gewerkschaftsentwicklung in den achtziger Jahren: ein Vergleich der OECD-Länder.' *Politische Viertalsjahrschrift*, 30, pp. 603–28.

Aron, R. (1957) *The Opium of the Intellectuals*. London: Secker and Warburg.

Ashford, D. (1983) 'Reconstructing the French "Etat": Progress of the loi Defferre.' *West European Politics*, 6, pp. 263–70.

Austen, J. et al. (1987) 'Referendums, 1978–1986.' *Electoral Studies*, 6, pp. 139–47.

Axelrod, R. (1970) *Conflict of Interest*. Chicago: Markham.

Bacalhau, M. (1988) 'Movilidad y Transferencia de Voto a Través de los Sondeos.' *Revista de Estudios Politicos*, 60–1, pp. 231–52.

Bachrach, P. and Baratz, M.S. (1963) 'Decisions and Nondecisions: An Analytical Framework.' *American Political Science Review*, 57, pp. 632–42.

Bakvis, H. (1981) *Catholic Power in the Netherlands*. Kingston: McGill-Queen's University Press.

Ballerstedt, E. et al. (1977) *Soziologischer Almanach*. Frankfurt am Main: Campus.

Banks, A.S. (1970) 'Modernization and Political Change: The Latin-American and Amer-European Nations.' *Comparative Political Studies*, 2, pp. 405–18.

Banks, A.S. (1971) *Cross-polity Time-series Data*. Cambridge, MA: MIT Press.

Banks, A.S. (1974) 'Industrialization and Development: A Longitudinal Analysis.' *Economic Development and Cultural Change*, 22, pp. 320–37.

Banks, A.S. (1981) 'An Index of Socio-Economic Development 1869–1975.' *Journal of Politics*, 43, pp. 390–411.

Baran, P. (1957) *The Political Economy of Economic Growth*. New York: Monthly Review Press.

Barnes, S. (1974) 'Italy', in Rose, R. (ed.), pp. 171–225.

Barrett, D.B. (ed.) (1982) *World Christian Encyclopaedia: A Comparative Study of Churches and Religions in the Modern World AD 1900–2000*. Nairobi: Oxford University Press.

Barry, B. (1970) *Sociologists, Economists and Democracy*. London: Collier-Macmillan.

Barry, B. (1975) 'Political Accommodation and Consociational Democracy.' *British Journal of Political Science*, 5, pp. 477–505.

Bartolini, S. and Mair, P. (eds) (1984) 'Party Politics in Contemporary Western Europe.' *West European Politics*, 7, no. 4.

Bashevkin, S. (ed.) (1985) 'Women and Politics in Western Europe.' *West European Politics*, vol. 8, no. 4.

Bassand, M. (1976) 'Le séparatisme jurassien: un conflit des classes et/ou un conflit ethnique?' *Cahiers internationaux de sociologie*, 61, pp. 221–46.

Bauer, M. et al. (1980) *Schweizerische Arbeiterbewegung: Dokumente zur Lage. Organisation und Kämpfen der Arbeiter von der Frühindustrialisierung bis zur Gegenwart*. Zürich: Limmat Verlag.

Baumgarten, J. (ed.) (1982) *Linkssozialisten in Europa: Alternativen zu Sozialdemokratie und Kommunistischen Parteien*. Hamburg: Junius.

Bealey, F. (1987) 'Stability and Crisis: Fears about Threats to Democracy.' *European Journal of Political Research*, 15, pp. 687–715.

Bell, D. (1960) *The End of Ideology*. New York: Free Press.

Bell, D. (1973) *The Coming of Post-industrial Society*. New York: Basic Books.

Bell, D. (1976) *The Cultural Contradictions of Capitalism*. New York: Basic Books.

Bell, D.S. (ed.) (1983) *Democratic Politics in Spain: Spanish Politics after Franco*. London: Frances Pinter.

Bendix, R. and Lipset, S.M. (1957) 'Political Sociology.' *Current Sociology*, 6, pp. 79–99.

Berelson, B. et al. (1954) *Voting: A Study of Opinion Formation in a Presidential Campaign*. Chicago: The University of Chicago Press.

Berger, M. et al. (1986) 'Legitimierung des Regierungswechsels: eine Analyse der Bundestagswahl 1983', in Klingemann, H.-D. and Kaase, M. (eds) *Wahlen und politischer Prosess: Analysen aus Anlass der Bundestagswahl 1983*. Opladen: Westdeutscher Verlag, pp. 251–88.

Bergh, T. et al. (1977) *Vekst og velstand: norsk politisk historie 1945–1965*. Oslo: Universitetsforlaget.

Berglund, S. (1988) 'The 1987 Eduskunta Election in Finland.' *Scandinavian Political Studies*, 11, pp. 69–76.

Berglund, S. and Lindström, U. (1978) *The Scandinavian Party System(s)*. Lund: Studentlitteratur.

von Beyme, K. (1970) *Die parlamentarische Regierungssysteme in Europa*. München: Piper.

von Beyme, K. (1979) *Das Politische System der Bundesrepublik Deutschland: eine Einführung*. München: Piper.

von Beyme, K. (1980) *Challenge to Power: Trade Unions and Industrial Relations in Capitalist Countries*. London: Sage.

von Beyme, K. (1982) *Parteien in westlichen Demokratien*. München: Piper.

von Beyme, K. (ed.) (1988) 'Right-Wing Extremism in Western Europe.' *West European Politics*, vol. 11, no. 2.

Bill, J.A. and Hardgrave, R.L. Jr. (1973) *Comparative Politics: The Quest for Theory*. Columbus, Ohio: Merrill.

Birch, A. (1978) 'Minority Nationalist Movements and Theories of Political Integration.' *World Politics*, 30, pp. 325–44.

Birgersson, B.O. et al. (1984) *Sverige efter 1900: en modern politisk historia*. Stockholm: Bonnier.

Birnbaum, P. (1975) *La fin du politique*. Paris: Seuil.

Blais, A. (1988) 'The classification of election systems.' *European Journal of Political Research*, vol. 16: 99–110.

Blalock, H. B. (1960) *Social Statistics*. New York: McGraw-Hill.

Blanco, J.J. et al. (1977) *La consciencia regional en Espana*. Madrid: Centro de investigaciones sociologicas.

Blaschke, J. (ed.) (1980) *Handbuch der westeuropäischen Regionalbewegungen*. Frankfurt am Main: Syndikat.

Blaustein, A. and Flanz, G. (eds) (1972–) *Constitutions of the Countries of the World*. New York: Oceana Publications.

Blondel, J. (1968) 'Party Systems and Patterns of Government in Western Democracies.' *Canadian Journal of Political Science*, 1, pp. 180–203.

Blondel, J. (1969) *An Introduction to Comparative Government*. London: Weidenfeld and Nicolson.

Bluhm, W.T. (1973) *Building an Austrian Nation: The Political Integration of a Western Nation*. New Haven: Yale University Press.

Bogason, P. (1987) 'Denmark', in Page, E.C. and Goldsmith, M.J. (eds) *Central and Local Government Relations*. London: Sage Publications, pp. 46–67.

Bogdanor, V. (1983) 'Introduction', in Bogdanor, V. and Butler, D. (eds) *Democracy and Elections*. Cambridge: Cambridge University Press, pp. 1–19.

Bogdanor, V. (ed.) (1985) *Representatives of the People? Parliamentarians and Constituents in Western Democracies*. Aldershot: Gower.

Bollen, K.A. (1980) 'Issues in the Comparative Measurement of Political Democracy.' *American Sociological Review*, 45, pp. 370–90.

Borella, F. (1977) *Les partis politiques dans la France d'aujourd'hui*. Paris: Ed. Seuil.

Bornischer, V. (1978) 'Einkommensungleichheit innerhalb von Ländern in Komparativer Sicht.' *Schweizerischer Zeitschrift für Soziologie*, 4, pp. 3–45.

Borre, O. (1980) 'Electoral Instability in Four Nordic Countries, 1950–1977.' *Comparative Political Studies*, 13, pp. 141–71.

Borre, O. et al. (1976) *Vaelgere i 70'erne: resultater fra interviewsundersoegelser ved folketingsvalgene i 1971, 1973 og 1975*. Koebenhavn: Akademisk forlag.

Bottomore, T. (1966) *Classes in Modern Society*. New York: Vintage.

Brams, S.J. (1975) *Game Theory and Politics*. New York: Free Press.

Brezzi, C. (1979) *I partiti democratici cristiani d'Europa*. Milano: Teti.

Britannica World Data (1989) Chicago: Encyclopaedia Britannica.

Bruneau, T.C. (1984) *Politics and Nationhood: Post-Revolutionary Portugal*. New York: Praeger.

Bruneau, T.C. and Macleod, A. (1986) *Politics in Contemporary Portugal: Parties and the Consolidation of Democracy*. Boulder: Lynne Rienner.

Buchanan, W. and Cantril, H. (1953) *How Nations See Each Other: A Study in Public Opinion*. Urbana, IL: The University of Illinois Press.

Budge, I. and Farlie, D.J. (1977) *Voting and Party Competition: A Theoretical Critique and Synthesis Applied to Surveys from Ten Democracies*. London: Wiley.

Budge, I. and Farlie, D.J. (1978) 'The Potentiality of Dimensional Analyses for Explaining Voting and Party Competition.' *European Journal of Political Research*, 6, pp. 203–31.

Budge, I. and Farlie, D.J. (1981) 'Predicting Regime Change: A Cross-national Investigation with Aggregate Data 1950–1980.' *Quality and Quantity*, 15, pp. 335–64.

Budge, I. and Farlie, D.J. (1983) *Explaining and Predicting Elections: Issue Effects and Party Strategies in Twenty-three Democracies*. London: Allen and Unwin.

Budge, I. et al. (1983) *The New British Political System: Government and Society in the 1980s*. London: Longman.

Budge, I. et al. (eds) (1987) *Ideology, Strategy and Party Change: Spatial Analyses of Post-war Election Programmes in 19 Democracies*. Cambridge: Cambridge University Press.

Butler, D. and Ranney, A. (eds) (1978) *Referendums: A Comparative Study of Practice and Theory*. Washington: American Enterprise Institute.

Buton, P. (1988) 'Les Effectifs Communistes en Europe Occidentale depuis 1968.' *Communisme*, 17, pp. 6–20.

Cahiers du communisme. Paris, monthly.

Cameron, D.R. (1978) 'The Expansion of the Public Economy. A Comparative Analysis.' *American Political Science Review*, 72, pp. 1243–61.

Campbell, A. et al. (1954) *The Voter Decides*. Evanston, IL: Row, Petersen and Co.

Campbell, A. et al. (1960) *The American Voter*. New York: Wiley.

Campiche, R. (1972) 'Switzerland', in Mol, H. (ed.) pp. 511–28.

Carlsson, G. (1969) *Social Mobility and Class Structure*. Lund: Gleerup.

Carr, R. and Fusi, J.P. (1979) *Spain: Dictatorship to Democracy*. London: Allen and Unwin.

Carstairs, A. (1980) *A Short History of Electoral Systems in Western Europe*. London: Allen and Unwin.

Castles, F.G. (1978) *The Social Democratic Image of Society: A Study of the Achievements and Origins of Scandinavian Social Democracy in Comparative Perspective*. London: Routledge and Kegan Paul.

Castles, F.G. (ed.) (1982) *The Impact of Parties: Politics and Policies in Democratic Capitalist States*. London: Sage.

Castles, F.G. (1986) 'Whatever Happened to the Communist Welfare State?' *Studies in Comparative Communism*, 19, pp. 213–26.

Castles, F.G. and Mair, P. (1984) 'Left–right Political Scales: Some "Expert" Judgments.' *European Journal of Political Research*, 12, pp. 73–88.

Castles, F.G. and Wildenmann, R. (eds) (1986) *Visions and Realities of Party Government*. Berlin: Walter de Gruyter.

Castles, S. (1984) *Here for Good: Western Europe's New Ethnic Minorities*. London: Pluto.

Castles, S. and Kosack, G. (1973) *Immigrant Workers and Class Structure in Western Europe*. London: Oxford University Press.

Cawson, A. (ed.) (1985) *Organized Interests and the State: Studies in Meso-corporatism*. London: Sage.

Chapsal, J. (1984) *La vie politique sous le Ve république*. 2nd ed. Paris: PUF.

Charlot, M. (1986) 'L'Émergence du Front National.' *Revue Française de Science Politique*, 36, pp. 30–45.

Choi, K. (1983) 'A Statistical Test of Olson's Model', in Mueller, D.C. (ed.), pp. 57–78.

Chubb, B. (1982) *The Government and Politics of Ireland*. 2nd ed. Stanford: Stanford University Press.

Church, C.H. (1989) 'Behind the Consociational Screen: Politics in Contemporary Switzerland.' *West European Politics*, 12, pp. 35–54.

Clark, M. (1984) *Modern Italy 1871–1982*. London: Longman.

Clegg, T. (1987) 'Spain', in Page, E.C. and Goldsmith, M.J. (eds) *Central and Local Government Relations*. London: Sage Publications, pp. 130–55.

Clogg, R. (1979) *A Short History of Modern Greece*. Cambridge: Cambridge University Press.

Clogg, R. (ed.) (1983) *Greece in the 1980s*. London: Macmillan.

Club of Rome (1972) *The Limits to Growth*. London: Earth Island.

Cole, A. and Campbell, P. (1989) *French Electoral Systems and Elections Since 1789*. Aldershot: Gower.

Colliard, J.-C. (1982) 'The Giscardians', in Layton-Henry, Z. (ed.) *Conservative Politics in Western Europe*. London: Macmillan, pp. 204–35.

Compton, P.A. (1976) 'Religious Affiliation and Demographic Variability in Northern Ireland.' *The Institute of British Geographers: Transactions*, N.S., 1, pp. 433–52.

Connor, W. (1977) 'Ethnonationalism in the First World: The Present in Historical Perspective', in Esman, M.J. (ed.), pp. 19–45.

Converse, P. (1966) 'The Concept of a Normal Vote', in Campbell, A. et al. (eds) *Elections and the Political Order*. New York: Wiley, pp. 9–39.

Coverdale, J.F. (1979) *The Political Transformation of Spain after Franco.* New York: Praeger.

Crewe, I. and Denver, D. (eds) (1985) *Electoral Change in Western Democracies: Patterns and Sources of Electoral Volatility.* London: Croom Helm.

Cromwell, T. (1977) 'The Size Distribution of Income: An International Comparison.' *Review of Income and Wealth*, 23, pp. 291–308.

Crouch, C. (1977) *Class Conflict and the Industrial Relations Crisis.* London: Heinemann.

Crouch, C. and Pizzorno, A. (eds) (1978) *The Resurgence of Class Conflict in Western Europe since 1968.* 2 vols. London: Macmillan.

Crozier, M. (1964) *The Bureaucratic Phenomenon.* Chicago: The University of Chicago Press.

Courtois, S. (ed.) (1986) 'Le Communisme en Europe Occidentale: Declin ou Mutation?' *Communisme*, 11–12.

Criddle, B. (1987) 'The French Parti Socialiste', in Paterson, W.E. and Thomas, A.H. (eds) *Social Democratic Parties in Western Europe.* London: Croom Helm, pp. 11–24.

Cutright, P. (1963) 'National Political Development: Measurement and Analysis.' *American Sociological Review*, 28, pp. 253–64.

Cutright, P. (1967) 'Inequality: A Cross-national Analysis.' *American Sociological Review*, 32, pp. 562–78.

Daalder, H. (1966a) 'Parties, Élites, and Political Developments in Western Europe', in LaPalombara, J. and Weiner, M. (eds), pp. 43–77.

Daalder, H. (1966b) 'The Netherlands: Opposition in a Segmented Society', in Dahl, R.A. (ed.), pp. 188–236.

Daalder, H. (1971) 'Cabinets and Party Systems in Ten European Democracies.' *Acta Politica*, 6, pp. 282–303.

Daalder, H. (ed.) (1987a) *Party Systems in Denmark, Austria, Switzerland, The Netherlands and Belgium.* London: Frances Pinter.

Daalder, H. (1987b) 'The Dutch Party System: From Segmentation to Polarization – and Then?' in Daalder, H. (ed.) (1987a) *Party Systems in Denmark, Austria, Switzerland, The Netherlands and Belgium.* London: Frances Pinter, pp. 193–284.

Daalder, H. (1989) 'The Mould of Dutch Politics: Themes for Comparative Inquiry.' *West European Politics*, 12, pp. 1–20.

Daalder, H. and Irwin, G.A. (eds) (1989) 'Politics in the Netherlands: How Much Change?' *West European Politics*, 12, no. 1, pp. 1–20.

Daalder, H. and Mair, P. (eds) (1983) *Western European Party Systems: Continuity and Change.* London: Sage.

Daalder, I.H. (1983) 'The Italian Party System in Transition: The End of Polarised Pluralism?' *West European Politics*, 6, pp. 216–36.

Dahl, R.A. (1956) *A Preface to Democratic Theory.* Chicago: The University of Chicago Press.

Dahl, R.A. (1961) *Who Governs?* New Haven: Yale University Press.

Dahl, R.A. (ed.) (1966) *Political Oppositions in Western Democracies.* New Haven: Yale University Press.

Dahl, R.A. (1971) *Polyarchy: Participation and Opposition.* New Haven: Yale University Press.

Dahrendorf, R. (1959) *Class and Class Conflict in Industrial Society.* London: Routledge and Kegan Paul.

Dalton, R.J. et al. (eds) (1985) *Electoral Change in Advanced Industrial Democracies: Realignment or Dealignment?* Princeton: Princeton University Press.

Dalton, R.J. (1989) *Politics in West Germany.* Glenview, IL.: Scott, Foresman and Co.

Danziger, J. (1978) *Making Budgets: Public Resource Allocation*. Beverly Hills: Sage.

Day, A.J. and Degenhardt, H.W. (eds) (1984) *Political Parties of the World*. 2nd ed. Harlow: Longman.

Delruelle-Vosswinkel, N. and Frognier, A.P. (1980) 'L'opinion publique et les problèmes communautaires.' *Courrier hebdomadaire du CRISP*, no. 880.

De Ridder, M. and Fraga, L. (1986) 'The Brussels Issue in Belgian Politics.' *West European Politics*, 9, pp. 376–92.

De Swaan, A. (1973) *Coalition Theories and Cabinet Formations: A Study of Formal Theories of Coalition Formation Applied to Nine European Parliaments after 1918*. Amsterdam: Elsevier.

Deutsch, K. (1961) 'Social Mobilization and Political Development.' *American Political Science Review*, 55, pp. 493–514.

Deutsch, K. (1963) *The Nerves of Government: Models of Political Communication and Control*. New York: Free Press.

Deutsch, K. (1980) *Politics and Government: How People Decide Their Fate*. 3rd ed. Boston: Houghton Mifflin.

De Vos, G.A. (ed.) (1975) *Ethnic Identity: Cultural Continuities and Change*. Palo Alto: Mayfield.

Dewachter, W. (1987) 'Changes in a Particratie: The Belgian Party System from 1944 to 1986', in Daalder, H. (ed.) *Party Systems in Denmark, Austria, Switzerland, The Netherlands and Belgium*. London: Frances Pinter, pp. 285–363.

DiPalma, G. (1970) *Apathy and Participation: Mass Politics in Western Societies*. New York: Free Press.

DiPalma, G. (1973) *The Study of Conflict in Western Society: A Critique of the End of Ideology*. Morristown, NJ: General Learning Press.

Dodd, L.C. (1976) *Coalitions in Parliamentary Government*. Princeton: Princeton University Press.

Dogan, M. (1967) 'Political Cleavage and Social Stratification in France and Italy', in Lipset, S.M. and Rokkan, S. (eds), pp. 129–95.

Dogan, M. (ed.) (1975) *The Mandarins of Western Europe*. Beverly Hills: Sage.

Dogan, M. and Derivry, D. (1988) 'France in Ten Slices: An Analysis of Aggregate Data.' *Electoral Studies*, 7, pp. 251–67.

Dogan, M. and Pelassy, D. (1984) *How to Compare Nations: Strategies in Comparative Politics*. Chatham, NJ: Chatham House.

Dogan, M. and Rokkan, S. (eds) (1969) *Quantitative Ecological Analysis in the Social Sciences*. Cambridge, MA: MIT Press.

Donaghy, P.J. and Newton, M.T. (1987) *Spain: A Guide to Political and Economic Institutions*. Cambridge: Cambridge University Press.

Dowding, K.M. and Kimber, R. (1983) 'The Meaning and Use of "Political Stability".' *European Journal of Political Research*, 11, pp. 229–43.

Dowding, K.M. and Kimber, R. (1985) 'Conceptual Problems in Research on Democratic Stability.' Paper presented to the ECPR Joint Sessions of Workshops, Barcelona (mimeo).

Dowding, K.M. and Kimber, R. (1987) 'Political Stability and the Science of Comparative Politics.' *European Journal of Political Research*, 15, pp. 103–22.

Downs, A. (1957) *An Economic Theory of Democracy*. New York: Harper and Brothers.

Dryzek, J. (1978) 'Politics, Economics and Inequality: A Cross-national Analysis.' *European Journal of Political Research*, 6, pp. 399–410.

Duchacek, I.D. (1973) *Rights and Liberties in the World Today: Constitutional Promise and Reality*. Santa Barbara: ABC-Clio.

Dunleavy, P. (1985) 'Bureaucrats, Budgets and the Growth of the State: Reconstructing an Instrumental Model.' *British Journal of Political Science*, 15, pp. 299–328.

Duocastella, J. (1975) 'El mapa religioso de España', in Almerich, P. et al. *Cambio social y religion en España*. Barcelona: Fontanella, pp. 130–65.

Duverger, M. (1954) *Political Parties: Their Organization and Activity in the Modern State*. London: Methuen.

Duverger, M. (1959) *Droit constitutionnel et institutions politiques. 1: Theorie générale des régimes politiques*. Paris: PUF.

Dye, T. (1966) *Politics, Economics and the Public*. Chicago: Rand McNally.

Easton, D. (1965) *A Systems Analysis of Political Life*. New York: Wiley.

Eckart, C. et al. (1975) 'Arbeiterbewusstsein, Klassenzusammensetzung und ökonomische Entwicklung: Empirische Thesen zum "instrumentellen Bewusstsein".' *Gesellschaft: Beiträge zum Marxschen Theorie*, no. 4, pp. 7–64.

Eckstein, H. (1966) *Division and Cohesion in Democracy: A Study of Norway*. Princeton: Princeton University Press.

Eckstein, H. (1968) 'Party Systems', in Sills, D.L. (ed.), Vol. 11, pp. 436–53.

Eckstein, H. (1971) *The Evaluation of Political Performance: Problems and Dimensions*. Beverly Hills: Sage.

Eckstein, H. (1988) 'A Culturalist Theory of Political Change.' *American Political Science Review*, 82, pp. 791–804.

Eckstein, H. and Gurr, T.R. (1975) *Patterns of Authority: A Structural Basis for Political Inquiry*. New York: Wiley.

Edinger, L.J. (1977) *Politics in West Germany*. 2nd ed. Boston: Little, Brown and Company.

Ehrmann, H.W. (1976) *Politics in France*. 3rd ed. Boston: Little, Brown and Company.

Eight Nation Study (1979) *Political Action: An Eight Nation Study 1973–1976*. Köln: Zentralarchiv für empirische Sozialforschung.

Eisenstadt, S.N. and Rokkan, S. (eds) (1973) *Building States and Nations*. 2 vols. Beverly Hills: Sage.

Elder, N. et al. (1982) *The Consensual Democracies? The Government and Politics of the Scandinavian States*. Oxford: Martin Robertson.

Elklit, J. et al. (1972) 'Om måling av nationalt tilhoerstorhold i Nordslesvig.' *Okonomi og politik*, 46, pp. 375–95.

Engels, F. (1958) *The Condition of the Working Class in England*. Oxford: Blackwell.

Enloe, C. (1973) *Ethnic Conflict and Political Development*. Boston: Little, Brown and Company.

Epstein, L.D. (1980) *Political Parties in Western Democracies*. New Brunswick, NJ: Transaction Books.

Ersson, S., Janda, K. and Lane, J.E. (1982) 'The Logic of Political Ecology Analysis', in Anckar, D. et al. (eds) *Partier, Ideologier, Väljare: En Antologi*. Åbo: Åbo Akademi, pp. 211–63.

Esman, M.J. (ed.) (1977) *Ethnic Conflict in the Western World*. Ithaca, NY: Cornell University Press.

Euro-Barometer 5 and 6 (1978) Ann Arbor: ICPSR.

Eurostat (1979) *Regional Statistics: Main Regional Indicators 1970–1977*. Luxembourg: Eurostat.

European Values Survey (1982) *Codebook*. Colchester: ESRC.

Evans, P., Rueschmeyer, D. and Skocpol, T. (eds) (1985) *Bringing the State Back In*. Cambridge: Cambridge University Press.

Farneti, P. (1985) *The Italian Party System*. London: Frances Pinter.

Featherstone, K. (1990a) 'The "Party-State" in Greece and the Fall of Papandreou.' *West European Politics*, vol.13, pp. 101–15.

Featherstone, K. (1990b) 'Political Parties and Democratic Consolidation in Greece', in Pridham, G. (ed.) *Securing Democracy*, pp. 179–202.

Featherstone, K. and Katsoudas, D.K. (eds) (1987) *Political Change in Greece: Before and After the Colonels*. London: Croom Helm.

Feierabend, I.K. and Feierabend, R.L. (1971) 'Aggressive Behaviors within Polities, 1948–1962: A Cross-national Study', in Gillespie, J.V. and Nesvold, B.A. (eds), pp. 141–66.

Fernandez Stock, M.J. (1988) 'El Centrismo Politico y los Partidos del Poder en Portugal.' *Revista de Estudios Politicos*, 60–61, pp. 139–92.

Fevolden, T. and Sörensen, R. (1987) 'Norway', in Page, E.C. and Goldsmith, M.J. (eds) *Central and Local Government Relations*. London: Sage Publications, pp. 29–45.

Franca, L. de (1980) *Comportamento Religioso de Populacao Portugesa*. Lisboa: Moraes.

Frears, J. (1988) 'Liberalism in France', in Kirchner, E.J. (ed.) *Liberal Parties in Western Europe*. Cambridge: Cambridge University Press, pp. 124–50.

Finer, S.E. (1970) *Comparative Government*. London: Allen Lane.

Fischer, H. (ed.) (1982) *Das Politische System Österreichs*. 3rd ed. Wien: Europa Verlag.

Fitzmaurice, J. (1980) 'Reflections on the European elections'. *West European Politics*, 3, 230–41.

Fitzmaurice, J. (1981) *Politics in Denmark*. London: Hurst.

Fitzmaurice, J. (1983) *The Politics of Belgium: Crisis and Compromise in a Plural Society*. London: Hurst.

Flanagan, S.C. (1973) 'Models and Methods of Analysis', in Almond, G.A. et al. (eds) *Crisis, Choice and Change: Historical Studies of Political Development*. Boston: Little, Brown and Company, pp. 43–102.

Flanz, G. (1974) 'Federal Republic of Germany', in Blaustein, A. and Flanz, G. (eds), Vol. VI.

Fogarty, M.P. (1957) *Christian Democracy in Western Europe, 1820–1953*. London: Routledge and Kegan Paul.

Frank, A.G. (1967) *Capitalism and Underdevelopment in Latin America: Historical Studies of Chile and Brazil*. New York: Monthly Review Press.

Friedrich, C. (1963) *Man and His Government: An Empirical Theory of Politics*. New York: McGraw-Hill.

Frognier, A.-P. (1975) 'Vote, Classe Sociale et Religion/Pratique Religieuse.' *Res Publica*, 17, pp. 479–90.

Galbraith, J.K. (1958) *The Affluent Society*. Boston: Houghton.

Galbraith, J.K. (1967) *The New Industrial State*. Harmondsworth: Pelican.

Gallagher, M. (1975) *Electoral Support for Irish Political Parties 1927–1973*. London: Sage.

Gallagher, M. (1985) *Political Parties in the Republic of Ireland*. Manchester: Manchester University Press.

Gallagher, T. (1982) *Portugal: A Twentieth-century Interpretation*. Manchester: Manchester University Press.

Gallagher, T. (1988) 'Goodbye to Revolution: The Portuguese Election of July 1987.' *West European Politics*, 11, pp. 139–45.

Galtung, J. (1971) 'A Structural Theory of Imperialism.' *Journal of Peace Research*, 8, pp. 81–117.

Gastil, R. (ed.) (1979) *Freedom in the World: Political Rights and Civil Liberties 1978.* Boston: G.K. Hall and Co.

Gastil, R.D. (1987) *Freedom in the World: Political Rights and Civil Liberties 1986–1987.* New York: Greenwood Press.

Geertz, C. (ed.) (1963) *Old Societies and New States: The Quest for Modernity in Asia and Africa.* New York: Free Press.

Gerlich, P. (1981) 'Government Structure: The Principles of Government', in Steiner, K. (ed.), pp. 209–21

Gerlich, P. (1987) 'Consociationalism to Competition: The Austrian Party System since 1945', in Daalder, H. (ed.) *Party Systems in Denmark, Austria, Switzerland, The Netherlands and Belgium.* London: Frances Pinter, pp. 61–106.

Ghini, C. (1982) 'Gli Iscritti al Partito e alla FGCI: 1943–1979' in Ilardia, M. and Accornero, A. (eds) *Il Partito Communista Italiano: Struttura e Storia dell'Organizzazione 1921/1979.* Milano: Feltrinelli, pp. 227–92.

Gidengil, E.L. (1978) 'Centres and Peripheries: An Empirical Test of Galtung's Theory of Imperialism.' *Journal of Peace Research,* 15, pp. 51–66.

Gillespie, J.V. and Nesvold, B.A. (eds) (1971) *Macro-quantitative Analysis: Conflict Development, and Democratization.* Beverly Hills: Sage.

Gillespie, R. (1990) 'Regime Consolidation in Spain: Party, State and Society' in Pridham, G. (ed.) *Securing Democracy,* pp. 126–46.

Gladdish, K. (1990) 'Portugal: An Open Verdict', in Pridham, G. (ed.) *Securing Democracy,* pp. 104–25

Goldsmith, M.J. and Page, E.C. (1987) 'Britain', in Page, E.C. and Goldsmith, M.J. (eds) *Central and Local Government Relations.* London: Sage Publications, pp. 68–87.

Goldthorpe, J.H. et al. (1969) *The Affluent Worker in the Class Structure.* London: Cambridge University Press.

Gollwitzer, H. (ed.) (1977) *Europäische Bauernparteien im 20. Jahrhundert.* Stuttgart: Gustav Fischer Verlag.

Gourevitch, P.A. (1979) 'The Reemergence of "Peripheral Nationalisms": Some Comparative Speculations on the Spatial Distribution of Political Leadership and Economic Growth.' *Comparative Studies in Society and History,* 21, pp. 303–22.

Gourevitch, P.A. (1981) *Paris and the Provinces: The Politics of Local Government Reform in France.* London: Allen and Unwin.

Graham, L.S. and Makler, H.M. (eds) (1979) *Contemporary Portugal: The Revolution and Its Consequences.* Austin: The University of Texas Press.

Graham, L.S. and Wheeler, R. (eds) (1983) *In Search of Modern Portugal: The Revolution and Its Consequences.* Madison: The University of Wisconsin Press.

Graham, R. (1983) *Spain: Change of a Nation.* London: Michael Joseph.

Grant, W. (1990) 'Government-industry Relations' in Urwin, D.A. and Paterson, W.E. (eds). London: Longman, pp. 59–84.

Gross, D.A. and Sigelman, L. (1984) 'Comparing Party Systems: A Multidimensional Approach.' *Comparative Politics,* 16, pp. 463–79.

Gruner, E. (1969) *Die Parteien in der Schweiz.* Bern: Francke.

Gunther, R. et al. (1986) *Spain after Franco: The Making of a Competitive Party System.* Berkeley: University of California Press.

Gurr, T.R. (1972) *Politimetrics: An Introduction to Quantitative Macropolitics.* Englewood Cliffs, NJ: Prentice-Hall.

Gurr, T.R. (1974a) 'The Neo-Alexandrians: A Review Essay on Data Handbooks in Political Science.' *American Political Science Review,* 68, pp. 243–52.

Gurr, T.R. (1974b) 'Persistence and Change in Political Systems, 1800–1971.' *American Political Science Review*, 68, pp. 1482–1504.

Haarman, H. (1975) *Soziologie und Politik der Sprachen*. München: dtv.

Hall, A.D. and Fagen, R.E (1956) 'Definition of System.' *General Systems*, 1, pp. 18–28.

Halpern, S.M. (1986) 'The Disorderly Universe of Consociational Democracy.' *West European Politics*, 9, pp. 181–97.

Hammond, J.L. (1979) 'New Approaches to Aggregate Electoral Data.' *Journal of Interdisciplinary History*, 9, pp. 473–92.

Hand, G. et al. (1979) *European Electoral Systems Handbook*. London: Butterworth.

Hanf, K. and Scharpf, F.W. (eds) (1978) *Interorganizational Policy Making: Limits to Coordination and Central Control*. London: Sage.

Hansen, T. (1981) 'Transforming Needs into Expenditures', in Newton, K. (ed.) *Urban Political Economy*. London: Pinter, pp. 27–47.

Hargens, L. (1976) 'A Note on Standardized Coefficients as Structural Parameters.' *Sociological Methods and Research*, 5, pp. 247–56.

Harmel, R. and Janda, K. (1982) *Parties and Their Environments: Limits to Reform?* New York: Longman.

Harrop, M. and Miller, W.L. (1987) *Elections and Voters: A Comparative Introduction*. London: Macmillan.

Hartmann, J. (1984) *Politische Profile der westeuropäischen Industriegesellschaft: Ein vergleichendes Handbuch*. Frankfurt am Main: Campus.

Haue, H. et al. (1981) *Det ny Danmark 1890–1980: udviklingslinier og tendens*. Koebenhavn: Munksgaard.

Håstad, E. et al. (1950) *'Gallup' och den svenska väljarkåren: några studier om opinionsmätningar*. Stockholm: Gebers.

Heald, D. (1988) 'The United Kingdom: Privatisation and its Political Context.' *West European Politics*, 11, pp. 31–48.

Heath, A. et al. (1985) *How Britain Votes*. Oxford: Pergamon Press.

Hebbert, M. and Machin, H. (eds) (1984) *Regionalisation in France, Italy and Spain*. London: London School of Economics.

Hechter, M. (1971) 'Towards a Theory of Ethnic Change.' *Politics and Society*, 2, pp. 21–45.

Hechter, M. (1975) *Internal Colonialism: The Celtic Fringe in British National Development, 1536–1966*. London: Routledge and Kegan Paul.

Heckscher, G. (1957) *The Study of Comparative Government and Politics*. London: Allen and Unwin.

Heidar, K. (1983) *Norske Politiske Fakta 1884–1982*. Oslo: Universitetsforlaget.

Heidenheimer, A.J., Heclo, H. and Adams, C.J. (1983) *Comparative Public Policy: The Politics of Social Choice in Europe and America*. London: Macmillan.

Helander, V. and Anckar, D. (1983) *Consultation and Political Culture: Essays on the Case of Finland*. Helsinki: Societas Scientiarum Fennica.

Héraud, G. (1974) *L'Europe des ethnies*. Paris: Presses d'Europe.

Hernes, G. (ed.) (1978) *Forhandlingsoekonomi og blandningsadminstrasjon*. Oslo: Universitetsforlaget.

Hermet, G., Rose, R. and Rouguié, A. (1978) *Elections without Choice*. London: Macmillan.

Hewitt, C. (1977) 'The Effect of Political Democracy and Social Democracy on Equality in Industrial Societies: A Cross-national Comparison.' *American Sociological Review*, 42, pp. 450–64.

Hibbs, D.A. and Fassbender, H. (eds) (1981) *Contemporary Political Economy*. Amsterdam: North-Holland.

Hicks, A. et al. (1989) 'Welfare Expansion Revisited: Policy Routines and Their Mediation by Party, Class and Crisis, 1957–1982.' *European Journal of Political Research*, 17, pp. 401–30.

Hidén, M. and Saraviita, I. (1978) *Statsförfattningsrätten i huvuddrag*. Helsingfors: Finlands Juristförbunds Förlags AB.

Highet, J. (1972) 'Scotland' in Mol, H. (ed.), pp. 249–69.

Hill, K. (1974) 'Belgium: Political Change in a Segmented Society', in Rose, R. (ed.), pp. 29–107.

Hine, D. (1977) 'Social Democracy in Italy', in Paterson, W.E. and Thomas, A.H. (eds) *Social Democratic Parties in Western Europe*. London: Croom Helm, pp. 25–66.

Hine, D. (1990) 'The Consolidation of Democracy in Post-war Italy', in Pridham, G. (ed.) *Securing Democracy*, pp. 62 83.

Hobsbawm, E. (1964) *Labouring Men*. London: Weidenfeld and Nicolson.

Hobsbawm, E. (1977) 'Some Reflections on "The Break-up of Britain".' *New Left Review*, no. 105, pp. 3–23.

Hofferbert, R.I. (1968) 'Socioeconomic Dimensions of the American States: 1890–1960.' *Midwest Journal of Political Science*, 12, pp. 401–18.

Hogwood, B. and Peters, B.G. (1983) *Policy Dynamics*. Brighton: Wheatsheaf Books.

Holmberg, S. (1981) *Svenska väljare*. Stockholm: Liber.

Holmberg, S. (1984) *Väljare i förändring*. Stockholm: Liber.

Holmberg, S. and Gilljam, M. (1987) *Väljare och Val i Sverige*. Stockholm: Bonniers.

Humana, C. (1983) *World Human Rights Guide*. London: Hutchinson.

Humes, S. and Martin, E. (1969) *The Structure of Local Government*. The Hague: International Union of Local Governments.

Humphreys, P. and Steed, M. (1988) 'Identifying Liberal Parties', in Kirchner, E.J. (ed.) *Liberal Parties in Western Europe*. Cambridge: Cambridge University Press, pp. 396–435.

Huntington, S. and Dominguez, J.I. (1975) 'Political Development', in Greenstein, F.I. and Polsby, N.W. (eds) *Handbook of Political Science*. Volume 3: Macropolitical Theory. Reading, MA: Addison-Wesley, pp. 1–114.

Hurwitz, L. (1971) 'An Index of Democratic Political Stability: A Methodological Note.' *Comparative Political Studies*, 4, pp. 41–68.

Hurwitz, L. (1973) 'Contemporary Approaches to Political Stability.' *Comparative Politics*, 5, pp. 449–63.

ILO, *Yearbook of Labour Statistics*. Geneva: ILO.

Inglehart, R. (1977) *The Silent Revolution: Changing Values and Political Styles among Western Publics*. Princeton: Princeton: Princeton University Press.

Inglehart, R. (1988a) 'The Renaissance of Political Culture.' *American Political Science Review*, 82, pp. 1203–30.

Inglehart, R. (1988b) 'Politische Kultur und stabile Demokratie.' *Politische Viertalsjahrschrift*, 29, pp. 369–87.

Inglehart, R. and Klingemann, H.D. (1976) 'Party Identification, Ideological Preference and the Left-right Dimension among Western Mass Publics', in Budge, I. et al. (eds) *Party Identification and Beyond*. London: Wiley, pp. 243–73.

Inglehart, R. and Sidjanski, D. (1975) 'Electeurs et Dimension Gauche-Droite' in Sidjanski, D. et al. *Les Suisses et la Politique: Enquète sur les Attitudes d'Électeurs Suisses* (1972). Berne: Lang, pp. 83–124.

Irving, R.E.M. (1979) *The Christian Democratic Parties of Western Europe*. London: Allen and Unwin.

Irwin, G.A. and van Holsteyn, J.J.M. (1989) 'Towards a More Open Model of Competition.' *West European Politics*, 12, pp. 112–38.

Isambert, F. and Terrenoire, J. (1980) *Atlas de la pratique religieuse des catholiques en France*. Paris: Presses de la Fondation Nationale des Sciences Politiques.

Jackman, R.W. (1975) *Politics and Social Equality: A Comparative Analysis*. New York: Wiley.

Jackman, R.W. (1985) 'Cross-national Statistical Research and the Study of Comparative Politics.' *American Journal of Political Science*, 29, pp. 161–82.

Jain, S. (1975) *Size Distribution of Income: A Compilation of Data*. Washington, DC: World Bank.

Janda, K. (1980) *Political Parties: A Cross-National Survey*. New York: Free Press.

Janda, K. (1989) 'Regional and Religious Support of Political Parties and Effects on their Issue Positions.' *International Political Science Review*, 10, 249–70.

Janda, K. and Gillies, R. (1983) 'How Well Does "Region" Explain Political Party Characteristics?' *Political Geography Quarterly*, 2, pp. 179–203.

Janin, B. (1975) 'Le val d'Aoste.' *Annales de géographie*, 84, pp. 78–86.

Janowitz, M. (1968) 'Political Sociology', in Sills, D.L. (ed.), Vol. 12, pp. 298–307.

Janson, C.-G. (1969) 'Some Problems of Ecological Factor Analysis' in Dogan and Rokkan (eds), pp. 301–41.

Jennings, I. (1951) *Cabinet Government*. Cambridge: Cambridge University Press.

Jennings, I. (1961) *Parliament*. Cambridge: Cambridge University Press.

Jodice, D.A. and Taylor, C.L. (1981) *Codebook Political Protest and Government Change, 1948–1977: The Third World Handbook of Political and Social Indicators*. Berlin: International Institute for Comparative Social Research (mimeo).

Johnson, N. (1983) *State and Government in the Federal Republic of Germany*. Oxford: Pergamon Press.

Katzenstein, P.J. (1977) 'Ethnic Conflict in South Tyrol', in Esman, M.J. (ed.), pp. 287–323.

Kellas, J.G. (1975) *The Scottish Political System*. 2nd ed. Cambridge: Cambridge University Press.

Kerr, H.K. (1974) *Switzerland: Social Cleavages and Partisan Conflict*. London: Sage.

Kerr, H.H. (1987) 'The Swiss Party System: Steadfast and Changing' in Daalder, H. (ed.) (1987a) *Party Systems in Denmark, Austria, Switzerland, The Netherlands and Belgium*. London: Frances Pinter, pp. 107–92.

Key, V.O. (1966) *The Responsible Electorate*. Cambridge, MA: Belknap Press.

Kirchheimer, O. (1966) 'The Transformation of the Western European Party Systems', in Lapalombara, J. and Weiner, M. (eds), pp. 177–200.

Kirchner, E.J. (ed.) (1988) *Liberal Parties in Western Europe*. Cambridge: Cambridge University Press.

Kjellberg, A. (1983) *Facklig organisering i tolv länder*. Lund: Arkiv.

Klockare, S. (1971) *Från generalstrejk till folkfront: söndring och samling i Kekkonens tid*. Stockholm: Prisma.

Knapp, A.F. (1985) 'Orderly Retreat: Mitterand Chooses PR.' *Electoral Studies*, 4, pp. 255–60.

Knutsen, O. (1989) 'Cleavage Dimensions in 10 West European Countries: A Comparative Empirical Analysis.' *Comparative Political Studies*, 21, pp. 495–534.

Kohler, B. (1982) *Political Forces in Spain, Greece, and Portugal*. London: Butterworth.

Kolinsky, E. (ed.) (1987) *Opposition in Western Europe*. London: Croom Helm.

Korpi, W. (1978) *The Working Class in Welfare Capitalism: Work, Unions and Politics in Sweden*. London: Routledge and Kegan Paul.

Korpi, W. (1983) *The Democratic Class Struggle*. London: Routledge and Kegan Paul.

Korpi, W. (1989) 'Power, Politics, and State Autonomy in the Development of Social Citizenship: Social Rights during Sickness in Eighteen OECD countries since 1930.' *American Sociological Review*, 54, pp. 309–28.

Kousoulas, G. (1974) *Modern Greece: Profile of a Nation*. New York: Scribners.

Krejci, J. and Velimsky, V. (1981) *Ethnic and Political Nations in Europe*. London: Croom Helm.

Kreuzer, M. (1990) 'New Politics: Just Post-Materialist? The Case of the Austrian and Swiss Greens', *West European Politics*, 12, pp. 12–30.

Kruijt, J.P. (1974) 'The Netherlands: The Influence of Denominationalism on Social Life and Organizational Patterns', in McRae, K. (ed.), pp. 128–36.

Kurian, G.T. (ed.) (1979) *The Book of World Rankings*. New York: Facts on File.

Kvistad, G.O. (1987) 'Between Party and State: Green Political Ideology in the Mid-1980s', *West European Politics*, 10, pp. 211–28.

Laakso, M. and Taagepera, R. (1979) 'Effective Number of Parties: A Measure with Application to West Europe.' *Comparative Political Studies*, 12, pp. 3–27.

Lakeman, E. (1974) *How Democracies Vote: A Study of Electoral Systems*. London: Faber.

Lancaster, T.D. and Prévost, G. (eds) (1985) *Politics and Change in Spain*. New York: Praeger.

Lane, J.-E. and Magnusson, T. (1987) 'Sweden', in Page, E.C. and Goldsmith, M.J. (eds) *Central and Local Government Relations*. London: Sage Publications, pp. 12–28.

Lane, R.E. (1965) *Political Life: Why and How People Get Involved in Politics*. New York: Free Press.

Langholm, S. (1971) 'On the Concepts of Center and Periphery.' *Journal of Peace Research*, 8, pp. 273–8.

LaPalombara, J. (1987) *Democracy, Italian Style*. New Haven: Yale University Press.

LaPalombara, J. and Weiner, M. (eds) (1966a) *Political Parties and Political Development*. Princeton: Princeton University Press.

LaPalombara, J. and Weiner, M. (1966b) 'The Origin and Development of Political Parties', in LaPalombara, J. and Weiner, M. (eds), pp. 3–42.

Larkey, P.D., Stolp, C. and Winer, M. (1981) 'Theorizing About the Growth of Government in Sweden: A Research Assessment.' *Journal of Public Policy*, 1, pp. 157–220.

Laver, M. et al. (eds) (1987) *How Ireland Voted: The Irish General Election 1987*. Dublin: Poolbeg.

Lawson, K. and Merkl, P.M. (eds) (1988) *When Parties Fail: Emerging Alternative Organizations*. Princeton: Princeton University Press.

Layton-Henry, Z. (ed.) (1982) *Conservative Politics in Western Europe*. London: Macmillan.

Layton-Henry, Z. (1988) 'The Political Challenge of Migration for West European States.' *European Journal of Political Research*, 16, pp. 587–95.

Layton-Henry, Z. (1990) 'Race and Immigration', in Urwin, D.A. and Paterson, W.E. (eds), pp. 162–81.

Lecaillon, J. et al. (1984) *Income Distribution and Economic Development: An Analytical Survey*. Geneva: ILO.

Legg, K. (1969) *Politics in Modern Greece*. Stanford: Stanford University Press.

Lehmbruch, G. (1967) *Proporzdemokratie: Politisches System und Politische Kultur in der Schweiz und in Österreich*. Tübingen: Mohr.

Lehmbruch, G. (1979) 'Liberal Corporatism and Party Government', in Schmitter and Lehmbruch (eds), pp. 147–83.

Lehmbruch, G (1982) 'Introduction: Neo-corporatism in Comparative Perspective', in Lehmbruch and Schmitter (eds), pp. 1–28.

Lehmbruch, G. and Schmitter, P. (eds) (1982) *Patterns of Corporatist Policy-making*. London: Sage.

Lehner, F. (1983) 'Pressure Politics and Economic Growth: Olson's Theory and the Swiss Experience', in Mueller, D.C. (ed.), pp. 203–14.

Lenski, G. (1963) *The Religious Factor: A Sociological Study of Religion's Impact on Politics, Economics and Family Life*. Garden City, NY: Doubleday.

Lenski, G. (1966) *Power and Privilege: A Theory of Social Stratification*. New York: McGraw-Hill.

Lepszy, N. (1979) *Regierung, Parteien und Gewerkschaften in den Niederlanden: Entwicklung und Strukturen*. Düsseldorf: Droste.

Lerner, D. (1968) 'Modernization: Social Aspects', in Sills, D.L. (ed.), Vol. 14, pp. 489–95.

Le Roy Laduaire, E. (1977) 'Occitania in Historical Perspective.' *Review*, 1, pp. 21–30.

Levy, M.J. (1952) *The Structure of Society*. Princeton: Princeton University Press.

Lewin, L. (1970) *Folket och éliterna: en studie i modern demokratisk teori*. Stockholm: Rabén and Sjögren.

Lewin, L. (1980) *Governing Trade Unions in Sweden*. Cambridge, MA: Harvard University Press.

Lewin, L. (1984) *Ideologi och strategi: svensk politik under 100 år*. Stockholm: Norstedt.

Lichbach, M.I. (1982) 'Governability in Interwar Europe: A Formal Model of Authority and Performance.' *Quality and Quantity*, 16, pp. 197–216.

Liebert, U. (1990) 'From Polarization to Pluralism: Regionalist-nationalist Parties in the Process of democratic consolidation in Post-Franco Spain', in Pridham, G. (ed.) *Securing Democracy*, pp. 147–78.

Lijphart, A. (1968) 'Typologies of Democratic Systems.' *Comparative Political Studies*, 1, pp. 3–44.

Lijphart, A. (1971) 'Class Voting and Religious Voting in the European Democracies: A Preliminary Report.' *Acta Politica*, 6, pp. 158–71.

Lijphart, A. (1974a) 'Consociational Democracy', in McRae, K. (ed.), pp. 70–89.

Lijphart, A. (1974b) 'The Netherlands: Continuity and Change in Voting Behavior', in Rose, R. (ed.), pp. 227–68.

Lijphart, A. (1975) *The Politics of Accommodation: Pluralism and Democracy in the Netherlands*. 2nd ed. Berkeley: University of California Press.

Lijphart, A. (1977a) *Democracy in Plural Societies: A Comparative Exploration*. New Haven: Yale University Press.

Lijphart, A. (1977b) 'Political Theories and the Explanation of Ethnic Conflict in the Western World: Falsified Predictions and Plausible Postdictions', in Esman, M.J. (ed.), pp. 46–64.

Lijphart, A. (1979) 'Consociation and Federation: Conceptual and Empirical Links.' *Canadian Journal of Political Science*, 12, pp. 499–515.

Lijphart, A. (1981) 'Political Parties: Ideologies and Programs', in Butler, D. et al. (eds) *Democracy at the Polls: A Comparative Study of Competitive National Elections*. Washington, DC: American Enterprise Institute. pp. 26–51.

Lijphart, A. (1984a) *Democracies: Patterns of Majoritarian and Consensus Government in Twenty-one Countries*. New Haven: Yale University Press.

Lijphart, A. (1984b) 'Measures of Cabinet Durability: A Conceptual and Empirical Evaluation.' *Comparative Political Studies*, 17, pp. 265–79.

Lijphart, A. (1985) 'The Field of Electoral Systems Research: A Critical Survey.' *Electoral Studies*, 4, pp. 3–14.

Lijphart, A. (1989) 'From The Politics of Accommodation to Adversarial Politics in the Netherlands: A Reassessment.' *West European Politics*, 12, pp. 139–54.

Lijphart, A., Bruneau, T.C., Diamandouros, P.K. and Gunther, R. (1988) 'A Mediterranean Model of Democracy? The Southern European Democracies in Comparative Perspective.' *West European Politics*, 11, pp. 7–25.

Linz, J.J. (1976) 'Patterns of Land Tenure, Division of Labor, and Voting Behavior in Europe.' *Comparative Politics*, 8, pp. 365–430.

Linz, J.J. (1979) 'Some Notes Toward a Comparative Study of Fascism in Sociological Historical Perspective', in Laqueur, W. (ed.), *Fascism: A Reader's Guide.* Harmondsworth: Penguin, pp. 13–78.

Linz, J.J. (1980) 'Religion and Politics in Spain: From Conflict to Consensus above Cleavage.' *Social Compass*, 27, pp. 255–77.

Lipset, S.M. (1959) *Political Man*. Garden City, NY: Doubleday.

Lipset, S.M. (1964) 'The Changing Class Structure and Contemporary European Politics.' *Daedalus*, 93, pp. 271–303.

Lipset, S.M. and Rokkan, S. (1967a) 'Cleavage Structures, Party Systems, and Voter Alignments: An Introduction', in Lipset, S.M. and Rokkan, S. (eds), pp. 1–64.

Lipset, S.M. and Rokkan, S. (eds) (1967b) *Party Systems and Voter Alignments: Cross-national Perspectives*. New York: Free Press.

Lively, J. (1975) *Democracy*. Oxford: Blackwell.

Lobo da Conceiçao, M.M. (1975) *Consideracoes sobre o projeto 'Reparticao regional do prodoto: essaio para 1970'*. Lisboa: Instituto nacional de estatisica.

Lodge, J. (1990) 'European Community Decision-making: Towards the Single Common Market", in Urwin, D.W. and Paterson, W.E. (eds).

Loewenberg, G. (1971) 'The Influence of Parliamentary Behavior on Regime Stability: Some Conceptual Clarifications.' *Comparative Politics*, 3, pp. 177–200.

Logan, J.R. (1977) 'Affluence, Class Structure and Working-class Consciousness in Modern Spain.' *American Journal of Sociology*, 83, pp. 386–402.

Lorwin, V.R. (1971) 'Segmented Pluralism: Ideological Cleavages and Political Cohesion in the Smaller European Democracies.' *Comparative Politics*, 3, pp. 141–75.

Lorwin, V.R. (1974) 'Belgium: Conflict and Compromise', in McRae, K. (ed.), pp. 179–206.

Lovenduski, J. (1990) 'Feminism and West European Politics: An Overview', in Urwin, D.A. and Paterson, W.E. (eds), pp. 206–26.

Lowell, A.L. (1896) *Governments and Parties in Continental Europe*. Cambridge, MA: Harvard University Press.

Luebbert, G.M. (1984) 'A Theory of Government Formation.' *Comparative Political Studies*, 17, pp. 229–64.

Lustick, I. (1979) 'Stability in Deeply Divided Societies: Consociationalism versus Control.' *World Politics*, 31, pp. 325–44.

Lybeck, J.A. (1985) 'Is the Lipset-Rokkan Hypothesis Testable?' *Scandinavian Political Studies*, 8, pp. 105–13.

Lybeck, J.A. and Henrekson, M. (eds) (1988) *Explaining the Growth of Government*. Amsterdam: North-Holland.

MacIver, R. (1947) *The Web of Government*. London: Macmillan.

Mackie, T.T. and Hogwood, B.W. (eds) (1985) *Unlocking the Cabinet: Cabinet Structures in Comparative Perspective.* London: Sage.

Mackie, T. and Rose, R. (1982) *The International Almanac of Electoral History.* 2nd ed. London: Macmillan.

MacMullen, A.L. (1979) 'Belgium', in Ridley, F.F. (ed.), pp. 204–26.

MacRae, D. Jr. (1967) *Parliament, Parties and Society in France 1946–1958.* New York: St Martin's Press.

Macridis, R.C. (1955) *The Study of Comparative Government.* New York: Random House.

Maddison, A. (1964) *Economic Growth in the West: Experience in Europe and North America.* New York: Twentieth Century Fund.

Madsen, E.S. and Paldam, M. (1978) *Economic and Political Data for the OECD Countries 1948–1975.* Aarhus University: Institute of Economics.

Madsen, H.J. (1978) 'POETICS: A Political Economic Time-series Cross-section System of Data: 1920–75.' Aarhus: Department of Political Science.

Maguire, M. (1983) 'Is There Still Persistence? Electoral Change in Western Europe, 1948–1979', in Daalder, H. and Mair, P. (eds), pp. 67–94.

Mair, P. (1987) *The Changing Irish Party System: Organisation, Ideology and Electoral Competition.* London: Frances Pinter.

Mair, P. (1989) 'Ireland: From Predominance to Moderate Pluralism and Back Again?' *West European Politics*, 12, pp. 129–42.

Mair, P. and Smith, G. (eds) (1989) *Understanding Party System Change in Western Europe. West European Politics*, 12, no. 4.

Mann, M. (1973) *Consciousness and Action among the Western Working Class.* London: Macmillan.

Maravall, J. (1982) *The Transition to Democracy in Spain.* London: Croom Helm.

March, J.G. and Olsen, J.P. (1984) 'The New Institutionalism: Organizational Factors in Political Life.' *American Political Science Review*, 78, pp. 734–49.

March, J.G. and Olsen, J.P. (1989) *Rediscovering Institutions. The Organizational Basis of Politics.* New York: The Free Press.

Marradi, A. (1981) 'Factor Analysis as an Aid in the Formation and Refinement of Empirically Useful Concepts', in Jackson, D.J. and Borgatta, E.F. (eds) *Factor Analysis and Measurement in Sociological Research.* London: Sage, pp. 11–49.

Martin, D. (1972) 'England', in Mol, H. (ed.), pp. 229–47.

Martin, D. (1978) 'The Religious Condition of Europe', in Giner, S. and Archer, M.S. (eds) *Contemporary Europe: Social Structure and Cultural Patterns.* London: Routledge and Kegan Paul, pp. 228–87.

Martin, J.D. and Gray, L.N. (1971) 'Measurement of Relative Variation: Sociological Examples.' *American Sociological Review*, 36, pp. 496–502.

Matheson, D.K. (1979) *Ideology, Political Action and the Finnish Working Class: A Survey Study of Political Behavior.* Helsinki: Societas Scientiarium Fennica.

Matzner, E. (1982) 'Sozialpartnerschaft', in Fischer, H. (ed.), pp. 429–51.

Mavrogordatos, G. (1983) *Stillborn Republic: Social Coalitions and Party Strategies in Greece, 1922–1936.* Berkeley: The University of California Press.

Mayer, L.C. (1980) 'A Note on the Aggregation of Party Systems', in Merkl, P. (ed.) *Western European Party Systems: Trends and Prospects.* New York: Free Press, pp. 515–20.

Mayer, N. and Perrineau, P. (eds) (1989) *Le Front National a Decouvert.* Paris: Presses de la F.N.S.P.

McGranahan, D. (1971) 'Analysis of Socio-economic Development through a System of Indicators.' *Annals of the American Academy of Political and Social Science*, 393, pp. 65–81.

McHale, V.E. (ed.) (1983) *Political Parties of Europe*. Westport, Conn.: Greenwood Press.

McKenzie, N. (1977) 'Center and Periphery: The Marriage of Two Minds.' *Acta Sociologica*, 20, pp. 55–74

McRae, K.D. (ed.) (1974) *Consociational Democracy: Political Accommodation in Segmented Societies*. Toronto: McClelland and Stewart.

McRae, K.D. (1983) *Conflict and Compromise in Multilingual Societies: Switzerland*. Waterloo: Wilfrid Laurier University Press.

Meadwell, H. (1989) 'Ethnic Nationalism and Collective Choice Theory.' *Comparative Political Studies*, 22, pp. 139–54.

Mellors, C. and Pijnenburg, B. (eds) (1989) *Political Parties and Coalitions in European Local Government*. London: Routledge.

Mény, Y. (1987) 'France', in Page, E.C. and Goldsmith, M.J. (eds) *Central and Local Government Relations*. Sage Publications, pp. 88–106.

Merkl, P.M. (1970) *Modern Comparative Politics*. New York: Holt, Rinehart and Winston.

Michelat, G. and Simon, M. (1971) 'Classe sociale objective, classe sociale subjective et comportement électoral.' *Revue française de sociologie*, 12, pp. 483–527.

Michelat, G. and Simon, M. (1977a) *Classe, religion et comportement politique*. Paris: Presses de la Fondation Nationale des Sciences politiques.

Michelat, G. and Simon, M. (1977b) 'Classe, religion, comportement politique.' *La Pensée*, no 192, pp. 71–92.

Mielke, S. (ed.) (1983) *Internationales Gewerkschaftshandbuch*. Opladen: Leske and Budrich.

Milbrath, L. (1965) *Political Participation: How and Why do People Get Involved in Politics?* Chicago: Rand McNally.

Miller, K. (1968) *Government and Politics in Denmark*. Boston: Houghton Mifflin.

Miller, W.E. and Stouthard, P.C. (1975) 'Confessional Attachment and Electoral Behaviour in the Netherlands.' *European Journal of Political Research, 3, pp. 219–58*.

Minkin, L. and Seyd, P. (1977) 'The British Labour Party', in Paterson, W.E. and Thomas, A.H. (eds) *Social Democratic Parties in Western Europe*. London: Croom Helm, pp. 101–52.

Mitchell, B.M. (1981) *European Historical Statistics 1750–1975*. 2nd ed. London: Macmillan.

Mitra, S.K. (1980) 'A Theory of Governmental Instability in Parliamentary Systems.' *Comparative Political Studies*, 13, pp. 235–63.

Mol, H. (ed.) (1972) *Western Religion: A Country by Country Sociological Inquiry*. The Hague: Mouton.

Morgan, D.R. and Lyons, W. (1975) 'Industrialization and Affluence Revisited: A Note on Socioeconomic Dimensions of the American States.' *American Journal of Political Science*, 19, pp. 263–76.

Morgan, R. and Silvestri, S. (eds) (1982) *Moderates and Conservatives in Western Europe: Political Parties, the European Community and the Atlantic Alliance*. London: Heinemann.

Morlino, L. (1984) 'The Changing Relationship Between Parties and Society in Italy.' *West European Politics*, 7, pp. 46–66.

Moulin, H. (1983) *The Strategy of Social Choice*. Amsterdam: North-Holland.

Mouzelis, N. and Attalides, M. (1971) 'Greece', in Archer, M.S. and Giner, S. (eds)

Contemporary Europe: Class, Status and Power. London: Weidenfeld and Nicolson, pp. 162–97.

Mueller, D.C. (ed.) (1983) *The Political Economy of Growth.* New Haven: Yale University Press.

Mughan, A. (1979) 'Modernization and Ethnic Conflict in Belgium.' *Political Studies*, 27, pp. 21–37.

Muller, E.N. (1985) 'Income Inequality, Regime Repressiveness, and Political Violence.' *American Sociological Review*, 50, pp. 47–61.

Muller, S.H. (1964) *The World's Living Languages: Basic Facts of their Structure, Kinship and Number of Speakers.* New York: Ungar.

Musgrave, R.A. and Jarrett, P. (1979) 'International Redistribution.' *Kyklos*, 32, pp. 541–58.

Musgrave, R.A. and Musgrave, P. (1980) *Public Finance in Theory and Practice.* New York: McGraw-Hill.

Müller-Rommel, F. (ed.) (1989) *New Politics in Western Europe.* Boulder: Westview Press.

Müller-Rommel, F. (1982) 'Ecology Parties in Western Europe.' *West European Politics*, 5, no. 1, pp. 68–72.

Müller-Rommel, F. (1985) 'The Green in Western Europe: Similar but Different.' *International Political Science Review*, 6. pp. 483–99.

Myrdal, G. (1957) *Economic Theory and Underdeveloped Regions.* London: Duckworth.

Myrdal, G. (1961) *Beyond the Welfare State.* London: Duckworth.

Naess, A. et al. (1956) *Democracy, Ideology and Objectivity: Studies in the Semantics and Cognitive Analysis of Ideological Controversy.* Oslo: Universitetsforlaget.

Nassmacher, K.H. (1968) *Das österreichische Regierungssystem: Grosse Koalition oder alternierende Regierung.* Köln: Westdeutscher Verlag.

Naustdalslid, J. (1977) 'A Multi-level Approach to the Study of Center–periphery Systems and Socio-economic Change.' *Journal of Peace Research*, 14, pp. 203–22.

Neumann, S. (ed.) (1956) *Modern Political Parties: Approaches to Comparative Politics.* Chicago: The University of Chicago Press.

Newland, R.A. (1982) *Comparative Electoral Systems.* London: McDougall Fund.

Nick, R. (1988) 'Die Bundesländer und das österreichische Parteiensystem' in Pelinka, A. and Plasser, F. (eds) *Das Österreichische Parteiensystem.* Wien: Böhlau, pp. 401–18.

Nick, R. and Pelinka, A. (1983) *Bürgerkrieg – Sozialpartnerschaft: Das politische System Österreichs 1. und 2. Republik: ein Vergleich.* Wien: Jugend und Volk.

Nicola, J. (1975) 'L'abstetionnisme en Suisse' in Sidjanski, D. et al. *Les Suisses et la Politique: Enquête sur les Attitudes d'Électeurs Suisses* (1972). Berne: Lang, pp. 187–210.

Nordlinger, E.A. (1972) *Conflict Regulation in Divided Societies.* Cambridge, MA: Harvard University.

Nousiainen, J. (1971) *The Finnish Political System.* Cambridge, MA: Harvard University Press.

O'Connor, J.S. (1988) 'Convergence or Divergence?: Change in Welfare Effort in OECD Countries 1960–1980.' *European Journal of Political Research*, 16, pp. 277–99.

O'Connor, J.S. and Brym, R.J. (1988) 'Public Welfare Expenditure in OECD Countries: Towards a Reconciliation of Inconsistent Findings.' *British Journal of Sociology*, 39, pp. 47–68.

O'Donnell, J.D. (1974) *How Ireland Is Governed.* 5th ed. Dublin: Institute of Public Administration.

OECD *OECD Observer.* Paris: OECD, quarterly.

OECD (1988) *Labour Force Statistics.* Paris: OECD.

OECD (1986) *Living Conditions in OECD Countries: A Compendium of Social Indicators.* Paris: OECD.

OECD (1985) *Measuring Health Care 1960–1983: Expenditure, Costs and Performance.* Paris: OECD.

OECD (various years) *National Accounts.* Paris: OECD.

OECD (various years) *Revenue Statistics.* Paris: OECD.

OECD (1985) *OECD Employment Outlook.* Paris: OECD.

OECD (1985) *Social Expenditure 1960–1990: Problems of Growth and Control.* Paris: OECD.

O'Leary, C (1979) *Irish Elections 1918–77: Parties, Voters and Proportional Representation.* Dublin: Gill and Macmillan.

Olsen, J.P. (1983) *Organized Democracy: Political Institutions in a Welfare State – the Case of Norway.* Bergen: Universitetsforlaget.

Olson, M. (1963) 'Rapid Growth as a Destabilizing Force.' *Journal of Economic History,* 23, pp. 529–52.

Ozbudun, E. (1970) *Party Cohesion in Western Democracies: A Causal Analysis.* Beverly Hills: Sage.

Page, E. and Goldsmith, M. (eds) (1987) *Central and Local Government Relations.* London: Sage.

Paloheimo, H. (1984) *Governments in Democratic Capitalist States 1950–1983: A Data Handbook.* University of Turku: Department of Sociology and Political Science.

Pampel, F.C. and Williamson, J.B. (1988) 'Welfare Spending in Advanced Industrial Democracies, 1950–1980.' *American Journal of Sociology,* 93, pp. 1424–56.

Papadopoulos, Y. (1989) 'Parties, the State and Society in Greece: Continuity within Change.' *West European Politics,* 12, pp. 55–71.

Park, T. (1973) 'Measuring the Dynamic Patterns of Development: The Case of Asia 1949–1968.' *Multivariate Behavioral Research,* 8, pp. 227–51.

Parry, R. (1990) 'The Viability of the Welfare State', in Urwin, D.A. and Paterson, W.E. (eds), pp. 12–32.

Parsons, T. (1951) *The Social System.* New York: Free Press.

Parsons, T. and Shils, E. (eds) (1951) *Towards a General Theory of Action.* Cambridge, MA: Harvard University Press.

Parsons, T. and Smelser, N. (1956) *Economy and Society.* London: Routledge and Kegan Paul.

Pasquino, G. (1990) 'Party Elites and Democratic Consolidation: Cross-national Comparison of Southern European Experience', in Pridham, G. (ed.) *Securing Democracy,* pp. 42–61.

Pateman, C. (1970) *Participation and Democratic Theory.* Cambridge: Cambridge University Press.

Paterson, W.E. (1990) 'Britain, France, West Germany and the Development of the European Community', in Urwin, D.W. and Paterson, W.E. (eds), pp. 184–205.

Paterson, W.E. and Thomas, A.H. (eds) (1977) *Social Democratic Parties in Western Europe.* London: Croom Helm.

Paterson, W.E. and Thomas, A.H. (eds) (1986) *The Future of Social Democracy: Problems and Prospects of Social Democratic Parties in Western Europe.* Oxford: Clarendon Press.

Paukert, F. (1973) 'Income Distribution at Different Levels of Development: A Survey of Evidence.' *International Labour Review,* 108, pp. 97–125.

Pedersen, M. (1979) 'The Dynamics of European Party Systems: Changing Patterns of Electoral Volatility.' *European Journal of Political Research*, 7, pp. 1–26.

Pedersen, M. (1980) 'On Measuring Party System Change: A Methodological Critique and a Suggestion.' *Comparative Political Studies*, 12, pp. 387–403.

Pedersen, M. (1982) 'Towards a New Typology of Party Lifespans and Minor Parties.' *Scandinavian Political Studies*, 5, pp. 1–16.

Pedersen, M. (1983) 'Changing Patterns of Electoral Volatility in European Party Systems, 1948–1977: Explorations in Explanation', in Daalder, H. and Mair, P. (eds), pp. 29–66.

Pedersen, M. (1987) 'The Danish "Working Multiparty System": Breakdown or Adaptation?', in Daalder, H. (ed.) *Party Systems in Denmark, Austria, Switzerland, The Netherlands and Belgium*. London: Frances Pinter, pp. 1–60.

Peillon, M. (1982) *Contemporary Irish Society: An Introduction*. Dublin: Gill and Macmillan.

Pelinka. A. (1980) *Sozialdemokratie in Europa: Macht ohne Grundsätze oder Grundsätze ohne Macht?* Wien: Herold.

Penniman, H. (ed.) (1977) *Italy at the Polls: The Parliamentary Elections of 1976*. Washington, DC: American Enterprise Institute.

Penniman, H. (ed.) (1978) *Ireland at the Polls: The Dáil Elections of 1977*. Washington, DC: American Enterprise Institute.

Penniman, H. (ed.) (1981) *Greece at the Polls: The National Elections of 1974 and 1977*. Washington, DC: American Enterprise Institute.

Pesonen, P. (1973) 'Dimensions of Political Cleavage in Multi-party Systems.' *European Journal of Political Research*, 1, pp. 109–32.

Pesonen, P. (1974) 'Finland: Party Support in a Fragmented System', in Rose, R. (ed.), pp. 271–314.

Peters, B.G. (1978) *The Politics of Bureaucracy*. New York: Longman.

Petersson, O. (1977) *Väljarna och valet 1976*. Stockholm: Statistiska centralbyrån.

Petersson, O. (1984) *Folkstyrelse och statsmakt i Norden*. Uppsala: Diskurs.

Pilat, J.F. (1980) *Ecological Politics: The Rise of the Green Movement*. Beverly Hills: Sage.

Plasser, F. and Ulram, P.A. (1988) 'Grossparteien in der Defensive: die Österreichische Parteien- und Wählerlandschaft nach der Nationalratswahl 1986' in Pelinka, A. and Plasser, F. (eds) (1988) *Das Österreichische Parteiensystem*. Wien: Böhlau, pp. 79–102.

Plenel, E. and Rollat, A. (1984) *L'effet Le Pen: dossier prèsenté et établi*. Paris: Editions la Découverte.

Polsby, N. (1963) *Community Power and Political Theory*. New Haven: Yale University Press.

Powell, G.B. (1970) *Social Fragmentation and Political Hostility: An Austrian Case Study*. Stanford: Stanford University Press.

Powell, G.B. (1980) 'Voting Turnout in Thirty Democracies: Partisan, Legal and Socio-economic Influences', in Rose, R. (ed.), pp. 5–34.

Powell, G.B. (1982) *Contemporary Democracies: Participation, Stability and Violence*. Cambridge, MA: Harvard University Press.

Power, J. (1978) *Western Europe's Migrant Workers*. London: Minority Rights Group.

Pride, R.A. (1970) *Origins of Democracy: A Cross-national Study of Mobilization, Party Systems and Democratic Stability*. Beverly Hills: Sage.

Pridham, G. (ed.) (1984) 'The New Mediterranean Democracies: Regime Transition in Spain, Greece and Portugal.' *West European Politics*, 7, no. 2.

Pridham, G. (ed.) (1986) *Coalitional Behaviour in Theory and Practice: An Inductive Model for Western Europe*. Cambridge: Cambridge University Press.

Pridham, G. (1988) 'Two Roads to Italian Liberalism: The Partito Repubblicano Italiano (PRI) and the Partito Liberale Italiano (PLI)', in Kirchner, E.J. (ed.) *Liberal Parties in Western Europe*. Cambridge: Cambridge University Press, pp. 29–61.

Pridham, G. (ed.) (1990) *Securing Democracy: Political Parties and Democratic Consolidation in Southern Europe*. London: Routledge.

Pryce, H. (ed.) (1987) *The Dynamics of European Union*. London: Croom Helm.

Przeworski, A. (1975) 'Institutionalization of Voting Patterns, or Is Mobilization the Source of Decay?' *American Political Science Review*, 69, pp. 49–67.

Przeworski, A. and Teune, H. (1970) *The Logic of Comparative Social Inquiry*. New York: Wiley.

Pulzer, P.J. (1974) 'Austria: The Legitimizing Role of Political Parties', in McRae, K.D. (ed.), pp. 151–78.

Querido, A. (1972) 'Portugal', in Mol, H. (ed.), pp. 427–36.

Rae, D. (1971) *The Political Consequences of Electoral Laws*. 2nd ed. New Haven: Yale University Press.

Rae, D.W. and Taylor, M. (1970) *The Analysis of Political Cleavages*. New Haven: Yale University Press.

Ragin, C.C. (1979) 'Ethnic Political Mobilization: The Welsh Case.' *American Sociological Review*, 44, pp. 619–35.

Rallings, C.S. and Andeweg, R.B. (1979) 'The Changing Class Structure and Political Behaviour: A Comparative Analysis of Lower Middle-class Politics in Britain and the Netherlands.' *European Journal of Political Research*, 7, pp. 27–47.

Raschke, J. (ed.) (1978) *Die politische Parteien in Westeuropa: Geschichte – Programm – Praxis: Ein Handbuch*. Hamburg: Rowohlt.

Rayside, D.M. (1977) 'Les relations des groupes linguistiques au Canada et en Belgique.' *Recherches sociologiques*, 8, pp. 95–131.

Rhodes, R.A.W. and Wright, V. (eds) (1987) 'Tensions in the Territorial Politics of Western Europe'. *West European Politics*, 10, no. 5.

Richardson, J.J. (ed.) (1982) *Policy Styles in Western Europe*. London: Allen and Unwin.

Richardson, J.J. and Jordan, A.G. (1979) *Governing under Pressure: The Policy Process in a Post-parliamentary Democracy*. Oxford: Martin Robertson.

Ridley, F.F. (1966) 'Chancellor Government as a Political System and the German Constitution.' *Parliamentary Affairs*, 19, pp. 446–61.

Ridley, F.F. (ed.) (1979) *Government and Administration in Western Europe*. London: Martin Robertson.

Ridley, F.F. (ed.) (1984) *Policies and Politics in Western Europe: The Impact of the Recession*. London: Croom Helm.

Riker, W.H. (1962) *The Theory of Political Coalitions*. New Haven: Yale University Press.

Riker, W.H. (1982) *Liberalism Against Populism*. San Francisco: Freeman.

Riker, W.H. and Ordeshok. P. (1973) *An Introduction to Positive Political Theory*. Englewood Cliffs, NJ: Prentice-Hall.

Roberti, P. (1974) 'Income Distribution: A Time-series and a Cross-section Study.' *Economic Journal*, 84, pp. 629–38.

Robinson, R.A.H. (1979) *Contemporary Portugal: A History*. London: Allen and Unwin.

Rokkan, S. (1966) 'Norway: Numerical Democracy and Corporate Pluralism', in Dahl,

R.A. (ed.), pp. 70–115.

Rokkan, S. (1980) 'Territories, Centres and Peripheries: Toward a Geoethnic-Geoeconomic-Geopolitical Model of Differentiation Within Western Europe', in Gottman, J. (ed.) *Centre and Periphery: Spatial Variation in Politics*. Beverly Hills: Sage, pp. 163–204.

Rokkan, S. and Merrit, R.L. (eds) (1966) *Comparing Nations: The Use of Quantitative Data in Cross-national Research*. New Haven: Yale University Press.

Rokkan, S. and Meyriat, J. (eds) (1969) *International Guide to Electoral Statistics*. Paris: Mouton.

Rokkan, S. and Urwin, D. (eds) (1982) *The Politics of Territorial Identity: Studies in European Regionalism*. London: Sage.

Rokkan, S. and Urwin, D. (1983) *Economy, Territory, Identity: Politics of West European Peripheries*. London: Sage.

Rokkan, S. and Valen, H. (1962) 'The Mobilization of the Periphery: Data on Turnout, Party Membership and Candidate Recruitment in Norway.' *Acta Sociologica*, 6, no. 1/2, pp. 111–58.

Rokkan, S. et al. (1970) *Citizens, Elections, Parties: Approaches to the Comparative Study of the Process of Development*. Oslo: Universitetsforlaget.

Rose, R. (1969) 'Dynamic Tendencies in the Authority of Regimes.' *World Politics*, 21, pp. 602–28.

Rose, R. (1971) *Governing without Consensus: An Irish Perspective*. London: Faber and Faber.

Rose, R. (1974a) *Politics in England Today*. London: Faber and Faber.

Rose, R. (ed.) (1974b) *Electoral Behavior: A Comparative Handbook*. New York: Free Press.

Rose, R. (1974c) 'Britain: Simple Abstractions and Complex Realities', in Rose, R. (ed.) (1974b), pp. 481–541.

Rose, R. (1976) *Northern Ireland: A Time of Choice*. London: Macmillan.

Rose, R. (ed.) (1980) *Electoral Participation: A Comparative Analysis*. London: Sage.

Rose, R. (1981) 'What if Anything is Wrong with Big Government?' *Journal of Public Policy*, 1, pp. 5–36.

Rose, R. (1984) *Understanding Big Government: The Programme Approach*. London: Sage.

Rose, R. and Mackie, T. (1988) 'Do Parties Persist or Disappear? The Big Tradeoff Facing Organizations' in Lawson, K. and Merkl, P.H. (eds) *When Parties Fail. Emerging Alternative Organizations*. Princeton: Princeton University Press.

Rose, R. and McAllister, I. (1982) *United Kingdom Facts*. London: Macmillan.

Rose, R. and Peters, B.G. (1978) *Can Government Go Bankrupt?* New York: Basic Books.

Rose, R. and Urwin, D. (1969) 'Social Cohesion, Political Parties and Strains in Regimes.' *Comparative Political Studies*, 2, pp. 7–67.

Rose, R. and Urwin, D. (1970) 'Persistence and Change in Western Party Systems Since 1945.' *Political Studies*, 18, pp. 287–319.

Rose, R. and Urwin, D. (1975) *Regional Differentiation and Political Unity in Western Nations*. London: Sage.

Rubbi, A. (1979) *I Partiti Communiste dell Europa Occidentale*. Milano: Teti.

Rudolph, J.R. Jr. and Thompson, R.J. (eds) (1989) *Ethnoterritorial Politics, Policy, and the Western World*. Boulder: Lynne Rienner.

Ruin, O. (1982) 'Sweden in the 1970s: Policy-making Becomes More Difficult', in Richardson, J.J. (ed.), pp. 141–67.

Rummel, R.J. (1971) 'Dimensions of Conflict Behavior within Nations, 1946–1959', in Gillespie, J.V. and Nesvold, B.A. (eds), pp. 39–48.

Ruscoe, A. (1982) *The Italian Communist Party, 1976–1981: On the Threshold of Government*. London: Macmillan.

Russett, B. (1964) 'Inequality and Instability: The Relation of Land Tenure to Politics.' *World Politics*, 16, pp. 442–54.

Rustow, D.A. (1955) *The Politics of Compromise: A Study of Parties and Cabinet Governments in Sweden*. Princeton: Princeton University Press.

Rustow, D.A. (1967) *A World of Nations: Problems of Political Modernization*. Washington: Brookings.

Samuelsson, K. (1961) *Religion and Economic Action*. New York: Harper and Row.

Sanantonio, E. (1987) 'Italy', in Page, E.C. and Goldsmith, M.J. (eds) *Central and Local Government Relations*, pp. 107–29.

Sanders, D. (1981) *Patterns of Political Instability*. London: Macmillan.

Sanders, D. and Herman, V. (1977) 'The Stability and Survival of Governments in Western Democracies.' *Acta Politica*, 12, pp. 346–77.

Sani, G. and Sartori, G. (1980) 'Polarization, Fragmentation and Competition in Western Democracies' (mimeo).

Sani, G. and Sartori, G. (1983) 'Polarization, Fragmentation and Competition in Western Democracies', in Daalder, H. and Mair, P. (eds), pp. 307–40.

Särlvik, B. (1974) 'Sweden: The Social Bases of the Parties in a Developmental Perspective', in Rose, R. (ed.), pp. 371–434.

Särlvik, B. and Crewe, I. (1983) *Decade of Realignment*. Cambridge: Cambridge University Press.

Sartori, G. (1962) *Democratic Theory*. Detroit: Wayne State University Press.

Sartori, G. (1969) 'From Sociology of Politics to Political Sociology', in Lipset, S.M. (ed.) *Politics and the Social Sciences*. New York: Oxford University Press, pp. 65–100.

Sartori, G. (1976) *Parties and Party Systems: A Framework for Analysis*. Volume 1. Cambridge: Cambridge University Press.

Sassoon, D. (1990) 'The Role of the Italian Communist Party in the Consolidation of Parliamentary Democracy in Italy', in Pridham, G. (ed.) *Securing Democracy*, pp. 84–103.

Sawyer, M. (1976) 'Income Distribution in OECD Countries.' *OECD Economic Outlook: Occasional Studies*, July, pp. 3–36.

Schmidt, M.G. (1982) *Wohlfartsstaatliche Politik und bürgerlichen und sozialdemokratischen Refierungen*. Frankfurt: Campus.

Schmidt, M.G. (ed.) (1983) *Westliche Industriegesellschaften: Wirtschaft – Gesellschaft – Politik*. München: Piper.

Schmidt, M.G. (1985) *Der Schweizerische Weg zur Vollbeschäftigung: Eine Bilanz der Arbeitslosigkeit und der Arbeitsmarkspolitik*. Frankfurt am Main: Campus.

Schmidt, M.G. (1989) 'Social Policy in Rich and Poor Countries: Socio-economic Trends and Political-institutional Determinants.' *European Journal of Political Research*, 17, pp. 641–59.

Schmitter, P.C. (1979) 'Still the Century of Corporatism?', in Schmitter, P.C. and Lehmbruch, G. (eds), pp. 7–52.

Schmitter, P.C. (1981) 'Interest Intermediation and Regime Governability in Contemporary Western Europe and North America', in Berger, S. (ed.) *Organizing Interests in Western Europe*. Cambridge: Cambridge University Press, pp. 285–327.

Schmitter, P.C. (1982) 'Reflections on Where the Theory of Neo-corporatism Has Gone and Where the Praxis of Neo-corporatism May Be Going', in Lehmbruch, G. and Schmitter, P.C. (eds), pp. 259–79.

Schmitter, P.C. (1983) 'Democratic Theory and Neo-corporatist Practice.' *Social Research*, 50, pp. 885–928.

Schmitter, P.C. (1984) 'Neo-corporatism and the State.' Firenze: European University Institute (mimeo).

Schmitter, P.C. and Lehmbruch, G. (eds) (1979) *Trends towards Corporatist Intermediation*. London: Sage.

Schofield, N. (1984) 'Coalitions in West European Democracies' (mimeo).

Scholten, I. (1980) 'Does Consociationalism Exist? A Critique of Dutch Experience', in Rose, R. (ed.), pp. 329–54.

Schumann, K. (1971) *Das Regierungssystem der Schweiz*. Köln: Heymanns.

Schumpeter, J.A. (1944) *Capitalism, Socialism and Democracy*. London: Allen and Unwin.

Seers, D. et al. (eds) (1979) *Underdeveloped Europe: Studies in Core–periphery Relations*. Hassocks, Sussex: Harvester Press.

Senelle, R. and Van de Velde, E. (1981) *The Reform of the Belgian State*. Vol. III. Brussels: Ministry of Foreign Affairs.

Shamir, M. (1984) 'Are Western Party Systems 'Frozen'? A Comparative Dynamic Analysis.' *Comparative Political Studies*, 17, pp. 35–79.

Sharpe, L.J. (ed.) (1979) *Decentralist Trends in Western Democracies*. London: Sage.

Sharpe, L.J. (1985) 'Central Coordination and the Policy Network.' *Political Studies*, 33, pp. 361–81.

Sharpe, L.J. (1988) 'The Growth and Decentralisation of the Modern Democratic State.' *European Journal of Political Research*, pp. 16, 365–80.

Sharpe, L.J. and Newton, K. (1984) *Does Politics Matter?* Oxford: Clarendon Press.

Shils, E. (1958) 'The Intellectuals and the Power: Some Perspectives for Comparative Analysis.' *Comparative Studies in Society and History*, 1, pp. 5–23.

Shils, E. (1975) *Center and Periphery: Essays in Macrosociology*. Chicago: The University of Chicago Press.

Siegfried, A. (1956) 'Stable Instability in France.' *Foreign Affairs*, 34, pp. 394–404.

Sigelman, L. and Yough, S.N. (1978) 'Left–right Polarization in National Party Systems: A Cross-national Analysis.' *Comparative Political Studies*, 11, pp. 355–79.

Sills, D.L. (ed.) (1968) *International Encyclopedia of the Social Sciences*. New York: Macmillan and Free Press.

SIPRI (various years) *World Armaments and Disarmament: SIPRI Yearbook*. Oxford: Oxford University Press.

Sjöblom, G. (1968) *Party Strategies in a Multiparty System*. Lund: Studentlitteratur.

Sked, A. and Cock, C. (1979) *Post-war Britain: A Political History*. Harmondsworth: Penguin.

Smith, A.D. (1983) *Theories of Nationalism*. 2nd ed. London: Duckworth.

Smith, G. (1979a) 'Western European Party Systems: On the Trail of a Typology.' *West European Politics*, 2, pp. 128–43.

Smith, G. (1979b) *Democracy in Western Germany: Parties and Politics in the Federal Republic*. London: Heinemann.

Smith, G. (1980) *Politics in Western Europe: A Comparative Analysis*. 3rd ed. London: Heinemann.

Smith, (1984)

Smith, G. (1986) 'The Futures of Party Government: A Framework for Analysis', in Castles, F.G. and Wildenmann, R. (eds), pp. 205–35.

Smith, G. (1989) *Politics in Western Europe*. 5th ed. London: Gower.

Smith, G., Paterson, W.E. and Merkl, P.M. (eds) (1989) *Developments in West German Politics*. London: Macmillan.

Smithson, M. (1982) 'On Relative Dispersion: A New Solution for Some Old Problems.' *Quality and Quantity*, 16, pp. 261–71.

Social Compass (1972) 'Foi, religion, morale et vie familiale dans dix pays d'Europe.' *Social Compass*, 18, pp. 279–84.

Statesman's Yearbook. London: Macmillan, annually.

Statistical Yearbook of Finland. Helsinki: Central Statistical Office, annually.

Statistical Yearbook of Greece. Athens: Central Statistical Office, annually.

Statistisches Handbuch für dir Republik Österreich. Wien: Statistisches Zentralamt, annually.

Statistisches Jahrbuch der Schweiz. Bern: Bundesamt für Statistik, annually.

Statistisches Jahrbuch für die Bundesrepublik Deutschland. Wiesbaden: Statistisches Bundesamt, annually.

Statistisk årsbog. Koebenhavn: Danmarks statistik, annually.

Statistisk årsbok. Stockholm: Statistiska centralbyrån.

Steed, M. (1979) 'France', in Henig, S. (ed.) *Political Parties in the European Community*. London: Allen and Unwin, pp. 51–89.

Steed, M. and Hearl, D. (1985) *Party Families*. London: Liberal European Action Group.

Steinberg, J. (1980) *Why Switzerland?* Cambridge: Cambridge University Press.

Steiner, J. (1974) *Amicable Agreement versus Majority Rule: Conflict Resolution in Switzerland*. Chapel Hill: The University of North Carolina Press.

Steiner, K. (1972) *Politics in Austria*. Boston: Little, Brown and Company.

Steiner, K. (ed.) (1981) *Modern Austria*. Palo Alto: SPOSS.

Stephens, M. (1976) *Linguistic Minorities in Western Europe*. Llandysul: Gomer Press.

Straka, M. (ed.) (1970) *Handbuch der europäischen Volksgruppen*. Wien: Braumüller.

Streeck, W. and Schmitter, P.C. (eds) (1985) *Private Interest Government: Beyond Market and State*. London: Sage.

Strom, K. (1984) 'Minority Governments in Parliamentary Democracies: The Rationality of Nonwinning Cabinet Solutions.' *Comparative Political Studies*, 17, pp. 199–227.

Strom, K. (1985) 'Party Goals and Government Performance in Parliamentary Democracies.' *American Political Science Review*, 79, pp. 738–54.

Strom, K. (1989) *Minority Government and Majority Rule*. Cambridge: Cambridge University Press.

Sully, M. (1981) *Political Parties and Elections in Austria*. London: Hurst.

Summers, R. and Heston, A. (1988) 'A New Set of International Comparisons of Real Product and Price Levels Estimates for 130 Countries, 1950–1985.' *Review of Income and Wealth*, 34, 1–25.

Sundberg, J. (1989) *Lokala Partiorganisationer i Kommunala och Nationella Val: Förändringar i Organisatorisk Styrka och Medlemsaktivitet i Politiska Lokalföreningar i Finland åren 1945–1987*. Helsingfors: Societas Scientiarum Fennica.

Sutton, F.X. (1963) 'Social Theory and Comparative Politics', in Eckstein, H. and Apter, D.A. (eds) *Comparative Politics: A Reader*. New York: Free Press, pp. 67–81.

Svåsand, L. (1985) *Politiske Partier*. Oslo: Tiden.

Swank, D.H. (1988) 'The Political Economy of Government Domestic Expenditure in the Affluent Democracies, 1960–80.' *American Journal of Political Science*, 32, pp. 1120–50.

Tamames, R. (1977) *Historia de Espana Alfaguara: La Republica: La Era de Franco*. Madrid: Alianza.

Tarschys, D. (1975) 'The Growth of Public Expenditures – Nine Modes of Explanation.' *Scandinavian Political Studies*, 10, pp. 9–31.

Tawney, R.H. (1938) *Religion and the Rise of Capitalism*. Harmondsworth: Pelican.

Taylor, C.L. (1981) *Codebook to World Handbook of Political and Social Indicators: Volume 1: Aggregate Data*. 3rd ed. Berlin: International Institute for Comparative Social Research (mimeo).

Taylor, C.L. and Hudson, M. (1972) *World Handbook of Political and Social Indicators*. 2nd ed. New Haven: Yale University Press.

Taylor, M. and Herman, V.M. (1971) 'Party Systems and Government Stability.' *American Political Science Review*, 65, pp. 28–37.

Taylor, S. (1990) 'The Politics of Unemployment' in Urwin, D.A. and Paterson, W.E. (eds) *Politics in Western Europe Today*. London: Longman, pp. 33–58.

Tesnière, L. (1928) 'Statistiques des langues de l'Europe', in Meillet, A., *Les langues dans l'Europe nouvelle*. Paris: Payot, pp. 291–484.

Therborn, G. (1984) 'The Prospects of Labour and the Transformation of Capitalism.' *New Left Review*, no. 145, pp. 5–38.

Therborn, G. et al. (1978) 'Sweden before and after Social Democracy: A First Overview.' *Acta Sociologica*, 21, Supplement, pp. 37–58.

Thomas, J.C. (1975) *The Decline of Ideology in Western Political Parties: A Study of Changing Policy Orientations*. London: Sage.

Thompson, D. (1969) *Democracy in France since 1870*. Oxford: Oxford University Press.

Thompson, M., Ellis, R. and Wildavsky, A. (1990) *Cultural Theory*. Boulder: Westview Press.

Thung, M.A., Peelen, G.J. and Kingmans, M.C. (1982) 'Dutch Pillarisation on the Move? Political Destabilisation and Religious Change.' *West European Politics*, 5, no. 2, pp. 127–48.

Tilly, C. (ed.) (1975) *The Formation of National States in Western Europe*. Princeton: Princeton University Press.

Timmermann, H. (1987) *The Decline of the World Communist Movement: Moscow, Beijing, and Communist Parties in the West*. Boulder: Westview Press.

Tinbergen, J. (1967) *Economic Policy: Principles and Design*. Amsterdam: North-Holland.

Tingsten, H. (1955) 'Stability and Vitality in Swedish Democracy.' *Political Quarterly*, 26, pp. 140–51.

Tingsten, H. (1965) *The Problems of Democracy*. Totowa, NJ: Bedminster Press.

Tschäni, H. (1979) *Parteien, Programme, Parolen*. Aarau: Sauerländer.

Tsokou, S. et al. (1986) 'Some Correlates of Partisan Preference in Greece 1980: A Discriminant Analysis.' *European Journal of Political Research*, 14, pp. 441–63.

Tsurutani, T. (1968) 'Stability and Instability: A Note in Comparative Political Analysis.' *Journal of Politics*, 30, pp. 910–33.

Tufte, E. (1978) *Political Control of the Economy*. Princeton: Princeton University Press.

Ucakar, K. (1982) 'Die Entwicklung der Intressenorganisationen', in Fischer, H. (ed.), pp. 397–428.

UNESCO, *Statistical Yearbook*. Paris: UNESCO, annually.

United Nations, *Demographic Yearbook*. New York: United Nations, annually.

United Nations, *Statistical Yearbook*. New York: United Nations, annually.

United Nations, *Yearbook of National Accounts Statistics*. New York: United Nations, annually.

Urwin, D.W. (1974) 'Germany: Continuity and Change in Electoral Politics', in Rose, R. (ed.), pp. 109–70.

Urwin, D.W. (1990) 'The Wearing of the Green: Issues, Movements and Parties', in Urwin, D.W. and Paterson, W.E. (eds) *Politics in Western Europe Today*. London: Longman, pp. 116–36.

Urwin, D.W. and Paterson, W.E. (eds) (1990) *Politics in Western Europe Today: Perspectives, Policies and Problems since 1980*. London: Longman.

Uusitalo, H. (1975) *Income and Welfare: A Study of Income as a Component of Welfare in the Scandinavian Countries in the 1970s*. Helsinki: Research Group for Comparative Sociology.

Valen, H. (1981) *Valg of politikk: et samfunn i endring*. Oslo: NKS-forlaget.

Valen, H. and Martinussen, W. (1972) *Velgere og politiske frontlinjer: stemmegivning og stridsspoersmål 1957–1969*. Oslo: Gyldendal.

Van Hassel, H. (1982) 'New Forms of Executive Regionalization in Belgium.' Paper Presented to the ECPR Joint Sessions of Workshop in Aarhus (mimeo).

Van Schendelen, M.P.C.M. (ed.) (1984) *Consociationalism, Pillarisation and Conflict-management in the Low Countries*. Rotterdam: Erasmus Universiteit.

Vickers, J. and Wright, V. (eds) (1988) 'The Politics of Privatisation in Western Europe.' *West European Politics*, 11.

Wahlbäck, K. (1967) *Från Mannerheim till Kekkonen*. Stockholm: Aldus.

Walker, J. (1966) 'A Critique of the Élitist Theory of Democracy.' *American Political Science Review*, 60, pp. 285–95.

Waller, M. and Fennema, M. (eds) (1988) *Communist Parties in Western Europe: Decline or Adaptation?* Oxford: Blackwell.

Wallerstein, I. (1974) *The Modern World-system*. New York: Academic Press.

Ward, C.K. (1972) 'Ireland', in Mol, H. (ed.), pp. 295–303.

Warwick, P. (1979) 'The Durability of Coalition Governments in Parliamentary Democracies.' *Comparative Political Studies*, 11, pp. 465–98.

Weber, M. (1947) *The Theory of Social and Economic Organization*. New York: Free Press.

Weber, M. (1965) *The Protestant Ethic and the Spirit of Capitalism*. London: Allen and Unwin.

Weber, M. (1968) *Economy and Society: An Outline of Interpretative Sociology*. New York: Bedminster Press.

Weil, G. (1970) *The Benelux Nations: The Politics of Small-country Democracies*. New York: Holt, Rinehart and Winston.

Weinzerl, E. and Skalnik, K. (eds) (1972) *Österreich: Die zweite Republik*. Graz: Styria.

Wende, F. (ed.) (1981) *Lexikon zur Geschichte der Parteien in Europa*. Stuttgart: Alfred Kröner Verlag.

Whiteley, P. (ed.) (1980) *Models of Political Economy*. London: Sage.

Whyte, J. (1974) 'Ireland: Politics without Social Bases', in Rose, R. (ed.), pp. 619–51.

Wildavsky, A. (1979) *Speaking Truth to Power: The Art and Craft of Policy Analysis*. Boston: Little, Brown and Company.

Wildavsky, A. (1980) *How to Limit Government Spending*. Berkeley: The University of California Press.

Wildavsky, A. (1986) *Budgeting*. Boston: Little, Brown and Company. 2nd ed.

Wildavsky, A. (1987) 'Choosing Preferences by Constructing Institutions: A Cultural Theory of Preference Formation.' *American Political Science Review*, 81, 3–22.

Wilensky, H. (1975) *The Welfare State and Equality*. Berkeley: The University of California Press.

Wilensky, H. (1976) *The 'New Corporatism', Centralization, and the Welfare State.* London: Sage.

Williams, A. (ed.) (1984) *Southern Europe Transformed: Political and Economic Change in Greece, Italy, Portugal and Spain.* London: Harper and Row.

Williamson, J.G. (1965) 'Regional Inequality and the Process of National Development: A Description of Patterns.' *Economic Development and Cultural Change,* 13, no. 4: 2, pp. 3–84.

Winch, R.F. and Campbell, D.T. (1969) 'Proof? No. Evidence? Yes: The Significance of Tests of Significance.' *American Sociologists,* 4, pp. 140–3.

Wolfinger, R.E. (1971) 'Nondecisions and the Study of Local Politics.' *American Political Science Review,* 65, pp. 1063–80.

Wolf-Philips, L. (1983) 'A Long Look at the British Constitution.' *Statsvetenskaplig Tidskrift,* 86, pp. 273–85.

Wolinetz, S.B. (ed.) (1988) *Parties and Party Systems in Liberal Democracies.* London: Routledge.

World Bank: World Development Report. New York: Oxford University Press, annually.

World Bank (1980) *World Tables.* 2nd ed. Baltimore: Johns Hopkins University Press.

Worre, T. (1982) *Det politiske system i Danmark.* Koebenhavn: Akademisk forlag.

Worre, T. (1989) 'Folketingsvalget 1987.' *Ökonomi og Politik,* 62, 3, pp. 39–54.

Wright, G. (1950) *The Reshaping of French Democracy.* London: Methuen.

Wright, V. (1983) *The Government and Politics of France.* 2nd ed. London: Hutchinson.

Wright, V. (ed.) (1984) *Continuity and Change in France.* London: Allen and Unwin.

Wörlund, I. et al. (1989) *Sveriges Politiska Partier: En Presentation.* Umeå: Department of Political Science.

Yinger, M. (1970) *The Scientific Study of Religion.* London: Macmillan.

Yough, S.N. and Sigelman, L. (1976) 'Mobilization, Institutionalization, Development and Instability: A Note of Reappraisal.' *Comparative Political Studies,* 9, pp. 223–32.

Zapf, W. and Flora, P. (1973) 'Differences in Paths of Development: An Analysis for Ten Countries', in Eisenstadt, S.N. and Rokkan, S. (eds) Vol 1, pp. 161–211.

Zariski, R. (1989) 'Ethnic Extremism among Ethnoterritorial Minorities in Western Europe: Dimensions, Causes, and Institutional Responses.' *Comparative Politics,* 21, pp. 253–72.

Zimmermann, E. (1989) 'Political Unrest in Western Europe: Trends and Prospects.' *West European Politics,* 12, pp. 179–96.

Zolberg, A. (1977) 'Splitting the Difference: Federalization without Federalism in Belgium', in Esman, M.J. (ed.), pp. 103–42.

Zuckerman, A. (1975) 'Political Cleavage: A Conceptual and Theoretical Analysis.' *British Journal of Political Science,* 5, pp. 231–48.

Zuckerman, A. (1982) 'New Approaches to Political Cleavages: A Theoretical Introduction.' *Comparative Political Studies,* 15, pp. 131–44.

Zuckerman, A. and Lichbach, M.I. (1977) 'Stability and Change in European Electorates.' *World Politics,* 29, 523–51.

Åslund, A. (1989) *Gorbachev's Struggle for Economic Reform. The Soviet Reform Process 1985–88.* London: Pinter.

Appendices

Appendix 4.1 Average Electoral Outcomes of the Political Parties in Western Europe in the 1970s

Austria
Elections: 1962, 1971, 1975
Data on the independent variables: 1970s; German-speaking from the 1950s
Parties: Sozialistische Partei Österreichs (SPÖ): 48.1%
        Österreichische Volkspartei (ÖVP): 43.8%
        Freiheitliche Partei Österreich (FPÖ): 6.0%
        Kommunistische Partei Österreichs (KPÖ): 1.9%

Belgium
Elections: 1968, 1971, 1974
Data on the independent variables: 1970s; linguistic data from 1947
Parties: Parti Social Chretien (PSC): 31.4%
        Parti Socialiste Belge (PSB): 27.3%
        Parti de la Liberté et du Progrés (PLB): 19.4%
        Parti Communiste de Belgique (PCB): 3.1%
        Volksunie (CVU): 10.4%
        Rassemblement Wallon-Front Democratique des Francophones Bruxellois (RW-FDF): 7.4%

Denmark
Elections: 1971, 1973, 1975
Data on the independent variables: 1970s
Parties: Socialdemokratiet (SD): 30.9%
        Radikale Venstre (RV): 10.9%

Appendix 4.1   (continued)

Det Konservative Folkeparti (KF): 10.5%
Retsforbundet (RFB): 2.1%
Socialistisk Folkeparti (SF): 6.7%
Danmarks Kommunistiske Parti (DKP): 3.1%
Kristeligt Folkeparti (KRF): 3.8%
Venstre (VE): 17.1%
Venstresocialister (VS): 1.7%
Centrum-Demokraterne (CD): 5.0%
Fremskridtspartiet (FRP): 14.7%

F R Germany
Elections: 1961, 1965, 1969
Data on the independent variables: 1960s
Parties: Sozialdemokratische Partei Deutschlands (SPD): 39.4%
Christlich-Demokratische Union (CDU): 46.3%
Freie Demokratsche Partei (FDP): 9.4%

Finland
Elections: 1966, 1970, 1972
Data on the independent variables: 1970s
Parties: Suomen Kansan Demokraattinen Liitto (SKDL): 18.3%
Työväen ja Pienviljelijäin Sosialidemokraattinen Liitto (TPSL): 1.7%
Suomen Sosialidemokraattinen Puolue (SDP): 25.5%
Suomen Maaseudun Puolue (SMP): 6.9%
Suomen Kristillinen Liitto (SKL): 1.8%
Keskustapuolue (KESK): 18.2%
Liberaalinen Kansanpuolue (LKP): 5.9%
Kansallinen Kokoomus (KOK): 16.5%
Svenska Folkpartiet (RKP): 5.7%

France
Elections: 1967, 1968, 1973
Data on the independent variables: 1970s
Parties: Parti Communiste Français (PCF): 21.3%
Parti Socialiste (PS): 18.6%
Parti Socialiste Unifié (PSU): 3.2%
Réformateurs (REF): 11.8%
Union des Démocrates Pour la République (UDR): 38.6%

Great Britain
Elections: 1966, 1970, 1974F
Data on the independent variables: mid-1960s; cultural data from the 1950s and the 1930s
Parties: Conservative Party (CONS): 42.1%
Labour Party (LAB): 42.8%
Liberal Party (LIB): 11.8%
Scottish National Party (SCOT): 1.2%
Plaid Cymru (WELSH): 0.4%

Appendix 4.1 (continued)

Greece
Elections: 1974, 1977, 1981
Data on the independent variables. 1970s
Parties: New Democracy (ND): 44.0%
  Union of the Democratic Center (EDHIK): 11.3%
  Panhellenic Socialist Movement (PASOK): 29.0%
  Communist Party of Greece (KKE): 11.2%

Ireland
Elections: 1969, 1973
Data on the independent variables: 1970s
Parties: Fianna Fáil (FF): 45.9%
  Fine Gael (FG): 34.6%
  Labour Party (LAB): 15.3%

Italy
Elections: 1968, 1972, 1976
Data on the independent variables: 1970s
Parties: Democrazia Cristiana (DC): 38.8%
  Partito Comunista Italiano (PCI): 29.5%
  Partito Socialista Italiano (PSI): 11.0%
  Partito Socialista Democratico Italiano (PSDI): 4.9%
  Movimento Sociale Italiano-Destra Nazionale (MSI): 6.4%
  Partito Liberale Italiano (PLI): 3.7%
  Partito Repubblicano Italiano (PRI): 2.7%

The Netherlands
Elections: 1967, 1971, 1972
Data on the independent variables: 1970s; religious data from 1960.
Parties: Boerenpartij (BP): 2.6%
  Anti-Revolutionaire Partij (ARP): 9.1%
  Christelijk-Historische Unie (CHU): 6.4%
  Katholieke Volkspartij (KVP): 22.0%
  Volkspartij voor Vrijheid en Demokratie (VVD): 11.8%
  Partij van de Arbeid (PVDA): 25.2%
  Communistische Partij Nederland (CPN): 4.0%
  Demokraten '66 (D'66): 4.8%
  Staatkundig Gereformeerde Partij (SGP): 2.2%
  Pasifistisch-Socialistische Partij (PSP): 1.9%

Norway
Elections: 1969, 1973, 1977
Data on the independent variables: 1970s
Parties: Det Norske Arbeiderparti (DNA): 41.4%
  Hoeyre (HOE): 20.6%

Appendix 4.1 (continued)

> Kristeligt Folkeparti (KRF): 11.0%
> Norges Kommunistiske Parti (NKP): 0.9%
> Senterpartiet (SP): 10.0%
> Socialistisk Venstreparti (SV): 6.3%
> Venstre (VE): 5.4%
> Fremskrittspartiet (FRP): 3.4%

Portugal
Elections: 1975, 1976, 1980
Data on the independent variables: 1970s; agrarian census from 1968
Parties: Partido Socialista Portuges (PSP): 35.4%
          Partido Communista Portuges (PCP): 15.4%
          Aliança Democrática (AD): 42.6%

Spain
Elections: 1977, 1979, 1982
Data on the independent variables: 1970s
Parties: Partido Socialista Obrero Espanol (PSOE): 35.6%
          Unión de Centro Democrático (UCD): 25.7%
          Partido Communista de Espana (PCE): 8.0%
          Alianza Popular (AP): 13.4%
          Ethnic Parties (ETHNIC): 5.0%

Sweden
Elections: 1976, 1979, 1982
Data on the independent variables: mid-1970s
Parties: Moderata Samlingspartiet (MOD): 19.8%
          Centerpartiet (CP): 19.2%
          Folkpartiet (FP): 9.2%
          Socialdemokratiska Arbetarpartiet (SAP): 43.8%
          Vänsterpartiet Kommunisterna (VPK): 5.3%
          Kristen Demokratisk Samling (KDS): 1.6%

Switzerland
Elections: 1967, 1971, 1975
Data on the independent variables: 1970s
Parties: Freisinnig-Demokratische Partei der Schweiz (FDP): 22.4%
          Christlich-Demokratische Volkspartei der Schweiz (CDV): 21.2%
          Sozialdemokratische Partei der Schweiz (SPS): 23.8%
          Schweizerische Volkspartei (SVP): 10.6%

Appendix 4.2 Environmental Influences on Party Electoral Outcomes: Regression Analyses for Sixteen Countries

Austria

Party	Independent variables	r	Beta	t-stat	R2D	R2	R2A	E2	CV	SCVw
ÖVP	I: Industrial employment	-.51	-.49	-15.61	.03	.67	.67	.98	.281	.269
	A: Small units	.31	.16	4.57	.19					
	W: Income	-.28	.00	0.07	.22					
	C: Catholics	.63	.56	17.01	.14					
	RO: —									
	L: German	.11	.18	5.66	.09					
SPÖ	I: Industrial employment	.52	.35	9.76	.14	.63	.62	.93	.256	.224
	A: Small units	-.29	-.00	-0.08	.35					
	W: Income	.18	-.13	-3.48	.25					
	C: —									
	RO: Secular	.66	.65	14.66	.46					
	L: German	-.14	-.28	-8.29	.07					
FPÖ	I: Industrial employment	-.04	-.05	-0.97	.08	.18	.16	.90	.539	.494
	A: Big units	.21	.21	4.17	.02					
	W: Income	.32	.43	7.34	.29					
	C: Evangelicals	.03	-.16	-2.67	.33					
	RO: —									
	L: German	.03	-.04	-0.72	.07					
KPÖ	I: Industrial employment	.29	.10	2.14	.14	.36	.35	.61	.826	.692
	A: Small units	-.27	.04	0.70	.35					
	W: Income	.17	-.11	-2.31	.25					
	C: —									
	RO: Secular	.58	.63	10.72	.46					
	L: German	.06	-.04	-0.93	.07					

Note: I = Industry; A = size or type of agricultural units; W = wealth; C = confession, RO = religious orientation; L = language or regional–cultural orientation; * = the variable is not relevant for the country studied; — = data is not available for the variable

Belgium

Party	Independent variables	r	Beta	t-stat	R2D	R2	R2A	E2	CV	SCVw
PSC	I: Industrial employment	.27	.09	1.94	.21	.87	.86	.98	.342	.602
	A: Small units	.44	.03	0.57	.25					
	W: Index	-.39	.02	0.45	.27					
	C: *									
	RO: Index	.89	.72	13.42	.47					
	L: Dutch	.72	.28	5.39	.42					
PSB	I: Industrial employment	.04	.17	2.50	.18	.67	.65	.94	.281	.504
	A: Small units	-.39	-.11	-1.57	.26					
	W: Index	.08	-.24	-3.31	.28					
	C: *									
	RO: Index	-.71	-.60	-7.16	.44					
	L: French	.60	.35	4.44	.38					
PLB	I: Industrial employment	-.47	-.40	-3.88	.21	.29	.25	.71	.312	.525
	A: Small units	.08	.13	1.23	.25					

Belgium (continued)

Party	Independent variables	r	Beta	t-stat	R2D	R2	R2A	E2	CV	SCVw
	W: Index	.03	.05	-0.45	.27					
	C: *									
	RO: Index	.01	.13	1.03	.47					
	L: Dutch	-.32	-.29	-2.36	.42					
PCB	I: Industrial employment	.08	.21	3.31	.18	.73	.72	.97	1.158	1.740
	A: Small units	-.21	.15	2.32	.26					
	W: Index	.10	-.18	-2.75	.28					
	C: *									
	RO: Index	-.77	-.77	-10.17	.44					
	L: French	.57	.32	4.54	.38					
CVU	I: Industrial employment	.31	-.08	-2.30	.21	.91	.91	.99	.952	1.446
	A: Small units	.29	.02	0.41	.25					
	W: Index	-.26	-.05	-1.43	.27					
	C: *									
	RO: Index	.48	-.11	-2.45	.47					
	L: Dutch	.95	1.02	23.82	.42					
RW	I: Industrial employment	-.33	.03	0.49	.21	.77	.76	.89	1.217	2.065
	A: Small units	-.46	-.12	-2.03	.25					
	W: Index	.55	.31	5.11	.27					
	C: *									
	RO: Index	-.61	-.06	-0.80	.47					
	L: Dutch	-.80	-.66	-9.65	.42					

Denmark

Party	Independent variables	r	Beta	t-stat	R2D	R2	R2A	E2	CV	SCVw
SD	I: Industrial employment	.41	.41	13.73	.06	.31	.30	.69	.269	.145
	A: Small units	.17	.05	1.78	.05					
	W: Index	-.00	-.36	-9.75	.39					
	C: —									
	RO: Index	-.29	-.44	-11.93	.39					
	L: —									
RV	I: Agricultural employment	.18	.26	4.48	.66	.05	.05	.52	.298	.171
	A: Big units	-.15	-.13	-3.66	.13					
	W: Index	-.12	.08	1.44	.59					
	C: —									
	RO: Index	.08	-.07	-1.35	.54					
	L: —									
KF	I: Agricultural employment	-.38	-.16	-3.05	.66	.17	.16	.44	.421	.238
	A: Big units	.13	.02	0.56	.13					
	W: Index	.39	.23	4.64	.59					
	C: —									
	RO: Index	-.31	-.05	-1.15	.54					
	L: —									
RFB	I: Agricultural employment	-.19	-.16	-2.74	.66	.08	.08	.57	.300	.138
	A: Small units	-.04	-.04	-1.06	.05					

Denmark (continued)

Party	Independent variables	r	Beta	t-stat	R2D	R2	R2A	E2	CV	SCVw
	W: Index	.24	.25	4.99	.56					
	C: —									
	RO: Index	-.06	.20	4.14	.54					
	L: —									
SF	I: Industrial employment	.33	.19	8.86	.05	.63	.63	.79	.642	.348
	A: Big units	.15	-.00	-0.08	.13					
	W: Index	.64	.27	9.32	.46					
	C: —									
	RO: Index	-.73	-.54	-19.83	.39					
	L: —									
DKP	I: Industrial employment	.26	.15	5.79	.06	.45	.45	.63	.651	.415
	A: Small units	.09	-.02	-0.90	.05					
	W: Index	.48	.10	3.04	.39					
	C: —									
	RO: Index	-.65	-.57	-17.16	.39					
	L: —									
VS	I: Industrial employment	.04	-.13	-5.95	.06	.62	.62	.84	.605	.369
	A: Small units	.10	.04	1.71	.05					
	W: Index	.70	.46	16.95	.39					
	C: —									
	RO: Index	-.70	-.43	-15.78	.39					
	L: —									
KRF	I: Industrial employment	-.23	-.14	-4.79	.06	.29	.29	.75	.639	.380
	A: Small units	-.26	-.17	-5.81	.05					
	W: Index	-.31	-.03	-0.56	.39					
	C: —									
	RO: Index	.49	.43	11.34	.39					
	L: —									
VE	I: Agricultural employment	.71	.68	16.82	.66	.54	.54	.72	.349	.306
	A: Big units	-.20	-.11	-4.37	.13					
	W: Index	-.48	.18	4.86	.59					
	C: —									
	RO: Index	.59	.20	5.79	.54					
	L: —									
CD	I: Industrial employment	.06	-.01	-0.26	.05	.12	.12	.36	.445	.252
	A: Big units	.15	.05	1.05	.13					
	W: Index	.34	.32	5.79	.46					
	C: —									
	RO: Index	-.22	-.02	-0.43	.39					
	L: —									
FRP	I: Industrial employment	-.11	-.10	-2.46	.06	.18	.18	.79	.174	.129
	A: Small units	-.19	-.11	-2.72	.05					
	W: Index	.02	.33	6.60	.39					
	C: —									
	RO: Index	.31	.47	9.59	.39					
	L: —									

FR Germany

Party	Independent variables		r	Beta	t-stat	R2D	R2	R2A	E2	CV	SCVw
SPD	I:	Industrial employment	.25	.26	10.13	.06	.55	.54	.90	.237	.148
	A:	Small units	.30	-.00	-0.15	.34					
	W:	Index	.48	.40	14.49	.18					
	C:	Protestants	.55	.59	18.86	.38					
	RO:	—									
	L:	Refugees	.21	-.16	-4.79	.44					
CDU	I:	Industrial employment	-.13	-.14	-7.31	.07	.74	.74	.95	.230	.146
	A:	Small units	-.37	-.06	-2.82	.33					
	W:	Index	-.53	-.36	-17.38	.18					
	C:	Catholics	.74	.74	30.77	.38					
	RO:	—									
	L:	Refugees	-.27	.14	5.73	.42					
FDP	I:	Industrial employment	-.10	-.12	-2.64	.06	.23	.22	.51	.343	.213
	A:	Small units	.25	.15	3.77	.34					
	W:	Index	.26	.17	4.79	.18					
	C:	Protestants	.38	.37	9.14	.38					
	RO:	—									
	L:	Refugees	.11	-.08	-1.80	.44					

Finland

Party	Independent variables		r	Beta	t-stat	R2D	R2	R2A	E2	CV	SCVw
SKDL	I:	Industrial employment	.21	.19	6.82	.36	.26	.26	.93	0.588	0.206
	A:	Small units	.25	.21	8.83	.11					
	W:	Index	.10	-.08	-2.63	.39					
	C:	—									
	RO:	Index	-.40	-.28	-10.51	.32					
	L:	Swedish	-.29	-.20	-8.65	.09					
TPSL	I:	Industrial employment	.33	.30	10.03	.36	.15	.15	.75	1.214	0.432
	A:	Medium-sized units	-.12	-.08	-2.97	.14					
	W:	Index	.23	.03	0.97	.43					
	C:	—									
	RO:	Index	-.22	-.04	-1.29	.30					
	L:	Swedish	-.17	-.18	-7.30	.09					
SDP	I:	Industrial employment	.63	.48	20.01	.36	.46	.45	.96	0.570	0.187
	A:	Small units	-.06	.05	2.53	.11					
	W:	Index	.53	.25	10.30	.39					
	C:	—									
	RO:	Index	-.38	-.05	-2.32	.32					
	L:	Swedish	-.06	-.09	-4.48	.09					
SMP	I:	Industrial employment	-.35	-.24	-8.31	.36	.22	.21	.42	0.585	0.333
	A:	Small units	.13	.02	0.63	.11					
	W:	Index	-.32	-.16	-5.47	.39					
	C:	—									
	RO:	Index	.12	.01	0.36	.32					
	L:	Swedish	-.29	-.27	-11.10	.09					

Finland (continued)

Party	Independent variables	r	Beta	t-stat	R2D	R2	R2A	E2	CV	SCVw
KESK	I: Industrial employment	-.57	-.33	-19.46	.36	.73	.73	.95	0.597	0.427
	A: Medium-sized units	.35	.19	13.33	.14					
	W: Index	-.60	-.28	-15.80	.43					
	C: —									
	RO: Index	.27	.08	5.06	.30					
	L: Swedish	-.55	-.52	-36.68	.09					
LKP	I: Industrial employment	.27	-.01	-0.47	.36	.46	.46	.88	0.787	0.279
	A: Medium-sized units	-.37	-.21	-10.40	.14					
	W: Index	.54	.48	18.99	.43					
	C: —									
	RO: Index	-.37	-.05	-2.05	.30					
	L: Swedish	-.32	-.35	-17.32	.09					
KOK	I: Industrial employment	.30	.11	4.71	.36	.47	.47	.94	0.617	0.211
	A: Medium-sized units	-.08	.04	2.09	.14					
	W: Index	.46	.52	20.83	.43					
	C: —									
	RO: Index	-.20	.17	7.62	.30					
	L: Swedish	-.44	-.52	-26.29	.09					
SKL	I: Industrial employment	.08	.11	2.91	.36	.10	.09	.70	0.831	0.272
	A: Medium-sized units	-.03	-.04	-1.31	.14					
	W: Index	.06	.05	1.35	.43					
	C: —									
	RO: Index	-.02	.12	3.38	.30					
	L: Swedish	-.27	-.31	-9.86	.09					
RKP	I: Commercial employment	-.05	.01	1.12	.60	.96	.96	.99	2.767	1.105
	A: Small units	-.15	.01	2.40	.11					
	W: Index	.05	-.00	-0.17	.62					
	C: —									
	RO: Index	.25	.05	8.19	.30					
	L: Swedish	.98	.97	184.43	.09					

France

Party	Independent variables	r	Beta	t-stat	R2D	R2	R2A	E2	CV	SCVw
PCF	I: Industrial employment	.11	-.03	-0.53	.23	.48	.47	.96	.371	.369
	A: Sharecroppers	.21	.09	1.98	.14					
	W: Index	.31	.18	3.78	.17					
	C: Protestants	.01	.16	3.55	.08					
	RO: Index	-.64	-.60	-12.21	.24					
	L: *									
PS	I: Industrial employment	-.13	-.10	-1.67	.20	.18	.16	.83	.385	.404
	A: Small units	-.19	-.17	-2.48	.35					
	W: Index	-.25	-.20	-2.75	.42					
	C: Protestants	.02	.11	1.91	.09					
	RO: Index	-.23	-.35	-5.96	.13					
	L: *									

France (continued)

Party		Independent variables	r	Beta	t-stat	R2D	R2	R2A	E2	CV	SCVw
PSU	I:	Industrial employment	.21	.09	1.43	.20	.16	.15	.65	.913	.803
	A:	Small units	.09	-.07	-1.04	.35					
	W:	Index	.34	.38	5.27	.42					
	C:	Protestants	-.09	-.10	-1.69	.09					
	RO:	Index	.06	.17	2.91	.13					
	L:	*									
REF	I:	Industrial employment	-.01	-.01	-0.13	.20	.08	.07	.66	.502	.458
	A:	Small units	.04	.05	0.65	.35					
	W:	Index	.06	.10	1.38	.42					
	C:	Protestants	-.00	-.07	-1.22	.09					
	RO:	Index	.25	.30	4.94	.13					
	L:	*									
UDR	I:	Industrial employment	.02	.05	0.85	.23	.27	.26	.64	.192	.183
	A:	Sharecroppers	-.32	-.23	-4.23	.14					
	W:	Index	-.16	-.09	-1.63	.17					
	C:	Protestants	.00	-.07	-1.30	.08					
	RO:	Index	.45	.41	7.33	.17					
	L:	*									

Great Britain

Party		Independent variables	r	Beta	t-stat	R2D	R2	R2A	E2	CV	SCVw
CONS	I:	Employers & managers	.61	0.46	12.09	.48	.63	.63	.89	0.293	0.146
	A:	Employment	-.03	-0.23	-6.98	.30					
	W:	Car density	.49	0.28	6.71	.56					
	C:	Anglicans	.21	0.15	4.24	.37					
	RO:	—									
	L:	English-speaking	.40	0.43	14.03	.20					
LAB	I:	Employers & managers	-.76	-0.51	14.32	.48	.69	.68	.87	0.298	0.195
	A:	Employment	-.50	-0.26	-8.37	.30					
	W:	Car density	-.66	-0.20	-5.27	.56					
	C:	Anglicans	-.41	-0.08	-2.60	.37					
	RO:	—									
	L:	English-speaking	-.01	-0.17	-6.04	.20					
LIB	I:	Employers & managers	.41	0.17	3.22	.48	.30	.29	.63	0.748	0.426
	A:	Employment	.46	0.32	6.95	.30					
	W:	Car density	.42	0.13	2.22	.56					
	C:	Anglicans	.34	0.11	2.34	.37					
	RO:	—									
	L:	English-speaking	-.10	0.08	1.81	.20					
SCOT	I:	Prof. workers	-.14	0.04	0.77	.31	.33	.32	.97	2.647	2.560
	A:	Employment	.37	0.65	11.40	.35					
	W:	Car density	-.12	-0.21	-3.19	.53					
	C:	Anglicans	-.19	-0.28	-4.85	.38					
	RO:	—									
	L:	English-speaking.	11	0.19	3.82	.17					

Great Britain (continued)

Party		Independent variables	r	Beta	t-stat	R2D	R2	R2A	E2	CV	SCVw
WELSH	I:	Unskilled workers	-.00	-0.11	-2.23	.55	.63	.62	.98	3.484	4.416
	A:	Employment	.21	0.06	1.50	.29					
	W:	Car density	.03	-0.14	-2.42	.64					
	C:	Non-conformists	.49	-0.39	-5.61	.76					
	RO:	—									
	L:	English-speaking	-.75	-1.08	-17.25	.70					

Greece

Party		Independent variables	r	Beta	t-stat	R2D	R2	R2A	E2	CV	SCVw
ND	I:	Industrial employment	.03	.09	1.05	.18	.05	.03	.46	.174	.227
	A:	Size of units	-.11	-.10	-1.26	.04					
	W:	Index	-.17	-.21	-2.46	.15					
	C:	*									
	RO:	—									
	L:	—									
PASOK	I:	Industrial employment	.02	-.00	-0.05	.15	.00	.00	.10	.175	.200
	A:	Number of	.00	.01	0.17	.02					
	W:	Index	.06	.07	0.77	.17					
	C:	*									
	RO:	—									
	L:	—									
EDHIK	I:	Industrial employment	-.07	-.08	-0.93	.15	.04	.02	.16	.346	.675
	A:	Number of	.17	.17	2.14	.02					
	W:	Index	-.01	.05	0.52	.17					
	C:	*									
	RO:	—									
	L:	—									
KKE	I:	Industrial employment	.10	.06	0.67	.18	.15	.13	.90	.583	.429
	A:	Size of units	.26	.27	3.61	.04					
	W:	Index	.27	.26	3.22	.15					
	C:	*									
	RO:	—									
	L:	—									

Ireland

Party		Independent variables	r	Beta	t-stat	R2D	R2	R2A	E2	CV	SCVw
FF	I:	Service employment	-.37	-.18	-1.43	.11	.53	.49	.89	.104	.264
	A:	—									
	W:	—									
	C:	Catholics	.48	.15	1.08	.32					
	RO:	—									
	L:	Irish	.70	.56	3.71	.38					
FG	I:	Service employment	-.67	-.68	-5.84	.11	.59	.55	.88	.167	.340
	A:	—									
	W:	—									

Ireland (continued)

Party	Independent variables	r	Beta	t-stat	R2D	R2	R2A	E2	CV	SCVw
	C: Catholics	-.31	-.42	-3.18	.32					
	RO: —									
	L: Irish	.06	.08	0.58	.38					
LAB	I: Service employment	.77	.69	7.47	.11	.74	.72	.90	.582	1.204
	A: —									
	W: —									
	C: Catholics	.16	.44	4.14	.32					
	RO: —									
	L: Irish	-.35	-.38	-3.43	.38					

Italy

Party	Independent variables	r	Beta	t-stat	R2D	R2	R2A	E2	CV	SCVw
DC	I: Industrial employment	-.04	-.10	-1.72	.48	.54	.54	.98	.230	.243
	A: Small units	.39	.41	8.97	.17					
	W: Index	-.20	.44	6.13	.66					
	C: —									
	RO: Index	.61	.77	12.95	.51					
	L: *									
PCI	I: Industrial employment	.12	.15	2.37	.47	.45	.44	.89	.344	.340
	A: Sharecroppers	.55	.60	12.43	.12					
	W: Index	.17	-.39	-5.12	.64					
	C: —									
	RO: Index	-.35	-.47	-8.35	.35					
	L: *									
PSI	I: Industrial employment	.29	.25	3.18	.47	.11	.10	.53	.299	.255
	A: Sharecroppers	-.06	-.15	-2.40	.12					
	W: Index	.21	.14	1.41	.64					
	C: —									
	RO: Index	-.04	.08	1.14	.35					
	L: *									
PSDI	I: Industrial employment	.29	.12	1.51	.48	.18	.17	.62	.346	.311
	A: Big units	-.22	-.25	-4.43	.03					
	W: Index	.32	.22	2.40	.62					
	C: *									
	RO: Index	-.24	-.11	-1.57	.34					
	L: *									
PLI	I: Industrial employment	.27	.18	2.35	.48	.16	.15	.63	.418	.407
	A: Big units	-.18	-.19	-3.39	.03					
	W: Index	.27	.04	0.41	.62					
	C: *									
	RO: Index	-.30	-.24	-3.54	.34					
	L: *									
PRI	I: Commercial employment	.16	.26	2.75	.64	.13	.12	.86	.681	.598
	A: Sharecroppers	.20	.27	4.48	.12					

Italy (continued)

Party		Independent variables	r	Beta	t-stat	R2D	R2	R2A	E2	CV	SCVw
PRI	W:	Index	-.00	-.37	-4.39	.55					
	C:	*									
	RO:	Index	-.18	-.17	-2.15	.51					
	L:	*									
MSI	I:	Industrial employment	-.48	-.18	-2.84	.48	.45	.44	.72	.516	.563
	A:	Small units	.44	.27	5.50	.17					
	W:	Index	-.59	-.45	-5.79	.66					
	C:	*									
	RO:	Index	.18	-.16	-2.85	.34					
	L:	*									

The Netherlands

Party		Independent variables	r	Beta	t-stat	R2D	R2	R2A	E2	CV	SCVw
ARP	I:	Agricultural employment	.42	-.04	-1.09	.24	.90	.90	.98	0.561	0.881
	A:	Freeholders	-.28	-.00	-0.01	.12					
	W:	Index	-.16	-.04	-1.26	.07					
	C:	Gereformeerde	.95	.96	27.01	.30					
	RO:	—									
	L:	*									
CHU	I:	Agricultural employment	.43	.20	3.09	.13	.61	.60	.88	0.668	1.082
	A:	Freeholders	-.09	-.07	-1.22	.02					
	W:	Index	-.19	-.13	-2.09	.06					
	C:	Hervormde	.74	.67	10.87	.09					
	RO:	—									
	L:	*									
KVP	I:	Industrial employment	.27	-.02	-0.52	.25	.92	.91	.94	0.791	1.166
	A:	Freeholders	.32	.08	2.63	.16					
	W:	Index	-.20	-.07	-2.30	.14					
	C:	Catholics	.95	.93	32.22	.10					
	RO:	—									
	L:	*									
SGP	I:	Agricultural employment	.23	.08	0.81	.24	.20	.17	.99	1.419	1.980
	A:	Freeholders	.00	.16	1.76	.12					
	W:	Index	.12	.21	2.37	.07					
	C:	Gereformeerde	.38	.42	4.15	.30					
	RO:	—									
	L:	*									
PVDA	I:	Industrial employment	-.04	.19	3.12	.25	.68	.67	.94	0.304	0.479
	A:	Freeholders	-.25	-.11	-1.81	.16					
	W:	Index	.00	-.05	-0.95	.14					
	C:	No affiliation	-.80	-.83	-14.72	.10					
	RO:	—									
	L:	*									
CPN	I:	Agricultural employment	-.18	-.11	-1.93	.05	.64	.63	.96	0.970	1.486

The Netherlands (continued)

Party		Independent variables	r	Beta	t-stat	R2D	R2	R2A	E2	CV	SCVw
CPN	A:	Freeholders	-.14	.13	2.07	.13					
	W:	Index	.13	-.27	-4.26	.22					
	C:	No affiliation	.75	.90	13.48	.28					
	RO:	—									
	L:	*									
PSP	I:	Commercial employment	.36	.07	0.73	.34	.39	.37	.50	0.460	0.687
	A:	Freeholders	-.21	.01	0.08	.12					
	W:	Index	.36	.08	0.87	.32					
	C:	No affiliation	.62	.56	6.16	.33					
	RO:	—									
	L:	*									
VVD	I:	Commercial employment	.41	.12	1.35	.34	.38	.36	.69	0.277	0.432
	A:	Freeholders	-.14	-.05	-0.61	.12					
	W:	Index	.61	.53	5.95	.32					
	C:	No affiliation	.32	.01	0.08	.33					
	RO:	—									
	L:	*									
D'66	I:	Commercial employment	.43	.19	1.96	.34	.33	.31	.58	0.325	0.460
	A:	Freeholders	-.11	-.01	-0.14	.12					
	W:	Index	.55	.45	4.80	.32					
	C:	No affiliation	.30	.01	0.12	.33					
	RO:	—									
	L:	*									
BP	I:	Agricultural employment	-.12	-.16	-1.83	.05	.14	.11	.29	.386	.653
	A:	Freeholders	.20	.09	0.91	.13					
	W:	Index	-.17	-.06	-0.60	.22					
	C:	No affiliation	-.33	-.29	-2.85	.28					
	RO:	—									
	L:	*									

Norway

Party		Independent variables	r	Beta	t-stat	R2D	R2	R2A	E2	CV	SCVw
DNA	I:	Industrial employment	.21	.22	8.30	.35	.45	.45	.87	0.330	.131
	A:	Forest land	.33	.22	9.51	.08					
	W:	Index	.01	-.22	-8.47	.34					
	C:	—									
	RO:	Anti-abortion	-.53	-.34	-13.77	.23					
	L:	New Norwegian	-.50	-.31	-12.89	.19					
SV	I:	Industrial employment	.21	.18	5.51	.35	.19	.19	.45	0.622	.218
	A:	Forest land	.13	.05	1.69	.08					
	W:	Index	.08	-.10	-3.08	-.34					
	C:	—									
	RO:	Anti-abortion	-.38	-.28	-9.19	.23					
	L:	New Norwegian	-.31	-16	-5.60	.19					

Norway (continued)

Party		Independent variables	r	Beta	t-stat	R2D	R2	R2A	E2	CV	SCVw
NKP	I:	Industrial employment	.16	.20	6.13	.35	.21	.21	.73	1.853	.617
	A:	Forest land	.29	.22	8.28	.08					
	W:	Index	.01	-.17	-5.39	.34					
	C:	—									
	RO:	Anti-abortion	-.36	-.24	-8.11	.23					
	L:	New Norwegian	-.27	-.12	-4.15	.19					
VE	I:	Industrial employment	-.00	.02	0.55	.33	.10	.10	.61	0.733	.340
	A:	Big units	-.22	-.17	-5.14	.12					
	W:	Index	-.01	.07	1.76	.36					
	C:	—									
	RO:	Anti-abortion	.17	.07	1.91	.21					
	L:	New Norwegian	.27	.20	5.64	.22					
SP	I:	Agricultural employment	.68	.85	21.37	.67	.53	.53	.92	0.699	.514
	A:	Small units	-.42	-.02	0.45	.55					
	W:	Index	-.30	.33	9.67	.55					
	C:	—									
	RO:	Anti-abortion	.33	.03	1.10	.23					
	L:	New Norwegian	.36	.11	4.15	.22					
KRF	I:	Industrial employment	-.12	.09	3.33	.35	.52	.52	.94	0.758	.395
	A:	Forest land	-.30	-.12	-5.02	.08					
	W:	Index	-.20	-.12	-4.22	.34					
	C:	—									
	RO:	Anti-abortion	.64	.47	18.71	.23					
	L:	New Norwegian	.54	.32	13.08	.19					
HOE	I:	Industrial employment	.20	-.16	-4.77	.43	.26	.26	.79	0.578	.266
	A:	Small units	.36	.16	4.21	.54					
	W:	Index	.45	.41	11.35	.50					
	C:	—									
	RO:	Anti-abortion	-.15	.02	0.58	.22					
	L:	New Norwegian	-.25	-.21	-7.45	.20					
FRP	I:	Industrial employment	.14	-.04	-0.87	.44	.09	.08	.54	0.547	.232
	A:	Small units	.22	.11	2.13	.54					
	W:	Index	.26	.22	4.63	.49					
	C:	—									
	RO:	Anti-abortion	.06	.15	3.97	.20					
	L:	New Norwegian	-.06	-.09	-2.36	.19					

Portugal

Party		Independent variables	r	Beta	t-stat	R2D	R2	R2A	E2	CV	SCVw
PSP	I:	—					.16	.16	.80	0.339	.164
	A:	Number of	-.33	-.22	-6.16	.19					
	W:	Emigration rate	-.21	-.12	-3.55	.07					
	C:	*									
	RO:	Index	-.32	-.21	-5.92	.18					
	L:	*									

Portugal (continued)

Party		Independent variables	r	Beta	t-stat	R2D	R2	R2A	E2	CV	SCVw
PCP	I:	—					.64	.64	.97	1.109	.558
	A:	Small units	-.58	-.28	-11.64	.25					
	W:	Emigration rate	-.29	-.10	-4.44	-.08					
	C:	*									
	RO:	Index	-.74	-.59	-24.87	.22					
	L:	*									
AD	I:	—					.66	.66	.90	0.477	.250
	A:	Small units	.58	.26	11.00	.25					
	W:	Emigration rate	.36	.17	8.18	.08					
	C:	*									
	RO:	Index	.75	.60	26.00	.22					
	L:	*									

Spain

Party		Independent variables	r	Beta	t-stat	R2D	R2	R2A	E2	CV	SCVw
PSOE	I:	Industrial employment	-.07	.27	2.01	.68	.15	.12	.42	0.254	.335
	A:	Latifundias	.31	.30	3.84	.01					
	W:	Index	-.18	-.25	-1.59	.77					
	C:	*									
	RO:	Index	-.12	-.04	-0.36	.59					
	L:	Unitarian orientation	.18	.14	1.41	.39					
UCD	I:	Industrial employment	-.36	-.35	-2.65	.69	.20	.17	.28	0.319	.540
	A:	Latifundias	-.22	-.26	-3.43	.02					
	W:	Index	-.30	.02	0.14	.76					
	C:	*									
	RO:	Index	.14	.01	0.15	.38					
	L:	Unitarian orientation	.25	.09	0.94	.40					
AP	I:	Agricultural employment	.21	.19	0.99	.82	.10	.07	.21	0.362	.522
	A:	Latifundias	-.22	-.21	-2.54	.11					
	W:	Index	-.17	.02	0.09	.88					
	C:	*									
	RO:	Index	.07	-.05	-0.49	.57					
	L:	Unitarian orientation	.14	.11	1.04	.43					
PCE	I:	Industrial employment	.10	.13	1.01	.69	.23	.20	.69	0.634	.727
	A:	Latifundias	.45	.47	6.37	.02					
	W:	Index	.10	.00	-0.01	.76					
	C:	*									
	RO:	Index	-.07	-.09	-0.99	.38					
	L:	Unitarian orientation	-.06	.03	0.28	.40					
ETN	I:	Industrial employment	.57	.41	3.53	.68	.39	.37	.82	2.124	2.516
	A:	Big units	-.15	.08	1.09	.23					
	W:	Index	.52	.05	0.39	.77					
	C:	*									
	RO:	Index	.37	-.06	-0.57	.60					
	L:	Unitarian orientation	-.51	-.33	-3.64	.48					

Sweden

Party	Independent variables	r	Beta	t-stat	R2D	R2	R2A	E2	CV	SCVw
MOD	I: Independent employment	-.30	-.18	-6.00	.08	.33	.32	.83	.423	.221
	A: Big units	.29	.23	7.51	.16					
	W: Tax capacity	.41	.50	13.84	.38					
	C: Non-conformists	-.17	-.00	-0.32	.11					
	RO: Church attendance	-.01	.35	9.76	.37					
	L: *									
CP	I: Agricultural employment	.67	.33	9.35	.56	.55	.55	.81	.349	.241
	A: Small units	.20	-.00	-0.09	.09					
	W: Tax capacity	-.56	-.12	-3.63	.48					
	C: Non-conformists	.23	.08	3.33	.08					
	RO: Church attendance	.67	.37	11.45	.49					
	L: *									
FP	I: Industrial employment	-.18	-.16	-4.84	.08	.14	.14	.66	.363	.179
	A: Big units	.12	.11	3.18	.16					
	W: Tax capacity	.21	.28	6.91	.38					
	C: Non-conformists	.16	.27	8.02	.11					
	RO: Church attendance	-.03	.12	2.90	.37					
	L: *									
SAP	I: Industrial employment	.38	.35	13.50	.08	.49	.48	.98	.231	.114
	A: Small units	.13	.21	7.94	.10					
	W: Tax capacity	.05	-.25	-7.70	.39					
	C: Non-conformists	-.17	-.24	-9.10	.10					
	RO: Church attendance	-.48	-.62	-20.17	.34					
	L: *									
VPK	I: Industrial employment	-.15	-.14	-4.62	.08	.31	.31	.97	.624	.309
	A: Small units	.19	.35	11.44	.10					
	W: Tax capacity	.31	.12	3.23	.39					
	C: Non-conformists	-.22	-.16	-5.25	.10					
	RO: Church attendance	-.40	-.39	-10.82	.34					
	L: *									
KDS	I: Industrial employment	.10	-.06	-3.01	.08	.70	.70	.92	.796	.422
	A: Small units	.24	.10	5.03	.10					
	W: Tax capacity	-.29	-.04	-1.51	.39					
	C: Non-conformists	.83	.81	40.30	.10					
	RO: Church attendance	.20	.03	1.18	.34					
	L: *									

Switzerland

Party	Independent variables	r	Beta	t-stat	R2D	R2	R2A	E2	CV	SCVw
FDP	I: Agricultural employment	-.19	-.28	-1.92	.38	.08	.02	.79	0.811	0.852
	A: Small units	.17	.12	0.93	.17					
	W: —									
	C: Protestants	-.04	-.18	-1.28	.33					
	RO: —									
	L: German	-.04	.07	0.58	.16					

Switzerland

Party		Independent variables	r	Beta	t-stat	R2D	R2	R2A	E2	CV	SCVw
CDV	I:	Agricultural employment	.71	.48	5.32	.43	.68	.66	.94	0.981	1.776
	A:	Big units	-.24	.10	2.11	.37					
	W:	—									
	C:	Protestants	-.72	-.48	-5.84	.30					
	RO:	—									
	L:	German	.19	.10	1.16	.28					
SPS	I:	Industrial employment	.49	.31	3.17	.28	.52	.49	.67	0.726	0.644
	A:	Big units	.13	.01	0.94	.35					
	W:	—									
	C:	Protestants	.66	.52	5.43	.25					
	RO:	—									
	L:	French	.14	.18	1.79	.33					
SVP	I:	Commercial employment	.11	-.07	-0.53	.25	.22	.17	.35	1.256	1.114
	A:	Small units	-.03	.01	0.13	.14					
	W:	—									
	C:	Protestants	.46	.48	4.23	.14					
	RO:	—									
	L:	German	-.00	-.00	-0.03	.21					

Appendix 6.1   Structure of government: levels and number of units in the 1980s

Austria	Land	Gemeinde			
	9	2 300			
Belgium	Communautés	Provins	Arrondisement	Commune	
	3	9	44	596	
Denmark	Amr	Kommun			
	14	275			
Finland	Lääni	Kommun			
	12	461			
France	Région	Départment	Arrondisement	Canton	Commune
	22	96	325	3 714	36 394
F R Germany*	Länder	Regierurgs-bezinke	Kreisfreie Staedte	Landkreis	Gemeinde
	11	26	91	237	8 502
Greece	Nomos	Demos			
	52	6 023			
Ireland	Province	County/ Corporation	District/Board		
	4	38	75		
Italy	Regione	Provincia	Communi		
	20	94	8 075		
Netherlands	Provins	Gemeente			
	12	714			

Norway	Fylke	Kommune	
	19	454	
Portugal	Distrito	Concelho	Freguesia
	20	305	4 050
Spain	Communidad	Provincia	Municipio
	Autōnoma		
	17	50	8 056
Sweden	Län	Kommun	
	24	284	
Switzerland	Kanton	Kommune	
	26	3 029	
United Kingdom	County	District	Parishes/
			Communities**
	53	369	10 000/1 000

Note: *'Old' FRG. **This applies to England and Wales. Scotland is divided into 9 regions and 3 island areas. The next level of government is the district, which number 53, and community councils.

Index